The
Galapagos Islands

A Natural History Guide

To Mei Fang,
who had to get up every
morning to type the book
on the computer, instead of
sleeping until noon, as usual.

THE GALAPAGOS ISLANDS

Pierre Constant

Nothing gets lost,
nothing is created,
everything transforms
—Lavoisier

Odyssey Publications Ltd, 1004 Kowloon Centre, 29–43 Ashley Road,
Tsim Sha Tsui, Kowloon, Hong Kong
Tel. (852) 2856 3896; Fax. (852) 2565 8004; E-mail: odyssey@asiaonline.net

Distribution in the United Kingdom, Ireland and Europe by
Hi Marketing Ltd, 38 Carver Road, London SE24 9LT, UK

Distribution in the United States of America by
W.W. Norton & Company, Inc., New York

Library of Congress Catalog Card Number has been requested.

(This edition first published in 1994 in French by Calao Life Experience, under the title
Archipel des Galapagos)

ISBN: 962-217-580-5

Editor: Mark Morris
Series Co-ordinator: Jane Finden-Crofts
Cover Concept: Margaret Lee

Photography/illustrations by Pierre Constant

Production by Twin Age Ltd, Hong Kong
Printed in China

(*Front cover*)   *Juvenile frigate*
(*Back cover*)   (*top*) *Portrait of flightless cormorant;* (*bottom*) *Sea lion*

CONTENTS

6

FOREWORD

I shall never forget the vision of the stone arch, emerging slowly above the surface of the Pacific Ocean at first light, after a long night on a sailingboat in Galápagos waters. This monumental arch, made of volcanic tuff—a haven for snow-white masked boobies—is the Great Arch of Darwin Island, at the extreme northwest of the archipelago. Swept by surf and foam, which roll at its foot, and looking like an oceanic Arc de Triomphe, Darwin Arch, oriented east-west, is the symbol of the 'Gate'. Silent witness of time forgotten, it shows the direction from which the first unsuspecting discoverers of history came: an archbishop from Panama, drifting with the currents, lost on an ocean in the middle of the XVIth century.

The first name given to the islands, Las Islas Encantadas or 'the Enchanted Isles', evokes the magical aura that has always surrounded the Galápagos. Since I first came to the archipelago in 1980—as a a young trainee of an Ecuadorian tourism company but soon to become a naturalist guide for the Galápagos National Park—the islands have changed, under the influence of man. The human population has increased fourfold in 15 years, and has doubled in the last five years. Today, the population is estimated at 20,000 people, scattered on four main islands. Tourism has been booming tremendously on this chain of volcanic isles, and the number of visitors, about 17,500 people in 1980—though limited to 25,000 visitors by the 'Master Plan' of 1981—eventually passed the record mark of 60,000 persons at the end of 1997. Souvenir shops multiply in Puerto Ayora, and hotels are sprouting like mushrooms after the rain (of dollars).

The fire on the slope of the Sierra Negra volcano in 1985 not only devastated hundreds of hectares of vegetation but, following a worldwide ad campaign, provoked a blaze of tourism, which saw a dramatic boom in 1986. The same year, a second airport was inaugurated on San Cristóbal Island, and the Reserve of Marine Resources was created by presidential decree. Since then, a lot of ink has been spilt; this includes my book, *Marine Life of the Galápagos*, a guide to the fish, whales, dolphins and other marine animals, published in 1992. Even though it stimulated the development of scuba diving, it also invited all sorts of abuses. Among these are the intensive plundering of the submarine riches and schools of sharks by Japanese commercial fishing boats, which first became interested in shark fins, then in *pepinos*, or sea cucumbers. The scandal broke in 1992, despite laws passed by the Ecuadorian government for the protection of sharks and *pepinos*, but illegal fishing continued in 1996, under the very noses of the authorities.

The economic stake for Galápagos fishermen is enormous. They went knocking on the door of the president in Quito to lift a ban on fishing. Eventually they won in July

1994, and the government gave them the go ahead to fish lobsters for three months, sea cucumbers for three months, and even sharks for three months. The number of tourism boats, which was limited in the Galápagos to avoid a 'tidal wave', was soon exceeded. Nowadays, about 100 boats operate in the archipelago. Will the hen that lays the golden eggs be exploited to the point of exhaustion? There are profits to be made, but the economic pressures that they bring are so unavoidable that one may fear that the Galápagos have already lost their sacred aura, their image of a lost, unviolated, natural paradise. UNESCO became ultimately concerned in 1995-96, and now puts pressure on the Ecuadorian government to bring a change and to effectively protect the Marine Reserve, already 'Whale Sanctuary' and newly declared a 'Biological Reserve' by INEFAN, (Instituto Ecuatoriano Forestal, de Aereas Naturales y de Vida Silvestre) in November 1996.

Nevertheless, the Darwin Station goes on with its research programme as if everything were fine, and the Galápagos National Park continues with programmes of protection, conservation, environmental education and the breeding of giant tortoises. Not to mention the training of multilingual naturalist guides, who are, to some extent, the 'arrowhead' of integrity in the Galápagos National Park. It is pleasant to imagine the Galápagos as a kind of Noah's ark in the middle of the deluge.

But I do not wish to darken the picture more than I should. The magic and the spell of the Enchanted Isles really do exist. They are found in the inquisitive look of the blue-footed boobies; in the sweetness and the frolic of the sea lions on land or in the water; in the peaceful and detached somnolence of marine iguanas flat on the rocks under the equatorial sun; in the enigmatic smiles of the land iguanas under the opuntia cacti; in the eternal immobility of the giant tortoises in their centenarian shells, overlooking the world from the rim of the volcanoes; in the mystical contemplation of the pelican standing on its rock, facing the glowing ocean at sunset; in the grace and innocence of the flightless cormorant during the courtship display; in the comical duel of the albatrosses fencing with their beak in the mating season; in the joyful gamboling of the bottlenose dolphins, for which each boat is a pretext to play; in the wave that crashes against the Great Arch and turns into one thousand drops of iridescent light...

For all that, I pay my respects to these islands. The Galápagos must be safeguarded as the innocence of the world. For the sun rises east on Noah's ark or on the arch of Darwin, and glows west on the great blue yonder of the Pacific. The magic of 'Las Encantadas' may one day disappear under the surface of the waves, but until then, men would have gone long before.

Pierre Constant

If I was asked to give advice to someone about to undertake a long journey, my answer would totally depend on that traveller's liking for one science or another, and on the advantages th... ...und for his own studies. Doubtless, one experiences great satisfo... ...plating such diverse lands, and to review, so to speak, the vari... ...this satisfaction far from compensates for all the hards... ...refore, one must have an aim, and this aim sho... ...unveil. In short this aim must support yo...

If... ...e visions of a journey are am... ...night. Over the last 60 ...ook, a man would ...lf to the hardest ...e greatest of ...dertaking ...days;

The Galápago...

Tropic of Cancer

Equator

Galapagos Islands

Tropic of Capricorn

Pacific ocean

os Archipelago

PIROCO 1994

SCIENTIFIC AND HISTORICAL DATA

CHAPTER ONE

General Setting of the Islands
Geology and Origin of the Galápagos
Volcanism; Glacial Ages

The Galápagos Islands stretch over a 320-kilometre (174-mile) axis from east to west, and the equator passes precisely across the crater of Wolf volcano in the north of Isabela Island. The archipelago is made up of 19 islands and 42 islets or surfacing rocks. San Cristóbal, the easternmost island of the Galápagos group, lies about 1,100 kilometres (600 miles) west of the mother country, Ecuador, on the South American mainland.

The total land surface of the archipelago is just over 8,000 square kilometres. Isabela, the largest island, has an area of 4,588 square kilometres; Santa Cruz, the second in size and the most central, is only 986 square kilometres; James is 585 square kilometres; San Cristóbal is 558 square kilometres; Floreana is 173 square kilometres. Among the tiniest islands, with a land surface between one and five square kilometres, are Rábida, Seymour, Wolf, Bartolomé, Tortuga and Darwin. Forty-two islets have a landmass smaller than one square kilometre, and 26 emerging rocks are numbered.

Oceanic Islands

The islands are purely oceanic, which means that they have never been connected to the mainland by any sort of land bridge. In the past, it was assumed that the Cocos and Carnegie ridges, underwater mountain ranges rising up to 2,000 metres above the sea floor, once connected the islands to the mainland of either Central America or South America, but this has been disproved, because of the sheer drop of the Peru-Chile trench. The conspicuous absence of land mammals in the Galápagos also helps to confirm the oceanic island theory.

The islands rise on the Galápagos Platform, a basaltic submarine plateau located between 200 and 500 fathoms (ie, between 360 and 900 metres; 1 fathom being equal to 1.82 metres) under the surface of the ocean. The archipelago is entirely volcanic, and Isabela Island alone is made up of six volcanoes side by side. Five of them are typical shield volcanos, the craters of which are huge 'calderas'.

Calderas

Caldera means 'cauldron' in Spanish. This geological name is used to define the aging of a shield volcano. This huge craterlike depression is formed by the subsidence of the

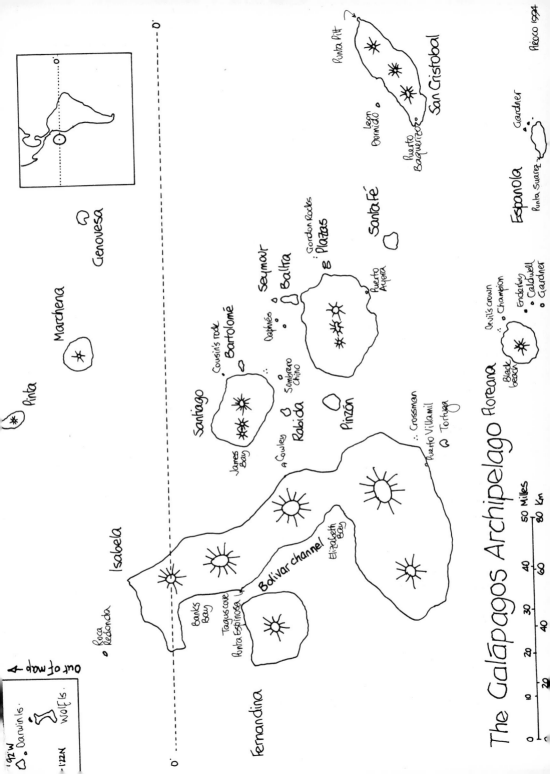

The Galápagos Archipelago

upper part of the volcano when the inner walls of the central crater fall in, widening the cross section of the crater over time.

Following repeated eruptions and regular volcanic activity, the magma chamber gets larger and swells up each time the magma rises. As magma creates pressure on the roof of the magma chamber, circumferential fissures form around the crater. Sometimes the lava spreads out through the cracks and creates parasitic cones on the slopes of the volcano. When the eruption comes to an end, the level of the magma subsides. The roof of the magma chamber is no longer supported and it collapses. Through successive collapses of the crater, the caldera is formed.

The most recent example was the collapse of the Fernandina volcano in 1968. The crater floor—800 metres deep at first—collapsed another 350 metres after a violent explosion. Ashes were launched 25 kilometres high into the sky and spread over an area of a few hundred square kilometres. Fernandina is the youngest caldera in the Galápagos, with a diameter of 6.5 kilometres. Sierra Negra, the oldest caldera of Isabela Island, measures 10 kilometres across. Santa Cruz and the southern part of San Cristóbal are also large shield volcanoes, whose summits have been eroded.

GEOLOGICAL ZONING

A deep oceanic trench, 3,000 metres under the ocean surface, separates the small northern islands of Darwin, Wolf, Marchena, Pinta and Genovesa from the rest of the archipelago to the south. MacBirney and Aoki (1966) show that the Galápagos are divided in three zones, comprising islands of like structure and of similar petrography.

The first zone to the southeast is made of Fernandina, Isabela and Floreana Islands. The second zone is made up of the northern islands mentioned above, adding Cerro Pitt, the northeastern tip of San Cristóbal Island. The third zone is made of the central islands of Santiago, Rábida, Santa Cruz, Pinzón, Baltra, Santa Fé, Española and the south of San Cristóbal.

PLATE TECTONICS

According to the theory of plate tectonics, the Galápagos archipelago is located in the north of the Nazca Plate, just under the Cocos Plate, and east of the South East Pacific mid-oceanic ridge, also called the East Pacific Rise (see map of Tectonic Plates, page 15). The islands are connected by two submarine ridges: the Carnegie Ridge to the east and the Cocos Ridge to the northeast.

The S E P mid-oceanic ridge (SEPMOR) stretches roughly north-south from California (San Andreas fault) to Easter Island and farther west into the southwestern Pacific. It spreads magma on the ocean floor, westward and eastward, pushing the oceanic Nazca

SCIENTIFIC AND HISTORICAL DATA

CHAPTER ONE

GENERAL SETTING OF THE ISLANDS
GEOLOGY AND ORIGIN OF THE GALÁPAGOS
VOLCANISM; GLACIAL AGES

The Galápagos Islands stretch over a 320-kilometre (174-mile) axis from east to west, and the equator passes precisely across the crater of Wolf volcano in the north of Isabela Island. The archipelago is made up of 19 islands and 42 islets or surfacing rocks. San Cristóbal, the easternmost island of the Galápagos group, lies about 1,100 kilometres (600 miles) west of the mother country, Ecuador, on the South American mainland.

The total land surface of the archipelago is just over 8,000 square kilometres. Isabela, the largest island, has an area of 4,588 square kilometres; Santa Cruz, the second in size and the most central, is only 986 square kilometres; James is 585 square kilometres; San Cristóbal is 558 square kilometres; Floreana is 173 square kilometres. Among the tiniest islands, with a land surface between one and five square kilometres, are Rábida, Seymour, Wolf, Bartolomé, Tortuga and Darwin. Forty-two islets have a landmass smaller than one square kilometre, and 26 emerging rocks are numbered.

OCEANIC ISLANDS

The islands are purely oceanic, which means that they have never been connected to the mainland by any sort of land bridge. In the past, it was assumed that the Cocos and Carnegie ridges, underwater mountain ranges rising up to 2,000 metres above the sea floor, once connected the islands to the mainland of either Central America or South America, but this has been disproved, because of the sheer drop of the Peru-Chile trench. The conspicuous absence of land mammals in the Galápagos also helps to confirm the oceanic island theory.

The islands rise on the Galápagos Platform, a basaltic submarine plateau located between 200 and 500 fathoms (ie, between 360 and 900 metres; 1 fathom being equal to 1.82 metres) under the surface of the ocean. The archipelago is entirely volcanic, and Isabela Island alone is made up of six volcanoes side by side. Five of them are typical shield volcanos, the craters of which are huge 'calderas'.

CALDERAS

Caldera means 'cauldron' in Spanish. This geological name is used to define the aging of a shield volcano. This huge craterlike depression is formed by the subsidence of the

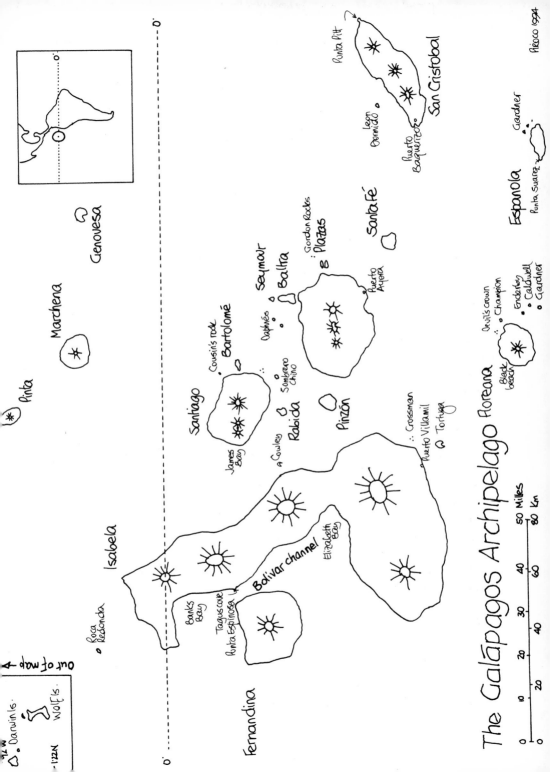

The Galápagos Archipelago

Arroco 1994

upper part of the volcano when the inner walls of the central crater fall in, widening the cross section of the crater over time.

Following repeated eruptions and regular volcanic activity, the magma chamber gets larger and swells up each time the magma rises. As magma creates pressure on the roof of the magma chamber, circumferential fissures form around the crater. Sometimes the lava spreads out through the cracks and creates parasitic cones on the slopes of the volcano. When the eruption comes to an end, the level of the magma subsides. The roof of the magma chamber is no longer supported and it collapses. Through successive collapses of the crater, the caldera is formed.

The most recent example was the collapse of the Fernandina volcano in 1968. The crater floor—800 metres deep at first—collapsed another 350 metres after a violent explosion. Ashes were launched 25 kilometres high into the sky and spread over an area of a few hundred square kilometres. Fernandina is the youngest caldera in the Galápagos, with a diameter of 6.5 kilometres. Sierra Negra, the oldest caldera of Isabela Island, measures 10 kilometres across. Santa Cruz and the southern part of San Cristóbal are also large shield volcanoes, whose summits have been eroded.

GEOLOGICAL ZONING

A deep oceanic trench, 3,000 metres under the ocean surface, separates the small northern islands of Darwin, Wolf, Marchena, Pinta and Genovesa from the rest of the archipelago to the south. MacBirney and Aoki (1966) show that the Galápagos are divided in three zones, comprising islands of like structure and of similar petrography.

The first zone to the southeast is made of Fernandina, Isabela and Floreana Islands. The second zone is made up of the northern islands mentioned above, adding Cerro Pitt, the northeastern tip of San Cristóbal Island. The third zone is made of the central islands of Santiago, Rábida, Santa Cruz, Pinzón, Baltra, Santa Fé, Española and the south of San Cristóbal.

PLATE TECTONICS

According to the theory of plate tectonics, the Galápagos archipelago is located in the north of the Nazca Plate, just under the Cocos Plate, and east of the South East Pacific mid-oceanic ridge, also called the East Pacific Rise (see map of Tectonic Plates, page 15). The islands are connected by two submarine ridges: the Carnegie Ridge to the east and the Cocos Ridge to the northeast.

The S E P mid-oceanic ridge (SEPMOR) stretches roughly north-south from California (San Andreas fault) to Easter Island and farther west into the southwestern Pacific. It spreads magma on the ocean floor, westward and eastward, pushing the oceanic Nazca

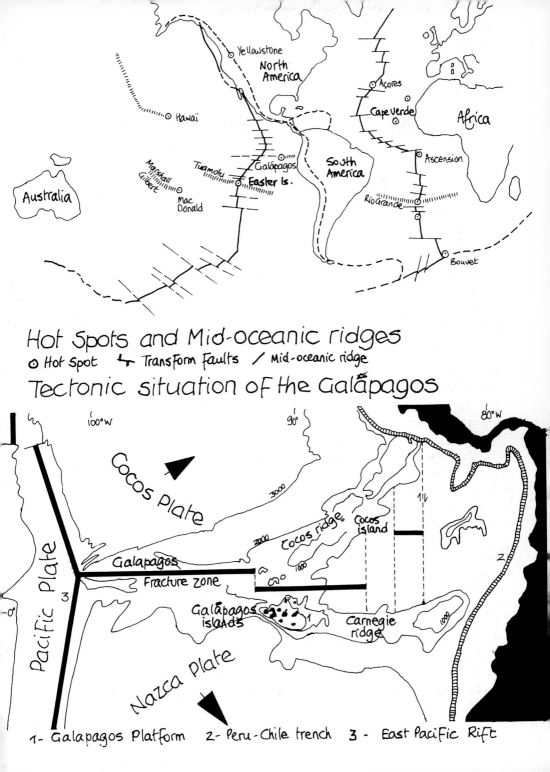

Hot Spots and Mid-oceanic ridges

○ Hot Spot   ⊥ Transform Faults   / Mid-oceanic ridge

Tectonic situation of the Galápagos

1- Galápagos Platform   2- Peru-Chile trench   3 - East Pacific Rift

Plate east, towards South America. At the same time, we have an extension of the SEP-MOR from west to east, called the Galápagos Fracture Zone (GFZ) or Galápagos Rift, which eventually evolves in a transformation fault* between the Carnegie and Cocos ridges. The GFZ also expands magma on the ocean floor, northward and southward, thus pushing the Nazca Plate southward.

We understand now that the Galápagos are located on an oceanic plate that receives pressure from the west (SEPMOR) and from the north (GFZ). What happens next? Well, think of a window pane on which you exert pressure from two adjacent sides. Crack. Get the picture?

HOT SPOT

The archipelago is a 'hot spot', an area of high thermic flux* and intense seismic and volcanic activity, subject to almost annual eruptions. A hot spot is related to a weakness of the oceanic crust, a zone of remarkable fragility in the tectonic plate, which leads to fissures on the ocean floor. In the Galápagos there is a system of parallel and orthogonal fractures*, which resemble a checkerboard. Under the Nazca Plate, the hot magma is always in motion due to convection currents. The hot spot, being a more sensitive area, creates a magmatic plume which pierces the oceanic crust in a weak part of the plate. The magma rises upward into the ocean (see figure Hot Spot, page 15). Upon contact with the cold ocean water, the lava cools off rapidly, builds a platform and keeps rising. It eventually creates a volcanic cone, which in a few years reaches the surface of the ocean. We then have an 'aerial volcano', a volcanic island born of the ocean. The base of the volcanic construction of the Galápagos could be 10 to 15 million years old. The hot spot is now responsible for the making of an archipelago, ie, a chain of volcanic islands more or less aligned. Hawaii is a classic example which is much older than the Galápagos, with an age of about 20 million years.

The magma rising up from the SEPMOR creates the expansion of the oceanic floor and the migration of the Nazca Plate to the southeast at a rate of five centimetres per year. The Nazca Plate will be forced under the continental plate of South America. The point of contact between the two plates (continental and oceanic) forms a trench, which is called the subduction zone. The Nazca Plate will then be in subduction under South America, and the Cocos Plate will migrate northeast and dive in the subduction zone of Central America (see Appendix 1).

If the hot spot does not move, the tectonic plate will shift. An island is created, then the oceanic plate moves east. A second island will be made later on, when the plume pierces the oceanic crust again, which in turn will migrate eastward with the plate. And so on, forming a chain of islands, that is to say, an archipelago.

THE AGE OF THE GALÁPAGOS

The consequence of this phenomenon is that, logically, the eldest islands will lie to the east and the youngest to the west. That is where the volcanic activity is resumed nowadays in the archipelago, mainly on Isabela and Fernandina islands. This brings us to determining the age of the Galápagos.

Various methods, including potassium-argon (P A) and paleomagnetism, have been used to date the age of volcanic rocks, essentially basalts. The first dating technique, P.A., shows that the Galápagos have a maximum age of three million years. The oldest basalts analyzed, using the radioactivity of the elements gave the following results: 3.2 million years (+/- 0.2) on Española; 2.7 million years (+/- 0.1) on Santa Fé; 4.2 million years (+/- 1.8) on South Plaza.

Many of the analyzed rocks come from submarine lava like Santa Cruz (1 million years), basalts of Wolf volcano (0.72 million years) and San Cristóbal (0.66 million years). Isabela Island was dated at about 700,000 years, and so are the islands of Fernandina, Santiago, Genovesa, Marchena and Darwin (Culpepper).

Wolf, Santa Cruz, Baltra, Rábida, Pinzón and Floreana are between 0.7 and 1.5 million years old, while the age of San Cristóbal is between 2.4 million years (Cox) and about 4 million years (Paul Colinvaux).

Former studies on magnetism also proved the young age of the islands. Most samples analyzed were dated in the period of Bruhnes (between 0 and 0.7 million years) and the period of Matuyama (0.7 to 2.4 million years). The age of the archipelago stands of course for the aerial part of the islands, ie, the date when the volcanoes surfaced above sea level. The islands' submerged bases could be of Miocene geological times, about 15 million years.

The Galápagos archipelago is one of the largest and most active groups of oceanic volcanoes in the world. The islands, never connected to the mainland, were built on a large but shallow platform 2,000 kilometres east of the SEPMOR. The localization of the main volcanoes seems to have been controlled by two systems of quite orthogonal fractures: one has a north-northwest direction; the other is rather east-west.

UPLIFTS

Numerous examples of island uplift have been observed on Santa Fé, Española and Santa Cruz. Cerro Colorado, facing Plazas Islands, is a rocky hill east of Santa Cruz Island which was uplifted in the past, bringing up tuff formations bearing fossils of Miocene times. Most recently, in Urvina Bay, on the west coast of Isabela Island, a tectonic uplift in 1954 brought coral heads and marine life five metres above sea level. It was followed a few months later by an eruption on the slope of Alcedo volcano.

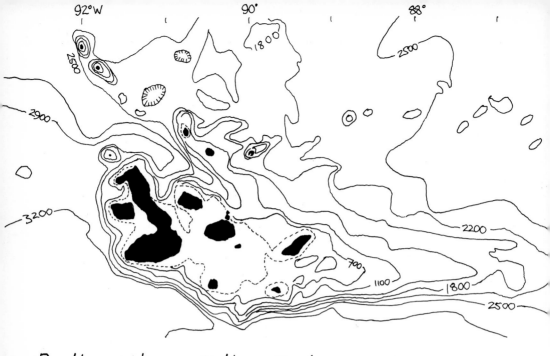

Bathymetry of the Galapagos
(after "Bureau of Commercial Fisheries", 1962) - Soundings in metres - Dotted line < 360 m.

The submerged islands
(source: "Nature" magazine and New York Times News.)

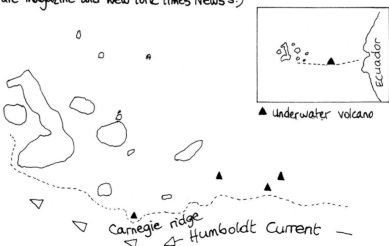

▲ Underwater volcano

Carnegie ridge

◁ Humboldt Current —

▲ Supposed sites of the submerged islands.

THE SUNKEN ISLANDS

In the beginning of 1992, in an issue of the English magazine *Nature*, American scientists from Oregon, California, Cornell University and the NOAA (National Oceanic and Atmospheric Administration) on a 26-day expedition discovered submarine mountains along the Carnegie Ridge, to the south and southeast of the Galápagos, in the direction of South America. David Christie and his colleagues gathered samples of volcanic cobblestones (typical of the shoreline) resulting from aerial and marine erosion. This demonstrated the existence of a chain of islands that were once above sea level and which were later submerged. The submarine mountain closest to the continent, only 590 kilometres away, had an estimated age of nine million years. Obviously, there should be even older sunken islands of the Galápagos group, which, according to the latest thinking, could now be as old as 90 million years (see drawing, page 18).

PETROLOGY

Chemically speaking, the petrology of the Galápagos is different from Hawaii's, for the magma of our archipelago is typical of the southeast Pacific ridge. The plutonic rocks and the effusive tholeïtes (subalkaline basalts, ie those rich in silicon) follow similar modes of differentiation, being enriched in iron and magnesium, in alkaline products and with an excess of silicon.

The islands are composed of basaltic lava, rich in iron and magnesium. Black at first, the lava becomes gradually brown, then brick red after alteration when iron becomes oxidized over time. This erosion process is typical of the 'basic' kind of lava; in the 'acid' kind, it is totally different.

VOLCANISM OF THE GALÁPAGOS ISLANDS

If the Galápagos Islands are well known for their extraordinary fauna, let us not forget that their appearance depends first on volcanic phenomena. A few elements of vocabulary will be essential for the proper understanding of the volcanic activity. Let us consider, first of all, volcanic activity in general, then the volcanic materials or volcanic products and, finally, where the magma comes from.

VOLCANIC ACTIVITY

It is divided into the aerial and the submarine activities. The aerial eruption depends on two factors: the viscosity of the magma and the quantity of liberated gases. Four major types of volcanoes are usually distinguished:

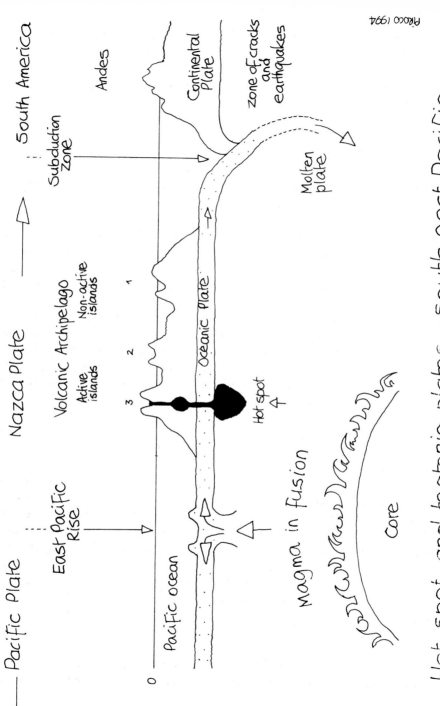

Hot spot and tectonic plates ~ South east Pacific

- the explosive or Vulcanian type: where the gas phase is predominant.
- the explosive or Domean type: where the magma is viscous and acid.
- the effusive or Hawaiian type: where the magma is fluid and basic. This is precisely the case of the Galápagos.
- the mixed or Strobolian type: the eruption is rich in gases, liquids and solid products.

This can be represented in a triangular diagram, where the three poles would be gases, fluid magma and acid viscous magma.

In submarine activity, the magma coming out of the ocean floor explodes violently when it contacts the cool water. Pieces of lava are torn apart and pulverized. Vitreous fragments spread over the ocean floor, cement and form submarine volcanic tuffs or 'hyaloclastites' (a Greek word meaning 'broken pieces of glass'), which can build real mountains. The submarine tuff cones thus formed are called 'guyots'. Their summit is flat, for the crater is soon to be filled by marine sediments.

The submarine lava flows come from aerial flows which have reached the shore. Steaming at the point of penetration, these flows once underwater are known as a 'giant's highway', for their surface is made of blocks (resembling tiles) with a polygonal structure. This is true when the slope is mild. When the slope is steep at the point of entry, however, the flow gives way to 'pillow lava', or lava cushions, which roll downhill and pile up at the bottom of the ocean.

VOLCANIC MATERIALS

FUMAROLES

Gas emanations are called fumaroles. These are seen on the slope of the crater and within the crater itself. Gases are important, as they help the magma to come out, pushing upward and acting on the viscosity of the lava. The two main components of fumaroles are water and carbon dioxide (CO_2). Nevertheless, their classification is based on chemical composition and temperature, which can rise up to 500° C. Thus we may distinguish chlorated, chlorhydrated, ammoniacal, sulphurhydated, 'mofettes' (CO_2), thermomineral waters, geysers (H_2O) and 'soffionis' (sprays of steaming water). Sulphurhydrated fumaroles can be seen on Isabela Island, in the craters of Alcedo and Sierra Negra volcanoes.

LAVAS

Lavas are molten materials which pour out of the crater. The movement of a flow depends on the viscosity, the push-up action of the magma in the chimney of the volcano, and the substratum. The speed of the flow, a few kilometres per hour at the exit of the vent, can be reduced to a few metres per hour at the bottom of the slope. The cooling action is quick at the surface of the lava flow, in which two types are distinguished:

- the 'aa' type: (Hawaiian word, meaning 'to hurt'), where the chaotic aspect of the surface of the flow is due to the gas explosions, having torn apart the external crust. We have there a fluid lava, rich in gas. This can be seen when climbing volcan Alcedo.
- the 'pahoehoe' type: or ropey lava (after the Hawaiian word meaning 'ropey'). Here the surface is smooth, and shows 'ripple marks', 'intestinal figures', waves in the directions of the flow, and 'ropes'. The lava progresses by tongues; it is not as fluid and has lost its gas (eg on Sullivan Bay, Santiago Island). The hardening of the basalts is generally quick under the crust. The cooling process often generates prismatic figures in columns. These are the organ pipe basalts, with four, five or six faces.

LAVA TUBES

These tunnels are frequent in the Galápagos. When lava spreads out of the crater, the surface of the flow cools off rapidly, while the inner flow rushes downhill quickly. When no more lava comes out of the crater, an empty tube is often left behind, surrounded by a solid outside crust. These natural tunnels, usually five to six metres wide and up to ten metres in height, can be seen at Puerto Ayora and Bellavista, on Santa Cruz Island.

TEPHRAS

Also called 'pyroclastites' or broken fire pieces (from the Greek), tephras are volcanic projectiles, mainly bombs, shapeless fragments or ashes. In the shapeless fragments, we have 'pumice', pieces of acid magma, viscous and grey-white in colour. These are ejected following violent explosions (eg Alcedo volcano, Isabela Island).

The 'scoriae', pieces of fluid magma with no set shape, are the most common volcanic projectiles. The red-purple colour is due to iron oxidation. Cinder cones are frequent in the Galápagos. Among 'bombs', we may distinguish 'spindle bombs' (rotated in flight), or 'spatter bombs', formed by the ejection of fluid magma. Spatter cones are seen on Bartolomé Island. Ashes appear because of violent volcanic projections up in the air. These consist of pieces of crystal or glass. The white colour of the ashes persists in acid lava, but in basic lava, the black ash may turn to red or orange-brown with time.

'Lapilli' and volcanic sands are scoriae fragments, which vary in size from 2 to 20 millimetres in 'lapilli' and from 0.2 to 2 millimetres in sands. Little bombs, drops of glass, are part of the same family, and may form hardened layers of crystals.

'Volcanic tuffs' (0.2 to 20 millimetres) are lapilli and sands cemented by ashes. 'Cinerites', or hardened ashes, form distinct, stratified layers.

PARASITIC CONES

Frequent in the Galápagos (James Bay, Santiago Island, or Bartolomé Island), tuff cones are always found near the coast or on the shoreline, for they are created in shallow sea water. Magma is blown up in small grains and ashes, which cement later on. Spatter cones are formed on firm land by projections of fluid magma patches, lava fountains (Bartolomé Island). Cinder cones are made of light small volcanic bombs cooling off in the air, after a dry explosion.

WHERE DOES MAGMA COME FROM?

If we consider the chemical composition of magma, we could simply say that they differentiate into two main groups: the acid and the basic.

The 'Basic Group' (basalts, gabbros)

Also called basaltic magma, it is black in colour, poor in silica (SiO_2) and alumina (Al_2O_3), with mean contents of 60-70 per cent, but rich in iron (Fe), magnesium (Mg), calcium (Ca), sodium (Na) and potassium (K). Thus, when the content in 'bases' is superior to the amount of silicon, we talk about 'basic' rocks.

The 'Acid group' (rhyolites, granites)

Comes from the granitic magma, rich in silica and alumina (80 to 90 per cent of the contents) and poor in bases: Na, K, Fe, Ca, Mg. When the silicon content is greater than the base content, the term used is 'acid' rocks.

Theory of Bimagmatism (last century)

According to this theory, there are two sources from which magma comes. In the crust is the acid magma (SiAl), at a depth of less than 20 kilometres. In the mantle is the basic magma (SiMg), at a depth between 35 kilometres and 100 kilometres.

The MOHO or 'Mohorovic discontinuity line' separates the crust and the mantle at a depth of 15 to 35 kilometres. The theory of bigmagmatism explains simply where the magma comes from, be it in the crust: SiAl (silicon-aluminum) or SiMa in the mantle (silicon-magnesium).

Later on, as the process became better understood, it was theorized that there is a common origin for the magma ('monomagmatism'). Furthermore, a more recent theory was posited by Yoder and Tilley (1962), based on the differentiation of the basalts.

SUMMARY OF MAGMAS

CHEMISTRY	BASALTIC	ANDESITIC	GRANITIC
	Basic	Calco-alkaline	Acid
Depth of Formation	35-100 km	10 to 35 km (mantle)	less than 20 km (crust)
Temperature of Formation	1200-1500° C	1200-1300° C	550-750° C
Effusive Products	Frequent	Frequent	Rare
Petrography	(+) Basalts (-) Gabbros	(+) Andesites Diorites (-)Rhyolites	(+) Granites (-) Basalts

(+)= more of (-)= less of

Basalts and rhyolites are eruptive rocks (surface); granites and gabbros are plutonic rocks (deep).

GLACIAL AGES IN THE GALÁPAGOS

It has been proved that the age of the Galápagos is between three and five million years. For the last two million years, glaciations have been important on earth and have contributed to modifying the geography of the continents. Today, ice covers 10 per cent of the planet's surface. Twenty thousand years ago, in Pleistocene times, that ice surface was three times as extensive as it is now. Ice comes from the ocean. If the ice of the poles should melt today, the sea level would rise up as much as 65 metres. In the Pleistocene, the ice cover had a volume of 77 million cubic kilometres, which means that the sea level then was at least 120 metres below its present level. Many islands in the Galápagos would have been joined together then.

The glacial ages of the Galápagos have been studied by Paul Colinvaux (1984) and measured by the study of sediments in ancient lakes. The Galápagos appeared to be more arid in glacial times. Four lagoons were investigated:
- Darwin Lake: in Tagus Cove (Isabela Island) had a bottom of salt and lava. No sediment, so quite young in age.
- Beagle Lake: (Isabela Island) possesses a 15-centimetres deep sandy bottom. The age is not significant.
- Arcturus Lake: (Genovesa Island) 30 metres of salt water cover a muddy sediment five metres in depth. The age was estimated to be 4,000 to 6,000 years.
- El Junco: (San Cristóbal Island) was the most interesting. With a diameter of 273 metres, this sweet-water lake, only six metres in depth, had a sediment depth of 16 metres, which was aged 40,000 years. A red clay sediment was also found which had a core more than 48,000 years old. This lake seems to have existed for at least 100,000 years. It was protected from evaporation by the cloud layer and the annual March rains.

CHAPTER TWO

OCEANIC CURRENTS
SEASONS AND CLIMATE
TEMPERATURES

Oceanic currents and trade winds have a determining action on the Galápagos, for they influence not only the climate but the two resulting seasons, which are:
- The *garua*, or dry season.
- The hot season, or wet season.

Even through they are located on the equator, the islands are classified as 'subtropical' rather than tropical. Nevertheless, the northern islands are almost tropical, because they are less affected by the cold waters of the south. The southern islands are more affected by the cold ocean stream of the Humboldt Current.

OCEAN CURRENTS

The confluence of many ocean currents in the Galápagos turned the islands into an unusual geographical spot on the world map. Even though on the equator, they do not have a characteristically equatorial climate and are therefore considered to have a micro-climate.

Logically, the ocean currents are a key to this phenomenon. The oceanic masses come primarily from the southeast, the northeast and the west. Some are cold, such as the Peruvian Coastal Current and the Peruvian Oceanic Current, with a mean temperature of 15° C. Upon arrival in the Galápagos, they surface from a depth of 100 metres.

Another important cold-water current is the Cromwell Current, also called the Sub-equatorial Countercurrent. With a front of 300 kilometres, it comes from the western Pacific, exactly under the equator and under the South Equatorial Current, which in turn flows west. The Cromwell Current is 150 to 200 metres thick, with a temperature of 13° C in its core, and flows at a speed of 25 centimetres per second. It upwells to the west of Fernandina and Isabela islands, then goes around these two islands towardss the center of the archipelago, where its action gradually fades away.

From the east, the South Equatorial Current flows at a speed of 50 centimetres per second. This water mass is influenced by the cold waters of the southeastern Pacific (Humboldt Current) and by the warm waters of the northeast coming from Panama (a flow sometimes called 'El Niño'). The border between the subtropical waters of the south and the tropical waters of the north is known as the 'Equatorial Front'. This diagonal line, southeast to northwest, stretches between 4° south latitude and 1° to 3° north latitude.

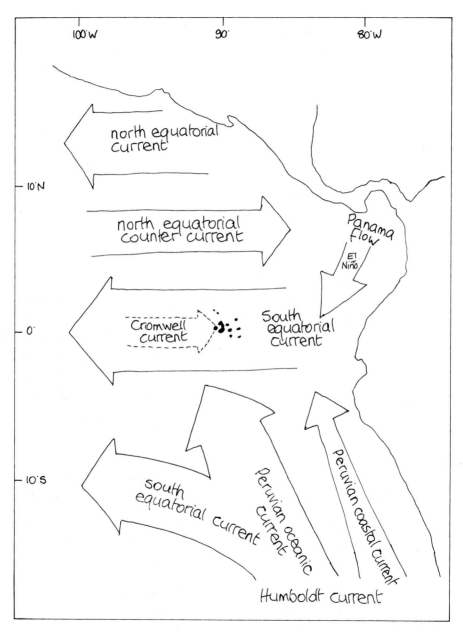

Distribution of the currents ~ Tropical East Pacific.

There is also a convergence of the trade winds, more or less parallel to the Equatorial Front. This is the Intertropical Convergence Zone (ITCZ), where the southeast trade winds and the northeast trade winds meet. This ITCZ is located at 10° north latitude in the dry season, and migrates down to 3° north latitude in the wet season.

Another important current, associated with the Panama flow or El Niño, is the North Equatorial Countercurrent (NECC), which places itself between the South Equatorial Current (SEC) and the North Equatorial Current (NEC), at about 5° north latitude. This superficial current brings warm tropical waters from the western Pacific and ends in the Gulf of Panama, where it splits in two. One part flows up north, along the coast of Central America towardss California. The other part flows south, where it meets the SEC. The NECC is the main conveyor of organisms coming from Asia and from the Panama-Colombia area.

THE GARUA SEASON

This cool and dry season lasts from May to December. Temperatures are lower than during the rest of the year, and the season brings a subtropical climate, when cold waters come up from the antarctic region.

A frequent mist covers the top of the islands, with some sort of fine rain or 'garua', which is more infrequent on the coast. During the garua season, the cold Peruvian Oceanic Current and Peruvian Coastal Current (known as the Humboldt Current) are dominant. This cold-water mass comes up from Antarctica along the western coast of South America, then heads west to the Galápagos upon reaching the equator. The southeast trade winds, very strong during the garua season, contribute to the process. The temperature of the water is about 18° to 20° C, with a salinity of 35 ppm. The marine fauna is rich. The Humboldt Current is strongest in September, and the sea surface rather rough (see map of Ocean Currents, page 26).

HOW IS THE GARUA FORMED?

The Intertropical Convergence Zone (ITCZ) is well north during the dry season. The southeast trade winds drive the waters of the Humboldt Current north. Warm air migrates over a cold-water current, at an elevation of a 100 or 200 metres, cools off upon contact, and becomes bottom heavy and loaded with humidity. An inversion is formed, with hot air above and cold air below. An equilibrium is reached, and the lower layer is saturated with condensed water. A stratus cloud is formed, which will travel horizontally above the ocean surface, with little precipitation.

If this layer meets an elevated island (eg Santa Cruz), an orographic elevation is created, with lower pressure. Hot air will cool off (since cold air cannot hold moisture as well as warm air), and precipitation will pour down in the form of garua.

THE WARM SEASON

It stretches from December to May. The annual rains occur during the first three months of the year. Nevertheless, the temperature is higher, and the sunny days are more numerous than during the garua season. The southeast trade winds vanish, as does the action of the Humboldt Current. The northeast trade winds become dominant, and warm waters head south from Panama and Colombia. Sea surface temperatures range from 24 to 27° C, with a low salinity of 33.5 ppm, and the waters are poor in organisms. The ITCZ migrates south, to a few degrees north of the equator. The warm waters again meet the Humboldt Current and form the South Equatorial Current, which flows across the Galápagos archipelago.

The climatic 'inversion' created during the garua season disappears, allowing for the formation of cumulus clouds. During the wet season, precipitation occurs as conventional rains—strong, but of short duration.

THE 'EL NIÑO' PHENOMENON

Some years the warm-water flow coming from the north is considerably increased. Since it happens around Christmas, it has been named 'El Niño' (after the infant Jesus). It is not a real current. Its action is mainly on the South American mainland, where it triggers heavy rains and disasters in the fishing industry. In fact, it doesn't really affect the Galápagos, where it is manifest every four to seven years.

In 1982-83, an exceptional Niño in the Galápagos brought nine months of continuous rain, an abnormal rate of ambient humidity, suffocating heat and a sea surface temperature of 30° C, followed by tremendous animal mortality. The climatologic effect of that Niño was felt worldwide. Scientists had to study the case seriously. What factors induce such an imbalance? After investigation, it seemed that the phenomenon simply resulted from the dynamics of the Pacific Ocean, and the displacement of considerable oceanic water masses.

During the dry season, the preponderant southeast trade winds push surface waters towards the west, away from the South American mainland. In the Pacific Ocean, the wind action does the same. This brings a conspicuous upheaval of the ocean level in the western Pacific, which means that the water column is higher in the west than it is in the east. Part of the 'return' system is made through the NECC and the Cromwell Current. With the start of the Galápagos' wet season in December, the ITCZ moves south. The water temperature rises with the arrival of warm waters coming from Panama. An enormous amount of warm water returns from the western Pacific towardss the east. It is believed that this is what triggered the 1982-83 Niño. These unusual conditions are associated with variations in pressure in the Pacific, allowing equatorial west winds to blow east. This would create surface waves that move across the Pacific, draining warm waters. Thus the floods in Ecuador, the abundant rains and the elevation of the ocean level in the Galápagos by 22 centimetres.

To conclude, the position of the ITCZ is slightly north of the equator, because the dominant winds come from the southeast. Since these bring humidity to the islands, the windward side of the islands is wetter than the leeward side. That is easily seen in the vegetation zones. The arid zone will rise up higher on the leeward side than on the windward side. Let us take the example of Santa Cruz Island, where the windward side is to the south: the arid zone stretches up from 80 to 120 metres maximum. On the north, leeward face, the arid zone rises up to 200–300 metres. The same applies to the transition zone. This phenomenon is called the 'rain shadow effect'. Fernandina Island is another example, lying in the 'rain shadow' of Isabela Island (see drawing of Vegetation Zones, page 69).

In 1997–98 another El Niño came to Galapagos. Abnormal sea surface temperatures were noticed as early as June 1997. The archipelago was effected and scientists warned that it could be the El Niño of the century. In April 1998, air temperatures were still high, and big waves were coming from afar to wash the south and west shores of the Galápagos islands.

Annual Temperatures After Six Years of Readings at the Darwin Station

	JAN	FEB	MAR	APR	MAY	JUN	JUL	AUG	SEP	OCT	NOV	DEC
Max Temp.° C	28	29.6	30.6	29.5	27.9	26	24.6	24.2	24.3	25.3	25.8	26.7
Min Temp.° C	22.8	23.2	22.7	22.7	22.1	19.1	19.8	19.1	19.6	19.5	20.4	20.9
Hours of sun	5.3	7.5	6.0	7.5	5.2	4.4	2.8	3.3	2.9	3.8	3.5	4.0
Sea Temp.° C	24.4	25.2	24.9	25	24.5	23.1	22	21.5	21.8	22.3	23	23.3

Temperatures in °C

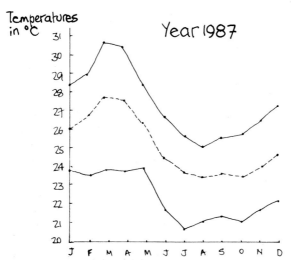

Year 1987

Month of the year

Air temperatures in Puerto Ayora
(Santa Cruz), equal to a "Niño"
[after "Carta Informativa", CDRS 1988].

Sea surface temperatures
Year 1987, for a possible "Niño".
[after CDRS, 1988].

Temperatures in °C

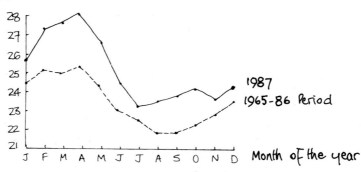

1987

1965-86 Period

Month of the year

CHAPTER THREE

HUMAN HISTORY OF THE GALÁPAGOS ISLANDS

Well before the Incas—that they ever visited the islands is doubtful—it seems that the first visitors to the islands were Indians who came from Ecuador on balsa rafts. Probably of Mantena or Huancavilca culture, they did not stay long. Pieces of pottery have been found on Santiago Island, on Santa Cruz (Whale Bay) and at Black Beach on the island of Floreana.

Around 1485, Tupac Inca Yupanqui, a prince from Cuzco (who would become the tenth inca), heard rumors about two uninhabited islands far to the west. He was then near the present site of Guayaquil with his army, and decided to build a fleet of balsa rafts equipped with sails. The expedition was gone for nine months to a year. The Inca Yupanqui returned with gold, a bronze seat, and the skin and jaws of a 'horse'. These trophies were kept in the fortress of Cuzco until the arrival of the Spaniards (after Cabello de Balboa, 1586). The two islands were called Nina-Chumbi (Fire Island) and Hahua Chumbi (Outer Island). According to Thor Heyerdahl, the Norwegian explorer, the trophies and the black men could have come from a raid on the mainland, north of the starting point. The skin and jaws of the so-called 'horse' could well have been that of a male sea lion.

The Galápagos bear no archeological remains of dwellings or other structures, so it is quite unlikely that a colony was ever established there, even in remote times.

After the discovery of the Americas by Christopher Columbus in 1492, and the liberation of Spain from the Moors by the Catholic King Ferdinand and Queen Isabela, trips beyond the Atlantic became popular. Conducted with the blessing of the Spanish kings, who were eager to discover new territories, the adventurers' declared aim was the conversion of pagan souls, and their exploits were undertaken under the high authority of the Borgia pope, Alexander VI, who divided the New World for that purpose between Spain and Portugal.

The year 1519 saw the conquest of Mexico by Hernan Cortez. Then in 1532 came the conquest of Peru by Francisco Pizzaro, who subdued the Inca empire. Far away from the kingdom of Spain, the conquistadors made their own laws in these new lands and without mercy enslaved all the Indians. Gradually, their thirst for gold and riches (one-fifth was given to the Spanish Crown) brought the conquistadors to quarrel among themselves for supreme power.

It was at that time that Fray Tomas de Berlanga, archbishop of Panama, was given a mission by King Charles V, to report on the anarchic situation in Peru. He and his crew set sail in a caravel for Lima on February 23, 1535. After seven days of navigation along the coast of South America, the wind dropped for six days. The vessel drifted 800 kilometres west into the Pacific Ocean, carried by the South Equatorial Current. Fray Tomas de Berlanga officially discovered the Galápagos archipelago on March 10, 1535. The bishop wrote to King Charles V, describing the giant tortoises, the iguanas, and the tameness of the birds. To him, the islands appeared very inhospitable.

Eleven years later, in 1546, a Spanish renegade named Diego de Rivadeneira, having deserted the army of Francisco Pizarro, fled with a dozen men on a stolen boat. He got lost just as the bishop had, and drifted away to the islands, where he eventually found water and turtles. He is the first visitor to mention the Galápagos hawk.

After their discovery, the islands still remained without a name. It was much later, during the second half of the XVIth century, that quite a number of navigators named them Islas Encantadas or 'Enchanted Islands', for they seemed to appear and disappear on the surface of the ocean by magic. The phantom silhouettes of the volcanoes were always bathed in fog, which made the islands hard to distinguish.

Nowadays, the official name is Archipelago de Colon, and was given to the islands by Ecuador in 1892 to commemorate the 400th anniversary of the discovery of the Americas by Christopher Columbus. The usual name, however, remains 'Galápagos'.

The first marine charts mentioning the islands date to 1570. In 1574, the 'Enchanted Islands' appeared on the map of Abraham Ortelius, with the name 'Archipelago de los Galopegos'. The pirate William Cowley, in 1684, followed by Captain Colnett, in 1793–94, brought English names to the islands. All the names, in English or Spanish, honor kings, admirals, pirates and numerous visitors of the islands.

In 1577, the English pirate Francis Drake cleared Cape Horn and arrived in the Pacific Ocean, where the situation becomes suddenly explosive. 'There is no peace beyond the line,' said he, referring to the boundary line drawn by Pope Alexander VI, which stretched north to south, 1,800 kilometres west of the Cape Verde Islands. Hostilities were declared between England and Spain. These would last from 1593 to 1710.

In the 17th century, English, French and Dutch pirates waged a war against Spain and used the Galápagos as a refuge. From there, they could easily attack the Spanish galleons sailing from the South American coast and sack the coastal ports of Guayaquil and Lima. Buccaneer's Cove and James Bay, on Santiago Island, became favourite hideouts of the pirates. There, they would collect water, wood and giant tortoises. The unfortunate reptiles that were piled in the hulls of the boats could survive a year without drinking water. The most famous of the English pirates were Cowley, Dampier, Davis, Wafer, Cook and Eaton. Among the French were Groguiet, l'Escuyer, Desmarais, Le Picard and Rose. The most visited islands were Santiago and Floreana, where volcanic caves served as primitive dwellings as well as a place to hide bounty and food.

TABLE OF THE NAMES OF THE ISLANDS

Spanish	English
Pinta	Abington
Isabela	Albemarle
Baltra	South Seymour
Santa Fé	Barrington
Beagle	Beagle
Marchena	Bindloe
Tortuga	Brattle
Bartolomé	Bartolomew
Caldwell	Caldwell
Champion	Champion
Floreana, Santa Maria	Charles
San Cristóbal	Chatham
Cowley	Cowley
Crossman	Crossman
Darwin	Culpepper
Wolf	Wenman
Daphné	Daphné
Pinzón	Duncan
Eden	Eden
Enderby	Enderby
Gardner	Gardner (Charles)
Gardner	Gardner (Hood)
Guy Fawkes	Guy Fawkes
Española	Hood
Santa Cruz	Indefatigable
Santiago, San Salvador	James
Rábida	Jervis
Sin Nombre	Nameless
Fernandina	Narborough
Onslow	Onslow
Plaza Sur	South Plaza
Genovesa	Tower
Watson	Watson

Another famous man who came to the Galápagos was 'Robinson Crusoe'. Alexander Selkirk was his real name. He was freed in February 1709 from his lone island—Juan Fernandez, off the coast of Chile—by Captain Woods Rodgers, another pirate. After four years and four months, Robinson Crusoe, who had been master of the ship *Cinque Ports*, was taken aboard Woods' ship. Three months later, he was in the Galápagos. There, he was given the command of a ship, and later on, he took part in the sack of Guayaquil, a port on the coast of Ecuador. Two years later, in 1711, he returned to England, where he became famous, thanks to *Robinson Crusoe* by Daniel Defoe.

Between 1780 and 1860, the waters of the Galápagos became a favourite place for British and American whalers. During the 19th century, thousands of fur sea lions were butchered. Captain Benjamin Morell confessed to having skinned 5,000 sea lions in two months. Thousands of turtles left the islands at that time, piled alive in the hulls of the boats, from which they were extracted periodically for their meat and their fat. In 1793, a strange barrel was erected on Floreana Island to facilitate communication between boats and the land. The barrel was put there by Captain James Colnett of the British Royal Navy, and officially marked the beginning of the era of the whaling industry. It is still in place today, at Post Office Bay.

The first man to live in the archipelago was Irish, and his name was Patrick Watkins. Nobody knows whether he was a castaway or if he deliberately chose to live on Floreana, in 1807. Anyway, he survived by growing vegetables, which he traded for rum with the passing whalers. His only wish was to drift permanently in the vapor of alcohol. Captain Porter of the navy frigate USS *Essex* described Watkins as a monster with devilish looks:

> *The most dreadful that can be imagined: ragged clothes, scarce sufficient to cover his nakedness, and covered with vermin; his red hair and beard matted, his skin much burnt from constant exposure to the sun, and so wild and savage in his manner and appearance that he struck everyone with horror.... But this man, wretched and miserable as he may have appeared, was neither destitute of ambition, nor incapable of undertaking an enterprise that would have appalled the heart of any other man; nor was he devoid of the talent of rousing others to second his hardihood.*

Two years later, in 1809, Watkins seized a whaling ship, the *Black Prince*, while the crew was on land in search of fresh water and turtles. He took with him five sailors that had landed on Floreana. Unable to find a way out without Watkin's help these five men became his 'slaves'. Watkins eventually made his way to Guayaquil on his own and no one ever discovered what became of his companions, whether he ate them or threw them overboard.

In 1813, the famous Captain David Porter of the USS *Essex,* who hated the English, captured the British whaling fleet in the Galápagos, taking 12 ships in five months. Porter wrote many interesting notes on the Galápagos environment. After Watkins, the islands were more or less uninhabited until 1832, when Ecuadorian General José Villamil founded a prosperous colony on Floreana. The population was mainly composed of convicts, political prisoners and other unwanted people, who traded meat and vegetables with the whalers. In February 1832, two years after the creation of the young republic, Colonel Ignacio Hernandez took official possession of the archipelago in the name of Ecuador. Spanish names were given to the islands, in addition to existing English names. After Villamil departed to San Cristóbal, the colony of Floreana was turned into a penitentiary and fell into chaos. In 1869, a cruel and tyrannical man named Manuel Cobos founded the penal colony of El Progresso on San Cristóbal Island. He regularly abused the wives of his men, and was eventually murdered with a machete by a Colombian convict in 1904.

Many colonies were established over the years, and nearly all collapsed. One succeeded, founded in 1893 by Don Antonil Gil, an honourable citizen of Guayaquil, in Puerto Villamil, on the southern coast of Isabela Island. People survived by selling cattle and by the exploitation of the sulphur mine of Sierra Negra volcano. A Norwegian colony settled on Floreana Island in 1926. Just like its predecessors, the attempt quickly went awry and the island was deserted.

Some years went by. In 1929, a strange German doctor, Friedrich Ritter—dentist, vegetarian and philosopher—arrived on the island with his female assistant, Dore Strauch. They built a house named 'Friedo' in the highlands of Floreana, near a freshwater spring, then created a cosmogonic orchard, following the elaborate theories of Dr Ritter. For the next three years, he wrote many articles for the press, which became well known in Europe. In 1932, the Wittmer family decided to settle on the island too, to practice agriculture and to lead a peaceful life. Floreana became so fashionable that luxurious yachts used to call in, and rich Americans dropped anchor at Black Beach to pay a visit to the 'Robinson Crusoes' of Floreana.

This was tremendously pleasing to the Baroness von Wagner de Bosquet, a young German woman who had a notion to build a hotel for 'millionaires' on the same island. With her two lovers, Lorenz and Philipson, she disembarked in 1932 and built the 'Hacienda Paraiso', a mere shack of planks and corrugated iron. Soon after, she proclaimed herself the 'Empress of Floreana' by virtue of the gun and the whip. Of course, this was not to the liking of Dr Ritter or the Wittmer family. Tensions rose.

The story ended in 1934, after the disappearance of the baroness and Philipson, and the tragic death of Lorenz, who was caught in a storm in a small boat and cast away on the shore of Marchena Island, where he died of thirst with a Norwegian sailor. Dr Ritter died, too, poisoned by tainted chicken. Dore Strauch left the island and returned to

Germany, where she wrote a book entitled *Satan Came to Eden* before she fell to the curse of Ritter some years later. At present, only Margret Wittmer has survived this untold drama, and the mystery lives on. She still lives at Black Beach on Floreana, and turned 90 on July 12, 1994. Her book, *Floreana, Poste Restante*, an extraordinary adventure tale of life at the end of the world, was published in 1961 and became a bestseller.

During the Second World War, an American Air Force base was built on the strategic island of Baltra (north of Santa Cruz Island), from where it was possible to defend the Panama Canal (see the Historical Index, in Appendix). Nowadays, Floreana and Isabela islands are inhabited, and bigger communities have been established on Santa Cruz and San Cristóbal. On Santa Cruz, the most central of all, two villages are occupied with agriculture in the tropical highlands. Puerto Ayora, in Academy Bay, is the touristic capital of the Galápagos. Puerto Baquerizo Moreno, on San Cristóbal, is the administrative capital and Ecuador's second naval base.

In 1981, the population of the islands was estimated at about 5,000 people. It reached 10,000 people in 1988, and was around 20,000 people in 1994 (see Appendix 3, page 292).

DARWIN AND THE GALÁPAGOS

Without any doubt, the most famous visitor to the Galápagos is Charles Darwin. His short stay in the archipelago has proved enormously significant for science and for the study of evolution (see map: the Route of Charles Darwin, page opposite). At the age of 26, the young British naturalist travelled around the globe on the HMS *Beagle* with Captain Fitzroy. Towardss the end of 1835, he sailed from Tierra del Fuego, along the coasts of Chile and Peru, and arrived in the islands for the most unforgettable five weeks of his life. One morning, after dropping anchor in a cove at San Cristóbal, he disembarked and would later write:

> *The surface of this part of the island seems to be punctured like a skimmer by subterranean steam; here and there, the lava, still soft, has puffed up in giant bubbles; elsewhere, the roof of the caverns thus formed has collapsed and one can see in the middle a well with perpendicular sides. The common shape of these numerous craters gives an artificial aspect to the land which reminds me of the furnaces of Staffordshire. It was incredibly hot. I felt extremely tired to walk on this rough surface, but the strange scene of this cyclopean country compensated far beyond my tiredness. During my wandering, I met two giant tortoises, each could have weighed at least 200 pounds; one was eating a cactus pad. When I approached, it stared at me conspicuously, then moved away slowly. The other one whistled formidably and retracted*

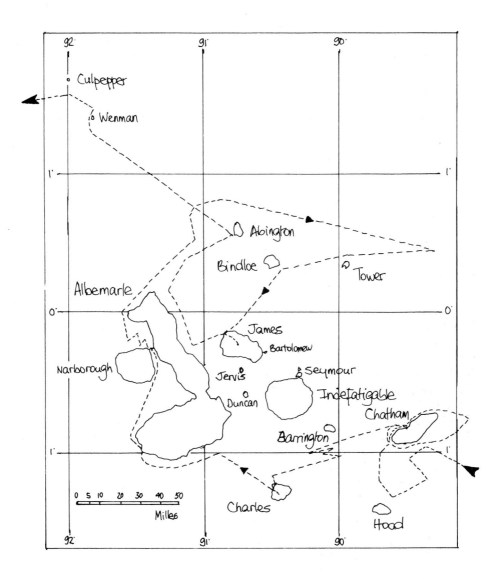

The Route of Charles Darwin
aboard HMS Beagle [Sept. 17 ~ Oct. 20 1835]

her head under the shell. These huge reptiles, surrounded by black lava, by shrubs with no leaves and tall cacti, looked like real antediluvian beasts. The few birds with dim colours than I met here and there, could not bother less about me than they would of the giant tortoises.

As he observed the fauna of the archipelago, one of Darwin's major discoveries was to realize that the species were not 'unchangeable', but that they were exposed to the irreversible process of evolution. Natural selection, adaptation to the environment and genetic mutation, became keywords that helped him to elaborate—thanks to the finches mainly—the celebrated theory of 'Evolution of the Species', which came to light in 1859, 24 years after his journey to the enchanted islands. A new revolution in the scientific mind was born.

CHAPTER FOUR

Arrival and Establishment of the Organisms

The first thing to consider is the difference between two fundamental concepts: 'continental island' and 'oceanic island'. A continental island is an island that has, at some time in the past, been connected to the continent by a land bridge, and which, therefore, possesses flora and fauna typical of the continental mass from which it originated. By contrast, an oceanic island is born from a submarine volcano which has emerged from the ocean without any life on it. The great distance between an oceanic island and the continent make if difficult for land organisms to reach it, even those having good means of dispersal. Logically, groups of plants and animals having an easy means of dispersal have a greater chance of reaching an oceanic island and thriving, if the conditions are favourable.

The consequence of this phenomenon is an unbalanced flora and fauna in comparison to the continental mass. The word 'disharmonic' is used to define this condition. The Galápagos Islands are therefore a good example of biotypic disharmony. The vertebrates are well represented by birds and reptiles; native mammals are poorly represented, while amphibians and freshwater fishes are totally absent. Among insects, only butterflies and beetles are well represented. A good number of land birds are totally absent in the archipelago.

Among plants, lichens, ferns, grasses, sedges and the Compositae family are well represented, whereas gymnosperms and palm trees are absent, and monocotyledons almost nonexistent. Very few trees are native to the islands. Orchids (11 species), Labiatae (mint family), Acanthacae (grasses, shrubs) are appreciated by the pollinating insects.

Groups of animal and plants well represented in the archipelago are therefore those most likely to cross an ocean frontier of hundreds of kilometres. Such a crossing could be made in three different ways:
- free floating on the sea, or on a natural raft.
- dispersal by wind, or in the air.
- transport in the body of another organism, by air or by sea.

Arrival

Let us consider first transport by sea. Seeds can be carried away passively by flotation. Legumes, even though intolerant of immersion, have an empty space between the embryo and the external shell of the seed. The Galápagos cotton (*Gossypium darwinii*) can withstand a lengthy stay in salt water, and may float for 10 weeks or longer (Stephens, 1958). The Humboldt and South Equatorial currents may carry these cotton seeds from the coast of Peru in less time than that.

Turtles have also a great capacity for flotation, for they have a pocket of air between the upper back and the shell. The second type of passive transport is 'rafting', by natural raft. These vegetation rafts have been seen drifting hundreds of kilometres from the coast, pushed by the sea winds towardss the Galápagos from Peru to Ecuador by the Humboldt or Panama currents. Even palm tree logs can carry various insects: ants, larvae, beetles. In 1892, Agassiz saw large rafts drifting from Panama to Cocos Island and the Galápagos, at a speed of about 130 kilometres (75 miles) a day. Such a raft could reach the archipelago in two weeks. Reptiles have a completely waterproof skin, and drink very little water. In 1880, a boa constrictor was seen (alive) in the Caribbean, coiled around the log of a cedar tree, floating 300 kilometres from Trinidad. Sea lions and fur sea lions also travel with the help of the currents. They came from the north (California) and from the southeast (Antarctic), and colonized the archipelago after a group migration.

The second type of transport is transport by air. Aerial dispersal is the best means by which insects reach the islands. It can be passive, as with spiders taken in air currents at an elevation of about 3,000 metres. Likewise, the seeds of orchids and spores of ferns, mosses and mushrooms, which can resist very low temperatures, are dispersed this way. When they arrive above the islands, the spores drop with the condensation of the air. The poor representation of butterflies in the Galápagos is due to the fact that adults have fragile wings, and the larvae are very sensitive.

Transport via other organisms, or active transport, is mainly carried out by birds. Seagulls for example, come from areas with abundant vegetation. They carry seeds in their stomachs, between their feathers or under their wings, even in the mud stuck to their feet. Seeds collected from riverbanks or swamps can be carried away in such a fashion.

Among 607 species of plants found in the Galápagos, it has been estimated that 59 per cent of them were transported as seeds by birds, 32 per cent by the wind, and nine per cent by ocean transport. If one considers the influence of man, then 40 per cent were transported by birds, 32 per cent by man, 22 per cent by wind and 6 per cent by flotation.

ESTABLISHMENT AND SURVIVAL

Once on the island, the organism has to establish itself, and before anything else it must find food to survive. Reproduction of the species comes later. The establishment is as vital as the arrival in order to colonize the island with success. Two major reasons explain why a group of animals or plants can be absent from an island:
- The organism has not reached there at all.

- After arriving, the organism has not been able to establish (importance of the season).

An airborne organism—unlike one carried by sea—is not conditioned to land on a particular island. It can drop on the soil of any habitat, and therefore has a greater chance to become established. Once the difficulties of arrival are overcome, the living being has to reproduce to ensure the survival of the species.

Hermaphroditic plants have no problems in reproducing, for the male and female principals are located on the same flower. By contrast, in dioecious plants, male and female principals are on different plants, as is the case with most animals, for whom reproduction is possible only if the complementary individual is present.

In the Galápagos, three plants are dioecious: Castela and Croton, which are shrubs of the arid zone, and Bursera, also called palo santo, which is a tree with white bark.

Lindsay (1966) thinks that the first plants introduced to the islands were self-reproducing. Later on, the presence of a wasp, as well as of some other pollinating insects, was important in the reproductive process of the plants. To illustrate the action of the wind in reproduction, studies have shown that 32 per cent of the flora are pollinated by the wind in Hawaii, 34 per cent in Juan Fernandez in the southeastern Pacific and 29 per cent in New Zealand.

Some factors are essential for a plant to establish. The majority of land plants need a soil rich in humus, and will not establish on an island where the soil is poor. Exceptions include the lichens Archicera, which can fix themselves upon lava on the shore.

Finally, animals are dependant on plants for food, therefore the plants must be established before the animal. We may talk about the vegetarian vertebrates, such as turtles, or marine iguanas, which need a good cover of vegetation to survive. Some sea birds need material to build their nests. The optimum moment chosen by an organism (eg a bird) to arrive is important when related to the arrival of another competing species. The 'ecological niche' (that is, all conditions necessary for survival and reproduction) of an arriving species may be already occupied by another organism which established itself earlier in the community. A morphological transformation will then take place. Otherwise, one of the two species is doomed to extinction. The arrival of an organism in an already overpopulated island is only possible if another species is going extinct or has already disappeared. The island reaches equilibrium when immigration is balanced by extinction. When they are near to the mainland, big islands have a high immigration rate and a low extinction rate, which means that they are soon saturated. Faraway islands, with a low immigration rate (even more if they are small), will be saturated less quickly. This is also due to a faster extinction rate.

MacArthur and Wilson (1963), authors of the equilibrium theory, take the example of Krakatoa Island, where fauna took 36 years to reach equilibrium after the devastating volcanic eruption. As a matter of fact, Krakatoa is very interesting, for it is a similar example to the Galápagos.

Krakatoa, a volcanic island of Indonesia, between Sumatra and Java, emerged from the ocean after a memorable explosion in 1883. In 1886, three years later, there were 11 species of ferns, two species of *Compositae* and two grasses. In 1894 (11 years later), the interior of the island was bedecked with grassy vegetation and a few shrubs. The year 1903 saw luxurious vegetation on the island. In 1908, 25 years after the eruption, one could find 13 species of birds, a species of monitor lizard, one gecko, 192 species of insects, ants, flies, beetles, dragonflies and butterflies; spiders and scorpions were also present.

The Galápagos followed the same pattern of population, and are today the home of unique organisms, including land and marine iguanas, giant tortoises, mockingbirds, lava gulls, Darwin's finches, the Galápagos dove, the flightless cormorant, the albatross and the Galápagos penguin, which are found nowhere else in the world.

GEOGRAPHIC AFFINITIES

Logically, most of the animals in the Galápagos originated from North, Central and South America and the Caribbean.
- from North America: some land birds like the 'yellow warbler' and the California sea lions.
- from the Caribbean: pink flamingos, Darwin's finches (the ancestor on Ste Lucie Island was transported by winds to Costa Rica, and later on to Cocos Island, before reaching the Galápagos).
- from South America: land iguanas, giant tortoises, pelicans, flightless cormorants, vermillion flycatcher.
- from the Antarctic: fur sea lions and penguins.

CHAPTER FIVE

The Theory of Evolution and the Galápagos

The Galápagos archipelago has been called the 'showcase of evolution', and truly, for the biologist, the islands are a living laboratory for the study of evolution. The closest example to the Galápagos is perhaps Hawaii, which, at 20 million years old, is six times older than the assumed age of our archipelago.

Evolution is the central topic of biology. Before Darwin, the creationist theory declared that life appeared on earth on Sunday 23 October 4004 BC, at nine in the morning. Darwin had been brought up to become an Anglican clergyman. He left England for a five-year journey around the planet, questioning himself for a long time, testing his ideas. He recognized variation within species and also that a gradual change was sometimes affecting a species. The world means change in the characteristics of living beings, which cannot be inherited. A living being is recognized by five essential characteristics, which are:
  - the ability to reproduce.
  - the ability to memorize information in their genes (in a molecular sense).
  - control of their environment.
  - excitability, or ability to respond to a stimulus.
  - excitability by/in producing energy.

A living organism knows how to adjust to specific conditions and is able to 'modify' itself. These evolutionary changes may be an answer to natural selection. Those which fail are doomed; those which succeed must change and evolve. 'The survival of the fittest', said Darwin. According to the theory of evolution, all living organisms have a phylogenetic heritage, in other words, a genetic heritage linked to the development of the group (Grzimek, *Encyclopedia of Evolution*, 1972). This phylogenetic process is stimulated by two factors:
  - genetic variation
  - natural selection

If organic evolution is a change in genetics, natural selection should not be mistaken for evolution. Evolution refers to temporal changes of all sorts, whereas natural selection brings about a particular way through which these changes are made (E.R. Pianka, 1974).

Another definition of evolution is: non-cyclic changes in the genetic pool (sum of the allele genes in a population). Two ideas come up next: the 'genotype' and the 'phenotype'. The genotype is the genetic asset of an individual as inherited from its parents' DNA. The phenotype is its morphology, physiology and real behavior after interaction of the genotype with the environment.

The evolutionary space-time (or time-free) frame of evolution is the mutation. Mutations within a population, and within a given time, play an important role in the future evolution of this population. Evolution is induced by mutations and natural selection. Mutations favor genetic variety. Natural selection, on the contrary, limits the genetic variety. Evolution is a continuum; it is not a number of species following one another. 'Speciation', or multiplication of the species, occurs when a genetic pool is divided in two isolated parts. This is to say that members of a given population become reproductively isolated from the other members of that population. Once evolution reaches such a level, where two populations cannot mate, then each turns into a unique species. The evolution process is so unique that the complex relationship between an organism and its environment changes with time. Three examples will bring some light to this idea:
- Evolution may occur when the biological entity (animal) stays within its habitat and does not substantially change its lifestyle.
- Organisms, having gone through mutations, even minor ones, may conquer a new habitat (a new ecological niche) by modification of their behavior, but still keeping their old structure. In other words, structures may accomplish new functions.
- Another possible evolution links the two cases mentioned above. Anatomic changes and new functions may occur simultaneously in the evolution of an animal group.

The original organism, having gone through the effects of natural selection, is transformed in such a way that its body is able to meet the functional demands of the environment. It evolves so that the last forms of individuals have more chances of survival and a higher rate of reproduction success than the earlier forms.

To conclude, let us quote Haeckel: 'Ontogeny recapitulates phylogeny', which means that the development of the individual within the egg sums up the development of the animal group to which it belongs. In the Galápagos, one important factor to consider is insularity. Islands differ from the continental landmass by their isolation, which implies not only the role of selection, but also that of the 'chance' factor in the evolutionary process. Mayr (1963) has shown the extreme importance of geographic isolation in speciation. Darwin is known for his famous saying: 'The survival of the fittest', which can be compared with 'the death of the weakest'. Considering fitness or adaptability, natural selection stresses an answer to the conditions of the environment.

For an animal, a change in behavior brings about a change in physiology, therefore a morphological change. Natural selection is the means through which organisms become gradually better adapted to their environment. Even though the majority of the species are doomed to extinction without the creation of a new evolutionary way, it is not impossible that a particular species can become a pioneer of evolution. Without differentiation of the species, there would not be any diversity in the organic world, and very little progress in evolution. The species is then the 'key' to evolution.

For insular populations, two common factors induce fragmentation and speed up speciation:
- the tendency for a well-established population to move out of the marginal habitats towardss more central habitats, therefore minimizing the capacity of dispersal of the population.
- the fact that island organisms have a tendency to form restricted and localized populations.

DARWIN'S FINCHES

Archipelagos are ideal for geographic isolation and speciation. In the Galápagos, 13 species of finches (in fact 14, counting the one on Cocos Island) have evolved from one original species, which migrated from Costa Rica. *Melanospiza richardsoni*, on Ste Lucie Island in the West Indies, is the nearest species.

For populations in isolation, various selective pressures on different islands lead to evolution and divergent adaptations. Occasional interactions between islands favour 'competition' which promotes the diversity of the 'niches'. (Niche: all the necessary conditions for an animal to survive and to reproduce in a given environment.) The competition may be 'interspecific', ie, between different species, or 'intraspecific', within the same species. The more individuals, the greater the competition. For the niches of the original island, the increasing population leads to the departure of a number of individuals towardss other habitats. Each newly colonized island will later yield as many unique species, adapted to a specific environment with adequate functions. The 'adaptive radiation' of the finches in the Galápagos has created four distinct genera, which differ by the following factors:
  - where they feed
  - how they feed
  - what they feed on

For the Darwin finches, the morphological changes are seen in the size and shape of the beak: ground finches, tree finches, cactus finches, vegetarian finch, warbler finch, sharpbill ground finch, carpenter finch... Some of these individuals migrate in the opposite direction, towardss islands already colonized by their ancestors, and live in perfect harmony with other species, each with its specific function and proper habitat. There would be no more competition for food. The 'allopatric' model of speciation (Peter Grant, 1981) explains the 'adaptive radiation' in four successive steps:

1) Colonization of an island in the Galápagos by a population coming from the continent (Central America), after crossing an oceanic barrier.

2) The population develops on the initial island. Some individuals migrate to nearby islands. Genetic changes occur in the new environment. The second step

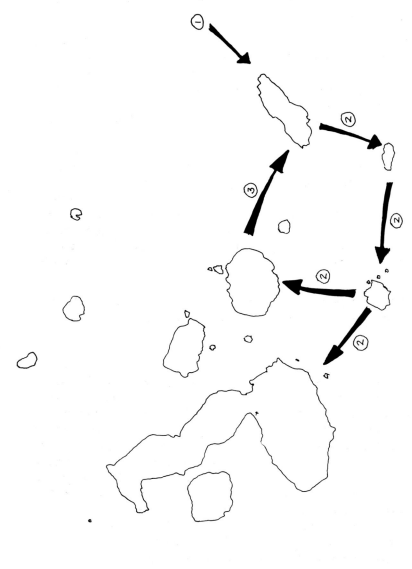

Allopatric model of the distribution of the species
e.g. the speciation of Darwin's finches [after Peter Grant, 1981].

may be repeated many times, resulting in the establishment of allopatric populations of one single species on many islands.

3) A secondary contact between the original population and the second population occurs. It is important to know how different the two groups are at the time of contact. If the differences are minor, the interaction goes freely and the two groups fuse. If the differences are moderate to wide, the individuals of the two groups may show a slight tendency to mix, and those which do so will leave offspring less fit than those which mate within the same group. Natural selection will favour those which reproduce in the tradition.

Differences between the new groups will be greater in the signals and responses related to mating. The result is that the reproductive isolation between groups initiated in 'allopatry' (ie, on different islands) will be perfected in 'sympatry' on the same island. In the end of the third step, two species have been produced out of one. Their coexistence is dependent on sufficient ecological differences: the selective process is similar to the one mentioned above. Selection acts against individuals of the two incipient species, which look so alike that they will certainly develop a competitive spirit for resources such as food. The consequence will be the divergence between the characters to exploit the resources.

4) The final step is the simple repetition of this cycle of events. This is how the 13 species of Darwin's finches were made (see the 'Allopatric model', page 46).

ENDEMISM

An organism, species or group, living and evolving in a specific place, which is found nowhere else is called endemic. It is important to remember this word, since it will be used frequently in the description of the flora and fauna of the archipelago. Oceanic islands have a high rate of endemism because of their isolation. If the island is small, such as Cocos Island, northeast of the Galápagos, speciation will not be as great as in an archipelago. The Cocos finch is endemic, but that is the only species. On bigger islands, where possibility for isolation is greater, differentiation may occur. In the Galápagos, 14 endemic races of tortoises, distinct and subspecific, have evolved on 11 islands. On the island of Isabela alone, five races were distinguished—one on each volcano. It is quite likely that these five volcanoes have been separate islands in the past, since in the Quaternary ice ages the level of the ocean rose and fell considerably.

Land iguanas have evolved on the central islands of the archipelago, and one distinct species has been recognized on Santa Fé Island. The lava lizard has distinct forms on Floreana, Española and San Cristóbal, as well as on the northern islands such as Marchena and Pinta. One single species is found on the central islands, with the exception of Pinzón, which has an endemic species.

The four species of mockingbirds have an easier dispersal ability than reptiles. They inhabit all islands, except on Floreana where they are extinct.

EXAMPLES OF ADAPTATION TO THE ENVIRONMENT

The flightless cormorant—whose ancestor came from equatorial America—lost its ability to fly. Without any predators, its wings became useless. The flightlessness is also due to the action of strong winds, which may take birds far away from the islands against their will. For those which keep their wings, the flight technique is to fly low above the ground. Marine iguanas feed on chloropyllian algae encrusted on the rocks, and may dive to a depth of 20 metres without breathing for half an hour. Some finches on Wolf Island suck blood from the wings of masked boobies. At first, finches were probably interested in the parasites on the boobies (such as horseflies) hidden between the feathers and around the neck of the seabirds.

In the tropical forest of the islands, the carpenter finch uses a wooden stick as a tool to dig larvae out of old stumps. Well-known reptiles such as tortoises and land iguanas feed on vegetation and not on insects. On the islands where these reptiles are found, opuntia cacti, with conspicuous pads, grow up like trees and develop a trunk, as tall as possible, to avoid being eaten by the reptiles. On islands where these reptiles are absent, opuntia grow close to the ground. It is amazing to realize that the cactus has developed an ability to 'think'—no more than a survival reaction—that some may call a 'conservation instinct'.

THE UNCERTAINTY OF THE FUTURE

Living organisms in the Galápagos are doomed to possible extinction. Islands deteriorate due to the erosion of wind, rain, sea. The worst factor, though, has been the arrival of man, who introduced unwanted species into the fragile ecosystem of the Galápagos: goats, rats, pigs, dogs and cats. These animals, at first domestic, turned feral and became a threat to the native species of the archipelago. Goats are very competitive and eat the food of the reptiles; dogs prey on iguanas; wild pigs on tortoise nests and young; fire ants destroy the population of invertebrates and become a plague.

Aerial view of Punta Pitt, San Cristobal 1992

Aerial view of the crater of Beagle Lake, Isabela 1990

Bartolomé and Sullivan Bay 1990

Spatter cones, Bartolomé 1993

The "pahoehoe" lava field of Sullivan Bay, Santiago 1990

Ropey lava on a "pahoehoe" surface, Sullivan Bay 1982

Hornito, Sullivan Bay 1990

Aerial view of Bartolomé 1990

Bartolomé at Sunset 1981

52

The garua on the rim of Sierra Negra volcano, Isabela 1988

Sulphur fumaroles, Sierra Negra, Isabela 1986

*Punta Vicente Roca, the sea lions' lagoon,
Isabela 1990*

Tuff cliffs, Punta Vicente Roca 1988

Volcan Ecuador, Isabela 1992

The blowhole of Punta Suarez Espanola 1989

Lava tube, Santa Cruz 1988

55

Darwin's Arch, Darwin Island 1993

The "Grottos", James Bay, Santiago 1990

Cathedral of tuff, "Leon Dormido" Cristobal 1992

Volcan Fernandina 1990

Salt mine and tuff cones, James Bay, Santiago 1992

Mangroves in "Divine's Bay", Puerto Ayora, Santa Cruz 1984

Opuntia *cacti and* sesuvium *flowerbeds in the dry season, Plaza 1993*

Giant opuntia *cactus, Buccaneer's Cove, Santiago 1990*

Flower of the opuntia *cactus, Punta Moreno 1986*

Jasminocereus *cactus, Pta. Moreno 1988*

Sesuvium *flowerbeds, Punta Pitt, San Cristobal* 1992

Red mangrove, Santa Cruz 1980

Jasminocereus *cacti, Darwin Station 1988*

Brachycereus (lava cactus), *Punta Espinosa* 1990

Nolana galapageia, *Floreana 1993*

Parkinsonia aculeata, *Floreana 1993*

Arid zone of the palo santos, Genovesa 1993

Agriculture zone of Santa Cruz, Santa Cruz 1993

Scalesia *forest, Los Gemelos, Santa Cruz 1993*

Scalesia *forest, Santa Cruz 1993*

Tree ferns, Sierra Negra, Isabela 1988

Lava lizard (female), Espanola 1992

Lava lizard (male), Punta Pitt Cristobal, 1992

Lava lizard (female), Punta Pitt 1992

CHAPTER SIX

FLORA AND VEGETATION ZONES

We mentioned earlier that the disharmony of the flora in the Galápagos is supported by the fact that the islands have never been connected to the continent. There are no native gymnosperms (cone-bearing trees), and 'monocotyledons' are poorly represented. Ferns represent a high percentage of the flora. Lichens are pioneer plants, which do not need any soil to grow.

Orchids, with only 11 species in the archipelago (as opposed to 3,000 species on the continent), are poorly represented. Their survival is limited by elevation, and they require a pollinating insect to ensure reproduction. The absence of such a pollinating insect considerably reduces the number of families and plants present on the islands.

In the Galápagos, 607 species of plants are found (or 736 taxa, if one considers species, subspecies and varieties). Out of that number, 412 species are native, and 195 species were introduced by man (32 per cent). Among natives, 242 species are indigenous and 170 species are endemic (34 per cent). If we consider the taxa, 312 taxa are indigenous, 229 are endemic, 195 are introduced. The number of introduced species rises with immigration of Ecuadorian settlers. In 1986, the new number of introduced plants was 240 species.

The distribution of plants on various islands is influenced by climate and soil. Larger islands, high in elevation, have many vegetation zones and therefore a greater number of species. The number of species depends therefore on surface and elevation, but more on elevation.

	PINTA	MARCHENA	ESPAÑOLA	SANTA FÉ
SURFACE	60 km2	30 km2	58 km2	24 km2
ALTITUDE	650 m	343 m	213 m	244 m
NUMBER OF SPECIES	200	60	110	70

Ninety-nine per cent of the flora of the Galápagos originated in South America, and only one per cent comes from Central America and Mexico. As we said earlier, the transport of seeds is carried out by birds (60 per cent), wind (31 per cent) and rafting (nine per cent).

Ferns, with spores dispersed by wind, are best represented in the archipelago (but endemic species are few). Lichens, grasses and mosses are also important due to their dispersal ability. Flowering plants, of the *Compositae* family, are very well represented (daisies and sunflowers belong to that family). With an excellent dispersal, they are pioneer plants in the colonization of faraway islands. In taxonomy, one considers:

- Phylum
- Class
- Order
- Family
- Genus
- Species
- subspecies   } Taxa
- variety

Seven endemic genera of plants are found in the Galápagos:

- *Scalesia*	(16 species)	
- *Lecocarpus*	(3 species)	Compositae family
- *Darwiniothamnus*	(3 species)	
- *Macrea*	(1 species)	
- *Jasminocereus*	(1 sp., 3 ssp.)	Cactae family
- *Brachycereus*	(1 species)	
- *Sicyocaulis*	(1 sp. of vine)	Cucumber family

SCALESIA

This genus is spread out and adapted to different zones: arid, humid, and cliffs. It is distinguished by the shape of the leaves, and flowering heads.

- *Scalesia pedunculata* (central islands) is a tree of the humid zone (ex: Santa Cruz). Branches have small flowering heads (see photo, page 63)
- *Scalesia dentatae*: shrub with large flowering heads (*Scalesia affinis* on Santa Cruz).
- *Scalesia lobatae* (*Scalesia helleri*) : shrub of the arid zone on Santa Cruz Island.
- *Scalesia foliosae*: shrub with flowering heads and arrow-shaped leaves.

CACTI

Two endemic genera: *Jasminocereus* and *Brachycereus*, and one endemic species: *Opuntia echios*.

- *Jasminocereus thouarsii*, also called the candelabra cactus, is a tall cactus found in the arid zone, and resembles Mexican organ pipe cacti. (see photo, page 59).
- *Brachycereus*, is a small cactus with white spines, 50-60 centimetres high, which grows directly on lava surfaces (see photo, page 60).
- *Opuntia* is the most common species of the arid zone. Rather small like a shrub, or tall like a tree with a trunk rising up to five metres, and spines at the base to discourage herbivores. The most impressive *Opuntiae* are found on Santa Fé Island, where the circumference of one trunk reached three metres (see photo, page 59).

VEGETATION ZONES

Seven vegetation zones are distinguished in the archipelago, but only big islands like Santa Cruz have them all (see drawing, page 60). From the bottom to the top, we may consider :

1) the Coastal or Littoral Zone
2) the Arid Zone
3) the Transition Zone
4) the Scalesia Zone
5) the Brown Zone
6) the Miconia Zone
7) the Pampa or Fern Zone

THE LITTORAL ZONE

A very narrow stretch a few metres wide, which is found on the coast or around saltwater lagoons. The vegetation is influenced by salt, and is made of shrubs and small trees. Mangroves are dominant, with four species:

- Red mangrove	*Rhizophora mangle* (see photo, page 60)
- Black mangrove	*Avicennia germinans*
- White mangrove	*Laguncularia racemosa*
- Button mangrove	*Conocarpus erecta*

The four mangroves are easily recognized by the shape of the leaves: oval in the white mangrove, elongated and pointed in the black mangrove. The red mangrove has bigger, arrow-shaped leaves and has stilt roots sticking out of the water. The button mangrove is distinguished by conspicuous white buttons at the base of the leaves, at the end of the branches.

The saltbush: *Cryptocarpus pyriformis* is a bush with fat, green leaves, very common in the islands, which may reach two metres in height. Local name: *monte salado*.

Sesuvium edmonstoneï or *Sesuvium portulacastrum*, of the succulent family, are very colourful annual plants which may cover large areas of the ground. Leaves are small sugar-almond type, red or green according to the dry or wet season. Flowers are pink or white, according to the species: *Sesuvium portulacastrum* (pink) or *Sesuvium edmostoneï* (white).

THE ARID ZONE

This rather large zone spreads up to an elevation of 80–120 metres. Dominant vegetation is represented by three cacti: *Opuntia, Jasminocereus* and *Brachycereus*. Most of the plants have a xerophytic adaptation (ie, adaptation to dry land), which is characterized by small leaves, a high rate of photosynthesis, spiny shrubs (eg *Scutia pauciflora*), deep roots (eg *Parkinsonia aculeata*), and leaves that may orient themselves towardss the sun (eg *Maytenus octogona*).

The arid zone is also the country of the palo santo, *Bursera graveolens* (see photo, page 62), a tree with white bark which has leaves only during the wet season. It is characteristic of the arid zone and found everywhere. Acacia are also seen, as shrubs or small trees (*Acacia rorudiana*), with tiny leaves, flowers like small yellow balls and a fruit like a brown bean. The almost identical *Prosopis juliflora* has bigger oblong leaves, typical of the acacias.

Chala: *Croton scouleri* is a shrub with grey stems, leaves are orange to yellow-green, and the fruit looks like a capsule. The sap of this plant stains clothes.
Manzanillo: *Hippomane mancinella* is a tree that develops at first near the ground, then grows quite tall. The fruit, green or yellow, resembles a small apple, but it is highly toxic, and may burn the skin and the eyes. If eaten, very painful stomach cramps may result.
Muyuyo: *Cordia lutea* is a nice tree with yellow flowers which is found frequently in Academy Bay, Santa Cruz Island.

During the wet season, the arid zone blooms with 'annual plants'. These plants are ephemeral.

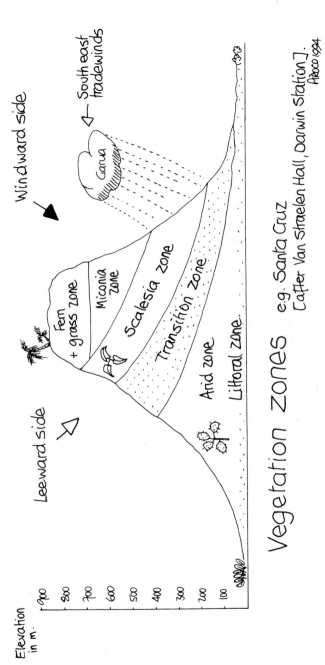

Vegetation zones   e.g. Santa Cruz

[after Van Straelen Hall, Darwin Station].

Aloco 1994

Windward side

← South east tradewinds

Garua

Leeward side

Fern + grass zone

Miconia Zone

Scalesia Zone

Transition zone

Arid zone

Littoral zone

Elevation in m.

900
800
700
600
500
400
300
200
100

THE TRANSITION ZONE

This zone climbs up between 100 and 200 metres in elevation, but may rise up to 500 metres on the leeward side. There again, palo santos are found. The characteristic plant of this zone is pega pega *(Pisonia floribunda)*, a tree with a short stem and spread-out branches. The coarse bark is covered with lichens. The local name pega pega means 'stick stick', because the leaves of this tree will 'grab' your fingers.

Guayabillo: *Psidium galapageium* is also spread out and conspicuous. The bark of this tree is soft and pinkish grey. Leaves are leathery and the fruit is similar to the guayaba *(Psidium guayava)* introduced to the islands, yellow and round with a pink flesh. The transition zone is intermediate between the arid and the humid zone.

THE SCALESIA ZONE

From 200 to 400 metres. A very humid zone with constant precipitation. This is where the garua concentrates during the dry season. Ferns, grasses and mosses are abundant, but the predominant species is *Scalesia pedunculata* (local name: *lechoso*). This sunflower tree may reach ten metres in height, and concentrates in dense forests, with mosses hanging from the branches and with flowers looking like white daisies. The scalesia forest climbing up the slopes of Santa Cruz volcanoes is a beautiful sight.

THE BROWN ZONE

This part ends the scalesia zone. Liverworts are the characteristic plants. Liverworts are epiphytes, which cling to the tree but do not depend on it. These brown mosses fall from the branches of scalesia, thus the name 'brown zone'.

THE MICONIA ZONE

Above the former zone, it rises up to 1,000 metres. This zone is represented by miconias, leafy bushes two to four metres tall. Leaves are long, rather oval shaped, and distinguished by three parallel central ribs. *Miconia robinsoniana* is also called 'cacaotillo', because the leaves resemble cacao. Flowering heads are pink or violet. The species is endemic, and is found only on Santa Cruz Island (Media Luna) and on San Cristóbal, towardss San Joaquin volcano.

THE PAMPA ZONE

The pampa finishes the scale of the vegetation zones and ranges from 650 metres' elevation up to the summit of the island. This windy and misty land with no trees is represented by ferns, grasses, sedges and other plants adapted to water; swamps and peat bogs are common. Waterholes within small collapsed lava tubes are often like green-houses, where mosses, ferns and four species of orchids grow. The only tree present is the tree fern, *Cyathea weatherbyana*, which may reach three metres in height. The moist pampa is a microclimate in itself (see photo, page 63).

THE INTRODUCED SPECIES

By 1986, 240 species of plants had been introduced by man to the Galápagos. These were found in the colonized, agricultural zone. The arrival of farmers and settlers on Santa Cristobal, Floreana and Santa Cruz, as well as in the south of Isabela, has created a few ecological disorders in the scalesia and miconia zones. As a matter of fact, many introduced species are taking over the native species.

Twenty per cent of the introduced species originate from North America or Europe. At least 10 species are aggressive in their active dispersal ability, ie, the ease with which they invade vegetation zones, to the detriment of the indigenous or endemic species. This is a major concern of the Galápagos National Park Service, in its efforts to protect and conserve the islands.

For two years the SPNG has used herbicides against guayaba, but the problem remains. No one knows exactly how much poison should be used to eradicate it efficiently. An attempt has been made to plant fast-growing teck or scalesia to counteract the slow-growing guayaba.

THE TEN PRINCIPAL INTRODUCED SPECIES OF PLANTS

FAMILY	SPECIES	LOCAL NAME	USE
Agavaceae	*Furcraea cubensis*	Cabuya (cactus)	Hedges
Crassulaceae	*Kalanchoe*	Pinnata	Ornamental
Lauraceae	*Persa americana*	Avocado, aguacate	Fruit
Mytaceae	*Psidium guayaba*	Guayaba	Fruit
Mytaceae	*Eujenia jambos*	Pomarosa	Fruit
Rustaceae	*Citrus spp*	Limon, Toronja	Fruit
Verbenaceae	*Lantana camara*	Lantana	Hedges
Poaceae	*Digitaria decumbens*	Pangola	Pasture
Poaceae	*Pennisetum purpureum*	Pasto elephante (elephant grass)	Pasture

"fou à pattes
bleues."

PART TWO

FAUNA

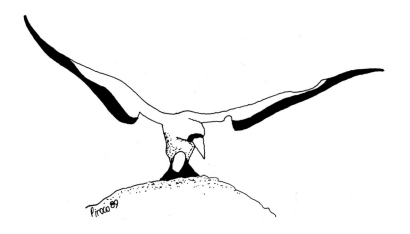

CHAPTER ONE

REPTILES

In the Galápagos archipelago, the dominant quadrupeds are reptiles. This is the reason that the islands were long considered a refuge for prehistoric, antediluvian beasts. These reptiles, related to South American forms, are represented by iguanas, lava lizards, geckos, snakes, and of course giant tortoises, which gave fame to the Galápagos. Sixty three per cent of the reptiles (17 species of 27) are endemic to the Galápagos.

GECKOS
Geckos are small lizards of the Geckonidae family. Three genera are found in the archipelago, and six species are endemic, all of the genus *Phyllodactylus:*
- *Gonatodes caudiscutatus* (1 species, on San Cristóbal only.)
- *Phyllodactylus* (6 endemic species, on Santa Cruz, Isabela, Baltra, Floreana, San Cristobal)
- *Lepidodactylus lugubris* (1 species, on Santa Cruz, Isabela, San Cristóbal).

The gecko is five centimetres long, with sand-coloured skin, and may climb smooth and vertical surfaces (such as windowpanes) thanks to the adhesive pads on its toes. With a vertical slit in its black eye, it is an essentially nocturnal reptile, but it may be seen during the daytime under rocks and in cracks. One or two eggs are laid in October and November. Geckos have permanent eyelids, like contact lenses. After eating, they lick their eyes with their tongue. They also swallow their dead skin after moulting. Some species change colour, like chameleons. Geckos have the ability of autotomy, ie they are able to part from their tail if necessary. Geckos are found in the central islands of the Galápagos.

SNAKES
Two snake species, a land snake and a sea snake, are found in the Galápagos:

The Galapagos Land Snake
This small, diurnal constrictor may catch prey up to 1.5 metres in length. Posteroglyphous, hardly venomous, it belongs to the family Colubridae and to the genus *Philodryas,* originating from the West Indies (Caribbean). Eight species were identified in the Galápagos:
- *Philodryas biserialis* (Española, Cristobal)   3 spp.
- *Philodryas slevini* (Central islands, except for Santa Fé)   2 spp.
- *Philodryas dorsalis* (Central islands)   3 spp.

Brown with yellow stripes, or grey-black with yellow spots in a zigzag pattern, it measures about 1.2 metres in length. It feeds on lizards, insects, small birds and young marine iguana hatchlings. The Galápagos snake is found on all islands, except in the five northern islands.

The Yellow-bellied Sea Snake *(Pelamis platurus)*

Belongs to the family Hydrophiidae. Dorsally black, ventrally yellow, with spots on the tail section. It measures up to 85 centimetres in length. Its venom is stronger than the cobra's. Rare, except during the Niño years when waters are warmer. Common from the west coast of Central America westward.

LAVA LIZARDS

family: Iguanidae
genus: *Microlophus*

This genus is found only in South America and the Galápagos. Seven species are endemic to the archipelago (one on each island). The biggest lizard is found on Española island, where it grows up to 25 centimetres. The smallest is half that size and is found on Floreana (south of the archipelago) (see photo, page 64). The male is bigger than the female, greyish black in colour with specks. The female has a conspicuous red-orange throat; sometimes, on Española, for example, the whole head is red.

Lizards feed on insects, seeds, flowers and leaves, and show a preference for vegetarian food. They love to bask in the sun on lava rocks, and have an excellent thermo-regulating system; by standing on all fours the are able to reduce their body temperature. At night, *Microlophus* retreats to its cosy nest, made of soil and leaves, in lava cracks.

Lizards are very territorial, but their aggressiveness is shown only to individuals of the same sex. In cases of conflict, males challenge each other by push-ups on their forelegs. They do not face each other, but sideways—displaying their spiny crest—and in opposite directions. They circle one another, sometimes biting each other on the mouth, spilling blood, but that is as far as it goes. Lava lizards have the ability of autotomy (the ability to cast off parts of the body), only once, but the tail will grow up again. This is a self-defense mechanism against predators.

Sexual maturity in the female is from nine months to one and a half years. For the male, it starts at three years. The mating season coincides with the hot season. The male mates with two or three females, after the garua season, in December. The female digs a shallow burrow, where she lays two to six eggs. The hatching will take place two to three months later. Lava lizards can live up to 10 years.

Predators of the lava lizards are snakes, hawks, owls, herons and mockingbirds. Lava lizards are absent on Genovesa, Darwin and Wolf.

Marine Iguanas

genus: Amblyrhynchus
species: cristatus

An endemic genus with one species and seven subspecies. The age of the iguana could be nine million years or more if we consider the fact that it is older than the islands existing today. It is descended from a land iguana from the South American mainland. It most probably reached the Galápagos via vegetation rafts that were drifting on the surface of the ocean. Consequently, it had to adapt to a strictly vegetarian seafood diet.

The only marine iguana in the world, the Galápagos species is found along shore on lava rocks. These creatures of another era gather in herds of a fantastic aspect, individuals packed one on top of another. The length, including the tail, ranges from 60 centimetres for the smallest variety (Genovesa Island) to one metre for the largest (Isabela Island). The tail is half the size of the body. A spiny crest runs along the back, from the top of the head to the tip of the tail (see photo, page 81).

The sooty-black skin—a mimetism with the black lava substrate—is a camouflage against predators and enables the iguana to absorb more heat during its exposure to the sun. Very lazy, even ugly to some people, the marine iguana spends most of its time warming up on the rocks. Flat in the morning, the body, with a prominent abdomen, changes orientation towards the sun as the day progresses. When it is too hot, the iguana raises the front of the body above the ground and allows the breeze to circulate under the stomach.

Like many reptiles, the marine iguana is poikilothermic; ie it may adapt to great temperature variations. It is also ectothermic, ie directly influenced by external heat (mammals, by contrast, are endothermic). Despite an optimal ambient temperature of 35–37° C, these cold-blooded reptiles may have an extreme body temperature 40° C at the hottest hour of the day, helping out in the digestive process, but at night its temperature drops to 24° C.

The iguana feeds on 'Ulva', a chlorophyllian algae, and sometimes on the faeces of sea lions or of its own species. It may easily dive to a depth of 20 metres (over 60 feet) to look for food on the rocks, and spend as much as one hour under water at a time. The compressed tail is well adapted to swimming, above or under water, and while doing so the legs have no use and stick to the sides of the body. The iguana tends to feed at low tide, when the ulva algae are exposed. They frequently eject a salt excess through the nostrils. The spray is thrown 50 centimetres, and may be used to warn off potential predators.

Extremely territorial, iguanas use their tongue and their olfactory sense to recognize their territory. They are sexually mature at around six to eight years, and have a life expectancy of 25 to 30 years. The mating season spreads over November and December, eggs are laid in February and March and will hatch in May or June. Females lay once every two years.

During the mating season, males—always larger than females—take on a red coloration (just like on Española, the southernmost island of the archipelago) and a green colour appears along the back, on the forelegs and hind legs. Males become very aggressive, and defend territories of one to two square metres. After mating, females are in competition to find the right nesting area. Sometimes a female waits for another one to finish a nest, then will try to take it over by force. Head to head fights are spectacular, and the strongest wins. On South Plaza Island, eggs are laid between early February and the end of March; two or three eggs will be left in a burrow of volcanic soil. On Española Island, where soil is scarce, iguanas dig their burrow under the pebbles of the beach. (The operation may be tragic at times, when a rock collapses over the animal and it dies in the nest). After covering the nest with soil, the female will guard it for 10 days.

Eggs have a thin white shell, and weigh from 80 to 100 grams. The gestation lasts about three months (between 84 and 91 days). Predators of the marine iguanas are hawks, herons, snakes and feral dogs.

During the disastrous Niño year 1982-83, the green ulva algae disappeared, leaving only a toxic brown alga. This increased the mortality rate of 60 per cent to the marine iguanas. The population is estimated today at about 200,000 to 300,000 individuals (Ebl-Eibesfeldt).

LAND IGUANAS

genus: *Conolophus*
species: *subcristatus* or *pallidus*

This endemic genus has officially two species, but may have one more if one considers the possibility of an endemic species on Fernandina Island.

Yellow-orange to brown, the land iguana differs from the green iguana, *Iguana iguana*, of South America and the Caribbean, ancestor of the Galápagos iguanas, by a lack of fear towards man. In the Galápagos, two species of land iguanas have been identified:
- *Conolophus subcristatus*: on Santa Cruz, Plaza, Isabela and Fernandina (yellow-orange in colour). Extinct on Santiago Island (see photos, page 85).
- *Conolophus pallidus*: on Santa Fé (whitish to chocolate brown). This is the biggest land iguana; the male weighs six to seven kilograms, the female three kilograms. The eyes are often red, as if injected with blood (see photos, page 87).

Land iguanas do not have a square nose like marine iguanas but a pointed one. Their length is about 1–1.2 metres. *Conolophus* feeds on grass, centipedes and annual plants in season, but its favorite food consists of the pads of the opuntia cactus. Especially the fruits and the yellow flowers, during the hot season. On Fernandina Island, at an elevation of 330 metres, 90 per cent of the food of the iguana is composed of the fruits and flowers of the creeping vine *Ipomea alba* (morning glory). Sometimes land iguanas feed on sea lion's afterbirth, grasshoppers or even dead birds.

Males have an impressive dorsal crest, more conspicuous than the female's, and are larger. Their body temperature ranges from 32.2° C (dry season) to 36° C (wet season). Females are sexually mature at 6 to 10 years. Land iguanas may reach 60 to 70 years old.

Land iguanas form small colonies. They keep to the driest part of the islands and dig burrows in the soil, sometimes under rocks (25 centimetres deep, 15 centimetres long). During the mating season males are territorial, and protect areas of 10 to 20 metres in diameter. Females choose the males. A male may have up to seven females. Each of the females comes back to the same nesting area. After a pair begins courtship the female stays in or around her mate's burrow while he keeps intruders away. After copulation, the female leaves the male for the nesting area, and digs several false nests before laying eggs in the right burrow—females fight over nesting sites. When ready to lay her eggs the female backs into the nest, partially sealing herself into it, and stays there for 24 hours. Thinner after emerging, she leaves the burrow and closes it; for the next week she will defend the nest.

On Fernandina Island, the females nest inside the caldera, near the fumaroles. From the coast, the round-trip takes 32 days. Egg laying peaks during the first two weeks of July. Nests are one to two metres deep. The ground temperature is 32 to 34° C. Clutches consist of 7 to 23 eggs, of a size smaller than those of the marine iguanas (50 grams).

Egg laying occurs during the hot season on Isabela and Plaza islands, and during the dry season on Fernandina, Santa Cruz and Santa Fé. Gestation lasts for three to four months, and the number of eggs ranges from 6 to 20, soft shelled.

Predators of the eggs are beetles; hawks, herons and snakes prey on hatchlings. The survival rate of a young land iguana in the wild is less than ten per cent.

EGG-LAYING OF THE LAND IGUANAS IN THE GALÁPAGOS

	Mating	Hatchings	Clutch	No. of eggs (average)
Isabela	January	May-June	10 to 25	14
Fernandina	June/July	Oct/Nov	8 to 22	10
Santa Cruz	September	January	5 to 17	12
Plaza	Jan/March	May/July	1 to 9	6
Santa Fé	Oct/Nov	Feb/March	7 to 10	8

On South Plaza Island, where marine iguanas are also present, Heidi and Howard Snell think that marine and land iguanas did at one time interbreed, producing hybrid offspring: 'Weirdo' in 1980 and 'Zebra' in 1985. On that particular island, it was common to see land iguanas climbing on shrubs and relaxing on the branches. The last hybrid iguana died of hunger in August 1993.

A symbiotic relationship exists between the small ground finch and land iguanas, in which the birds eat ticks off the iguanas. When the finch comes, the iguana stands on all fours, allowing the bird free access as it hunts for the pests.

Since 1976, and following the attack of wild dogs on the land iguana colonies of Conway Bay (Santa Cruz) and Cartago Bay (Isabela), the Galápagos National Park and the Charles Darwin Research Station have started a programme to protect and conserve the species. Eggs were brought to Puerto Ayora to be incubated, and young to be bred in captivity. Since 1980, more than 250 young iguanas have been returned to Cartago Bay (SPNG, 1988). The repatriation on Conway Bay started in 1987.

In 1991 and 1992, 50 land iguanas were reintroduced onto Baltra Island by the SPNG, after a 40-year absence. The initial source came from North Seymour, through the reproduction centre of the Darwin Station.

MARINE TURTLES

family: Chelonidae
genus: *Chelonia*
species: *agassizi*

There may be eight species of marine turtles in the world, but only four species have been seen in the Galápagos (see drawings, page 101).

- *Dermochelys coriacea*	Leatherback
- *Lepidochelys olivacea*	Olive ridley
- *Eretmochelys imbricata*	Hawksbill
- *Chelonia mydas*	Pacific green turtle

Until now, only one has been common to the islands, the subspecies *Chelonia mydas agassizi*, the Pacific green turtle, which has a circumtropical distribution. Nevertheless, found in the eastern Pacific region from Baja California to the Galápagos, a new species has been recognised by scientists. It is the 'black turtle', *Chelonia agassizi*, which, to some specialists, is a subspecies of the Pacific green turtle. It is precisely this marine turtle that is found in the Galápagos (cf *National Geographic*, February 1994).

The Black Turtle
This turtle feeds on ulva, the chlorophyll alga, on the roots of mangroves, as well as on the leaves of the red mangrove. Males are smaller than the females, with a concave plas-

tron, claws on the bend of the front flippers (to grasp the carapace of the female) and a long tail. The concave plastron facilitates copulation. Females have a convex plastron (see photo, page 91). Sexual maturity is reached at 20 to 25 years. The mating season starts with the hot season, and the peak reproduction and egg laying occur in December-January. Group mating is easily seen in the lagoon of Tortuga Negra (north of Santa Cruz) in November.

Egg laying takes place generally between January and June, but may occur all year-round. The female comes out of the water after dark, and starts digging on the beach (high on the dune) with her hind flippers. After about 20 minutes of digging, she lays 80 to 120 eggs about the size of ping-pong balls at the bottom of the nest. The hardest part is still to come, for she has to work another 30 to 60 minutes covering the nest with sand. Turtle tracks may be observed on the beach the following morning, if the tide has not erased them during the night.

Gestation lasts for about two months (55 days). The hatchlings have a soft black shell, five centimetres long, (the carapace (shell) of the adult is 84 centimetres long, but this measurement will decrease over the years). The temperature of incubation influences the sex of the individual. If it is over 30° C, the egg produces a female; below that temperature, the tendency is towards males. The egg-laying frequency is every two to three years. The main predators of the marine turtles are sharks, orcas and crabs (which feed on hatchlings), and the beetle *Trox suberosus* (which preys on eggs). A few sea birds and shore birds such as herons, frigates and lava gulls also prey on the young as they are crossing the beach towards the sea. This is why the nest usually comes to life after dark, because as soon as the day breaks, the baby turtles are blinded by the sunlight and cannot find their way to the ocean. This is when they become an easy catch for predators.

Between 1975 and 1980, a special programme that marked 7,400 green turtles proved that migrations occur from Costa Rica, Panama, Colombia, Peru and Ecuador.

GIANT TORTOISE OR 'GALÁPAGO'

family: Testudinae
genus: *Geochelone*
species: *elephantopus*

Only two island groups in the world are inhabited by giant tortoises: Aldabra Island in the Seychelles, and the Galápagos Islands. Giant tortoises would have to have reached the Galápagos by floating from South America, which seems unbelievable. The most likely ancestor, *Geochelone chiliensis*, originally came from Argentina, but nothing explains its arrival in the archipelago, which remains a total mystery. No one knows what size these tortoises were in the beginning.

In the Galápagos, female tortoises can weigh up to 50 kilograms and males up to 250

Marine iguana (male), North Seymour 1992

Colony of marine iguanas and crabs (zayapas), Pta. Espinosa, Fernandina 1990

Marine iguanas in the ventilated position, Pta. Espinosa 1989

Marine iguanas of Espanola 1989

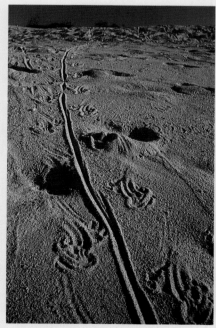

Track of a marine iguana, James Bay 1988

Track of a marine iguana, Las Bachas 1990

Marine iguana of Espanola, Punta Suarez 1992

Marine iguana in the mating season, Espanola 1991

Swimming marine iguana, Pta. Espinosa 1990

Land iguana, South Plaza 1993

Land iguana (male), Urvina Bay, Isabela 1986

Iguana iguana, *green iguana of South America, Guayaquil 1989*

Land iguana (male), South Plaza 1993

Land iguana and Opuntia cactus Plaza

Iguana eating a cactus pad, Plaza 1993

Land iguana, Santa Fé 1990

Land iguana, Santa Fé 1991

Land iguana, Santa Fé 1993

87

Giant tortoise, Volcan Alcedo, Isabela 1985

Giant tortoise digging a burrow against the sun Alcedo 1988

Giant tortoise, Urvina Bay, Isabela 1992

Giant tortoise on the rim of Alcedo volcano 1992

Giant tortoises in the rainy season, Alcedo 1991

Female giant tortoise on a volcano trail, Alcedo 1991

Giant tortoises, Alcedo 1991

Dome-shaped tortoise, Santa Cruz 1993

Saddle-shaped tortoise of Espanola, Station Darwin 1992

The black marine turtle, Chelonia agassizi, *Bartolomé 1993*

Black turtle after laying eggs, Floreana 1993

Marine turtle underwater, Gordon Rocks 1993

Galapagos penguins, Bartolomé 1990

Flightless cormorants in courtship display, Pta. Espinosa, Fernandina 1992

Flightless cormorants, Fernandina 1986

Flightless cormorants, Pta. Albemarle Isabela 1986

Flightless cormorant, Pta. Espinosa 1986

Swallowtail gull, South Plaza 1986

Lava gull, Tortuga Bay 1992

Swallowtail gulls mating, Genovesa 1990

Young swallowtail gull, Genovesa 1993

Albatrosses mating, Espanola 1989

Albatross, Punta Suarez, Espanola 1993

Young albatross, Espanola 1993

kilograms (see photo, page 88). In the past, the population of tortoises was estimated at about 250,000 individuals; In 1980 only 15,000 remained. Before man reached the islands in the time of the pirates, the tortoises had no predators. For the past four centuries, man has been responsible for the destruction of these reptiles. Now the danger comes from other introduced species.

The scientific name of the giant tortoise is *Geochelone elephantopus*. Zoologists have numbered 14 races or subspecies, but only 11 survive today (in fact, the real figure is ten since Lonesome George, the only survivor of Pinta Island, now lives at Darwin Station in Puerta Ayora on Santa Cruz island. The $10,000 reward offered to whoever could provide a female of the same species brought no results, and George will remain an old bachelor.) The giant tortoise is extinct on Fernandina, Floreana, Santa Fé. Contrary to what was once thought, there were never tortoises on Rábida.

Isabela Island, with more than 6,500 individuals, remains the island with the largest giant tortoise population. More than 4,000 Galápagos live in the caldera of Alcedo volcano; 1,000 survive on Wolf volcano, 700 on Cerro Azul, 500 on Darwin, and 400 on Sierra Negra (see map of Isabela). On Santiago Island, the western population was destroyed, and the eastern population numbers 500. There is still a strong population in the east and south of San Cristóbal (despite competition from feral goats), and 250 individuals on Española (compared with 15 in 1960), saved from extinction by the SPNG.

Very independent animals, the giant tortoises live mostly on the summits of the islands. Three groups are distinguishable, based on the shape of the shell:

The Saddleback Type (Española, Pinzón, Pinta and Fernandina)
The carapace is raised in the front, and the neck and legs are very long. By its morphology, this type of tortoise looks for food (cactus pads or leaves) high above the ground, extending its long neck forward like a periscope (see photo, page 90). It is found in the arid zone of the lowlands.

The Dome-shaped Type (Santa Cruz, Isabela)
Heavier and more voluminous than the former type, this tortoise grazes grass directly on the ground. It is found on islands with rich vegetation, in the highlands, around the rim of the volcanoes and in the calderas (see photo, page 89).

The Intermediate Type
This is a variation of the dome shape, including the other races (except those on Wolf volcano and Santa Fé).

Tortoises can survive in dry areas as they are able to conserve water and fat in their internal cavities. This ability first was noticed during their long survival on pirate boats. Nobody knows the maximum age of these land turtles. In the corral of the Darwin Sta-

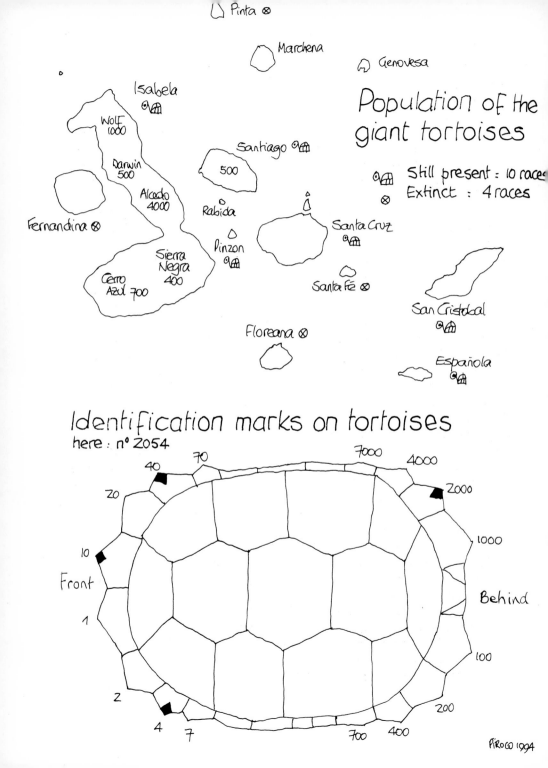

Pinta ⊗

Marchena

Genovesa

Isabela ◉▦

Wolf 1000

Population of the giant tortoises

◉▦ Still present: 10 races
⊗ Extinct: 4 races

Santiago ◉▦

Darwin 500

500

Alcedo 4000

Rabida

Fernandina ⊗

Santa Cruz ◉▦

Pinzon ◉▦

Sierra Negra 400

Cerro Azul 700

Santa Fe ⊗

San Cristobal ◉▦

Floreana ⊗

Española ◉▦

Identification marks on tortoises

here: n° 2054

70   7000   4000

40   20   2000

1000

10

Front

1

Behind

100

2

200

4   7   700   400

PIROCO 1994

tion, the oldest individual may be as much as 170 years old (and would have known Darwin himself).

Tortoises have a peaceful life. Throughout the year, they eat great quantities of grass, leaves, lower parts of bushes, and the cactus pads of the opuntia. Most of the time they sleep in open spaces, or wade in mudponds during the wet season. At night, they hide under the shrubs. When threatened, their first reaction is to retract head and legs under the shell with a conspicuous hiss. If, by misfortune, one is rolled upon its back, it is difficult for it to get back on its legs. Then it becomes vulnerable.

The mating season coincides with the wet season. Males engage in mock fighting, then look for a female. Later on, between February and May, females start the long journey downhill to the coast, and will look for the right nesting area, in the arid zone, about 20 metres above sea level. Egg laying lasts from June to December. The female digs a nest 30 centimetres deep and 20 centimetres wide, which will be cemented by a lid made of urine and excrement. This jelly is then covered with sand. The construction of the nest takes eight to 12 hours of work on Española, and four to five hours on Santiago Island.

The gestation period lasts from three to eight months, depending on the location of the nest. If it is at low elevation, it will take 120 days; if the elevation is high, then the incubation period may take as long as 200 days. The number of eggs depends on the species: 12 to 15 eggs on Santa Cruz, four to five eggs on Española and Pinzón.

Observation and research carried out by Linda Cayot at the Darwin Station has shown that the temperature of incubation influences the sex of the giant tortoise. If the temperature is higher or equal to 28.5 or 29° C, embryos turn into females. Below that temperature, the eggs produce males. The hatch occurs between mid-January and March. The clutch is of three to eight eggs for the saddleback tortoises and up to 16 eggs or the dome-shaped tortoises. According to some scientists, the sexual maturity of the giant tortoise could be reached at 20 to 30 years.

Predators are numerous. The black rat (*Rattus rattus*), introduced by the pirates, preys on eggs after digging out the nests. Wild pigs do the same. Feral dogs attack small tortoises after hatching (south of Isabela), and dig up the nests (San Cristóbal). As for feral cats, they do not harm tortoises, except in the south of Isabela.

Various means have been adopted by the Galápagos National Park to protect the nest:
- against the rats on Pinzón Island: nothing much can be done but to destroy the rats themselves. This was done in 1989 by the SPNG.
- against feral pigs: by building a stone wall around the nest.
- the incubation of eggs and the breeding of young tortoises at the Darwin Station, helps to develop the existing population.
- feral dogs are the 'plague' of the moment.

Programmes of protection, conservation and breeding of giant tortoises have begun at the Galápagos National Park and at the Darwin Station in 1960. At the time, 13 individuals (11 females and 2 males) from Española Island were the last survivors of a race doomed for extinction. By 1988, 200 saddleback tortoises had been reintroduced on Española, following the successful incubation programme.

Each year, park guards collect tortoise eggs on different islands. These are brought back and incubated at the Darwin Station, where the young will be raised for four years and then returned to their original island. Today, more than 1,000 tortoises have been reintroduced to various islands of the archipelago.

In July 1996 reports of nine dead and 11 sick tortoises were made at El Chato reserve in the highlands of Santa Cruz. Toxicological analysis led by Dr. Linda Cayot of the CDRS were negative, but coliform and anaerobic bacteria were found, as was fungus. The diet of the giant tortoise has been oriented towards the *maracuya*, or passion fruit. The likelihood of *maracuya* poisoning is under investigation, as is the possibility of pond infection by dead tortoises.

Marine Turtles

Black turtle
(Chelonia agassizi)

Hawksbill turtle
(Eretmochelys imbricata)

Leatherback turtle
(Dermochelys coriacea)

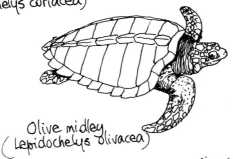

Olive ridley
(Lepidochelys olivacea)

Piroco 89

CHAPTER TWO

SEA BIRDS
SHORE AND LAGOON BIRDS

The bird life of the Galápagos is unique and diversified. In the beginning, migrating sea birds came from Ecuador, Peru, Colombia, and the Caribbean. Trade winds also helped introduced these migrants to the archipelago. Dependent not on the land but on the sea, most probably, sea birds were the first animals to colonize the islands. Half of the resident population of birds is endemic to the archipelago, but only five species of sea birds (of 19) are unique to the Galápagos: the Galápagos penguin, the flightless cormorant, the lava gull, the swallowtail gull and the Galápagos waved albatross. Therefore, 25 per cent of the sea birds are endemic to the islands.

GALÁPAGOS PENGUIN   *Spheniscus mendiculus*

Endemic. Belongs to the order Sphenisciformes, birds that cannot fly, and in which the wings evolved for use as fins (see photo, page 92).

The Galápagos penguin is related to the Magellan penguin, *Spheniscus magellanicus*, an ancestor thought to be found in southern Chile. It is also related to the penguin of the Falkland Islands and islands near Antarctica. This penguin came to the Galápagos by means of the Humboldt Current. In the islands, its population was 13,000 before the 1982-83 Niño, concentrated around Bartolomé, Rábida, Sombrero Chino, Floreana, the west coast of Isabela and the Bolivar Channel, as well as on the coast of Fernandina, the westernmost island.

The Galápagos penguin swims with its front fins, and its feet help in steering. Swimming slowly at the surface, it moves very fast underwater and sometimes leaps above the water happily; in dolphins, this behavior is known as 'porpoising'. On land the Galápagos penguin walks, hops from rock to rock, and goes 'tobogganing'. Before jumping, it stretches its neck forward as if studying the terrain.

Head and beak movements can be an appeasement response to threatening behavior. They are also a way of greeting without triggering aggression. Crossing beaks is done for the same purpose. During the mating season, Galápagos penguins preen one another's heads, and also slap themselves gently with the front flippers.

Galápagos penguins are opportunistic reproducers. They nest in cavities, where two eggs will be laid three to four days apart. On Fernandina, egg laying occurs in September. Incubation lasts from 38 to 40 days. Very shy animals, penguins nest in groupage They sleep on land and look for food during the day, returning to the shore between 4 and 6:30 pm. In the early morning, they can be seen in the water between 5 and 7 am. They leave a wake behind them, just like ducks.

The disastrous 1982-83 Niño year caused a loss of 77 per cent of the population. By 1985, their number had been slowly recovering and was estimated at 2,000-3,000 individuals. Predators of the Galápagos penguin include red crabs, rice rats, Galápagos snakes, short-eared owls and Galápagos hawks.

In late 1996, two penguin nests were found on Isla Floreana. In May of the same year a 'Penguin Expedition' spent five weeks on the northwest coast of Floreana from Post Office bay to Black Beach. A pair of penguins was found at the base of Cerro Daylight and a single adult was found at the islet of Piedra Dura. A second nest was found at Cerro Daylight the following August. A herd of six goats and a cat were also seen.

FLIGHTLESS CORMORANT   *Nannopetrum harrisi*

Endemic. Belongs to the order of Pelicaniformes. It is a large dark bird with atrophied wings and a strong, long beak with a hooked end. Adults are black above, brown underneath, and have turquoise-blue eyes. The young are black all over, with dull eyes. Males are larger than females (see photo, page 93).

Cormorants are often seen above the tideline, with wings spread out to dry in the wind. This is an ancestral habit which is useless, since the bird cannot fly. A lack of predators has influenced its flightlessness.

Like a penguin, it swims underwater and uses its webbed feet. It feeds on fishes, eels and octopus. This sedentary bird emits a grunt and nests in small colonies on rocks or sheltered beaches. The mating season lasts from November to March, but may be throughout the year since the flightless cormorant is an opportunistic breeder. The male chooses the female. Between March and September, she lays two or three big white eggs in a nest of twigs, algae and marine grass. The incubation time is about 35 days.

Being endemic to the Galápagos, it is one of the rarest bird in the world. Its population is estimated at 800 pairs. It is found on the shore of Fernandina and on the west coast of Isabela, where the nutrient-rich Cromwell current from the central Pacific brings an abundance of fish.

The largest colonies of flightless cormorants are located at Cape Douglas (37 nests), Cape Hammond (28 nests) on Fernandina and at Cape Berkeley (30 nests) on the northwest of Isabela. Visitor sites are Punta Espinosa (Fernandina), Puerta Moreno, Puerta Garcia and Puerta Albermarle (Isabela).

LAVA GULL   *Larus fuliginosus*

Endemic. Belongs to the order Charadriiformes and to the family Laridae (see photo, page 94). The population of this bird was once estimated at 400 pairs, but it is found everywhere in the Galápagos. Adults are sooty grey with a white ring around the eyes. Feet and beak are black. The lava gull has the funny habit of staring between its feet, head bent down. This submissive attitude means 'good intentions' to the protagonist. It also has a loud shriek that can be mistaken for a human laugh.

Frequently encountered in ports, the lava gull feeds on crabs and small marine iguanas, but mainly on dead fish and waste like sea lions' afterbirth. It is a scavenger. Solitary, it nests in rocky overhangs and at the bottom of cliffs near the waterfront. Two olive-green eggs speckled with brown are laid in a nest of twigs. Adults are very protective of the nest, and will scare off any intruder (even bigger than themselves), using their feet to hit the aggressor.

SWALLOWTAIL GULL   *Creagrus furcatus*

Endemic. The only other gull present in the Galápagos. It is differentiated from the lava gull by a black and white spotted swallowtail and a red eyering. The body is pale grey on its back, ventrally white. The beak is black with a white tip, and the feet are red (see photo, page 94). The white marks at the base and tip of the beak help the chick in the nest to see the arrival of its parent at night. Consequently, to obtain food, it will just knock on the beak of the adult. Big black eyes are characteristic of the swallowtail gull, which feeds only at night. Its nocturnal vision is made possible by the red eyering which serves as a sort of sonar. It feeds offshore, looking for fish and squid. This night-feeding habit has developed in response to competition from other sea birds during the daytime, in particular the tropicbird, which feeds during the day on the same food.

The swallowtail gull nests in cliffs and lays only one egg—white speckled with brown—which is easily mistaken with the composition of the nest, which is made of pieces of white coral and black lava gravels. Prosperous couples mate once every nine or ten months.

Swallowtail gulls are often seen at dawn and at dusk when they go or come back from fishing. Their cry is unique and resembles a clanking whose possible function which may be compared to echolocation.

In the Galápagos, other gulls may be seen occasionally migrating such as the Franklin's gull and the laughing gull (Genovesa, March 1995).

WAVED ALBATROSS   *Dimedea irrorata*

There are 13 species of albatross in the world. The albatross belongs to the order Procellariformes, which is recognized by the tube-nose on the top of the beak. This order comprises two families, which feed on plankton: the Diomedeidae (albatross) and the Procellaridae (petrels and puffins).

One of the most majestic birds in the archipelago, the waved albatross is endemic not only to the Galápagos, but also to the island of Española (Hood Island), for this is the only place in the world where it reproduces. Its life expectancy is about 20 years. This cousin of the petrels and the puffins, has a population of 24,000 individuals. Weighing four kilograms, and with a wingspan of 2.5 metres, this is the largest bird in the Galápagos (see photo, page 96).

The back, wings and tail are light brown, contrasting with the whiteness of the head, neck and belly. Its big yellow beak looks like a tube, hooked at the end.

With sufficient wind, the albatross in flight is a tremendous glider, but in calm weather it has to move its wings harder than other birds. It feeds offshore, on fish, squid and other invertebrates, and may also steal from boobies occasionally. Nevertheless, its feeding habits are nocturnal, and its big black eyes are the proof of it. It feeds on the surface of the water.

The waved albatross is found in the Galápagos only during the dry season, on Española; it arrives around mid-April and leaves around mid-December. It returns to its island to reproduce after six months spent in the open sea of the Pacific Ocean, and as far as Japan. Every year, the ritual is repeated: males arrive first to reconnoitre the terrain and the nesting site; when the females arrive a few days or weeks later, one may see a kind of collective rape. Afterward, serious matters start, and pairs are formed. Albatrosses are faithful to their mate for their whole life (see photo, page 95).

Generally, the courtship of the female by the male does not happen in the same year as nesting, but in two different seasons. The courtship display is remarkable. In their dance, albatrosses cross beaks as two fencers in a duel, then go for a 'sky-pointing display', with the beak opening and loudly snapping shut, and start the love fight again. This display is repeated over and over.

The mating occurs over a period of five days. The single egg, as large as a billiard ball, is laid between mid-April and mid-June. The whole colony reproduces at the same time. The eggs hatch between mid-June and mid-August, after an incubation of 63 days. Curiously, the waved albatross will roll its egg quite a distance between the rocks, pushing it with the beak, as if to give it exercise. Sometimes the egg breaks.

The albatross chick is a big, ugly, brown fluffy thing. It will take 167 days before it flies. The nesting site is abandoned between the end of November and mid-January.

The waved albatross of Española is sexually mature at the age of five or six years. Its lifespan may reach 30 to 40 years. Some albatrosses abandoned at Española have been found as far away as the shores of Japan. There was a massive abandonment of the nests during the Niño year 1982–83.

AUDUBON'S SHEARWATER   *Puffinus lherminieri*

Belongs to the order Procellariformes and to the family Procellaridae. Dorsally dark brown, ventrally white, the Audubon shearwater is originally from the Antilles, but it is also found in the Pacific and Indian oceans (see drawing, page 107). The Audubon shearwater is easily mistaken with the Hawaiian petrel, which is larger and has a white patch on the forehead.

Active during the day, it feeds on plankton and crustaceans. It often fishes in group and flies low above the water. It may dive to a depth of two metres, and uses its wings to swim after small fish.

The Audubon shearwater is an opportunistic breeder. On south Plaza Island, the reproduction cycle is nine months. One white egg is laid with an incubation time of 49 days. The juvenile may fly 75 days later. The population in the Galápagos is estimated at 10,000 pairs. Its predator is the short-eared owl.

HAWAIIAN PETREL   *Pterodroma phaeophygia*

Dorsally black, ventrally white (see drawing, page 107). Two species are found in Hawaii and in the Galápagos. This black bird with a white forehead and white under-wings may be seen in the highlands of Santa Cruz, San Cristóbal, Floreana, James and Isabela, where the vegetation is dense. The Hawaiian petrel nests on the ground, under rocks and in volcanic caves.

The reproduction season differs according to the island:

	Floreana	Santa Cruz	Santiago
Arrival:	end November	May	January
Egg laying:	end December/April	June/September	February/June
Hatch:	end February/June	August/November	April/August
Takeoff:	June/September	December/March	July/November

Hawaïan Petrel

Audubon
Shearwater

Storm
Petrels

Castro's
storm petrel

Galápagos
storm petrel

Elliot's
storm petrel

PIROCO 89

The reproduction cycle is annual, and only one egg is laid. The incubation time is 51 days, and 120 days are necessary for the juvenile to take off. It feeds on fish and squid, offshore.

The predators of the Hawaiian petrel are rats and cats (which pilfer eggs and chicks), feral dogs and feral pigs. These are a major problem in the Galápagos National Park, which has led a campaign for protection and conservation of the species in Floreana since 1982.

The population of the Hawaiian petrel has been estimated at between 10,000 and 50,000.

STORM PETRELS

Belong to the Procellariformes, easily recognized by the tube nose. Three species are found in the Galápagos:
- Castro's storm petrel   (*Oceanodroma castro*)
- Galápagos storm petrel   (*Oceanodroma tethys*)
- Elliot's storm petrel   (*Oceanites gracilis*)

Plankton feeders, these small black petrels skip across the surface of the water, fluttering about like butterflies. They are each differentiated by the white markings at the base of the tail (see drawing, page 107).

CASTRO'S STORM PETREL   *Oceanodroma castro*

Subtropical Atlantic and Pacific distribution. Conspicuous white band on the tail. Nests in cliffs, among rocks and under ledges, on Plaza Island, Daphne Mayor, Guy Fawkes, Cowley's Island, Devil's Crown, Isla Pitt and Genovesa (Tower Island).

This pelagic bird feeds at night, as well as during the day, on small fish and squid. Castro's storm petrel is an annual breeder; two seasons are distinguished: eggs are laid between March and June, or December-January (Plazas). A single white egg is laid. The incubation time is about 42 days.

Its predator is the short-eared owl, mostly during the cold season.

GALÁPAGOS STORM PETREL   *Oceanodroma tethys*

Distinguished by the white cuneiform (wedge-shaped) mark at the base of the tail. Pelagic, its feeding habit is nocturnal, on the surface. Annual reproduction; one single egg is laid between May and June. The population of Galápagos storm petrels is about 200,000 pairs, nesting on Genovesa, Isla Pitt and Rock Redonda.

ELIOT'S STORM PETREL *Oceanites gracilis*

Among all petrels, this is the most common. A white lens-shaped mark is conspicuous at the base of the tail. It feeds inshore. One single egg is laid between April and September.

The population of Elliot's storm petrels is several thousand pairs.

BROWN NODDI *Anous stolidous*

Also known as the noddi tern. Colour is sooty grey to brown, with the top of the head white. The black eye is circled in white (see photo, page 113). A resident tern in the Galápagos, the noddi builds its nest of twigs in the cliffs. It feeds on the surface of the water, inshore. It may enter the water, but generally hovers low above fish schools. It often associated with Audubon shearwater and brown pelicans; by sitting on the heads of these larger birds it can wait for the small fish they catch.

Known as the 'noddi' because of its courtship display, nodding its head in front of the mate, it is an opportunistic breeder. The noddi tern nests in caves and rocky over-hangs. One single egg is laid.

The following terns are present but rare: The royal tern, *Sterna maxima*, is white with the top of the head black and an orange beak. The sooty tern, *Sterna fuscata*, nests only on Darwin Island in the north of the archipelago.

GREAT FRIGATEBIRD *Fregata minor*

Belongs to the order of Pelicaniformes, which are recognized by reduced or absent external nasal slits.

Frigates, or 'vultures of the sea', are specially designed for life aloft. Their wingspan is as big as that of the albatross. This bird, having lost the waterproofing of its black plumage, never lands on the sea. The uropygial gland, which normally oils the feathers, is atrophied and useless.

Frigates spend time gliding in circles in the sky. When in pursuit of other birds—especially boobies, for example, which they frequently harass for food—they may be very fast. This is called 'cleptoparasitism'. Frigates may also catch small fish on the surface of the water with the mere swipe of the hooked beak.

Males are black with a greenish sheen. Wings are long and pointed, and the tail is scissorlike. During the courtship display, the male inflates a huge leathery red poach under his throat. This seduces and attracts the female to the nest, which the male has already prepared for the purpose of mating. This amazing ritual may be observed in March and April on Frigatebird Hill (San Cristóbal) or on Genovesa Island (Darwin Bay), or throughout the year on North Seymour Island.

Females also have black plumage, but the upper ventral part of the throat is white (see photos, pages 114 and 115). The eyering is conspicuously red on the female, while the male's is bluish green. Frigate chicks are all white at first, then the head and neck turn hazelnut in colour.

The reproduction cycle of the frigate is one and a half to three times longer than that of any other member of the order Pelicaniformes. Ten to 20 days of courtship display are necessary before mating. Frigatebirds reproduce in colony. One single egg is laid in a nest of twigs, always in a tree or a bush. The annual reproduction differs on various islands. Eggs are laid between February and August on Genovesa Island, between April and November on Española Island. The incubation time is 55 days. Maturity takes 130 to 160 days (even 180 days sometimes), before the juvenile can fly. The slow growth of the young, and its ability to fast, are remarkable adaptations to the irregularity of the food supply. The great frigate is therefore a 'tropical breeder', which means that it has a long reproduction cycle. Apparently the frigate reproduces every two years. It always returns to the same nesting site and does not show any sign of territorial aggressivity to other birds of the same species.

The great frigate is an 'offshore feeder', foraging far away from the coast and from the islands, thus avoiding competition with the magnificent frigate, which is an 'inshore feeder' feeding closer to the islands. The great frigate feeds on fish caught on the surface, and also 'hijacks' other sea birds (such as boobies), catching them by the tail and forcing them to regurgitate food in the air. Frigates also prey on turtle eggs and recently hatched young.

Great frigatebirds are found throughout the archipelago on the periphery of the islands. Main colonies are located on Genovesa, Darwin, Wolf, Española, Floreana (Gardner), Tortuga Island, Isla and Punta Pitt. The great frigate is pantropical.

Magnificent Frigate   *Fregata magnificens*

Very similar to the great frigate, but the male has a purple sheen on its black plumage, and the female has a black triangle on the white patch of the throat. The eyering is bluish green on both sexes. Unlike the great frigate, the magnificent frigate is an 'inshore feeder', and feeds near the islands. On North Seymour, where it is easily seen, courtship displays are observed throughout the year. It is also a 'tropical breeder', with long reproduction cycles. Only one egg is laid, with an incubation time of 55 days.

The magnificent frigate nests on the salt bush, *Cryptocarpus pyriformis* (North Seymour) or in the palo santos (San Cristóbal). The main colonies are found on Seymour, Darwin, Wolf, Isabela (Punta Moreno), San Cristóbal (Wreck Bay) and Genovesa.

Magnificent frigates are also found in the Caribbean, on the west coast of Central America and in the north of South America.

TROPICBIRD

Phaeton aethereus

Belongs to the order Pelicaniformes and to the family Phaetodontidae, which comprises one genus and three species: the small tropicbird, the great tropicbird and the white tropicbird. The first two are pantropical and the latter is found in the southern Pacific.

This beautiful white bird with short wings has two long and narrow feathers extending from the tail. A black line runs through the eyes, and the bill is coral red in adults. The juvenile lacks the two tail feathers. Its food being pelagic, the tropicbird is an 'offshore feeder'. It feeds on fish and squid by plunge-diving during the daytime.

The tropicbird reproduces in colonies, and lays only one red-brown, spotted egg in a crack of the cliff or between rocks (see photos, page 116). There is a noticeable difference between reproduction cycles of the tropicbirds on South Plaza, Genovesa and Daphné Island:

South Plaza:	annual reproduction, three eggs are laid between August and February
Genovesa:	eggs laid between July and November
Champion, Onslow, Enderby:	egg laying between August and December (islets of Floreana)
Daphné:	eggs are laid any time of the year. Severe intraspecific competition for the nesting sites. Opportunistic breeders, incubation time: 42 days.

Even though three eggs may be laid, only one usually develops into maturity. Chicks are fed until their first flight. They receive fish of an average size (20 centimetres) and squid.

Colonies of tropicbirds are found on Plaza, Seymour, Daphné, Rábida, Sombrero Chino, Tortuga and Floreana (Champion, Enderby, Caldwell, Gardner, Onslow). This bird does not like cold waters, and is therefore rare on Fernandina and Isabela.

BROWN PELICAN

Pelicanus occidentalis

One of the largest birds in the archipelago. Adults are grey-brown with the top of the head white. The nape is reddish hazelnut during the mating season. Young do not have these colours and are brown overall. Feet are webbed and grey-black. The beak is very long and hooked at the tipage The lower jaw has a large poach, which inflates with water after plunge-diving.

The pelican fishes along the shore. It will take in a few liters of saltwater, which is ejected later through holes in the beak, before it swallows its fish (see photo, page 117).

In flight, the pelican gives a few strokes of its wings, then glides for a long time. It often flies in formation with other pelicans.

This opportunistic breeder nests in the mangroves, or on the salt bushes. The reproduction cycle of nine months occurs during the hot season. Two or three chalk-white eggs are laid on a platform of twigs. A few juveniles die young after they learned how to fly, usually when they have not mastered the fishing technique.

The brown pelican nests on all central islands, but more easily on Marchena and Española.

BOOBIES   *Sula*

Boobies are very common in the islands. Three species are seen in the Galápagos: the blue-footed, the red-footed and the masked booby. All have an aerodynamic body and a long, pointed bill.

All three live in colonies, but with various habitats. The name 'booby' may derive from the fact that—once they have seen fish while flying—they drop on it like arrows from a height of fifteen metres. Unfortunately, they react in the same way towards fishing lures, plunge- diving on the surface of the ocean behind the boat.

Boobies belong to the family Sulidae, and the order Pelicaniformes (pelicans, frigates, cormorants, tropicbirds). All have webbed feet. The family Sulidae is divided into two groups:
- the genus *Morus* .... three gannets
- the genus *Sula* .... six boobies

The six boobies belong to the genus *Sula*. Three of these are common to the Galápagos. The three others are the Peruvian booby (creator of guano), the brown booby (pantropical) and the Abbott's booby (found in the Christmas Islands, near Java in Indonesia).

Blue-footed boobies are found north to the Gulf of California and south to the coastal islands of northern Peru. The two other boobies of the Galápagos are pantropical. Great concentrations of Sula exist in the regions of cold waters, which are rich in nutrients and organisms. The Humboldt current supports the booby colonies of the archipelago.

Well adapted to extensive flight when looking for food, boobies have the ability to plunge-dive and move underwater, when fishing.

Boobies incubate their eggs with their webbed feet and not with an abdominal pouch.

RED-FOOTED BOOBY   *Sula sula*

This is the lightest booby, with a weight of about one kiogram. Colour is light brown, with a bluish beak. There is also a white variety, called the 'morpho blanco'. The red feet

Noddi terns, Pta. Vicente Roca 1992

Great frigate (male), San Cristobal 1981

Pair of great frigates, Genovesa, 1990

Female great frigatebird and chick, Genovesa 1992

Young great frigate, Genovesa 1993

Young great frigates in flight 1988

Colony of great frigates in the salt bushes, Genovesa 1993

Tropicbird, Punta Suarez, Espanola 1984

Tropicbird in flight, Espanola 1984

Brown pelican (adult), Puerto Ayora 1984

Pelican and young, Pta. Moreno, Isabela 1988

Pelican nesting, Rabida 1989

117

Pelican feeding its young, Rabida 1990

Red-footed booby, Genovesa 1993

Red-footed booby, Morpho blanco variety, Genovesa 1990

Red-footed boobies (young), Genovesa 1990

Blue-footed boobies, Espanola 1980

Blue-footed booby (young), Espanola 1985

Nest of excreta of the blue-footed booby Punta Pitt 1993

Courtship display of the blue-footed boobies, Espanola 1984

Blue-footed booby and chicks, Espanola 1993

Masked booby, Espanola 1992

Pair of masked boobies, Daphné 1993

Masked booby, Espanola 1981

Ventilation posture of a booby, Daphné 1992

Great blue heron, Floreana 1990

Lava heron (juvenile), Bartolomé 1990

Yellow crowned night heron, Genovesa 1993

Cattle egret, Santa Fé 1990

Common egret, Urvina Bay 1992

Oystercatchers, Sullivan Bay 1990

Flamingo, Pta. Cormorant, Floreana 1992

Young flamingoes, Floreana 1992

Young flamingo, Floreana 1992

Common stilt, Santa Cruz 1991

Bahama pintail, Hotel Galapagos 1991

Whimbrel, Fernandina 1992

Ruddy turnstone, Fernandina 1992

Sanderlings, Seymour 1992

Ruddy turnstones feeding on a sea lion's afterbirth, Seymour 1993

are adapted to gripping branches; thus it is the only booby to nest in trees (eg palo santos or in the bushes) (see photo, pages 118 and 119). The reproduction season depends on the availability of food . The chicks may easily die of hunger during the first weeks of their life. Despite the high mortality rate, only one egg is laid. The time necessary to breed young does not allow an annual cycle of reproduction. Consequently, a period of 14 months elapses before the red-footed booby nests again.

The largest colony of red-footed boobies is on Genovesa Island. The population of the archipelago is 250,000. The red-footed boobies are the largest community of boobies in the Galápagos.

BLUE-FOOTED BOOBY   *Sula nebouxii*

This is the most common booby. Its lifespan is about 15 to 20 years. Unlike its red-footed relative, the blue-footed booby fishes inshore. It nests on the coast. The nesting site, on the ground, is marked by sprays of ejecta which draw a radiant white sun on the volcanic sand. Food is usually abundant, and allows two or sometimes three eggs to be laid.

The male is lighter than the female (1.28 kilograms and 1.80 kilograms respectively) and plunge-dives more easily than the female. It is recognized by the black pinpoint pupil of the eye, while the dark iris coloration of the female gives the impression that her pupil is larger. The male whistles, and the female honks (see photo, page 120).

During the mating season, the booby dances with its turquoise-blue feet, spreads out its wings, bring its tail up, point its bill to the sky and whistles loudly. This ceremony is known as 'sky pointing display'. Meanwhile, the female moves about, retracts her beak towards the body, and seems to respond 'no, no'. Sometimes a jealous pretender intrudes on the pair's courtship, trying its luck with the female. But conflict soon erupts, and very noisy beak fighting follows.

The second egg hatches five to seven days after the first, which puts the younger of the two chicks at a great disadvantage. If food is sufficient, the two chicks will be bred together. Otherwise, the stronger firstborn will survive and will kick its sibling out of the nest. Exposed to the fierce equatorial sun, or to the marauding frigates, the abandoned chick will die quickly.

The sexual dimorphism of the blue-footed boobies allows a partial division of activities. The small size and long tail of the male favour its mobility underwater. Consequently, it will be the one fishing while the female sits on the nest. In any case, a parent will always remain with the nest. The feet of the boobies are well irrigated with blood, and their thermo-regulating function insures perfect incubation.

An opportunistic breeder, the blue-footed booby avoids nesting in the hot season, between December and April. It prefers the cold season between May and December, for it needs dry and clear ground which is not covered with vegetation. Once the egg hatches, after one and a half months of incubation, the parent will stay with the chick until it is able to fly, giving it shade and protection. Finally, the juvenile must learn to plunge-dive and to fish. This takes 50 days for the blue-footed booby, and three months for the red-footed booby.

Since their food is abundant, blue-footed boobies may have more than one clutch a year. Nine months' time will be necessary, for the limiting factor is the moult.

The light weight of these birds allows them to build a nest inside a crater (eg Daphné Mayor), from where they may take off easily. Of the three boobies, the blue-footed is the only one to do this.

The population of the blue-footed boobies has been estimated at 10,000, but it may be much more. Large colonies are found on Española (Punta Suarez), Daphné, Tagus Cove and Punta Vicente Roca (west coast of Isabela), Cape Douglas (Fernandina).

MASKED BOOBY

Sula dactylatra

Heaviest of the three boobies, males weigh 1.63 kilograms, while females are larger at 1.88 kilograms. The plumage is white, wings are fringed with black, and the beak is orange yellow. The conspicuous black mask on the eyes makes it easy to recognize (see photo, page 122).

Like the blue-footed booby, the white or masked booby nests directly on the ground and surrounds its nest with waste. It chooses the site on clifftops, where the air streams allow it to take off easily. The fishing zone is intermediate between those of the other booby species, ie between islands. This adaptation to the environment illustrates the idea of the 'ecological niche'.

In masked boobies, sexual dimorphism is slight. Two eggs are laid five days apart. The incubation time is 43 days, but the clutch is quickly reduced to one chick following an unavoidable fratricide. Food sources are not as abundant as they are for the blue-footed boobies.

The season for reproduction is stable. On Genovesa Island, the masked booby mates from September to November, on Española Island, from November to February.

The population of masked boobies is about 25,000. The largest colonies are found at Punta Suarez (Española Island), where the nests are on the southern cliffs, at Darwin Bay (Genevesa Island), as well as on Wolf and Darwin Island in the north of the archipelago.

Shorebirds and Lagoon Birds

Great Blue Heron   *Ardea herodias*

Greyish blue, with a lighter head and neck, this tall wader nests in the mangrove. Frequently seen at Puerto Ayora (Santa Cruz Island), and around the kitchen of the Hotel Galápagos (an old one with a broken wing). They can be observed at Tortuga bay, strolling down the beach at low tide and looking for small fish. Preys on baby turtles as well (see photo, p 123).

Lava Heron   *Butoroides sundevalli*

Small grey-black heron, with yellow or red feet, which stalks on the shore and around tide pools. Young may be lighter, with a striated back and yellow legs. On the rocks near the waterline, lava herons look for crabs and small fish, and stands still for long spells, with an amazing stare (see photo, page 123).

Night Heron   *Nyctanassa violacea*

Of intermediate size between the two former species, this heron is streaked grey-brown. It has a black head with yellow and white feathers. Two thin white feathers run behind its head from the top of the skull. This nocturnal wader is found at night under the street lamps of Puerto Ayora (Santa Cruz Island), and can also be frequently seen during the daytime at the entrance of caves or under rock ledges overlooking tide pools, as in Darwin Bay (Genovesa Island) or Puerto Egas (Santiago Island) (see photo, page 124).

Cattle Egret   *Bubulcus ibis*

A little white heron, very majestic in flight, with black legs (juveniles) or yellow legs (adults). It is found on the shore at low tide, or even in the arid zone, where it catches lizards and grasshoppers. The nest is made in the mangrove.

It is found in the highlands of Santa Cruz, where it is seen in the company of cows. It also comes near sea lions in search of flies, which is not always to the liking of these mammals! (See photo, page 124).

Common or Great Egret   *Casmerodius alba*

A great white heron with a yellow bill and black legs. It concentrates in the central islands, on the coast, and nests in the mangroves, laying two eggs. The common egret feeds on fish, lizards, grasshoppers and other insects (see photo, page 124).

Shore and lagoon birds (1)

Common stilt

Common Egret

Wandering tattler

Semi-palmated plover

PIROCO 89

Sanderling

Shore and lagoon birds (2)

Northern phalarope

Ruddy turnstone

Common gallinule

Purple gallinule

Piroco 89

OYSTERCATCHER   *Haematopus ostralaegus*

A brown bird with a white belly, a black head and a red eyering. The bill is long, pencil-like, orange or red. The oystercatcher is the same size as the lava heron. It is found on the littoral (Punta Suarez, Española, Puerto Egas, Santiago Island), but is not common, due to the lack of proper habitat. Feeds on abalone, conical shaped shells fixed on the rocks of the intertidal zone, as well as on pencil sea urchins (see photo, page 125).

FLAMINGO   *Phoenicopterus ruber*

Rare in the Galápagos, it is found in seven saltwater lagoons, behind the mangroves of the littoral. Flamingos may only reside in places where the water is not too deep for wading (less than one metre).

Swinging its neck right and left, it searches for food in the silt, thanks to a sonar in the bill which enables it to detect organisms. These are mainly a small pink shrimp (*Artemia salina*), the water-boatmen (T*richocorixia reticulata*), larvae of coleoptera and diptera, organisms belonging to the ostracidae family and algae. Flamingos feed for seven to 12 hours a day. The tongue sucks the sediment and salt water; everything is filtered through sievelike plates inside the beak, then pumped out the sides.

Mud nests, like small towers, are erected on the border of the lagoon. These are sometime destroyed by floods or by wild pigs.

The flamingo reproduces at the age of five to six years, and mates every three to four years. A single egg is laid with an incubation time of 28 days. Only about 50 per cent of the hatchlings will survive. Of this number, 73 per cent will reach adulthood. Chicks are fluffy white, with big black legs. At the age of two months, they know how to filter food. At four months they become adults. Juveniles are preyed upon by hawks, suffer floods or get lost. A mortality rate of 20 per cent occurs during the first year.

Flamingos have a lifespan of 18 to 24 years. Easily disturbed, they take flight if approached noisily. Common stilts, usually present in the area, always warn flamingos of any potential danger.

The population in the archipelago is estimated at 400 to 600. Flamingos may be observed at Espumilla Beach (Santiago Island), Rocas Bainbridge, and lagoons of Villamil (Isabela Island), Punta Cormorant (Floreana Island) and Rábida Island (see photo, page 125).

COMMON STILT   *Himantopus himantopus*

Another bird of brackish lagoons, which feeds on small animals caught in the silt with its long thin black bill. The common stilt is a slender bird, black dorsally, white ventrally and up to the underparts of neck and head. Legs are long and red. Common stilts share the lagoon with flamingos and white-cheeked pintail ducks (see photo, page 126).

BAHAMA WHITE-CHEEKED PINTAIL   *Anas bahamensis*

Also known as the Bahama duck. This brown duck has white cheeks and a red mark at the base of the beak. It is the only duck to reproduce in the Galápagos. Blown to the islands by the northeast trade winds, this species originated in the Caribbean and is now found in freshwater pools and brackish lagoons (see photo, page 126).

WHIMBREL   *Numenius phaeopus*

This shoreline wader is distinguished by its long curved bill. Brown with white spots, it has a dark streak on the eye and other bands on the top of the head. Found on rocks and on beaches at the border of retreating waves. A very shy bird and easily frightened, it takes off with a conspicuous repetitive shriek (see photo, page 127).

WANDERING TATTLER   *Heteroscelus incanus*

A slate-grey bird with white eyebrows. Ventrally white or speckled, a long thin black bill, and long yellow legs. Usually found on the rocks of the shore at low tide (see photo, page 132).

SEMIPALMATED PLOVER   *Charadrius semipalmatus*

A small bird of the littoral. The back and top of head are brown. Ventrally white, with orange legs. A conspicuous black ring is noticeable around the neck. The bill is short and black, with an orange base. Walks quickly on the beach along the waterline, or on rocks (see drawing, page 132).

SANDERLING   *Calidris alba*

Dorsally grey speckled with white, ventrally white up to the throat. A long, pointed black bill, and black legs. Walks very fast on the beach along the waterline, after the dying wave (see photo, page 128).

Ruddy Turnstone *Arenaria interpes*

Dorsally brown, speckled with black and white, ventrally white. A conspicuous black collar under the throat. The legs are orange. The bill is small, sharp and curved upward. Its cry is a deep crackling. When in search of food, it turns over shells and rocks. It has also been observed feeding on sea lions' afterbirth, and sucking blood avidly (Seymour, December 1993). Usually found on the rocks near the water.

Northern Phalarope *Phalaropus lobatus*

Dorsally streaked, grey-blue and orange. The head is blue-grey, the throat is white, and a brown-red collar appears during the mating season. Ventrally white with black legs (see drawing, page 133; photo, page 161).

Common Gallinule *Gallinula chloropus*

A bird of brackish lagoons. Black to metallic blue, with a yellow-tipped red bill. Big yellow legs. A shy bird, quite rare. When it swims, the head moves back and forth. Feeds on plants and aquatic invertebrates. It may be observed in the lagoons of Puerto Villamil (Isabela Island) (see drawing, page 133).

Purple Gallinule *Porphyrula martinica*

Purple-blue on the top of the head and ventrally. Dorsally brownish green. The forehead is turquoise-blue. The bill is red and yellow tipped. Big yellow legs. Found in lagoons with abundant vegetation (see drawing, page 133).

CHAPTER THREE

LAND BIRDS

In the Galápagos, the endemism rate of land birds (76%) is three times higher than the endemism rate of sea birds (35%). This is easily explained by the fact that sea birds are migrants, and land birds are rather sedentary. The latter are also more shy towards man than sea birds.

All land birds in the Galápagos originated in North, Central or South America. They arrived in the islands by chance with the northeast or southeast trade winds. The impossibility of returning to the mainland forced them to adapt to their new environment. Later on, competition and natural selection brought diversification and speciation for some genera. Through evolution, some species became endemic, with no other possible choice (except extinction).

ENDEMIC SPECIES

Nowadays, 29 species of land birds can be identified in the Galápagos, 22 of which are endemic and seven non-endemic.

Among the endemic species: 13 species of Darwin's finches, four species of mockingbird, one dove, one flycatcher, one hawk, one martin, one rail. Among the non-endemic species are: one crake, one cuckoo, two owls, one ani, one warbler, one flycatcher (see Appendix 2, Geographical distribution of the land birds). Since the avifauna come mainly from South America, the distribution of the species is disharmonic. The 1,000 kilometres of the Pacific Ocean between the islands and Ecuador pose an almost impossible barrier to migrations.

EXAMPLES OF DISHARMONY:

	Number of species in world	Number of species in Ecuador	Number of species in Galápagos
Hummingbirds	319	120	0
Parrots	315	44	0
Eagles and Hawks	208	46	
(genus *Buteo*)		12	1
Flycatchers	347	153	2
Mockingbirds	31	6	4 + 7 ssp.
Finches	436	47	13

For some groups, the quality of the environment is the most important. For example, hummingbirds look for big flowers, and parrots look for succulent fruits, all of which are nonexistent in the Galápagos.

All the land birds in the Galápagos breed during the rainy season, at the beginning of the year (January). All, that is, except for one species, the Galápagos rail, which breeds in the cold season, between June and December. The rainy season brings plant growth and thus abundant food for the land birds. This immediate response to the presence of food is called 'opportunistic breeding'.

No land bird species has gone extinct throughout the islands, whereas in Hawaii the islandwide extinction rate is 40%. In the Galápagos, extinctions are localized. Three species have disappeared on Floreana: the mockingbird, the large-bill ground finch, and the barn owl (killed by man). The Galápagos hawk is also extinct on San Cristóbal (because of man), but a few pairs are left on Santa Cruz.

GALÁPAGOS MOCKINGBIRD   *Nesomimus*

The ancestor of the Galápagos mockingbird is the longtail mockingbird, *Mimus longicaudatus*, from Ecuador. In the Galápagos, the four species and six subspecies of mockingbirds are all endemic:
  - Galápagos mockingbird (on all islands except Pinzón)
  - Hood mockingbird (endemic to Española and Gardner)
  - Cristobal mockingbird (endemic to San Cristóbal Island)
  - Floreana mockingbird (only found on the satellite islands of Floreana: Champion and Gardner).
These noisy birds, very curious by nature, are greyish brown dorsally and cream-coloured ventrally. The beak is black and curved downward.

Predatory birds, they feed on small finches, lava lizards, centipedes and insects. They also crave the eggs of sea birds, such as boobies and albatrosses. Very social birds, they have no fear of man, and are quite common to the archipelago.

Out of the breeding season, mockingbirds establish communities, with up to nine individuals on Genovesa Island and up to 40 individuals on Española Island. All associate for the defense of the territory and for the search of food. Serious fights may occur at the border of two territories. Two rows of antagonists face one another, and the fighting is fierce between the opposing parties (see photo, page 161).

GALÁPAGOS DOVE   *Zenaida galapagoensis*

Endemic. This little dove, dorsally reddish brown, ventrally beige to pink, has a conspicuous turquoise-blue ring around the eye. Very tame towards man, as the pirate William

Dampier related in 1684: 'One could easily kill a few dozen with a stick, during the morning.' Obviously, this would not be possible nowadays.

The Galápagos dove feeds on the ground, on seeds, usually of the opuntia cactus and of the croton shrub (of which fruits are also eaten), and on caterpillars.

The optimal time of breeding is during the wet season. The Galápagos dove nests on the ground of the arid zone, sometimes under lava rocks. It uses also old nests of mockingbirds. During the breeding season, ritual fights and nodding ceremonies occur. Two eggs are laid.

The Galápagos dove is found on Genovesa, Española, Santiago, Rábida, but it became rare on the inhabited islands of Santa Cruz, Floreana and Cristobal (see photo, page 162).

VERMILLION FLYCATCHER   *Pyrocephalus rubinus*

A very colorful bird, red on the head and on the belly, dorsally black. It has a conspicuous black mask on the eyes. Vermillion flycatchers are found in the humid (scalesia) forest of the highlands, mostly in the central islands. Absent on Genovesa and Española.

The female is yellow ventrally, black dorsally, as is the juvenile male, which turns to red in a later phase.

Originally from South America, it is now found up as far as Mexico and southern California. Known locally as 'brujo' or sorcerer (see photo, page 162).

LARGE-BILLED FLYCATCHER   *Myiarchus magnirostris*

Endemic. May be observed in the highlands, and also in the transition and arid zones. Larger than the former species, it has a yellow belly and a grey throat. Dorsally brown, the top of the head may have a slight crest at times.

Inquisitive by nature, it has the habit of collecting human hair for the construction of its nest (see photo, page 163).

YELLOW WARBLER   *Dendroica petechia*

Originally from the North American mainland, and found from Alaska to southern Peru. This small, insect-eating bird is entirely yellow; the male has a reddish brown patch on the top of the head. The bill is sharp and pointed. Yellow warblers often enter houses to search for flies against the windowpanes.

Common to all these islands, it is found in mangroves, in arid zones and humid zones with dense vegetation. Confined to the Galápagos and Cocos Island (see photo, page 164).

GALÁPAGOS MARTIN   *Progne modesta*

Endemic. Distributed in small groups on central islands. Resembles a big dark swallow. The male is bluish black; the female is light grey. Although rare, it may be observed circling in the sky. Its flight alternates between quick wing flapping and periods of gliding.

The Galápagos martin nests in the holes of cliffs, in calderas and on the rim of volcanoes (Sugar Loaf, on Santiago Island and Daphné Island).

DARK-BILLED CUCKOO   *Coccyzus melacoryphus*

This is a rare bird. Twice as big as the yellow warbler, it is mainly speckled grey, with the top of the head black, and a long tail. Dorsally dark brown, ventrally pale. Widely distributed in South America, it arrived in the Galápagos recently, where it can be observed mainly in the highlands. Very frequent in the lowlands during the Niño year 1982/83. Related to the black-billed cuckoo of North America (see drawing, page 141).

SMOOTH-BILLED ANI   *Crotophaga ani*

Reached the Galápagos recently from Ecuador. It was probably introduced by settlers in 1962 to protect cattle from ticks. This black bird has a feathery black tail, and a smooth broad black bill humped on the topage Poorly adapted to long-distance flight, it was discovered on Genovesa Island, 90 kilometres away from Santa Cruz.

Anis are gregarious. They are found in the humid highlands, where they are company to cattle, from which they eat ticks and other parasites. The smooth-billed ani belongs to the Cuculidae family (cuckoos and anis). (See drawing, page 141.)

GALÁPAGOS RAIL   *Laterallus spilonotus*

Endemic. About 15 centimetres long, dark colour with hazelnut markings and white spots on the wings. Feeds on insects and other invertebrates on the ground, and on dead leaves. Omnivorous, it lost its ability to fly, due to its feeding habits. Nevertheless, it may fly ten to 15 metres. The rail lives in the highlands between 350 and 600 metres (San Cristóbal, Santa Cruz, Santiago, Isabela, Floreana, Pinta and Fernandina).

It is the only land bird to breed in the cold season between June and December. The incubation period of the egg is 23 to 25 days.

PAINT-BILLED RAIL   *Neocrex erythrops*

Slightly larger than the Galápagos rail, it is distinguished by dark plumage with no markings, a yellow and red bill, and red legs.

Land birds

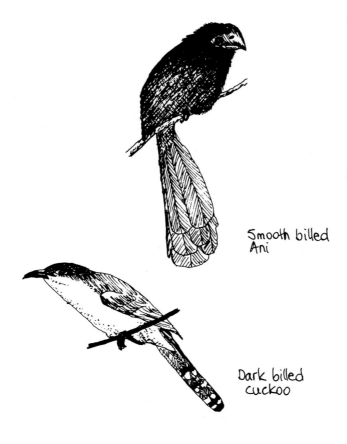

Smooth billed
Ani

Dark billed
cuckoo

Galápagos
rail

Paint-billed
crake

PIROCO 89

A poor flier, it was discovered in 1953 in the agricultural zone of Santa Cruz and Floreana Island (see drawing, page 141).

GALÁPAGOS HAWK   *Buteo galapagoensis*

Endemic. This magnificent predator was for a time extinct on Santa Cruz. But recently (Gemelos, November1993) the author observed the return of the hawks to the highlands of that island. Practically extinct on Floreana and San Cristóbal, due to hunting by the settlers. The hawk is common to Pinzón Island (for a long time infested with black rats), and to Santiago and Isabela islands.

The adult has dark brown plumage, a tail striped with white, and yellow legs. Juveniles are lighter and speckled with white. This bird of prey is unique, having no predators itself, and is therefore on the top of the 'food chain'. With its sharp eyesight, the hawk may detect prey—mainly lizards, iguanas, snakes, finches, boobies, flycatchers and young goats—from a great distance. It will also eat dead animals, such as sea lions, sea birds, marine iguanas, goats and fishes.

The Galápagos hawk builds its nest in trees and on rocks. Two or three eggs are laid, and the chicks may be bred simultaneously. The reproduction system, known as 'cooperative polyandry', is unusual. A female hawk will mate with up to four males and make four different nests. Each male will take care of a nest. The female is larger than the male. The reason for this polyandry may be due to the difficulty in finding an appropriate territory, or to the limited number of available territories (see photo, page 165).

SHORT-EARED OWL   *Asio flammeus*

Endemic subspecies. Present on all islands except Wolf. This diurnal hunter is seen in the highlands and close to the sea bird colonies. Short-eared owls feed on rats, land birds and sea birds such as storm petrels. It has no fear of man whatsoever, provided it is not approached too closely.

On Santa Cruz, it hunts early morning from 5 to 10 am, then in the evening from 4 to 10 pm. It nests on the ground, among high grasses. When hawks and barn owls inhabit the same island, the short-eared owl is rare (see photo, page 166).

BARN OWL   *Tyto alba*

Endemic subspecies. Unlike the short-eared owl, the barn owl is a nocturnal predator, feeding on rats and mice only. It is found on the big central islands: Fernandina, Isabela, Santiago, Santa Cruz and San Cristóbal. The barn owl is not afraid of man.

It nests in rock caves, holes in trees and in abandoned houses. The population is about 8,500 pairs (see photo, page 166).

DARWIN'S FINCHES

The theory of evolution brought fame to Darwin's finches. The dark-coloured birds are about the size of a sparrow and are distributed on all the islands. They are often very noisy birds and have no fear of man.

Although they belong to the finch family, they make a subfamily called Geospizae, which is found only in the Galápagos and on Cocos Island to the northeast. Thirteen species are endemic to the archipelago; all originated from an original species, *Melanospiza richardsonii,* found on Sainte Lucie Island in the Caribbean.

All the finches are strikingly alike, and it takes the trained eye of a specialist to distinguish them perfectly. The diversity of structure apparent in this little group of birds aroused Darwin's interest in 1835. He came to understand, long after his journey, that a mother species had modified to different ends and for specific functions (1845).

Finches may be classified in different genera, following the characteristic shape of their beak and feeding habits. Four main groups and six genera are distinguished, with the Cocos finch:

- Ground finches   (Geospiza, 6 species)
- Vegetarian finch   (Platyspiza, 1 species)
- Tree finches   (Camarynchus, 3 species; Cactospiza, 2 species)
- Warbler finch   (Certhidea, 1 species)

CLASSIFICATION OF THE 14 DARWIN'S FINCHES

Cocos finch	*Pinaroloxias inornata*
Cactus finch	*Geospiza scandens*
Large cactus finch	*Geospiza conirostris*
Small ground finch	*Geospiza fuliginosa*
Medium ground finch	*Geospiza fortis*
Large ground finch	*Geospiza magnirostris*
Sharpbill ground finch	*Geospiza difficilis*
Small tree finch	*Camarynchus parvulus*
Medium tree finch	*Camarynchus pauper*
Large tree finch	*Camarynchus psittacula*
Carpenter finch	*Cactospiza pallidus*
Mangrove finch	*Cactospiza heliobates*
Vegetarian finch	*Platyspiza cassirostris*
Warbler finch	*Certhidea olivacea*

Lack and Bowan, two scientists who studied finches after Darwin, each have their own views on their evolution. Lack thinks that isolation and competition were important factors in the evolution of the finches. Bowan thinks that only differences in food brought about a particular adaptation. Therefore, there was no competition between species. Ground finches are distributed in the dry arid zone, and look for seeds on the ground. Tree finches are more often in the humid zone. The medium tree finch is only found on Isabela Island. The sharpbill ground finch, also known as the 'blood-sucking' finch or 'vampire' finch (on Wolf Island), draws blood from the base of the feathers of masked and red-footed boobies. The cactus finch appears in the coastal and transition zones. The large cactus finch is only found on Genovesa and Española islands. The carpenter finch, which uses a stick as a tool, is found from the arid zone to the highlands. The mangrove finch is found in the elevated mangroves of Isabela and Fernandina islands.

Finches lay four eggs after the mating season. The incubation time is 14 days (see photo, page 167–69). See Appendix 2: Distribution of land birds according to vegetation zones.

Darwin's finches

Pinson de
Darwin.

1 Large billed ground Finch
2 Medium ground Finch
3 Small ground Finch
4 Sharpbilled ground Finch
5 Cactus Finch
6 Large cactus Finch
7 Small tree Finch
8 Medium tree Finch
9 Large tree Finch
10 Carpenter Finch
11 Mangrove Finch
12 Vegetarian Finch
13 Warbler Finch

CHAPTER FOUR

MAMMALS

Like most oceanic islands, the archipelago is poor in native mammals: two species of bats, a few species of rats and, of course, sea lions.

The paucity of native mammals in the islands is explained by the fact that the islands were never connected to the mainland. Today only mammals introduced by man can be considered the only existing mammals. Before the arrival of man the only mammals were rice rats. Later man brought goats, dogs, donkeys, horses and the black rat.

BATS   *Lasiurus*

Two species are present. They inhabit the mangroves, the crowns of opuntia cactus,and the hollow tree trunks introduced by man, such as the guayabillo (*Psidium galapageium*).

One of these bats, *Lasiurus brachyotis,* is endemic, related to the red bat of South America, but smaller and with short ears. The other species is the hoary bat (*Lasiurus cinereus*), with whitish grey hair and light brown fur. Feeding on insects, these bats are found on Santa Cruz (coast and highlands), on San Cristóbal, Floreana and West Isabela (mangroves).

GALÁPAGOS RICE RATS   *Oryzomis*

Endemic to the Galápagos Islands, these rodents belong to the genus *Oryzomis*, distributed on the American mainland. This small brown rat with big bulging black eyes has no fear of man. It digs nests under the rocks of the arid zone, as well as in the highlands. The rice rats are omnivorous. Seven species have been identified.

The Galápagos rice rats have been studied by Brosset (1963), a Frenchman, who divided them into two categories:

1) genus *Oryzomis*: two endemic species, found on San Cristóbal.
Oryzomis galapagoensis and on Santa Fé, and *Oryzomis bauri*. The latter, mainly vegetarian, feeds on seeds and vegetation.
2) genus *Nesoryzomis*: four species, found on Fernandina and Santiago Island.
Extinct on Baltra, Santa Cruz and Isabela.

A third genus, now extinct, was found in the highlands of Santa Cruz and Isabela. It is known as *Megaoryzomys*, the giant rice rat. The endemic rice rat of the Galápagos has been disappearing since the introduction of the black rat (*Rattus rattus*) during the time of the pirates. Three factors speed its extinction: competition and disease.The natural predators of the rice rat are the short-eared owl, the barn owl and the Galápagos hawk.

SEA LION   *Zalophus californianus*

Belonging to the family Otaridae the Galápagos sea lion is related to the California sea lion, but is smaller, and is different from the Peruvian sea lion (*Otaria flavescens*), which is from a more southern distribution.

Abundant in the archipelago, sea lions gather in colonies on sand or on the rocks. The male is polygamous, but there is no such thing as a 'harem' in the strict sense of the word, for the female is free to come and go as she pleases, in and out of the groupage. The male is distinguished from the female by its huge size and by a conspicuous hump on the forehead, while the female has a smooth forehead.

The male becomes adult at the age of 10 years and weighs up to 250 kilograms. The female matures at around six to eight years and weighs up to 120 kilograms.

The male is very territorial, especially at the beginning of the mating season, and patrols on the beach or in the water constantly to chase occasional intruders. He keeps an eye on the young, which may wander off too far from the safety of the beach, and may be attacked by sharks.

The mating season occurs between May and January, more or less the time of the garua. It stretches over a period of six to eight months, with a peak from September to November. The male defends a territory of 40 to 100 square metres with a group of up to 30 females. Those which do not have territories gather in 'bachelor clubs'. This is often a voluntary retreat, following a tiring period of holding a territory. A territorial male has very little time to feed, and he keeps his territory for about 14 to 29 days before it is taken over by another male.

Mating occurs in the water. The female gives birth on land—after retiring to a chosen site—and walks away from the afterbirth, with the pup in her mouth. Frigates, gulls, hawks, mockingbirds and ruddy turnstones have been seen feeding on the afterbirth. The newborn sea lion pup weighs about five to six kilograms; one year later it will weigh 20 to 30 kilograms.

Mother and pup recognize one another by cry and smell. The female stays five to six days with the young and teaches it to suck from her four teats. Then the mother goes back to the sea. The pup will lose its first fur five months later, and will have its adult pelt. It will suckle the female for one to two years maximum, before it is left on its own.

Four weeks after giving birth, the female mates again, but the fertilization of the new egg will be effective only two months later. This is known as the 'delayed implantation'. The next birth will occur after a gestation of nine months.

THE ANNUAL CYCLE OF THE GALÁPAGOS SEA LION

| Jan | Feb | March | April | May | June | July | Aug | Sept | Oct | Nov | Dec |

```
─────────── + ── + ─────── + ──────────────────────
──────────► B ── M ─────── I ──────── 9 months ──────────►
```
B: birth
M: mating
I: implantation

Seventy per cent of the sea lion's diet is composed of sardines. The sea lion may dive to a depth of 30 to 60 metres, and dives down to 100 metres have been recorded. It feeds during the day, as opposed to the fur sea lion, which feeds at night.

One of the sea lion's favourite games is surfing a big wave as it is about to crash on the shore (eg on North Seymour Island). Another game is 'water polo', using a marine iguana instead of a ball. The unfortunate reptile is caught by the tail and gleefully thrown up in the air.

The lifespan of sea lions is 18 to 20 years. Females are sexually active after three years. Males become sexually active at about six or seven years, when they can defend a territory against other males or challenge a dominant male.

Sea lion colonies are found on South Plaza, Santa Fé, Rábida, James Bay (Santiago Island), Española, San Cristóbal, Isabela. The global population is estimated at 20,000 to 50,000 individuals.

Since 1970, a viral disease, the 'seal pox', has affected sea lions, contributing to a loss of 50 per cent of the population. The disease is evidenced by an infection of the eyes and purulent warts all over the body. The natural predators of the sea lions are sharks and orcas (see photo, page 170–72).

FUR SEA LION   *Arctocephalus galapagoensis*

Whatever people may tell you, there are no fur seals in the Galápagos, but only fur sea lions. This species originated in the Southern Hemisphere, and reached the islands via the Humboldt current. The mother species is *Arctocephalus australis*, and the existing Galápagos subspecies, *Arctocephalus galapagoensis*, is endemic. Another branch of the genus *Arctocephalus* is found in South Africa and on the west coast of Namibia, *Arctocephalus capensis*, the Cape sea lion, which enjoys the cold Benguella current—the equivalent of the Humboldt current in the eastern Atlantic.

The fur sea lion of the Galápagos was near extinction at the beginning of the 20th century, following the plundering of their numbers by whalers and other skin hunters. It is the only tropical species of the genus, which was at first subantarctic. It is also the smallest (see photo, page 172).

Differences between seals and sea lions include the following:
- seals do not have external ears, sea lions do.
- seals cannot support themselves on their front flippers, and creep on the ground.
- seals swim with their posterior flippers, sea lions with the front flippers. Sea lions possess strong front flippers, on which they stand and which they use to swim.

The fur sea lion may be easily distinguished from the sea lion by its smaller size, its pointed nose, big round sad eyes with a glossy glare and apparent ears. Most of the time it lies under rocks or in lava cracks, hiding from the sun. Males weigh up to 75 kilograms and females up to 35 kilograms.

Fur sea lions feed at night on squid and schools of small fish. They may dive to depths of 40 to 100 metres. Mating occurs on land during the garua season, between mid-August and mid-November. Many pups are born in early October. The female is sexually mature at the age of three years, and takes care of the young for two or three years. The pup changes skin and fur at the age of six months.

As in the California sea lion, there is a delayed implantation, three months after the birth of the first pup, making for an annual breeding cycle. Males hold territories for between 27 and 51 days. Since they do not have time to feed, they lose up to 25 per cent of their original weight. For males defending a territory, the mortality rate is 30 per cent the first year. After the birth of the pups, the territorial structure disappears, and the males leave, exhausted.

These *lobos de dos pelos* ('double-fur sea wolves'), as they are known locally, are found in Puerto Egas (Santiago Island), on Fernandina Island and on the northern islands of Marchena, Pinta, Isabela, Fernandina, Wolf and Darwin.

At present, the global population is stable, with 30,000 to 40,000 individuals. The two species of sea lions suffer shark attacks, especially on full-moon nights. Therefore, these marine mammals avoid going out on these nights!

CHAPTER FIVE

MARINE LIFE

The Galápagos are bathed by three currents—the cold Humboldt and Cromwell currents, and the warm Panama flow (or El Niño)—providing the islands with a rich, diverse and unique underwater fauna. Organisms originated from three main regions or oceanic provinces:
- the southeastern Pacific, on the Peru-Chile coast
- the eastern Pacific, stretching from Panama to Baja California
- the western Pacific, or Indo-Pacific region, for the tropical species of warm waters.

In 1978, the number of species of fish was estimated at 306 (McCosker, Taylor and Warner). Of this number:

51 species,	or 17%,	are endemic to the Galápagos
177 species,	or 58%,	belong to the Panamic region
43 species,	or 14%,	belong to the Indo-Pacific province
21 species,	or 7%,	belong to the Peru-Chile province
7 species,	or 2%,	are insular endemic: Galápagos, Cocos, Revillagigedos, Malpelo
4 species,	or 1%,	belong to the Atlantic province

The number of fish above is far from exhaustive. According to the most recent research (1992) of Jack Grove and Dr. Lavenberg, of the Los Angeles County Museum in California, the number could easily go beyond 400 species, and the rate of endemism would be reduced to 7 per cent.

Among the numerous fish found in the archipelago, there are 18 species of morays, five species of rays (stingrays, golden ray, marbled ray, spotted eagle ray and manta rays). There are also about 12 species of sharks, which so far have not been harmful to man. No serious incidents have occurred, although some shark attacks have been reported from Pinzón Island. The dangerous great white shark is not an inhabitant of the archipelago; it is found farther north and away from the islands. The most common sharks are the white-tip reef shark, the black-tip reef shark, two species of hammerheads, the Galápagos shark, the grey reef shark, the tiger shark, the hornshark and the whale shark (Gordon Rock, 1984; Darwin Island).

Among the cetaceans, at least 16 species of whales and seven species of dolphins have been identified. Of the latter, the most common are the bottle-nosed dolphin (*Tursiops truncatus*) and the common dolphin. Whales include the sperm whale, the humpback whale, the pilot whale, the orca and the false killer whale, Sei whale, Minke whale, Bryde's whale, Cuvier's beaked whale and other beaked whales. All these whales are distributed throughout the archipelago and are easily observed in the west of Isabela and Fernandina due to the 'upwelling' of the Cromwell current, rich in organisms and plankton. Another species of whale was added to the list in 1993; a few sightings of blue whales were reported by the research sailboat *Odyssey* to the north of Isabela and Fernandina (David Day).

The littoral is also rich in various organisms such as sea stars and cushion stars, sea urchins, sea cucumbers and red crabs ('*zayapas*') with turquoise blue colorations. A few coral reefs—hermatypic hexacorallians and octacorallians—are present to the west of Santiago, south of Genovesa and Santa Cruz (Tortuga bay), north of Floreana. Ahermatypic solitary corals are also found. Corals need particular conditions for their development: clear water with a minimal temperature of 18° C to 20° C, and an optimal depth of 20 metres (see map and drawing, pages 186–87).

Among shells we may mention: cones (*Conidae*), mitre shells (*Mitridae*), cowries (*Cypraeidae*), nerites (*Neritidae*), periwinkles (*Littorinidae*), creepers (*Cerithiidae*), strombs (*Strombidae*), helmet shells (*Cassidae*), murex shells (*Muricidae*), horse conches.

CLASSIFICATION OF THE CETACEANS IN GALÁPAGOS   *Order of marine mammals*

SIZE	SUBORDER OF MYSTICETI (Baleen whales)	
	Rorquals (Family Balaenopteridae)	
19 metres	Sei whale	*Balaenoptera borealis*
15 metres	Bryde's whale	*Balaenoptera edeni*
10 metres	Minke whale	*Balaenoptera acutorostrata*
19 metres	Humpback whale	*Megaptera novaeangliae*
30 metres	Blue whale	*Balaenoptera musculus*
	SUBORDER OF THE ODONTOCETI (Toothed whales)	
	Sperm whales (Family Physeteridae)	
21 metres	Sperm whale	*Physeter catodon*
3.7 metres	Pygmy sperm whale	*Kogia breviceps*
2.7 metres	Dwarf sperm whale	*Kogia simus*

CLASSIFICATION OF THE CETACEANS IN GALÁPAGOS   *Order of Marine Mammals*

Size		
	Beaked whales (Family Ziphiidae)	
7 metres	Cuvier's beaked whale	*Ziphius cavirostris*
5 metres	Beaked whales	*Mesoplodon* sp.
	Marine dolphins (Family Delphinidae)	
10 metres	Orca, killer whale	*Orcinus orca*
2.7 metres	Pygmy killer whale	*Feresa attenuata*
6 metres	False killer whale	*Pseudorca crassidens*
7 metres	Shortfin pilot whale	*Globycephala macrorhynchus*
2.8 metres	Melon-headed whale	*Peponocephala electra*
2.4 metres	Fraser's dolphin	*Lagenodelphis hosei*
4.5 metres	Risso's dolphin or Grey grampus	*Grampus griseus*
2.6 metres	Common dolphin or White-bellied dolphin	*Delphinus delphis*
4 metres	Bottle-nosed dolphin	*Tursiops truncatus*
2 metres	Spotted dolphin	*Stenella attenuata*
2.7 metres	Striped dolphin	*Stenella coeruleoalba*
2 metres	Spinner dolphin	*Stenella longirostris*

(List of Cetaceans, after David Day, No*ticias de Galápagos*, April 1994).

List of the fishes, whales, dolphins and other marine animals of the Galápagos (368 species)   (E) = Endemic

1/ **Cornetfishes, trumpetfishes, pipefishes:**

Reef cornet fish	*Fistularia commersonii*
Trumpetfish	*Aulostomus chinensis*
Fantail pipefish	*Doryrhampus melanopleura*
Pacific seahorse	*Hippocampus ingens*

2/ **Needlefishes, halfbeaks, flying fishes:**

Pike needlefish	*Strongylura exilis*
Silverstripe halfbeak	*Hyporhampus unifasciatus*
Ribbon halfbeak	*Euleptorhamphus longirostris*
Longfin halfbeak	*Hemirhampus saltator*
Sharpchin flying fish	*Fodiator acutus*
Flying fish	*Cheilopogon dorsomaculata*
Flying fish	*Exocoetus monocirrhus*
Flying fish	*Prognichthys seali*

Baleen whales

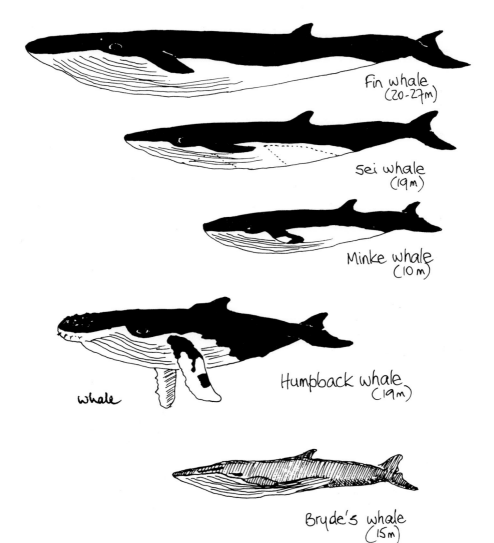

Fin whale
(20-27m)

Sei whale
(19m)

Minke whale
(10m)

Humpback whale
(19m)

whale

Bryde's whale
(15m)

Piroco 89

Toothed whales

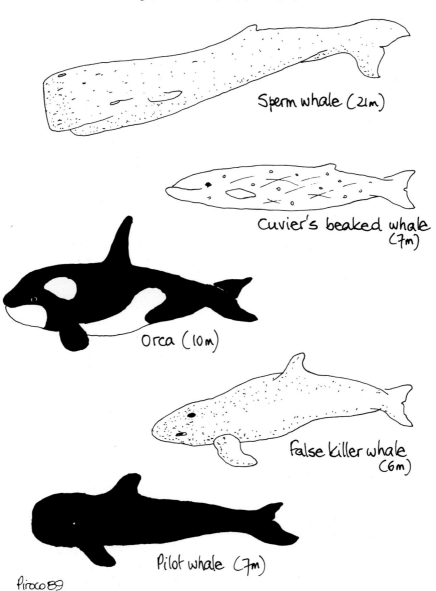

Sperm whale (21m)

Cuvier's beaked whale (7m)

Orca (10m)

False killer whale (6m)

Pilot whale (7m)

Piroco 89

3/ **Parrotfishes, wrasses:**

Bluechin parrotfish	*Scarus ghobban*
Bumphead parrotfish	*Scarus perrico*
Bicolor parrotfish	*Scarus rubroviolaceus*
Azure parrotfish	*Scarus compressus*
Loosetooth parrotfish	*Nicholsina denticulata*
Mexican hogfish	*Bodianus diplotaenia*
Harlequin wrasse	*Bodianus eclancheri*
Cortez rainbow wrasse	*Thalassoma lucasanum*
Sunset wrasse	*Thalassoma lutescens*
Chameleon wrasse	*Halichoeres dispilus*
Spinster wrasse (or goldspot wrasse)	*Halichoeres nicholsi*
Dragon wrasse	*Novaculichthys taeniourus*
Surge wrasse	*Thalassoma purpureum*
Galápagos sheephead	*Semicossyphus darwini*
Pacific beakfish, Tigris	*Oplegnathus insigne*

4/ **Surgeonfishes, angelfishes, damselfishes, butterflyfishes:**

Yellowtail surgeonfish	*Prionurus laticlavius*
Gold-rimmed surgeonfish	*Acanthurus glaucopareius*
Yellowfin surgeonfish	*Acanthurus xanthopterus*
Convict tang	*Acanthurus triostegus*
Spotted unicorn	*Naso brevirostris*
Vlaminck unicorn	*Naso vlamingii*
Moorish Idol	*Zanclus canescens*
King angelfish	*Holocanthus passer*
Barberfish	*Heniochus nigrirostris*
Scythe butterflyfish	*Chaetodon falcifer*
Three-banded butterflyfish	*Chaetodon humeralis*
Meyer's butterflyfish	*Chaetodon meyeri*
Raccoon butterflyfish	*Chaetodon lunula*
Threadfin butterflyfish	*Chaetodon auriga*
Duskybarred butterflyfish	*Chaetodon kleinii*
Longnose butterflyfish	*Foreipiger flavissimus*
Panama sergeant major	*Abudefduf troschelli*
Night sergeant	*Nexilarius concolor*
Rusty damselfish	*Nexilosus latifrons*
Yellowtail damselfish	*Eupomacentrus arcifrons*
Acapulco damselfish	*Eupomacentrus acapulcoensis*
Galápagos whitetail damsel	*Stegastes leucorus beebei*
Giant damselfish	*Microspathodon dorsalis*
Bumphead damselfish	*Microspathodon bairdii*
Whitespot chromis	*Chromis atrilobata*
Blackspot chromis	*Azurina eupalama*
White striped chromis	*Chromis alta*

5/ Puffers, porcupinefishes, boxfishes:

Galápagos pufferfish	*Spherodes angusticeps*
Concentric pufferfish	*Spherodes annulatus*
Guineafowl puffer	*Arothron meleagris*
White-spotted puffer	*Arothron hispidus*
Spotted sharpnosed pufferfish	*Canthigaster punctatissima*
Balloonfish	*Diodon holocanthus*
Porcupinefish	*Diodon hystrix*
Galápagos blue porcupinefish	*Chilomycterus affinis galapagoensis*
Yellow spotted burrfish	*Cyclichthys spilostylus*
Pacific boxfish	*Ostracion meleagris*

6/ Triggerfishes, filefishes:

Yellow bellied triggerfish	*Sufflamen verres*
Black triggerfish	*Melichthys niger*
Pink tail triggerfish	*Melichthys vidua*
Blunthead triggerfish	*Pseudobalistes naufragium*
Finescale triggerfish	*Balistes polyepsis*
Red tail triggerfish	*Xanthichthys mento*
Blue-striped triggerfish	*Xanthichthys caeruleolineatus*
Scrawled filefish	*Aluterus scriptus*
Vagabond filefish	*Cantherines dumerlii*

7/ Blennies, clinid blennies (klipfishes), combtooth blennies, gobies:

Large-banded blenny	*Ophioblennius steindachneri*	
Sabretooth blenny	*Plagiotremus azaleus*	
Castro's blenny	*Acanthemblemaria castroii*	(E)
Red-spotted barnacle blenny	*Hypsoblennius brevipinnis*	
Galápagos four-eyed blenny	*Dialommus fuscus*	(E)
Bravo clinid	*Labrisomus dentriticus*	(E)
Large mouth blenny	*Labrisomus xanti*	
Jenkins clinid	*Labrisomus jenkinsi*	(E)
Porehead blenny	*Labrisomus multiporosus*	
Galápagos triplefin blenny	*Enneapterygius corallicola*	(E)
Blenny sp.	*Malacoctenus afuerae*	
Belted blenny	*Malacoctenus zonogaster*	(E)
Throatspotted blenny	*Malacoctenus tetranemus*	
?	*Starksia galapagensis*	(E)
Ophidiid	*Caecogilbia galapagoensis*	
De Roy's ophidiid	*Caecogilbia deroyi*	
Tagus goby	*Chriolepis tagus*	(E)
Blackeye goby	*Coryphopterus urospilus*	
Goby species	*Eleotrica cableae*	(E)
Galápagos blue-banded goby	*Lythrypnus gilberti*	(E)
Goby species	*Lythryphus rizophora*	

Banded cleaner goby	*Elacatinus nesiotes*
?	*Gobisoma* species

8/ Groupers, seabasses, grunts, mojarras, snappers, seachubs:

Flag cabrilla	*Epinephelus labriformis*	
Spotted cabrilla grouper	*Epinephelus analogus*	
Panama graysby	*Epinephelus panamensis*	
Mutton hamlet	*Epinephelus afer*	
Leather bass	*Epinephelus dermatolepis*	
Misty grouper, mero	*Epinephelus mystacinus*	(E)
Rainbow basslet	*Liopropoma fasciatum*	
Bacalao, yellow grouper	*Mycteroperca olfax*	
Camotillo, white spotted seabass	*Paralabrax albomaculatus*	(E)
Barred serrano	*Serranus fasciatus*	
Creolefish	*Paranthias colonus*	
Gray threadfin seabass, plumero	*Cratinus agassizi*	
Galápagos grunt	*Orthopristis forbesi*	
Grey grunt, Golden-eye grunt	*Haemulon scudderi*	
Graybar grunt	*Haemulon sexfasciatum*	
Burrito grunt, yellowtail grunt	*Anisotremus interruptus*	
Peruvian grunt	*Anisotremus scapularis*	
Black-striped salema	*Xenocys jessiae*	
White salema	*Xenichthys agassizi*	
Pacific flagfin mojarra	*Eucinostomus californiensis*	
Spotfin mojarra	*Eucinostomus argenteus*	
Yellowfin mojarra	*Gerres cinereus*	
Stripe-tail aholehole	*Kuhila taeniura*	
Machete	*Elops affinis*	
Blue and gold snapper	*Lutjanus viridis*	
Yellowtail snapper	*Lutjanus argiventris*	
Mullet snapper	*Lutjanus aratus*	
Pacific dog snapper	*Lutjanus novemfasciatus*	
Barred pargo	*Hoplopagrus guentheri*	
Jordan's snapper	*Lutjanus jordani*	
Dusky chub	*Girella fremenvillei*	
Cortez sea chub	*Kyphosus elegans*	
Blue bronze chub	*Kyphosus analogus*	
Rainbow chub	*Sectator ocyurus*	
Shiner perch	*Cymatogaster aggregata*	

9/ Squirrelfishes, bigeyes, cardinalfishes:

Crimson soldierfish	*Myripristis leiognathos*	
Big eyed soldierfish	*Myripristis murdjan*	
Whitetip soldierfish	*Myripristis* species	(E)

Sun squirrelfish	*Sargocentron suborbitalis*
Glasseye	*Priacanthus cruentatus*
Popeye catalufa	*Pseudopriacanthus serrula*
Tail spot cardinalfish	*Apogon dovii*
Pacific cardinalfish	*Apogon pacificus*
Blacktip cardinalfish	*Apogon atradorsatus* (E)
Percelle	*Cheilodipterus species*

10/ Scorpionfishes, hawkfishes:

Spotted scorpionfish	*Scorpaena plumieri mystes*
Rainbow scorpionfish	*Scorpaenodes xyris*
Scorpionfish	*Scorpaena histrio*
Red scorpionfish	*Pontinus species*
Hieroglyphic hawkfish	*Cirrhitus rivulatus*
Coral hawkfish	*Cirrhitichthys oxycephalus*
Longnosed hawkfish	*Oxycirrhites typus*

11/ Goatfishes, searobins, lizardfishes:

Mexican goatfish	*Mullodichthys dentatus*
Galápagos searobin	*Prionotus miles* (E)
White margin searobin	*Prionotus albirostris*
Sauro lizardfish	*Synodus lacertinus*
California lizardfish	*Synodus lucioceps*
Spotted lizardfish	*Synodus scituliceps*
Lizardfish	*Synodus jenkinsii*
Marchena lizardfish	*Synodus marchenae* (E)
Galápagos clingfish	*Arcos poecilophtalmus* (E)

12/ Anchovies, herrings, remoras, silversides:

Anchovy	*Anchoa naso*
Galápagos thread herring	*Opisthonema berlangai* (E)
Peruvian Pacific sardine	*Sardinops sadax sadax*
Remora, sharksucker	*Remora remora*
Silverside	*Eurystole eriarcha*
Silverside	*Nectarges nesiotes* (E)

13/ Porgies, bonefishes, tilefishes, dolphins, sunfishes:

Pacific porgy	*Calamus brachysomus*
Galápagos porgy	*Calamus taurinus*
Galápagos seabrim	*Archosargus pourtalesi*
Bonefish	*Albula vulpes*
Ocean whitefish	*Caulolatilus princeps*
Dolphinfish	*Coryphaena hippurus*
Ocean sunfish	*Mola mola*
Pacific spadefish	*Chaetodipterus zonatus*

14/ Jacks, pompanos:

Gafftopsail pompano	*Trachinotus rhodopus*
Paloma pompano	*Trachinotus païtensis*
Steel pompano	*Trachinotus stilbe*
African pompano	*Alectis ciliaris*
Green jack	*Caranx caballus*
Pacific crevalle jack	*Caranx caninus*
Black jack	*Caranx lugubris*
Gold-spotted jack	*Carangodes orthogrammus*
Bigeye jack	*Caranx sexfasciatus*
Horse eye jack	*Caranx latus*
Blue fin jack	*Caranx melampygus*
Rainbow runner	*Elagatis bipinnulatus*
Mackerel jack	*Decapterus pinnulatus*
Bigeye scad, Chinchard	*Selar crumenophtalmus*
Pacific amberjack	*Seriola colburni*
= Almaco amberjack	*Seriola rivoliana*
Yellowtail	*Seriola lalandei*
Pilot fish	*Naucrates ductor*

15/ Barracudas, mackerels, tunas, marlins:

Pelican barracuda	*Sphyraena idiastes*
Wahoo	*Acanthocybium solanderi*
Sierra mackerel	*Scomberomorus sierra*
Pacific bonito	*Sarda chilensis*
Skipjack tuna	*Euthynnus pelamis*
Yellowfin tuna	*Thunnus albacares*
Chub mackerel	*Scomber japonicus*
Striped marlin	*Makaira mitsukurii*
Black marlin	*Makaira marlina*

16/ Croakers, drums, mullets, snooks:

Gungo drum, rock croaker	*Pareques viola*
Yelloweye croaker	*Odontoscion xanthops*
Bronze croaker	*Odontoscion eurymesops*
Galápagos croaker	*Umbrina galapagorum*
Striped mullet	*Mugil cephalus*
Yellowtail mullet, lisa	*Mugil cephalus rammelsbergii*
Orange-eyed mullet	*Xenomugil thoburni*
Galápagos mullet	*Mugil galapagensis*
Snook	*Centropomus nigrescens*

17/ Batfishes, frogfishes:

Galápagos redlips batfish	*Ogcocephalus darwinii*

Sanguine frogfish	*Antennarius sanguineus*
Bandtail frogfish	*Antennarius strigatus*

18/ **Flounders, soles, tonguefishes:**

Pacific sanddab	*Citharichthys sordidus*
Speckled sanddab	*Citharichthys stigmaeus*
Blue-eyed flounder	*Bothus mancus*
Striped sole	*Achirus fonsecensis*
Galápagos Sole	*Asergodes herrei*
Rainbow tonguefish	*Symphurus atramentatus*

19/ **Morays, snake eels, conger eels:**

Hardtail moray	*Anarchias galapagensis*	
Black-spot moray	*Muraena clepsydra*	
Panamic green moray	*Muraena castaneus*	
Magnificent moray	*Muraena argus*	
Lentil moray	*Muraena lentiginosa*	
Zebra moray	*Echidna zebra*	
Night moray	*Echidna nocturna*	
Yellowmargin moray	*Gymnothorax flavimarginatus*	
Whitish speckled moray	*Gymnothorax pictus*	
Black moray	*Gymnothorax buroensis*	
Masked moray	*Gymnothorax panamensis*	
Fine-spotted moray	*Gymnothorax dovii*	
Olive moray	*Gymnothorax funebris*	
Whitemouth moray	*Gymnothorax meleagris*	
Slenderjaw moray	*Enchelycore octaviana*	
Mosac moray	*Enchelycore lichenosa*	
Peppered moray	*Uropterygius polysticus*	
Rusty moray	*Uropterygius necturus*	
?	*Uropterygius species*	
Burrowing Galápagossnake eel	*Callechelys galapagensis*	(E)
Snake eel	*Paraletharchus opercularis*	(E)
Snake eel	*Caecula equatorialis*	(E)
Tiger snake eel	*Myrichthys tigrinus (M.maculosus)*	
Pacific snake eel	*Ophichthus triserialis*	
Galápagos cusk eel	*Ophidion species*	
Panama conger eel	*Anosoma gilberti*	
Galápagos garden eel	*Tanioconger klausewitzi*	

20/ **Stingrays, golden rays, eagle rays, mantas:**

Whiptail stingray	*Dasyatis brevis*
Longtail stingray	*Dasyatis longus*
Round stingray	*Urotrygon species*
Marbled ray	*Taeniura meyeri*
Pacific cownose ray	*Rhinoptera steindachneri*

Northern phalarope in winter plumage, Rabida 1993

Espanola mockingbird, Gardner Bay 1984

Galapagos dove, Sullivan Bay 1990

Vermillion flycatcher (male), Los Gemelos, Santa Cruz 1993

Vermillion flycatcher (female), Santa Cruz 1993

Large-billed flycatcher, Floreana 1990

Yellow warbler, James Bay 1990

Smooth-billed anis, Santa Cruz 1992

Galapagos hawk feeding on a marine iguana, Fernandina 1992

Galapagos hawk (young), Alcedo 1991

Hawk and mockingbird, Espumilla, Santiago 1990

Short-eared owl, Santa Cruz 1986

Barn owl, Santa Cruz 1982

Small-billed ground finch 1989

Large-billed ground finch, Darwin Station 1988

167

Cactus finch (male), Santa Cruz 1991

Large cactus finch, Espanola 1991

Small-billed tree finch, Gemelos 1988

Small-billed tree finch (young), Gemelos 1993

Sealions colony, Gardner Bay, Espanola 1992

Female sea lions, Cristobal 1989

Sea lion pups, Espanola 1993

Sea lion (male), Gardner Bay, Espanola 1992

Fur sea lion, James Bay, Santiago 1990

Fur sea lion, Santiago 1985

Slipper lobster, Tagus Cove, Isabela 1992

Red spiny lobster and slipper lobsters, Sombrero Chino 1986

Blue lobster, Elizabeth Bay, Isabela 1986

173

Sea cucumber or pepino, Isostichopus fuscus, *Santa Fé 1991*

Spotted eagle ray, Bartolomé 1992

Golden cownose rays, Tortuga Negra 1984

Marine turtles mating, Tortuga Negra 1990

Stingrays, Floreana 1990

False killer whales surfacing, Darwin 1993

Common dolphin, Banks Bay, Isabela 1992

Spotted eagle ray	*Aetobatus narinari*
Pacific manta	*Manta hamiltoni*

21/ **Sharks:**

Whitetip reef shark	*Triaenodon obesus*
Galápagos requiem shark	*Carcharhinus galapagensis*
Blacktip shark	*Carcharhinus limbatus*
Silvertip shark	*Carcharhinus albimarginatus*
Grey reef shark	*Carcharhinus amblyrhynchos*
Silky shark	*Carcharhinus falciformis*
Tiger shark	*Galeocerdo cuvieri*
Smooth hammerhead	*Sphyrna zygaena*
Scalloped hammerhead	*Sphyrna lewini*
Spotted houndshark	*Triakis maculata*
Galápagos hornshark	*Heterodontus quoyi*
Whale shark	*Rhincodon typus*
Shortfin mako	*Isurus oxyrinchus*
Great white shark	*Carcharodon carcharias*

22/ **Baleen whales: rorquals:**

Sei whale	*Balaenoptera borealis*
Bryde's whale	*Balaenoptera edeni*
Minke whale	*Balaenoptera acutorostrata*
Blue whale	*Balaenoptera musculus*
Humpback whale	*Megaptera novaeangliae*

23/ **Toothed whales, ocean dolphins:**

Sperm whale, cachalot	*Physeter catodon*
Pygmy sperm whale	*Kogia breviceps*
Dwarf sperm whale	*Kogia simus*
Cuvier's beaked whale	*Ziphius cavirostris*
Beaked whales species	*Mesoplodon species*
Melon-headed whale	*Peponocephala electra*
Pygmy killer whale	*Feresa attenuata*
Killer whale, orca	*Orcinus orca*
False killer whale	*Pseudorca crassidens*
Short-finned pilot whale	*Globicephala macrorhynchus*
Fraser's dolphin	*Lagenodelphis hosei*
Risso's dolphin, grey grampus	*Grampus griseus*
Common dolphin, white bellied	*Delphinus delphis*
Bottle nosed dolphin	*Tursiops truncatus*
Spotted dolphin	*Stenella attenuata*
Spinner dolphin	*Stenella longirostris*
Striped dolphin	*Stenella coeruleoalba*

(List of Cetaceans after David Day, *Noticias de Galápagos*, April 1994)

Total = 292 species

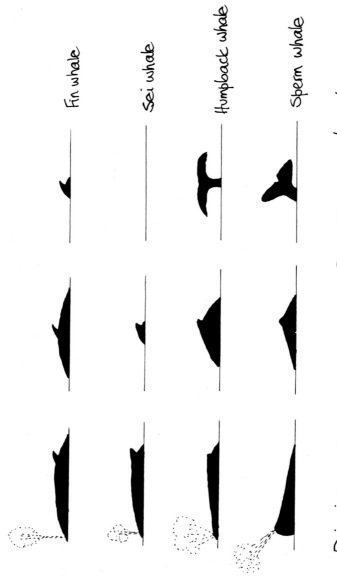

Fin whale

Sei whale

Humpback whale

Sperm whale

Diving sequence of a few whales
[after Gordon C. Pike, 1956].

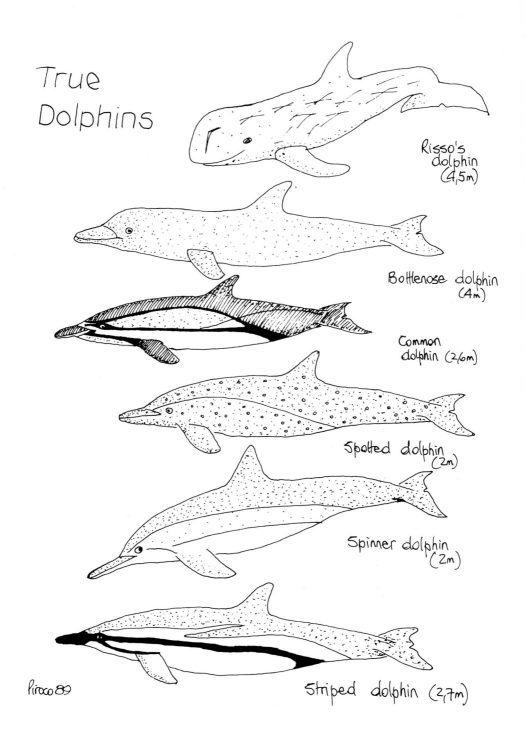

True
Dolphins

Risso's
dolphin
(4,5m)

Bottlenose dolphin
(4m)

Common
dolphin (2,6m)

Spotted dolphin
(2m)

Spinner dolphin
(2m)

Piroco 89

Striped dolphin (2,7m)

Sharks (1)

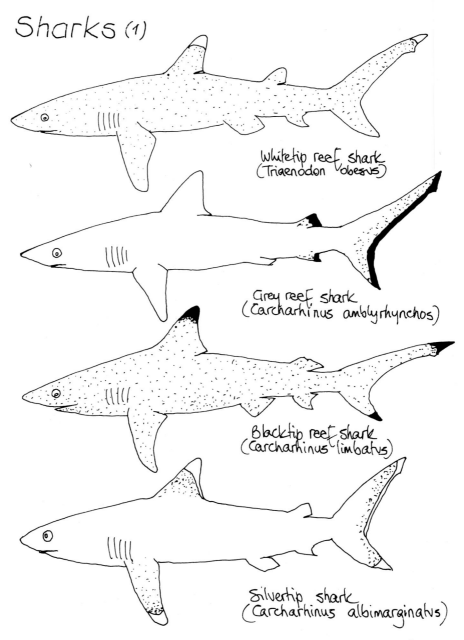

Whitetip reef shark
(Triaenodon obesus)

Grey reef shark
(Carcharhinus amblyrhynchos)

Blacktip reef shark
(Carcharhinus limbatus)

Silvertip shark
(Carcharhinus albimarginatus)

Piroco 89

Sharks (2)

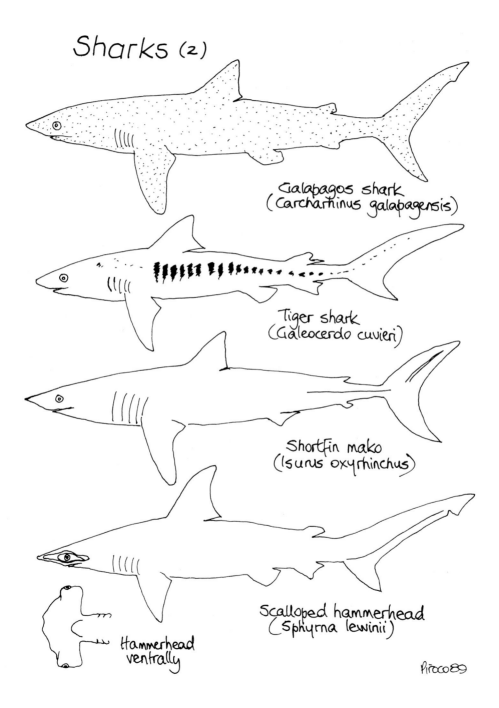

Galapagos shark
(Carcharhinus galapagensis)

Tiger shark
(Galeocerdo cuvieri)

Shortfin mako
(Isurus oxyrhinchus)

Scalloped hammerhead
(Sphyrna lewinii)

Hammerhead
ventrally

Pirocco89

Sharks (3)

Hornshark
(Heterodontus quoyi)

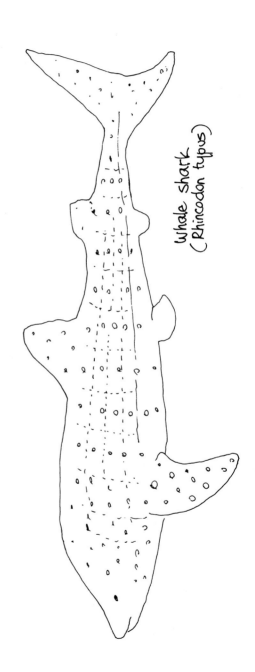

Whale shark
(Rhincodon typus)

OTHER MARINE ANIMALS

PHYLUM CNIDARIA
1/ Class Anthozoa: anemones, corals, gorgonians:

Pacific tube anemone	Pachycerianthus fimbriatus
Anemone	Bunodactis mexicana
Anemone	Bunodosoma species
Leopard spotted anemone	Antiparactis species
Anemone	Anthopleura species
Zoanthid	Palythoa species
Zoanthid	Zoanthus species
Golden sea fan	Muricea species
Orange cup coral	Tubastrea coccinea
Tagus cup coral	Tubastrea tagusensis
Pink cup coral	Tubastrea species
Yellow polyp black coral	Antipathes galapagensis
Panama black coral	Antipathes panamensis
	Cycloseris elegans
Pebble coral	Cycloseris mexicana
	Gardineroseris planulata
	Psammocora stellata
	Psammocora brighami
	Pocillopora damicornis
	Pocillopora elegans
	Pocillopora capitata
Corals	
	Agaricella species
	Porites lobata
	Pavona clavus
	Pavona gigantea
	Pavona varians

PHYLUM ANNELIDA
2/ Class Polychaeta: segmented worms:

Common fireworm	Eurythoe complanata
Ornate fireworm	Chloeia viridis

PHYLUM MOLLUSCA
3/ Class Polyplacophora: chitons

Rippled chiton	Chiton sulcatus	(E)
Chiton	Chiton goodallii	(E)

4/ Class Gastropoda: snails, sea slugs, sea hares, nudibranchs:

Panamic horse conch	Pleuroploca princeps
Galápagos black sea slug	Onchidella steindachneri (E)
Blue-striped sea slug	Tambja mullineri
Starry night nudibranch	Hypselodoris lapizlazuli
Carnivorous nudibranch	?
Sea hare	Dolabrifera dolabrifera
Purple sea hare	Aplysia sp

PHYLUM ARTHROPODA

5/ Class Crustacea: crabs, shrimps, lobsters:

Galápagos pebblestone crab	Mithrax sp
Giant hermit crab	Petrochirus californiensis
Hairy hermit crab	Aniculus elegans
Bar-eyed hermit crab	Dardanus fucosus
Swimming crab	Cronius ruber
Red crab	Cancer sp
Sally lightfoot crab	Grapsus grapsus
Princely fiddler crab	Uca princeps
Panamic arrowhead crab	Stenorhynchus debilis
Shamed face box crab	Calappa convexa
Ghost crab	Ocypode sp
Sea star shrimp	Periclimenes soror
Banded coral shrimp	Stenopus hispidus
Giant khaki shrimp	Penaeus californiensis
Yellowsnout red shrimp	Rhynchocinetes sp
Red spiny lobster	Panulirus penicillatus
Blue lobster	Panulirus gracilis
Slipper lobster	Scyllarides astori

PHYLUM ECHINODERMATA

6/ Class Asteroidea: seastars:

Armored sand star	Astropecten armatus
Panamic cushion star	Pentaceraster cummingi
(or Gulf star)	Oreaster occidentalis
Chocolate chipstar	Nidorellia armata
Pyramid sea star	Pharia pyramidata
Tan sea star	Phataria unifascialis
Troschel's sea star	Evasterias troschelii
Pacific comet star	Linckia columbiae
Sunstar	Heliaster multiradiata
Bradley sea star	Mithrodia bradleyi

7/ Class Ophiuroidea: brittle stars:
Alexander's spiny brittle star   Ophiocma alexandri
Multicolored brittle star   Ophioderma variegatum
8/ Class Echinoidea: sea urchins:
Pencil sea urchin   Eucidaris thouarsii
Crowned sea urchin   Centrostephanus coronatus
Galápagos green sea urchin   Lytechinus semituberculatus (E)
Flower sea urchin   Toxopneustes roseus
Giant sand dollar   Clypeaster europacificus
Heart urchin, sea porcupine   Lovenia cordiformis
Grooved heart urchin   Agassizia scobiculata
9/ Class Holothuroidea: sea cucumbers:
Brown spotted sea cucumber   Holothuria impatiens
Sulfur sea cucumber   Holothuria lubrica
Giant sea cucumber   Isostichopus fuscus
Reptiles
Sea snake   Pelamis platurus
Marine iguana   Amblyrhynchus cristatus
Pacific green sea turtle   Chelonia mydas agassizi
Other Mammals
Sea lion   Zalophus californianus
Fur sea lion   Arctocephalus galapagoensis

Total: 80 species

COMMERCIAL FISHING

Commercial fishing includes: artisanal fishing, industrial fishing and sport fishing.

Of the 30 species which are fished in the Galápagos, 90 per cent belong to the family Serranidae (groupers and seabasses). In the 1950s, mainly *bacalao* (yellow grouper), *lisa* (yellowtail mullet) and lobster were caught. Between the 1930s and 1950s, bacalao were caught on a line (*pinchagua*), then cut in half, salted, dried on the rocks, and exported to the mainland. In the 1980s, bacalao accounted for 50 per cent of industrial fishing, followed by *camotillo* and *mero* (two other groupers). Tuna fishing lagged far behind.

In 1986, annual fishing brought in 150 to 250 tons. Bacalao fishing occurs six months out of the year between October and March, mainly around Isabela Island (until the Marine Reserve was created).

The *norteno* fishing, during the first three months of the year, occurs in the northern islands of Marchena, Darwin and Wolf. The last three months of the year are the season for *camotillo* fishing.

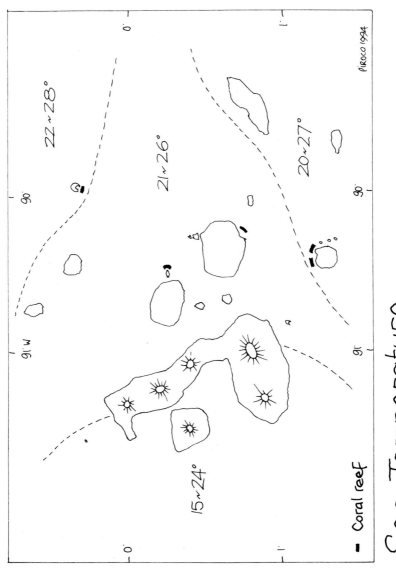

22~28°

21~26°

20~27°

15~24°

PIROCO 1994

- Coral reef

Sea Temperature

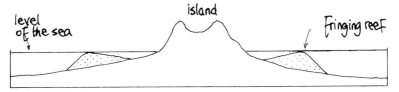

level of the sea

island

Fringing reef

1 - Volcanic island. Construction of a coral reef around it.

barrier reef

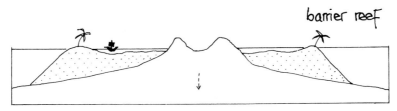

2 - The island sinks and is eroded. The reef builds up vertically. e.g. Bora Bora (Society islands).

lagoon

atoll

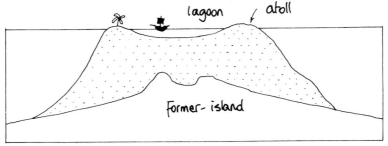

Former - island

3 - The island disappears totally, with the reef building up. The circular reef leaves an atoll.

Evolution of a coral reef
after Darwin

Piraco 1994

List of the fishes exploited by the fishing industry in the Galápagos

Family		Scientific name	Local name	English
Serranidae	(E)	*Mycteroperca olfax*	Bacalao	Yellow grouper
	(E)	*Paralabrax albomaculatus*	Camotillo	White-spotted rock grouper
	(E)	*Epinephelus mystacinus*	Mero	Misty grouper
	(E)	*Epinephelus sp*	Norteno	Norteno
		Epinephelus labriformis	Cabrilla	Flag cabrilla
		Epinephelus dermatolepis	Cagaleche	Leather bass
		Cratinus agassizi	Plumero, gallo	Threadfin seabass
Labridae		*Semicossyphus darwinii*	Vieja	Sheephead
Lutjanidae		*Lutjanus novemfasciatus*	Pargo	Pacific dog snapper
		Lutjanus argiventris	Pargo	Yellowtail snapper
Carangidae		*Seriola rivoliana*	Palometa	Pacific amberjack
Scorpaenidae		*Scorpaena sp*	Brujo	Scorpionfish
Scombridae		*Euthynnus lineatus*	Atun negro	Skipjack tuna
		Sarda chilensis	Atun blanco	Pacific bonito
		Scomberomorus sierra	Sierra	Sierra mackerel
		Acanthocybium solanderi	Guajo	Wahoo

Fishes for bait

Family		Scientific name	Local name	English
Clupeidae		*Opisthonema berlangai*	Sardina	Thread herring
Engraulidae		*Anchoa nasus*	Plástico	Anchovy
Haemulidae		*Xenocys jessiae*	Ojon	Black-striped salema
Mugilidae	(E)	*Mugil galapagensis*	Lisa	Yellowtail mullet

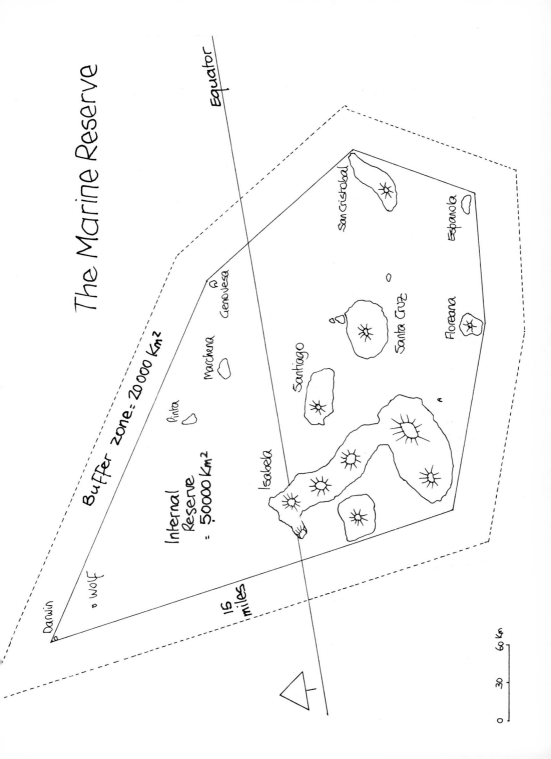

The Marine Reserve

Buffer zone = 20 000 Km²

Internal Reserve = 50000 Km²

Equator

Darwin

o Wolf

Pinta

Marchena

Genovesa

Isabela

Santiago

Santa Cruz

San Cristobal

Floreana

Española

15 miles

0   30   60 Km

LOBSTER AND BLACK CORAL

Three species of lobster are present in the Galápagos, which are commercially exploited:

Common name	Scientific name	Local name
Red lobster	*Panulirus penicillatus*	Langosta roja
Blue lobster	*Panulirus gracilis*	Langosta azul
Slipper lobster	*Scyllarides astori*	Langostino

The red lobster, found in the central and northern islands, and northeast of Isabela Island, once made up 60 per cent of the catch. The blue lobster, once 40 per cent of the catch, is larger, and is distributed mostly on the west coast of Isabela (Urvina and Elizabeth Bay) and around the southern coast, as far as Cartago Bay to the east of Isabela Island.

The minimum legal size is 25 centimetres from head to tail. In 1960, the production was 180 tons; in 1965, 65 tons, and in 1983, 94 tons (of which 33 tons consisted of tails). To allow annual reproduction and the survival of the species, a ban on lobster fishing was enforced each year January-February and June—July. Nevertheless, the abusive catch of recent years has brought a dramatic reduction of the resource and, as a result, the Ecuadorian government imposed a total ban for seven years—from January 1, 1993, until the year 2000—in order to restock the lobster species.

Nevertheless, after strikes and protests led by fishermen in 1993-94, the government reopened lobster fishing for three months per year, from July 15 to October15.

Another problem for the Park is the exploitation of the black coral, Antipathes panamensis, which is not endemic to the Galápagos, unlike Antipathes galapagensis which is endemic.

Black coral is sought by the craftsmen of Puerta Ayora (Santa Cruz) and Puerto Baquerizo Moreno (San Cristóbal). The coral is carved and polished to make jewellery and other fancy gifts which are then sold in shops as Galápagos souvenirs. At present the Galápagos National Park does not have the power to ban sales or stop this exploitation.

THE MARINE RESERVE

On May 13, 1986, the Ecuadorian government, by presidential decree of Leon Febrès Cordero, established the Reserve of the Galápagos Marine Resources. The 50,000 square kilometres of ocean surface comprises the internal waters of the archipelago. A strip of 15 nautical miles (28 kilometres), extending from the outlying points of the islands, was added. This 'buffer zone' represents another 20,000 square kilometres, bringing the total surface of the Marine Reserve to 70,000 square kilometres.

A committee was created to supervise and control the reserve. Its members are representative of the following departments: agriculture, foreign affairs, defense, industry and commercial fisheries, energy and mining, planning and the INGALA (Instituto Nacional Galápagos).

This biological reserve aims to protect and preserve a number of ecological aspects of the islands, as well as the interaction of the National Park with the Marine Reserve. Industrial fishing is not allowed, but local or artisanal fishing go on as before (see drawing of the Marine Reserve, page 189).

ILLEGAL FISHING AND THE 'PEPINOS' AFFAIR

As expected, abuses were not long in surfacing. Striking fishermen came to knock at the government's door to show their anger in 1993. At issue are illegal shark fishing and shark finning (which has caused a furor for some years now), as well as pepino (sea cucumber) fishing. All are pirate fisheries, conducted by sophisticated Japanese fishing boats. The 'pepino war' has gained considerable press attention since 1992.

The shark fishing, stimulated by the Japanese fishing industry, began to cause a stir as far back as 1983. In violation of Ecuadorian law, Japanese boats were penetrating Galápagos waters in the northern islands and around Isabela Island. They were seen on a number of occasions, then escorted away, after paying dubious fines'. The Japanese then conceived the following stratagem: They used Ecuadorian boats from Manta (Ecuador), which could be sent into Galápagos waters to fish, while the Japanese mother-ship would safely wait for the catch in international waters. The Japanese ship Choki Maru was nevertheless hailed in 1991, with a shipment of 5,000 shark fins, six kilometres from Cartago Bay, on the east coast of Isabela Island. In 1992, a patrol boat of the Ecuadorian navy captured the Donai, a fishing boat from Manta, near Pinta Island, with a load of 50 hammerhead sharks on board.

The scandal of the sea cucumbers or pepinos blew up in 1992, when pirate camps were discovered on the basaltic coast of Fernandina Island. Local fishermen had settled with their families and were collecting 130,000 to 150,000 pepinos per day. These sea cucumbers, of the species *Isostichopus fuscus,* are marine invertebrates of commercial value in eastern Asian countries. The larvae are an important part of the plankton, which is food for a great number of fish. The sea cucumbers live on rocky bottoms, at a depth of two to 20 metres, and are important for the purification of sea water. The exploitation of the pepinos is a worldwide business which lays waste to an area of the globe for two to four years; the fishermen plunder the resources, then start somewhere else. It started on the coast of Ecuador in 1988, before it spread out to the Galápagos (see photo, page 174).

PART THREE

DESCRIPTION OF THE ISLANDS

"Marine iguanas"

DESCRIPTION OF THE ISLANDS

Baltra - North Seymour
Santa Cruz
South Plaza
Santa Fé   CENTRAL ISLANDS
Daphné
Rábida
Pinzon

Floreana
Española   SOUTHERN ISLANDS
San Cristobal

Genovesa
Marchena
Pinta   NORTHERN ISLANDS
Wolf
Darwin

Santiago
Bartolomé
Sombrero
Chino   WESTERN ISLANDS
Isabela
Fernandina

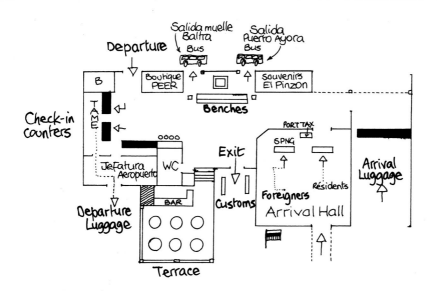

Baltra airport

PiROCO 1994

CHAPTER ONE

CENTRAL ISLANDS

BALTRA

The plane leaves Quito at 9:30 am and stops over at Guayaquil. It takes off again at around 11 am. After an hour and a quarter of cloudless flight, you'll be in sight of San Cristobal Island, which will appear on the port side, bedecked with a layer of cotton-shaped clouds. The black-indented shoreline is fringed with waves of white foam. A few minutes later, you may view the Gordon Rocks, then the Plaza Islands in the distant haze. Finally, you will fly over the luminous sandbar of Mosquera Island. The plane will tilt to port before landing on the island of Baltra. The B-747 of TAME airlines, inaugurated on October 22, 1980, stops in the heart of the arid zone, a land covered with cacti.

At Baltra Island, the Galápagos National Park customs will ask you to pay an entry fee of US$80 (since 1993), and you will be given a leaflet of visitor's rules. You are also expected to pay US$11 for port fees.

A small island north of Santa Cruz, Baltra is a basaltic plateau—which belongs geologically to Santa Cruz—faulted in an east-west direction. In the distant past, the island was once connected to Santa Cruz and North Seymour. Some fossiliferous tuff beds, between lava flows, are the proof of an ancient tectonic uplift. Sheer cliffs rise to the north, to the east and south. The entire island leans towards the west.

On the west coast, Aeolean Cove offers smooth sand beaches. This port is used by the Ecuadorian navy and is also the site of an air force base. Departures and arrivals of numerous tourist boats are made from there. A few cargo ships which visit the archipelago also call in. Baltra Airport was built by the Americans during World War II. The army base was intended to defend the Panama Canal against Japanese air raids, but the attack never came. Rumour has it that the Americans were partly responsible for the eradication of land iguanas on the island, aided by the presence of feral goats, which ate all the vegetation edible to iguanas. The Ecuadorian air force received the base at the end of the war; today it's a civil and military airport, as well as a naval base.

After a 40-year absence, land iguanas were reintroduced to Baltra by the Galápagos National Park. On June 19, 1991, 35 iguanas (five years old) from the breeding centre in Santa Cruz were freed on the island. The following year, in April 1992, 12 land iguanas (8 to 10 years old) were released. The first year of the project showed a survival rate of at least 40 per cent.

Baltra is connected to the island of Santa Cruz by a ferry that crosses daily the Itabaca Channel. From the landing site it is 40 kilometres to the town of Puerto Ayora, or one and a half hours by the minibus of CITTEG, the local transport company (see map of Baltra, page 194).

NORTH SEYMOUR

North of Baltra, Seymour is a small flat island with a land surface of two square kilometres, very similar to Baltra and typical of the arid zone. Palo santos are endemic to the island. Opuntia, the local prickly pear cactus, is the food of the land iguanas.
A trail, about two kilometres long, makes a loop to the southwest, inland and along the rocky coast, crossing the colony of blue-footed boobies then the colony of magnificent frigates. The nesting area of the frigatebirds mixes with that of the boobies. Two species of frigates share the same habitat in harmony. Their nests of twigs are made on the palo santos, as well as on the salt bushes bordering the beach. A few marine iguanas walk across the white coral sand, leaving tracks of their tail and claws. Sea lions bask on the black lava rocks, and the surf crashes on the rocky shore of the west coast at sunset. In the background, the eroded tuff cones of Daphné Mayor and Daphné Minor rise above the ocean surface.

At Seymour, the dry landing on rocks is sometimes difficult, depending on the tide and the season. Rocks may be slippery, and shoes should be worn. A short distance away, Mosquera Islet is an ideal place for a walk when the sun goes down. White sands host a colony of sea lions. Beware of the territorial males, which are known to be aggressive, even in the water. A cautious swim is highly recommended (see map, page 197).

SANTA CRUZ

land surface: 986 square km
elevation: 864 m
main town: Puerto Ayora

The most populous of the islands, Santa Cruz possesses a radio which emits at 1410 KHz (since 1974). Of the five inhabited islands of the Galápagos, Santa Cruz and particularly Puerto Ayora, the touristic capital, have for the last 15 years had the highest immigration rate in the archipelago. The population of the Galápagos is estimated at about 20,000 people—four times the number in 1980.

All the vegetation zones are represented on Santa Cruz, stretching from the littoral zone up to the fern zone at the top of Mount Crocker. The windward side is more humid and diversified than the leeward side, which is very dry. This is especially understandable when one considers that the dominant winds are the southeast tradewinds, and that the precipitation of garua falls on that side of the island.

North Seymour

Frigates

Palo santos and Opuntia

Blue Footed boobies

surf and sealions

marine iguanas

Frigates

Palos santos

S.T. gulls

Sea lions

Basalt cliff

Mosquera

↑ Seymour

sea lions

beach

sea lions

10 m

13 m

rocks

⬇ Baltra

0   100 m

Santa Cruz

Baltra

Tortuga negra

las Bachas

Venezia

Caleta Tiburon

Conway Bay

Eden

Whale Bay

Gordon rocks

Cerro Colorado

Plaza islands

Cerro Iguana

Cerro Ventana

Los Gemelos

Scalesia Forest

Camote

Cerro Ballena

Salasaca

Cerro Crocker

864m

Media Luna

Cascajo

Pta. Roca Fuerte

Santa Rosa

Mutiny

Tunnels

Reserve SPNG

rancho Mariposa

Bellavista

Caseta

Tunnel

Puerto Ayora

Darwin Station

Puerto Nuñez

Punta Nuñez

Punta Tamayo

Tortuga Bay

Pta. Estrada

isla Caamaño

Pieroco 1994

0 2 4 6 Km

Puerto Ayora ~ Santa Cruz

1. Main jetty
2. Peninsular supermarket
3. Correo – Post office
4. Catholic church
5. CITTEG – Minibus to Baltra
6. Hospital
7. INGALA
8. IMETEL
9. School
10. Hotel Palmeras
11. "Black lady" boutique
12. Boutique PEEK + minimarket "Myla"
13. Five Fingers-Bar, Restaurant, disco
14. "Rincon del alma" restaurant
15. Capitania del Puerto
16. Hotel Salinas
17. Hotel Vilmita
18. "mas y mas" restaurant
19. Municipio
20. Hotel Cabo de Mar
21. Police / Immigration
22. TAME
23. "La Garrapata" restaurant + "La Panga" disco
24. "El Reciclado" boutique
25. D'Toto
26. Hotel Solymar
27. Banco del Pacifico
28. Drugstore
29. Movie hall
30. "4 Linternas" restaurant
31. Galapagos Subaqua
32. Quasar Nautica
33. Pension Gloria
34. New Residencial Angermeyer
35. Gimnasio Formas
36. BAMBU artesanias
37. Mistral – Galeria Johanna
38. Tea shirt shop
39. "Iguanas-bananas" shop
40. Hotel Galapagos
41. Scuba Iguana
42. Galapagos Nat. Park
43. Kiosco Parque Nacional
44. M/N iguana wreck (1988)
45. ETICA
46. Hotel Dolfin
47. Red Mangrove Inn
48. Trattoria de Pipo

Baltra – 42 Km.

to Tortuga Bay

Laguna Las Ninfas

Cliff + Opuntia cacti

El Otro Lado

Pelican Bay

Cimetiere

Academy Bay

Pibaco 1994

The Galapagos National Park
and Darwin Station

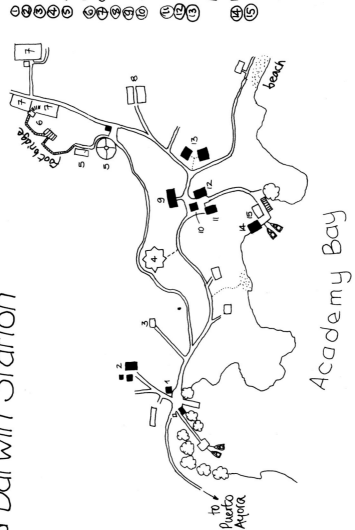

① National Park information
② National Park offices
③ Guide's course hall
④ Van Straelen exhibition hall
⑤ Breeding center of young tortoises
⑥ "Lonesome Georges" corral
⑦ Giant tortoises corral
⑧ Dormitories
⑨ Darwin Station workshops
⑩ Administrative building Darwin Station
⑪ Laboratories
⑫ Station Library
⑬ Tomas Fischer science building (1992-93)
⑭ Laboratories of introduced plants and animals
⑮ Darwin Station dining hall Oceanography + marine biology labs.

Academy Bay

to Puerto Ayora

beach

foot-bridge

PiRoco 1995

Geologically, Santa Cruz is well eroded, and the oldest formations are found to the northeast. Facing the Plazas Islands is Cerro Colorado (the Red Rock), a tectonically uplifted hill in which basaltic lava and fossiliferous tuff are layered with volcanic tuffs of Miocene geological times. The human history started in the 20th century, when European and American settlers arrived between the two world wars. The soil being fertile, the villages of Bellavista and Santa Rosa were founded in the tropical humid zone of the highlands. A great number of exotic plants were introduced: sugarcane, coffee, bananas, oranges, lemon trees and avocado trees. Domestic animals were also introduced. Most of them turned feral, creating a serious and disastrous impact on the native species of the island. But this will be explained later.

A colony of land iguanas may be observed at Conway Bay, on the northwest coast. Facing the bay, on Eden Island, is a small colony of sea lions. Marine iguanas are well represented on the shores all around Santa Cruz, but a colony is established on Isla Coamaño (facing Puerto Ayora), as well as in Punta Nunez, on the southern coast. Eight species of finch are found on the island, and the Hawaiian petrel nests in the highlands. Almost all the species of birds found in the Galápagos have been observed on Santa Cruz.

Punta Ayora is the commercial and tourist centre of the archipelago. From here, cattle and coffee are exported to the mainland. The southwestern part of the port is inhabited by a small colony of European immigrants, who arrived in the 1920s and 30s (see Appendix 3, Population of the Galápagos).

From Puerto Ayora, it is possible to make day trips or tours around the islands by chartering a small boat (with cook, captain and guide) among five to eight people. The cost involved is about $35–50 per person per day. The cruise usually lasts up to one week, and the itinerary is decided by the passengers.

HOTELS (PRICES IN US$)

Hotel Galápagos (on the way to Darwin Station), luxury bungalows facing Academy bay, single: $72; double: $120.

Hotel Sol y mar (Pelican Bay), on the waterfront, single: $24, double: $108.

Hotel Fernandina: $12 to $15, clean rooms and a little garden.

New Angermeyer (exotic), used to be the Garden of Eden pension of Lucrecia Angermeyer before she sold it to a German (in 1993), who reconstructed the whole place. Rooms at $50.

Residencial Las Ninfas (near port).

Hotel Salinas, $3 to $5.

Pension Gloria, ideal for backpackers, $3 to $5. There is also an abandoned camping ground behind the cemetery on the way to the Darwin Station.

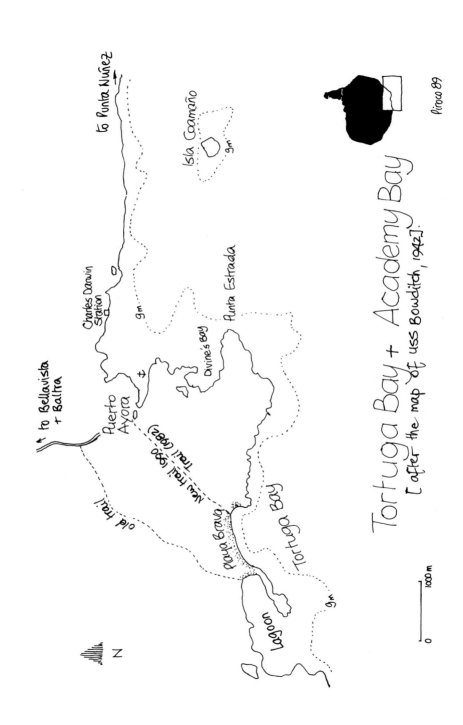

Tortuga Bay + Academy Bay
[after the map of USS Bowditch, 1942]

Piroca 89

N

to Bellavista
+ Baltra

to Punta Núñez

Isla Caamaño

9m

Charles Darwin
Station

9m

Puerto
Ayora

Old Trail

New trail (1986)
Old trail (1980)

Playa Brava

Lagoon

Tortuga Bay

9m

Divine's Bay

Punta Estrada

1000 m

0

RESTAURANTS

4 Linternas (Pelican Bay), run by an Italian woman called Sylvana. Good atmosphere.

La Trattoria de Pipo (Italian), Pelican Bay.

Five fingers, bar-restaurant with terrace and disco on the second floor, facing the Capitania del Puerto (naval base).

La Garrapata, near the disco-bar La Panga.

El Rincón del Alma, facing the naval base where there are more local restaurants and foodstalls.

Salvavidas Bar and Restaurant, on the harbour (since 1994).

Kathy's Kitchen, downtown, on the main place, road to Baltra.

OTHER

Banco del Pacifico (Pelican Bay), bank, near Hotel Sol y Mar.

Scuba Iguana, dive club operated at Hotel Galápagos by Matthias Espinosa and Jack Nelson, starting at US$78/2 dives.

Nautidiving, PADI dive school and club, run by Vicente and Polo Navarro, at the 'Red Mangrove Inn', near Hotel Galápagos, from US$75 to US$110/2 dives.

EMETEL, telephone office. Connections with the mainland since 1993, international calls available since 1994.

Port Captain (Capitania del Puerto), for visiting sailboats, the right to drop anchor is for 48 hours in Puerto Ayora (72 hours in San Cristobal). Port fees: the arrival tax (*arribo*) or departure tax (*salida*) are 2,400 sucres or slightly more than a dollar. Mooring fees (*Faros y boyas*): $3 per ton, mooring: $0.1/ton/day. The Galápagos National Park tax is not required, but if the crew plans to visit the islands of the National Park, that would be on a local boat only. For foreign vessels a longer anchoring time in port will only be allowed in case of damage to the boat, which has rendered it unsailable.

SIGHTSEEING

The Charles Darwin Research Station, open from 7 am to 5 pm, Monday to Friday, and Saturday 8 am to 12 pm.

Van Straelen Exhibition Hall (museum on Galápagos Natural History).

Breeding centre for young tortoises, with elevated walkways and tortoise corrals, including that of Lonesome George, the survivor of Pinta Island.

A few **sandy beaches** can be found beyond the Darwin Station, when you head towards the cliff of Punta Nunez. The dirt road leading to the Darwin Station is 1.5 kilometres long, bordered with red, black and white mangroves; giant cacti (Opuntia and Jasminocereus); spiny shrubs such as *Scutia pauciflora,* and other shrubs such as *Maytenus octogona*. The administrative building of the Galápagos National Park is on the way to the Darwin Station, at the first road crossing to the left (see maps of Puerto Ayora and of the Darwin Station, page 198–99).

EXCURSIONS FROM PUERTO AYORA

TORTUGA BAY (TURTLE BAY)
To reach this white sand beach, less than one hour away from Puerto Ayora, first take
the road to Baltra, in town, then turn left about 150 metres after leaving the main square
on the port. A volcanic gravel road climbs to the top of the *barranco* (canyon) along a
stairway before changing to a decent trail. An easy graveled way, opened in 1982,
replaces the old track on the lava rocks, crossing the arid zone of the palo santos and
cacti (sport shoes are advised). Don't forget your hat, sun protection and drinking
water, for the equatorial sun is fierce.

In Tortuga Bay, you may see nesting pelicans in the mangroves (warm season), and
maybe flamingos in the lagoon. If you go for a swim, do not venture beyond the last
wave, for the currents are dangerous at low tide, and sharks could be waiting. Return
before sunset (6 pm). The excursion is worth it (see map, page 200).

LOS GEMELOS (THE TWINS)
On the road to Baltra, beyond the village of Santa Rosa, in the humid tropical zone of
the scalesia (*Scalesia pedunculata*) forest. The Gemelos are two pit-craters over 30
metres deep located on either side of the road. They may be explosion craters, or they
may have been created by the collapse of the roof of some magma chamber, following
circumferencial fissures. A few trails wander around the craters. Many land birds may be
seen, such as the vermillion flycatcher, the large bill flycatcher, the short-eared owl, the
Galápagos dove, and a great number of Darwin's finches, including the carpenter finch,
which uses a stick as a tool to help extract larvae from old stumps.

It is advisable to go to Los Gemelos in the early morning, around 8 am, with the
minibus of CITTEG heading to Baltra. (There is no chance of finding a bus during the
daytime; transport is by hire only.) The village of Santa Rosa is about two kilometres
downhill.

THE TORTOISE RESERVE (CASETA AND EL CHATO)
In the humid zone, this is the ideal place to observe giant tortoises in the wild. From
Santa Rosa, a trail—five kilometres long and sometimes very muddy—leads to
Caseta and to El Chato. It takes two to three hours on foot. The vegetation is
composed of high scalesia, guayabillo (*Psidium galapageium*) and pega pega (*Pisonia
floribunda*) grasses. Darwin's finches are plentiful, as are flycatchers. There is a
camping site at Caseta, and it is possible to hire horses at Santa Rosa (see map of
Santa Cruz, page 197).

Alternatively, one may see tortoises in private farms, such as Poza Pamela or, even
better, at Rancho Mariposa, run by Steve and Jenny Divine, who have a cozy little country

N

Gordon Rocks

North-Plaza

Cerro Colorado (Santa Cruz)

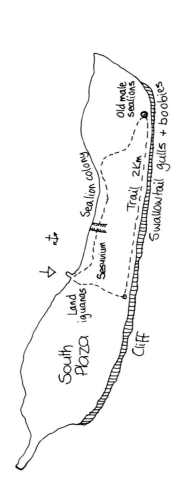

South Plaza

Land iguanas

Sesuvium

Sea lion colony

Old male sea lions

Trail 2 km

Cliff

Swallowtail gulls + boobies

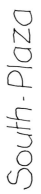

0   100   200 m

South - Plaza

restaurant (expect to pay about US$10 for a meal) with great scenery, and a pond where tortoises come to drink freely. An entry fee is charged.

Los Tunneles (the lava tunnels)

Lava tubes, a few hundred metres to a few kilometres long, are one of the curiosities of Santa Cruz. There is a small one, three kilometres away from Puerto Ayora on the left side of the road. With a diameter of about 10 metres, it is large enough for a subway train to go through. Another tunnel, two kilometres long, is found east of Bellavista on a private land. There is another in Salasaca, west of Santa Rosa, and a third on the land of Furio—an Italian man who has a ranch and a restaurant named Mutiny ($12 per meal)—facing the access road to Steve Divine, not far from Santa Rosa.

Media Luna and Mount Crocker

The trail which leads to the *zona alta* or highlands starts from Bellavista and crosses the agricultural zone (with coffee and avocado plantations) before it gets to the pampa of the miconias (see chapter on flora). It takes an hour to and hour and a half to see Media Luna, a half-moon volcanic cone covered with miconia bushes. In this garua-swept area, the trail is muddy and slippery so expect to get your feet wet. The garua may be so thick that nothing can be seen once the miconia zone is reached. Do not venture further or you may get lost. This walk is very good for observing the vegetation zones and the trees introduced by the settlers, including *Psidium guayaba*, with yellow fruit, or *goyava*, bordering the trail. Cows graze in the fields, in the company of cattle egrets (*Bubulcus ibis*), often sitting on their backs.

On a clear day you may walk farther up to Puntudo, a small volcano at the top of the island, with a conspicuous conical shape. Mount Crocker, the highest summit of Santa Cruz, culminates at 864 metres (two hours from Bellavista and three kilometres beyond Media luna). The site is extraordinary, with a 360-degree panorama, taking in Baltra and Seymour to the north and the two Daphnés to the northwest. This lunar landscape is utterly spectacular, with a chain of tuff cones, broken lava tubes (where volcanic water holes are numerous) and the scalesia forest sliding up the slopes like a wave up the beach (see map of Santa Cruz, page 197).

South Plaza

land surface: 13 square km
elevation: 25 m

The Plazas Islands (North and South) are east of Santa Cruz, a few hundred metres from the coast. There, Cerro Colorado (the Red Rock) rises up with its fossiliferous tuff beds. The two islands were uplifted by tectonic action at the same time as Cerro Colorado, and are both tilted towards the north.

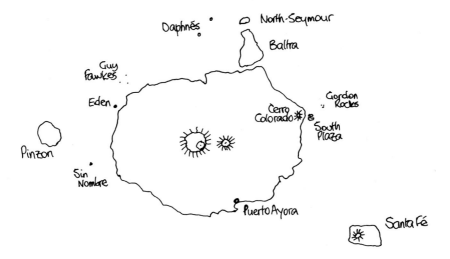

Daphnés
North-Seymour
Baltra
Guy Fawkes
Eden
Gordon Rocks
Cerro Colorado
South Plaza
Pinzon
Sin Nombre
Puerto Ayora
Santa Fé

Santa Fe ~ north east bay

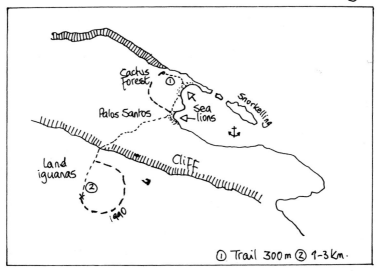

Cactus Forest
①
Snorkelling
Palos Santos
Sea lions
Land iguanas
②
CliFF

① Trail 300 m ② 1-3 km.

Only South Plaza Island is open to visitors, the other island being closed and reserved for scientific research (see drawing, page 204).

The vegetation belongs to the arid zone and is represented by annual plants such as sesuvium, and by opuntia cacti. *Sesuvium edmonstonei* (endemic) is a plant of the succulent family, with red or green almond-shaped leaves, depending on the dry or the wet season. The island wears a red carpet during the months of May to December.

A colony of about 1,000 sea lions inhabits the island. A great number of these marine mammals gather around the disembarking site, playing or porpoising out of the water like dolphins. Do not get close to the male named Charlie, who is known to be aggressive and even bites on occasion.

South Plaza is a good place for observing yellow-brown land iguanas. It is prohibited to feed the reptiles. Years back, when the rules of the Galápagos National Park were not so strict, visitors used to bring oranges and hand them over to the iguanas, who loved the fruit. They became conditioned to such an extent that when a group of tourists arrived at the landing site, land iguanas would run to meet the newcomers, and climb on the visitors' knees to eat the precious fruit. The food balance of the reptiles was seriously affected, and the Galápagos National Park had to bring an end to these illicit practices.

A dangerous cliff borders the south of the island, where many sea lions rest. You may observe swallowtail gulls, tropicbirds, frigates, blue-footed boobies, and masked boobies, Audubon shearwaters, pelicans gliding in the sky. From the top of the cliff (watch out: two guides fell over and ended up at the hospital or died), you may see turtles, rays, yellowtail mullets and sharks. The feral goats were eradicated from the island in 1961. South Plaza is an easy day trip from Puerto Ayora. Gordon Rocks, a short distance away, is a good diving site.

Santa Fé

land surface: 24 square km
elevation: 259 m

Another island uplifted by tectonic action, where some of the oldest basaltic rocks of the archipelago have been dated at 2.7 million years. Santa Fé is to the southeast of Santa Cruz, and can be easily seen from Puerto Ayora (see map, page 206).

In the middle of a sunny day, the lagoon of Santa Fé turns into an eye-catching turquoise blue. The white sandy bottom is only a few metres below the surface. On the beach, sea lions bask lazily in the sun. A trail leads inland to the top of a cliff, from where the view is breathtaking. Two species of land iguanas inhabit the archipelago, but one of these, the endemic *Conolophus pallidus*, dwells only on Santa Fé; it is bigger, with a whitish colour, sometimes chocolate brown when moulting. It sports a prominent dorsal crest, and the eyes are often blood shot.

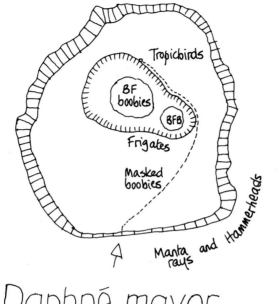

Tropicbirds

BF
boobies

BFB

Frigates

Masked
boobies

Manta and Hammerheads
rays

Daphné mayor

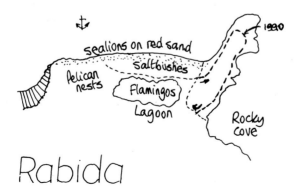

1990

sealions on red sand

saltbushes

Pelican
nests

Flamingos

Lagoon

Rocky
cove

Rabida

Bottlenose dolphins, Banks Bay, Isabela 1988

Surfing sealions, Seymour 1991

Mexican goatfishes, Marchena 1993

Yellowtail surgeonfishes, Marchena 1992

Sea lion in the black coral, Cousin's rock 1990

Cushion star, Tagus cove, Isabela 1991

Orange cup coral, 1990

Bluechin parrotfish (female), Bartolomé 1992

Whitetip reef shark, Devil's Crown 1989

Scalloped hammerhead shark, Darwin 1993

Barracudas, Roca Redonda 1990

School of hammerhead sharks, Darwin 1993

Rainbow scorpionfish, Isabela 1990

213

Pacific amberjacks, Devil's Crown 1990

Redtail triggerfish, Wolf 1992

Longnose hawkfish in black coral, Cousin's Rock 1991

Cerianthid anemone and red crab, Tagus Cove, Isabela 1990

215

Bigeye jacks, Darwin 1993

Yellowtail grunts and blue and gold snappers, Marchena 1993

Fine spotted moray, Gymnothorax dovii Marchena 1993

The vegetation is of the arid type. The forest of the giant prickly pear cacti, *Opuntia echios* var. *barringtonensis,* is striking for the size of the trunks.

The Galápagos hawk often overlooks the beach from the top of a salt bush or a palo santo. A species of endemic rice rat is also known to inhabit the island.

Sea lions, sea turtles, small white-tip reef sharks, spotted eagle rays and round stingrays are common to the small bay. Feral goats were eradicated in 1971. Watch out for stingrays in shallow water.

DAPHNÉ

land surface: 32 ha
elevation: 120 m

North of Santa Island and west of Baltra Island, Daphné is a tuff cone above the surface of the ocean, which can be observed from the airport. In fact there are two islands: Daphné Mayor and Daphné Minor. The latter is the older, and erosion has reduced the original cone to a cylinder-shaped island with sheer cliffs. Daphné Mayor has kept its full cone, with a main crater and a second lateral crater, on the south rim.

Vegetation is poor and mainly represented by croton, palo santos, opuntia cacti and sesuvium. The curiosity of Daphné is the colony of blue-footed boobies, dwelling on the floor of the crater, where the birds nest between April and December.

Magnificent frigatebirds are found on the slopes and on the rim, as well as masked boobies, finches and short-eared owls. Tropicbirds nest in the cliff of Daphné Minor, but fly over Daphné Mayor, too. The landscape is splendid in the early morning after sunrise. The palo santo of Daphné is endemic (see map, page 208).

RÁBIDA (JERVIS)

land surface: 5 square km
elevation: 367 m

Jervis, the English name of Rábida Island, is located near the geographic centre of the archipelago. The island is made of eroded hills and lava ejected from spatter cones. Rábida is more volcanically diversified than any other island of the Galápagos.

Vegetation is composed of palo santos, opuntias and spiny shrubs. Behind the red sand beach at the north of the island, a brackish lagoon shelters a population of flamingos, Bahama pintail ducks and common stilts. Pelicans nest by the beach in the salt bushes (*Cryptocarpus pyriformis*), locally known as *monte salado*. Blue-footed boobies and masked boobies are found in the cliffs.

A new trail leads to the top of a small hill, on the left of the beach. Downhill, on the the right side, portions of the purple-red cliff frequently crumble into the sea. Feral goats were exterminated in 1970 and 1975. (see map, page 208).

PINZÓN

land surface: 12 squarekm
max. elevation: 450 m

West of Santa Cruz, Pinzón is a small island of no apparent interest except, like Rábida, for its geological diversity. The west and southwest parts of the volcano collapsed due to marine erosion and volcanic fractures. On the west coast, the cliffs rise up to 150 metres. Disembarking on the island is therefore difficult.

The vegetation is represented by croton and by spiny shrubs. Inland, near the old crater, lives a population of giant tortoises. Finches are tame, and Galápagos hawks are plentiful. Lava lizards and snakes are also present. One of the great problems of Pinzón was until recently the proliferation of *Rattus rattus*, the black rat, which feeds on eggs and young reptiles. The SPNG, the Galápagos National Park Service, eradicated the rats by traps and poison in September-November 1989.

"Blue footed boobies"

CHAPTER TWO

THE SOUTHERN ISLANDS

FLOREANA

land surface: 24 square km
elevation: 864 m

The southernmost island of the archipelago, along with Española, Floreana is of volcanic origin, very old, and its numerous volcanoes have reached an advanced stage of erosion. No volcanic activity was reported for a long time. South of Post Office Bay, Cerro Paja, the summit of the island, seems to be lost in its eternal sleep. Puerto Velasco Ibarra, the capital, is a mere village under the sun, and its population was just 65 inhabitants in 1986.

In the highlands, the vegetation is diversified and luxurious. Since Floreana was the first colonized island in the 19th century, it contains many species of plants introduced by the settlers. The visitor sites are Punta Cormorant, Corona del Diablo (or Devil's Crown), Post Office Bay and Black Beach on the west coast.

PUNTA CORMORANT

North of Floreana, this is a beautiful green sand beach. The colour is due to the abundance of green olivine crystals in the volcanic tuff. The beach is fringed by white and black mangroves, behind which is a flamingo lagoon. These waders are easily frightened; be as quiet as possible when observing. Adults are pink and juveniles whitish. Flamingos feed on an aquatic insect, *Trichocorixia,* and a small lagoon shrimp *Artemia.* The site is also favorable for observing common stilts, Bahama pintails, whimbrels and ruddy turnstones.

A great number of plants are endemic to Punta Cormorant, such as *Lecocarpus pinnatifidus* and *Scalesia villosa,* with arrow-shaped leaves covered with white hair. On the top of the dune of the white sand beach grows *Nolana galapageia,* a dense shrub with fat yellow almond-shaped leaves (see photo, page 220).

CORONA DEL DIABLO

Also known as Onslow or Devil's Crown, the marine site is a short distance from Punta Cormorant, 250 metres offshore. It used to be good for skin or scuba diving.

The submarine life—Pocillopora, Pavona and Porites corals, pencil sea urchins, parrotfish, wrasses, king angelfishes, yellowtail surgeonfish, Mexican hogfish—is the main attraction here, but it was much visited in the last 10 years. Other creatures to be seen include amberjacks, blue and gold snappers, white-tip sharks, hammerhead sharks (sometimes), rays and turtles (see drawing, page 220). On the outside of the crown (to the north), the current is strong from east to west.

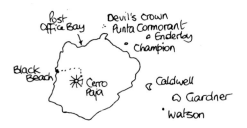

Floreana

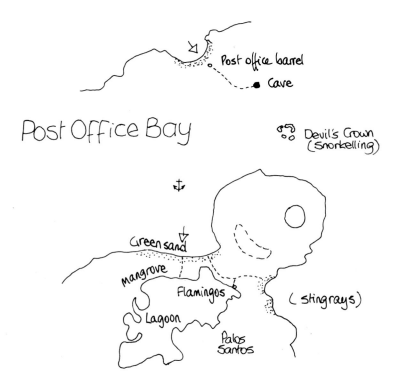

Post Office Bay

Post office barrel

Cave

Devil's Crown
(Snorkelling)

Green sand

Mangrove

Flamingos

Lagoon

Palos Santos

(stingrays)

Punta Cormorant + Devil's crown

POST OFFICE BAY

At this historic site a man named Hathaway erected a wooden barrel in 1793. It was used as a post office for passing ships, first by whalers and later by visiting yachts and tourists. A trail behind the barrel leads to a cave (lava tube) not far inland (see map, page 220).

In 1926, Norwegians settled on Floreana to start a fish-canning factory. Unfortunately, the experience ended two years later. Loberia Islet, near Post Office Bay, has a colony of sea lions.

BLACK BEACH AND PUERTO VELASCO IBARRA

In the early 20th century, Floreana was the theatre where tragic and mysterious events were played out which drew the attention of Europe to this faraway island in the eastern Pacific. One day in 1929, Dr. Friedrich Ritter, a German dentist by profession and a philosopher by nature, arrived on the deserted island with his assistant and mistress Dore Strauch, and asked to disembark at Black Beach, as if it were the most natural thing to do. Both of them lived as Robinson Crusoes for the next three years, before the arrival of the Wittmers in 1932, a German family of farmers from Bayern, with a poliomyelitic son.

This little world managed on its own until the arrival later that year of Baroness von Wagner de Bousquet, a German diva, with her two lovers, Lorenz and Philipson. She had it in mind to construct a hotel for 'millionaires', but built nothing more than a shack of planks and corrugated iron, which she proudly named Hacienda Paraíso. Soon, she claimed the island for her own and declared herself 'Empress of Floreana', intending to impose her rule by the whip and the revolver. Things rapidly turned bitter.

To make a long story short, the baroness and Philipson disappeared without a trace in 1935. Lorenz escaped with a Norwegian fisherman from San Cristobal and a few months later was found dead and mummified on a deserted beach of Marchena Island, after having capsized. Four days later, on November 21, Dr Ritter, learning about the drama, died on Floreana. It is suspected that he was poisoned by Dore Strauch with a rotten chicken, though he was known to be a strict vegetarian. The woman returned to Germany, where she published a book entitled *Satan Came to Eden*. Nobody knows the truth of the story, nor will ever know. But in the end, it seems that Lorenz killed the baroness and Philipson, with the help of Wittmer and Dr. Ritter. Margret Wittmer denies the fact, claiming that the cursed couple left the island for Tahiti on a private yacht (see *The Galapagos Affair*, by John Treherne, London 1983).

Margret Wittmer, the only survivor, celebrated her 90th birthday in 1994, and she certainly knows more than she wants to say. She lives at Black Beach with her daughters, where she owns a small hotel, a restaurant and a souvenir shop, and runs the local *correos*, the Ecuadorian post office. She does not make orange wine anymore, as in the

isla Gardner

Punta Suarez

Punta Cevallos

Española (Hood)

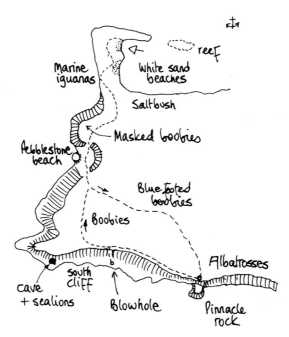

reef

Marine iguanas

White sand beaches

Saltbush

Masked boobies

Pebblestone beach

Blue-footed boobies

Boobies

Albatrosses

cave + sealions

south cliff

Blowhole

Pinnacle rock

Punta Suarez

N

past, but has recently opened an eight-room hotel with toilets and showers ($30 per day, full board).

It is possible to hire a pickup for $16 round-trip to visit the highlands of Floreana, as well as the freshwater spring used by pirates in the 17th century and the caves carved in the volcanic tuff where they found a refuge well before the arrival of the Wittmers.

ESPANOLA

land surface: 61 square km
max. elevation: 206 m

Known in English as Hood, this volcanic island has a central volcano. Another island was discovered recently, east of Española, submerged a few metres under the ocean surface. This proves that the archipelago is older than once thought, and that it has long been in subduction under the South American mainland.

Bordered by steep cliffs, the southern coast is washed by surf and spray. The vegetation is typical of the arid and transition zones, with a number of spiny shrubs. Feral goats were eradicated from Española in 1978. Under the programme started in 1970, the SPNG has reintroduced 369 small giant tortoises on Española over the course of 20 years.

The richness of the fauna is not only evidenced in the colonies of seabirds, such as the blue-footed and masked boobies, but also in the presence of the endemic albatross, *Diomedea irrorata*. Despite its inhospitable look, Punta Suarez hosts a great variety of seabirds and land birds. Albatrosses nest on the island between mid-March and mid-December. Boobies are inland or on the cliffs all year-round. swallowtail gulls, oyster-catchers, lava herons, night herons, Galápagos doves, the small ground finches, warbler finches, large cactus finches, Española mockingbirds (endemic to Española), Galápagos hawks, marine iguanas, lava lizards the Galápagos snakes are also found on Hood, as well as the saddleback turtle (which you will not see!).

There is a blowhole on the basaltic shore, at the end of the trail in Punta Suarez. The seawater rushes violently under the lava bedrock, then is ejected upward through cracks in a vaporous plume to a height of 25 metres.

To the northeast of Española, Gardner Bay has a very long sandy beach facing an island of the same name. Sea lions bask lazily in the sun and the Española mockingbirds swarm on the beach, eminently curious about all visitors (see drawing, page 222).

SAN CRISTOBAL

land surface: 558 square km
elevation: 730 m

The administrative centre of the archipelago, with Puerto Baquerizo Moreno as capital, San Cristobal is also the islands' second Ecuadorian naval base. The population was nearly 8,000 people in 1993 (versus 2,752 in 1986). The radio 'Voz de Galápagos' has broadcast since 1969.

The geography of the island is composed of two distinct parts. The west part has a central volcano culminating at about 700 metres (San Joaquin), with a few parasitic cones. The eastern part of the island, made of spatter cones and lava flows, does not rise above 160 metres. It was once thought that San Cristobal was the oldest island because it is the easternmost of the Galápagos, but there is no proof of this. The slopes exposed to the north are arid and desolated, while those oriented to the south are more humid, being exposed to the southeast tradewinds.

Wreck Bay, the southwest tip of San Cristobal, shelters the village of Puerto Baquerizo Moreno. The old wooden houses that faced the sea in the past, separated by lava flows and yellow sand beaches, has given way gradually to concrete buildings and houses made of volcanic rocks. Over the last 15 years the provincial town has gained some kind of charm and is definitely attached to its image of progress.

In the highlands, eight kilometres away, the village of Progreso was once the site of the penal colony founded by Manuel Cobos in 1888. Cobos created a sugarcane factory, where the convicts were put to hard labour. A notorious tyrant, Manuel Cobos abused the women of his men, and he was eventually killed by a Colombian convict with a machete in 1904.

The humid zone of San Cristobal does not produce sugarcane any longer, but bananas, oranges, grapefruits, lemons, guavas, avocados and coffee are grown. The settlers introduced animals such as goats, rats, cats, dogs, and a species of salamander.

The visitor's sites are Cerro de Las Tijeretas (Frigatebird Hill), the freshwater lake of El Junco. Kicker Rock (Leon Dormido) and Stephens Bay, the Loberia and Isla Lobos.

HOTELS *(see map of Puerto Baquerizo Moreno, opposite)*

Gran Hotel San Cristobal (Playa Mann), single $31, double $42, triple $54, with terrace and restaurant.
Hotel Northia, single $13, double $20.
Hotel Mar Azul
Hostal Galápagos
Cabanas Don Jorge (towards Playa Mann), friendly bungalows at $9.
Residencial San Francisco (on the waterfront). Rooms for $3.50.

RESTAURANTS

Hotel San Cristobal
Restaurant Rosita
Cevicheria Langostino
Soda-bar Nathaly and other small *comedores* in port.

Puerto Baquerizo Moreno - Cristobal

Wreck Bay

Frigate bird Hill

Ruins

Playa Mann

Gran Hotel San Cristobal

Cabañas Don Jorge

Galapagos Hostal

N

Pirolo 1994

Shipyard

New pier 1993

Ballena Cafeteria

Bar

Banco del Pacifico

Parc

Residencial San Francisco

Post office

Municipio

Min market

PAN

Ceviecheria Langostino

Soda bar Nathaly

Cruz Roja

Restaurant Rosita

School

Park

Hotel Northia

Progreso 7km.

Beach

Lagoon

Policia

Hospital Museo

EMETEL

Mercado municipal

Tortoise

Hotel Chatham

Capitania de Puerto

Zona Naval

Hotel Mar Azul

to la Loberia

Cristobal Airport

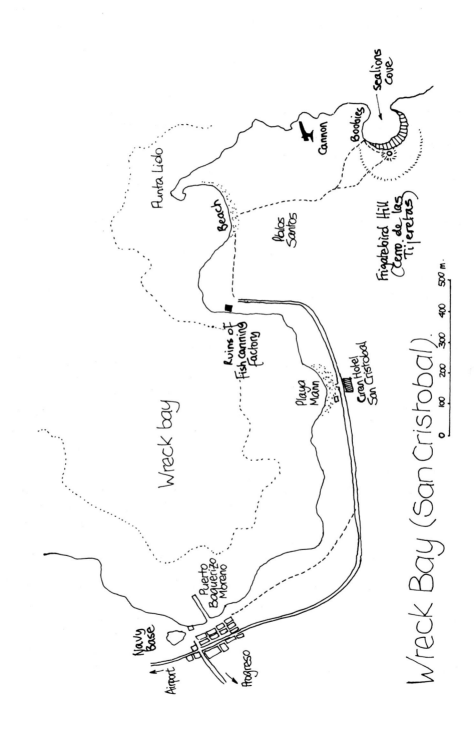

Wreck Bay (San Cristóbal).

Sealions Cove

Boobies

Cannon

Punta Lido

Beach

Palos Santos

Frigatebird Hill
(Cerro de las
Tijeretas)

Ruins of
fish canning
factory

Wreck bay

Playa
Mann

Gran Hotel
San Cristóbal

Puerto
Baquerizo
Moreno

Navy Base

Airport

Progreso

0   100   200   300   400   500 m.

Puerto Baquerizo has developed a lot since the opening of the new airport in 1986 and the influx of tourism. SAN Airlines has a daily flight to San Cristobal from Quito or Guayaquil (12 pm), except on Sundays. The return flight costs $375 from Quito, or $330 from Guayaquil. Foreign students younger than 26, with a bona fide student card, get a 25 per cent discount on the cost of the ticket ($328). To make you feel any better, nationals pay 396,000 sucres, or $203, roundtrip from Quito, and Galápagos residents pay 144,000 sucres, or $74, from Guayaquil. Hard to believe.

TO SEE

Museo de San Cristobal (opened in 1990), open Monday-Saturday 8:30–12:00 pm, and 3:30–5:30 pm. Little museum of natural history.
La Loberia, half an hour's walk beyond the airport, has a small colony of sea lions, on a white sand beach.

EXCURSIONS AROUND SAN CRISTOBAL

CERRO DE LAS TIJERETAS (FRIGATEBIRD HILL)

A short distance from the port of San Cristobal, beyond Playa Mann, is a hill covered with palo santos, overlooking an almost circular cove. The trail passes by an abandoned fish-canning factory and goes on to another beach. From there, turn right uphill. The track may be covered by vegetation in the hot season. Nevertheless, you may observe frigates having their courtship display in March-April. Birds are few, however, in the dry season. There's a beautiful panoramic view of the surrounding coastline, heading to the northeast.

LAGUNA EL JUNCO

This natural lagoon is located in the highlands at an elevation of 700 metres, 19 kilometres from Puerto Baquerizo Moreno. The only freshwater pool on the island. This crater lake has a diameter of 270 metres, a surface of 360,000 square metres and a depth of 6 metres. It is supplied by rain water only.

The sedimentary deposits of this lagoon were studied by the American geologist Paul Colinvaux (1966), who concluded that the age of El Junco was 48,000 years. The name 'Junco' comes from the sedges that invade the banks of the lake. In 1978, the lake even overflowed after the hard rains, and a small creek occasionally flows towards the south of the island. The best period to visit El Junco is from December to May during the hot season. A daily local bus links Pto. Baquerizo and Progreso, from where it is a two-hour walk to the lake. On a clear day, the view from the summit is excellent. A few resident birds live at the lake, including the Bahama pintail, the moorhen, the whimbrel and the semipalmated plover.

LEON DORMIDO

Also known as Kicker's Rock, this cathedral of tuff rises in the middle of the ocean, off Stephens Bay, to the northeast of Puerto Baquerizo. It is a three-hour trip by local boat. The 'Sleeping Lion' has vertiginous cliffs and hosts a number of seabirds, such as masked boobies, blue-footed boobies, great frigates and tropicbirds. Some sea lions rest on the rocks at the base of the cliff. A narrow channel allows a panga to go through Leon Dormido, between the sheer tuff walls, cutting through from east to west. Sharks are present in the troubled waters.

Facing Kicker's Rock on the coast, Cerro Brujo (the 'Sorcerer's Mountain') stands at the end of a long white sand beach. A sea lion colony, shorebirds, pelicans and boobies are seen. A beautiful place for a swim or for a stroll at sunset.

ISLA LOBOS

One hour by boat on the way to Leon Dormido. This insignificant island of basaltic rocks is separated from San Cristobal by a narrow arm of seawater. Sea lions inhabit the site, and blue-footed boobies nest on the white sand. A relaxing atmosphere in a landscape of primitive beauty. A 300-metre trail crosses the island from east to west.

PUNTA PITT

This site was opened by the Galápagos National Park in the beginning of 1989. It is the eastern tip of the Galápagos archipelago. The mountainous landscape is carved from the tuff formations of an ancient eroded volcano. The green sand cove where one disembarks is guarded by two tuff cones, furrowed by erosion. Behind the beach, where a few old sea lion males lie at times, the vegetation of saltbushes and spiny shrubs (*Scutia pauciflora*) gives way to a mini-canyon which climbs up a hill. The panorama from the viewpoint is magnificent. The trail draws a half moon around the site, goes over a pass, and climbs downhill and south to a vegetation of palo santos (where some frigates nest). *Muyuyos* (or *Cordea lutea*) trees and big yellow-green shrubs (*Nolana galapageia*) are often nesting sites for red-footed boobies. One may observe the 'morpho blanco' variety of red-footed boobies. Blue-footed boobies nest on the ground in the middle of the trail, marking their nesting site with a corona of their excrement. The trail climbs slightly, with good views on the sea, where at times dolphins porpoise along the coast. All around you the succulent plant sesuvium covers the ground with a red carpet in the dry season. The track makes a loop before returning to the starting point (see drawing, page 229).

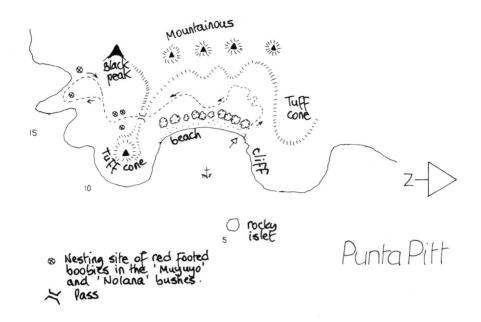

Mountainous

Black peak

Tuff cone

Tuff cone

beach

cliff

15

10

Z→

○ rocky islet

5

⊗ Nesting site of red footed boobies in the 'Muyuyo' and 'Nolana' bushes.

⋊ Pass

Punta Pitt

San Cristobal

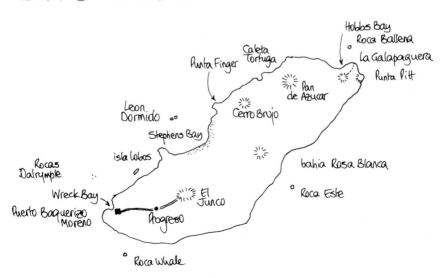

Hobbs Bay
○ Roca Ballena
La Galapaguera
Punta Pitt

Caleta Tortuga

Punta Finger

Pan de Azucar

Leon Dormido

Cerro Brujo

Stephens Bay

isla Lobos

bahia Rosa Blanca

Rocas Dalrymple

○ Roca Este

Wreck Bay

El Junco

Puerto Baquerizo Moreno

Progreso

○ Roca Whale

0   6 Km

Piroco 1994

A small rocky islet facing Punta Pitt is a fine spot for skin diving. The water is often crystal clear, but also chilly.

LA GALAPAGUERA

Not far from Punta Pitt and to the west, la Galapaguera is a site where you may meet giant tortoises. But one may walk a lot and get lost, since the trail is not clear and is covered with vegetation in the hot season. Not all guides know about the site, and many dare not venture there.

CHAPTER THREE

THE NORTHERN ISLANDS

GENOVESA
land surface: 14 square km
elevation: 75 m

This rather flat island to the northwest of the archipelago looks like a huge parrot beak, opened towards the rest of the Galápagos. The central volcano is now a big caldera filled with seawater to a depth of 65 metres. Darwin Bay, open to the ocean, is also a huge collapsed caldera submerged by seawater, 180 metres deep in the centre. A narrow and shallow passage allows sailboats and other ships to enter the bay by following an alignment of beacons. Cliffs rise up to 20 or 30 metres all around the bay.

DARWIN BAY

One disembarks on a small white coral beach, under the indifferent eye of the swallow-tail gulls. Salt bushes (*Cryptocarpus pyriformis*) border the beach, where red-footed boobies, masked boobies and great frigates nest throughout the year. The species do not always get along too well; frigates tend to steal the nests of the boobies, while boobies destroy the eggs of the frigates.

Some tide pools are hidden behind a lava ridge bordering the bay. Night and lava herons, looking for small fry, are common. Sea lions come to have a swim there at times. The trail climbs onto the cliff. Swallowtail gulls make a nest of white coral pieces and black volcanic gravel, where they lay a big white egg speckled brownish black (camouflaging it against the background). Opuntia cacti and *Croton scouleri* shrubs are everywhere. Red-footed boobies (juveniles), gulls and frigates hover above the cliff overlooking the bay, taking advantage of the rising winds.

PRINCE PHILIP'S STEPS

The name was given after the visit of Prince Philip of the United Kingdom some years ago. The site, south of Darwin Bay is on the top of a cliff. After a dry landing on rocks, one climbs up 25 metres through a *barranco* and reaches the arid zone of palo santos, where great frigates nest in the trees and masked boobies on the ground. The trail heads inland to the east coast, an old *pahoehoe* lava flow, reddish brown because of oxidation and erosion. One will notice a big crack, which was created when the lava was still hot and fluid and flowed back into the fracture, like icing on a chocolate cake. Storm petrels swarm the sky by hundreds. A colony of hundreds of thousands is believed to inhabit the area. Short-eared owls hide in the crack of the lava flow (see drawing, page 232) and prey on the storm petrels.

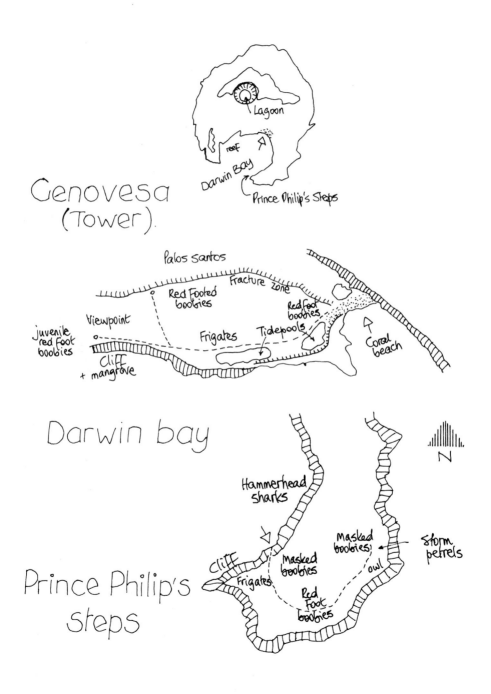

Genovesa
(Tower).

Lagoon

reef

Darwin Bay

Prince Philip's Steps

Palos santos

Fracture zone

Red Footed boobies

Red foot boobies

Viewpoint

juvenile red foot boobies

Frigates

Tidepools

Coral beach

Cliff + mangrove

Darwin bay

N

Hammerhead sharks

Masked boobies

Storm petrels

Cliff

Frigates

Masked boobies

owl

Red Foot boobies

Prince Philip's Steps

The Northern islands

O. Darwin

Out of Map

Wolf

1'23'N

1'N

50 W

Rocas Nerus

Pinta Is.

Cap Ibbetson

Pta. Mejia

Pta. Moutalvo

Marchena Is.

343 m

Pta. Espejo

Pta. Calle

Playa de los muertos

Genovesa Is.

Darwin Bay

Fur sealions

Great Arch

← Darwin

lava tubes

Frigates Boobies

reef

Bottle rock

current ← current

Cliff

Cave

N

isla de la Fresa

rock

wall 70 m.

53 m

current

N

Pavona + Porites coral

Old Light house

WOLF →

rough

Frigates Boobies

Pinnacle rock

Fur sea lions

Rock

N

current

PIROCO 1994

MARCHENA

land surface: 115 square km
elevation: 343 m

Desolated by its external aspect, Marchena is located 50 kilometres west of Genovesa. The island is the top of a large shield volcano, with numerous small volcanic cones in the caldera and on the slopes of the volcano. The first recorded eruption occurred on September 25, 1991, with incandescent clouds during the night and lava flows to the southwest.

Marchena is not officially open to visitors, even though it is possible to disembark on the black sand beach on the southwest of the island. The Playa de los Muertos is the place where Lorenz was found dead in 1934, after being shipwrecked with a Norwegian fisherman.

PINTA

Northwest of Marchena, Pinta rises to an elevation of 750 metres. Two geological areas are distinguished. The oldest is a narrow band on the west coast, the remains of an old volcano that collapsed into the ocean. Cliffs rise up to 90 metres. A crack separates this old cliff from a younger volcano (765 metres in elevation). No eruption has been recorded on Pinta.

It is possible to drop anchor at Cape Ibbetson, to the south of the island. The vegetation is dry on the coast, humid in the highlands. For a long time, Pinta was the home of Lonesome George, last survivor of the giant tortoises. He is now a resident of the Darwin Station.

DARWIN AND WOLF

Isolated like two black sheep to the northwest of the archipelago, Darwin and Wolf, also known as Culpepper and Wenman, seem to be outcasts. These islands are the eroded summits of two large calderas, which rise 1,800 metres from the bottom of the ocean (see drawings, page 233).

DARWIN

A flat island, 165 metres in elevation, surrounded on all sides by vertical cliffs, where the surf breaks. A helicopter landed on the high plateau of Darwin in 1964. Two hundred metres off the eastern shore of the island, a monumental arch is erected on a shallow platform. Like an Arc de Triomphe facing east, this symbolic gate reminds people of the first navigators, who came from that direction. Masked boobies and red-footed boobies dwell on Darwin Arch, while hammerhead sharks and whale sharks silently roam in the blue depths. False killer whales have been seen surfacing along the northeast coast of Darwin (author's own observation, December 1993). Royal terns and sooty terns are also frequent residents on Darwin.

WOLF

Very similar to its neighbour, Wolf rises up to 250 metres, with high cliffs, 225 metres in elevation. Even though it is not a visitor's site, it is possible to disembark on the island, but climbing to the top is risky. An old abandoned lighthouse has stood there for years.

Like Darwin, Wolf is a haven for seabirds, such as great frigatebirds, red-footed boobies, masked boobies, tropicbirds and swallowtail gulls, which nest in the cliff. Fur sea lions have a small colony in the north of the island, and also on a pile of rocks on the east coast. Hammerhead sharks cruise back and forth offshore. Dolphins often accompany boats approaching Wolf as far as the anchorage on the west coast.

The common vegetation is the croton shrub and the opuntia cactus. The sharpbill ground finch, known as the 'vampire finch', lives on Wolf and drinks the blood of masked boobies from the base of the wing feathers.

Both Darwin and Wolf are excellent diving sites.

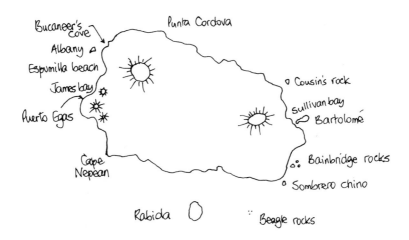

Bucaneer's Cove
Albany
Espumilla beach
James bay
Puerto Egas

Punta Cordova

Cousin's rock
Sullivan bay
Bartolomé

Bainbridge rocks

Cabo Nepean

Sombrero chino

Rabida

Beagle rocks

Santiago (James).

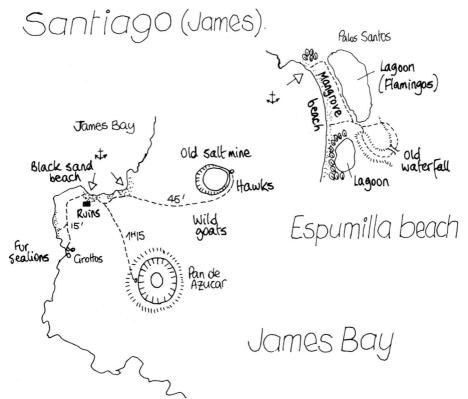

Palos Santos

Lagoon (Flamingos)

Mangrove beach

Old waterfall

Lagoon

Espumilla beach

James Bay

Black sand beach

Old salt mine

Hawks

45'

Ruins

15'

Wild goats

Fur sealions

Grottos

1H15

Pan de Azucar

James Bay

CHAPTER FOUR

THE WESTERN ISLANDS

SANTIAGO

Also known as James or San Salvador, the island, located west of Santa Cruz, is composed of a number of tuff cones and a central volcano bedecked with vegetation. Many volcanic eruptions were recorded in the last century. The vegetation is dense in the highlands, and a scalesia forest covers the northwest side of the central volcano. The southern coast, and a five-kilometres band inland, are only lava flows with arid vegetation.

Many animals were introduced by man in the time of the pirates, such as goats, pigs, donkeys and rats. The visitor's sites are James Bay (Puerto Egas), Espumilla Beach, Buccaneer's Cove and Sullivan Bay. James Bay Puerto Egas, on the west coast of Santiago, with a black sand beach and small cliffs of tuff formations, was once upon a time colonized by man. In the 1920s and again in the 1960s, salt was extracted from the crater of a tuff cone, a 45-minute walk away (three kilometres). The remains of some buildings still stand on the cliff. The vegetation around is poor and was destroyed by the population of feral goats that inhabit the area, except for the shrub *Castela galapageia*—with little oval-shaped leaves and round red fruits—which are poisonous to the goats.

A 'Sugar Loaf' rises above James Bay. It's hard to climb, but you'll be rewarded with a spectacular view of two craters of tuff cones and the panorama of the bay. An easier walk would be to 'the grottos', basaltic marine caves with open roof, on the littoral. These natural pools are an enchanting place, where sea lions and fur sea lions come to play.

Shorebirds are numerous, and include as lava herons, oystercatchers, whimbrels, semipalmated plovers and wandering tattlers. *Zayapas*, red and turquoise blue crabs, are everywhere. Galápagos doves and Galápagos hawks are also common in the area (see map, page 236).

PLAYA ESPUMILLA

North of James Bay, Espumilla (which means 'Foam' in Spanish) is a beautiful golden sand beach, fringed with mangroves. Two brackish lagoons lie behind, with a few resident birds: flamingos, common stilts, Bahama pintail ducks, semipalmated plovers. Many turtle nests may be found in the sand dunes under the mangrove trees. Sometimes turtles get lost in the lagoon, and die if they cannot find their way back to the sea. A trail to the right climbs over the hill, where land birds such as vermillion flycatchers and large-bill flycatchers can be seen.

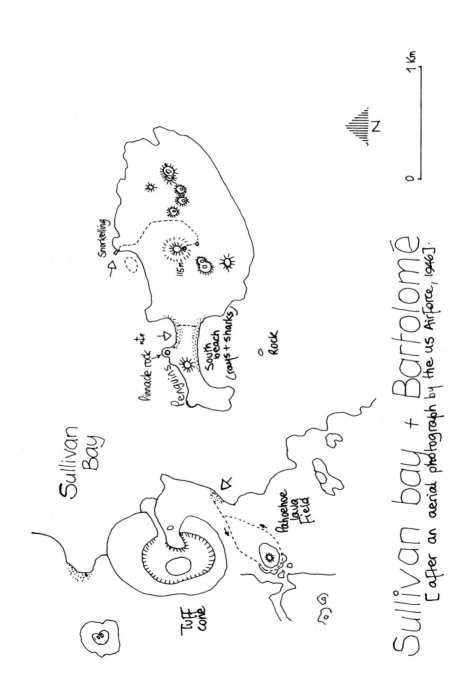

Sullivan Bay

Snorkelling

115 m

Pinnacle rock

Penguins

South beach
(rays + sharks)

Rock

Tuff
Cone

Pahoehoe
lava field

N

0   1 Km

Sullivan bay + Bartolomé
[after an aerial photograph by the US Airforce, 1946].

BUCCANEER'S COVE

Farther north is beautiful Buccaneer's Cove, with red-purple sand. Pirates used to come here to refit their boats and search for water and tortoises. Ceramic jars were found at the bottom of the bay; some had wine, others marmalade.

Sea lions bask on the beach. One should be aware of the dangerous surf that crashes on the beach when disembarking or embarking. Cliffs of tuff formations surround the cove, the natural statue of 'the Monk' guarding this magic site, and the small islet in the centre of the bay are all part of the fabulous landscape that is created in the warm light of sunset (see map of Santiago, page 236).

SULLIVAN BAY

Facing Bartolomé Island, on the east coast of Santiago. Two imposing tuff cones rise in the middle of an enormous lava field, of a *pahoehoe* surface type. The landscape of ropey lava, the intestinal figures created by the lava flow and the *hornitos* (pockets of gas and water trapped under a crust of lava, and later exploded) are among the curiosities of Sullivan Bay. The loop trail, marked with small black and white posts, can be walked in an hour and 15 minutes. Oystercatchers often wander along the shoreline.

BARTOLOMÉ

land surface: 1.2 squarekm
max. elevation: 114 m

A very impressive little island in front of Sullivan Bay, with a landscape of real volcanic desolation: tuff cones, spatter cones, scoria formations and black volcanic sand. A trail leads to the summit of the central volcano; a stairway made of *cedrela* wood was constructed by the Galápagos National Park to stop the island's quick erosion caused by daily visitors. From the top of the volcano, the view is extraordinary. Towards the east, a field of spatter cones punctuates the island. Towards the west, one is amazed by the isthmus of Bartolomé, covered by mangroves and bordered by two small coves of golden sand in the shape of half moons. On the north beach, the Pinnacle Rock stands like a finger pointed to the sky. This volcanic needle is the last remaining piece of a tuff cone, eroded and partially bombed by American pilots during the World War II. Today it is the most photographed part of the island (see drawing, page 238).

The only vegetation on the slopes of the volcano is *Tiquilia*, a little white plant which grows in the volcanic sand, and *Chamaesycae* (an Euphorbiacae), which forms a small tuft of green or red with tiny white flowers. The lava cactus, *Brachycereus*, an endemic genus, grows on the old lava flow uphill of the first stairway. One may notice some broken lava tubes which climb down the slope of the volcano. It is possible to swim and skin dive at the north cove, under Pinnacle Rock, where the underwater life is attractive. Maybe you will be lucky enough to meet some Galápagos penguins swimming

Roca Redonda

Cap Albemarle

Cap Berkeley   Ecuador   Equator

Punta Vicente Roca   Cap Marshall

Banks Bay   Wolf 1707 m.   James

Tagus cove   James Bay   Bartolomé

Punta Espinosa   Darwin 1330 m.

Cap Douglas   1495 m.   Punta Garcia

Bolivar channel

Fernandina   Punta Mangle   Urvina bay   Alcedo 1097 m.   Cowley   Rabida

Elizabeth bay   Perry isthmus   Cartago bay   Pinzon

Punta Moreno

Sierra Negra 1370 m   Crossman Is.

Punta Cristobal   Cerro Azul 1689 m   Santo Tómas

Iguana Cove   Puerto Villamil   Tortuga

Punta Essex   Cap Rosa

Isabela + Fernandina

about, porpoising at the surface, or speeding like torpedoes behind a school of fish. There is a small colony in a sheltered cove behind Pinnacle Rock.

The south beach is unsuitable for swimming due to stingrays, small whitetip and blacktip sharks. Spotted eagle rays can be observed at the surface, and black turtles are plentiful during the months of November and December, when they come to lay eggs on the beach. Herons prey on baby turtles running down the beach after they hatch.

Sombrero Chino

Only a hundred metres from the southeastern coast of Santiago island, Sombrero Chino ('Chinese Hat') is separated from the big island by a marvellous turquoise-blue lagoon. The island is made of a few adjacent craters and very old, fragile *pahoehoe* lava flows. The vegetation is meager, but some very colourful sesuvium plants are scattered around.

The trail, 350 metres long, runs from the northern white sand beach, where sea lions and penguins are common, to the western part of the island. There, the lava bedrock hosts a colony of marine iguanas, which often wallow in tide pools. The waves crash against the nearby cliffs, spraying the whole area with mist. Some Galápagos hawks overlook their kingdom from the top of the island.

Sombrero Chino is an ideal place for snorkelling or skin diving in the lagoon.

Isabela

land surface: 4,588 square km
elevation: 1,707 m

By far the biggest island of the archipelago, Isabela's land surface accounts for half of the archipelago's total. It measures 132 kilometres from north to south and 84 kilometres at its greatest width. The island is composed of six main volcanoes, five of which evolved in calderas, the old stage of a shield volcano. The largest caldera is 10 kilometres in diameter. From the oldest to the youngest these volcanoes are: Sierra Negra, Alcedo, Darwin, Wolf, Cerro Azul. The sixth is Ecuador volcano, at the northwestern tip of the island (the seahorse nose of Isabela), has been destroyed by erosion and wave action. It is estimated that more than 2,500 cones are present on Isabela. Wolf Volcano is the highest summit, culminating at 1,707 metres. The equator passes through both Ecuador and Wolf volcanoes. All these volcanoes are considered very active. The most recent eruptions occurred on Cerro Azul and Sierra Negra in 1979, on Wolf in 1982. Some earthquakes shook Alcedo in March 1991.

Alcedo Volcano

max. elevation: 1,150 m

The trail to Alcedo starts from the small black cove of Alcedo Beach (volcanic gravel), on the east coast of the island. It follows an *aa* lava flow and a canyon dug by rain water.

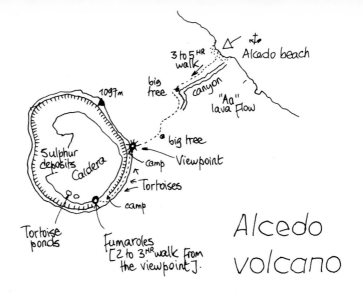

3 to 5 ᴴᴿ walk

Alcedo beach

big tree

canyon

"Aa" lava flow

1097m

big tree

Viewpoint

camp

Sulphur deposits

Caldera

Tortoises

camp

Tortoise ponds

Fumaroles [2 to 3 ᴴᴿ walk from the viewpoint].

Alcedo volcano

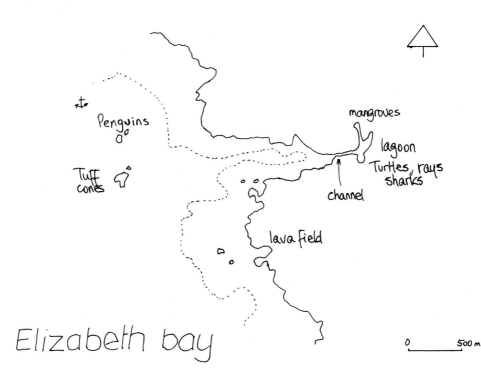

Penguins

Tuff cones

mangroves

lagoon

Turtles, rays sharks

channel

lava field

Elizabeth bay

0 ⎯⎯ 500 m

The track crosses the arid zone of palo santos and croton. The climb should be made early, before sunrise, because the heat becomes torrid during the day. Fortunately, some big trees provide shade along the way at two possible stops. Expect it to take three to five hours to reach the rim of the crater, depending on the individual. After a slow ascent for most of the hike, the last climb is very strenuous before you get to the top, and volcanic gravel slips under your feet. You may meet some female tortoises on the trail in the hot season, as they walk down to the lowlands to nest in June.

The caldera of Alcedo is seven kilometres wide; the crater floor, 200 metres below the rim, is an immense lava field bedecked with palo santos and spiny shrubs. The rim is covered with shrubs and small trees, such as cat's claws, Zan*thoxylum fagara* (local name *una de gato*), and *Tournefortia pubescens*. There are also some endemic tree ferns of the species *Cyathea weatherbyana*.

Fumaroles can be observed on the southern slope of the caldera (another two or three hours' walk). The 'geyser' is no more than a hot waterhole spewing vaporous fumes. Sulphur deposits are also seen farther away. On the rim and inside the caldera, thousands of tortoises gather during the wet season to wallow happily in muddy rain pools, which rehydrates them and protects them from ticks. With a population estimated at 5,000 individuals, the Alcedo tortoise is the most flourishing in the Galápagos. In the dry season, tortoises hide in the bushes, on the rim of the crater, or dig a sort of burrow to hide from the fierce sun.

The Galápagos hawk is very common in the hot season, and the inquisitive juveniles often hover over your head. Goats, donkeys and cats live on the slopes of the volcano, causing minor damage to the vegetation and to land birds.

It is possible to camp on Alcedo, but fires are prohibited. Bring your stove, enough water (two litres per day) and a flashlight if you spend the night (see map, page 242).

PUNTA GARCIA

This site used to be accessible by *panga* only. The aa landscape was once a breeding site of flightless cormorants, just above the waterline, but the birds seem to have deserted the place. This rare seabird of the Galápagos breeds from March to September. Brown pelicans are sometimes present. The lagoon is not very safe for swimming, due to troubled water and sharks.

PUNTA ALBEMARLE

At the northern tip of Isabela Island, this site was an American radar base during World War II. Disembarking is not easy because of the surf. The largest species of marine iguana in the Galápagos is found at Punta Albemarle. There are quite a few nests of flightless cormorants, and a little colony of fur sea lions.

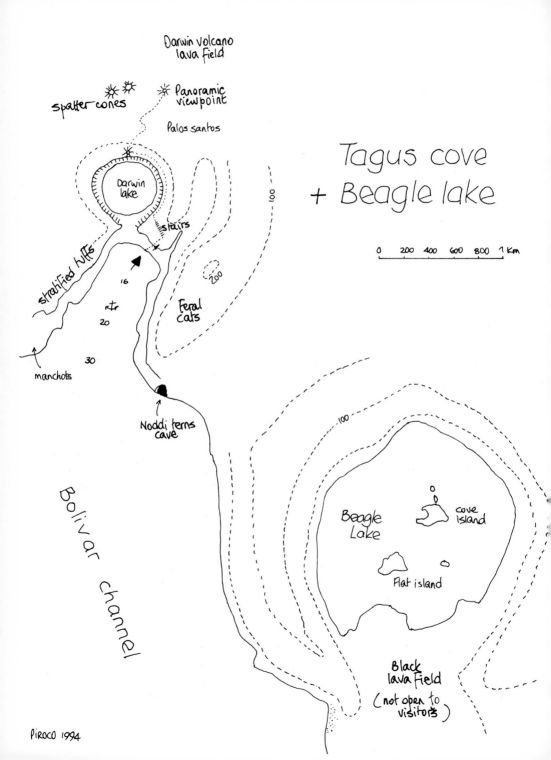

Darwin volcano
lava Field

spatter cones

Panoramic
viewpoint

Palos santos

Darwin
lake

stairs

stratified tuffs

16

20

30

manchots

Feral
cats

Noddi terns
cave

Bolivar channel

Tagus cove
+ Beagle lake

0   200 400 600 800 1 Km

100

200

100

Beagle
Lake

cove
island

Flat island

Black
lava Field
(not open to
visitors)

PIROCO 1994

Punta Tortuga

On the west coast, slightly north of Tagus Cove, Punta Tortuga is a beach of dark sand, behind which is a mangrove swamp. One may observe the mangrove finch, similar to the carpenter finch but with a shorter and sharper bill.

The area was tectonically uplifted in 1975. In 1825, the American ship *Tartar,* anchored in Banks Bay, north of the site, and witnessed a volcanic eruption on Fernandina, 15 kilometres to the south. The air temperature rose to 50° C, and the sea temperature reached 40° C, so warm that the tar on the riggings began to melt. The eruption lasted for two weeks.

Tagus Cove

This small, U-shaped cove was a refuge of pirates and whalers. It is still a historical site, if one considers all the graffiti on the surrounding cliffs. Today, any kind of painting is forbidden and punishable. The name 'Tagus' was given in 1814 by a British navy ship of the same name, which came to look for tortoises and found some.

The landing site is awkward and rather slippery on the rocks. Behind the tuff formations bordering the cove, a wooden stairway, constructed by the Galápagos National Park in 1990, climbs up to a viewpoint. From there one discovers Darwin Lake down below. The brackish lagoon is perfectly circular, and is elevated above sea level by tectonic uplift. The white palo santos are everywhere around Darwin Lake, and turn happily green during the wet season. Darwin's finches are found in swarms, to the benefit of the feral cats that inhabit the area. The cats were studied by Mike Konecny in 1980; this American scientist partially lost his vision due to a viral disease as he attached radio collars around the cats' necks.

The trail goes halfway around the lake, then heads inland up to a ridge with a few spatter cones. From the viewpoint, one may appreciate the impressive landscape of Darwin volcano's lava flow (aa surface type) and, on a clear day, the wide silhouette of Ecuador and Wolf volcanoes to the north. A man with solid ranger shoes, would lose the sole of his boots after four kilometres of hard walking on the lava of this convict's country. The feral dogs that live in the area have developed the ability to cross the basaltic surface, thanks to horny pads under their feet, which protect them against cuts—a remarkable example of adaptation to the environment. The most extraordinary fact is that these dogs can drink seawater without any ill effect (see drawing, page 244).

It is possible to take a *panga* ride along the cliffs of Tagus Cove to observe pelican nests, blue-footed boobies, noddi terns in a marine cave, Galápagos penguins standing peacefully on a rock by the water, marine iguanas basking in the sun and lazy sea lions. Snorkelling and skin diving in Tagus Cove are interesting, especially at night, when one may see hornsharks on the volcanic gravel bottom and redlip batfishes (at greater depth).

Urvina Bay

West of Alcedo volcano, Urvina Bay was tectonically uplifted in 1954. Coral heads (nowadays white) were thrust five metres above sea level, as were six kilometres of coastline. A lateral eruption of volcan Alcedo occurred a few months later.

After a wet landing on a white sand beach, Urvina is a good site for seeing giant tortoises, big land iguanas and marine iguanas. Half an hour away from the beach along the shore, one may discover a few nests of flightless cormorants around a sheltered lagoon, where common egrets and great blue herons are also present (see drawing, page 248).

Elizabeth Bay

South of Urvina Bay and west of the Perry Isthmus, Elizabeth Bay is a marine site where landing is not allowed. As you pass by the small islets in the middle of the bay, you may sight Galápagos penguins, but they are as rare as flightless cormorants. A narrow channel penetrates farther inland, in a dense mangrove area with unusually tall trees, and opens up on a big lagoon with many arms. It is a haven for green turtles, golden rays and spotted eagle rays, small white-tip sharks. Marine turtle mate in the lagoon in November-December (see drawing, page 242).

Punta Moreno

This is a typical *pahoehoe* lava flow, southwest of Elizabeth Bay, with numerous cracks and water holes, formed when the roof of gas pockets under the lava surface broke in. A rich life has developed in and around these natural pools. One may see flamingos, Bahama pintails, great blue herons. Pelicans nest in the mangroves. Feral dogs roam the region and attack marine iguanas and sea lions.

Puerto Villamil

Principal centre of Isabela district, on the south coast of the island. It is one of the least inhabited islands, with a population of about 800 people, and an 'end-of-the-world' feeling. The fishermen's village was founded in 1897 by Don Antonio Gil, an honorable citizen from Guayaquil. This is one of the most beautiful sites of the archipelago, with marvelous white sand beaches that stretch for kilometres. The historical past of Isabela is rich in fabulous and terrible stories. In fact, Turtle Bay (Bahia de la Tortuga) was used by pirates; buried treasure was hidden there, and some was discovered in 1974. Behind Villamil and along the coast, brackish lagoons are a refuge for flamingos, whimbrels, white-cheeked pintails, common stilts and gallinules.

Following the beach to the west, one passes by the cemetery of Puerto Villamil (one kilometre), with old graves and rotten crosses. The trail heads inland at the end of the beach, to the Muro de las Lacrimas, the Wall of Tears. It was erected from

road to
Santo Tomas
15 Km

Flamingo
lagoon

airfield

Lagoons

to
Cemetery + penitenciary

1 Main jetty
2 Capitania del Puerto
3 Soda bar
4 Colegio de la mision
5 Police station
6 Main square
7 School
8 Comedor Teresita
9 Medical dispensary
10 Hotel Alexandra
11 Casa Jaramillo
12 Parque Nacional Galápagos

0   40 m

Ingala

Puerto Villamil
~ Isabela.

Bahia Tortuga

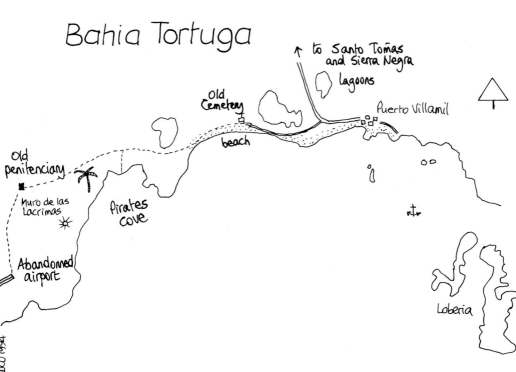

to Santo Tomás
and Sierra Negra

Lagoons

Old
Cemetery

Puerto Villamil

beach

Old
penitenciary

Muro de las
Lacrimas

Pirates
cove

Abandoned
airport

Loberia

Piroco 1994

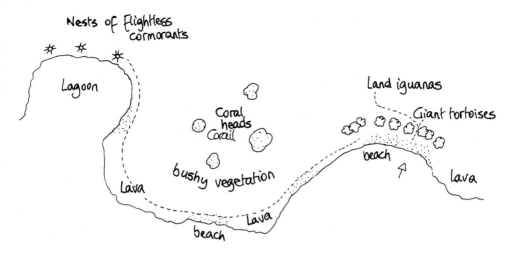

Nests of flightless cormorants

Lagoon

Coral heads
Corail

bushy vegetation

Land iguanas

Giant tortoises

beach

Lava

Lava

Lava

beach

Urvina bay

Punta Espinosa

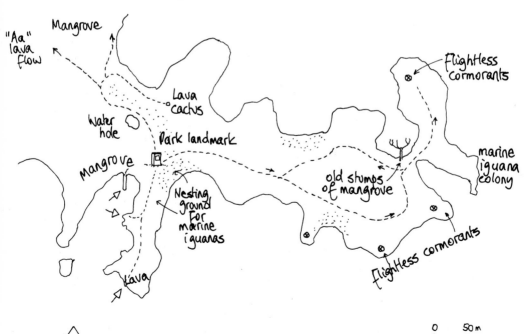

Mangrove

"Aa" lava flow

Water hole

Mangrove

Lava cactus

Park landmark

Nesting ground for marine iguanas

Lava

old stumps of mangrove

flightless cormorants

marine iguana colony

flightless cormorants

0   50m

PIROCO 1994

big lava blocks by convicts of the penal colony. The penitentiary of Isabela was opened in 1944 at a foot of a desolated hill, in the arid zone, two to three hours' walk from Villamil. Following a mutiny that was mentioned in the press at the time, it was definitively closed down and blown up in 1959. More than 200 convicts had been forced to hard labour. Life was horrible there and the cruelty of the guards was legendary. This period will remain forever in the memory of Isabela. Of the penitentiary itself, the only ruins are a standing cylinder of rusted iron, and a huge wall of basalt, 50 metres long, five metres wide and eight metres tall. Behind the Wall of Tears, a trail climbs up the hill, from where you may best contemplate the desolation and perhaps feel a chill run up your spine. In the far distance, the bay of Villamil shines from the timeless surf that crashes on the beach, and the magnificent turquoise-blue waters in the midday sun are an exotic image that help dispel the unhappy past.

On the way back, notice the solitary coconut tree on the right. A pirate's treasure was discovered there 20 years ago by a mysterious Frenchman who left no trace of his passage but for a big hole with some rusted pieces of iron. Puerto Villamil, a small paradise lost, not yet open for tourism, is like the black sheep of the Galápagos. An airport was built more than ten years ago with a landing strip of white coral, but it was found later on that it was not practical because it was wrongly oriented in respect to the southeast tradewinds, and the site was abandoned.

On the beach at the end of the village, the little Hotel Alexandra is swept by the ocean wind like a deserted house. The last time it was used, two Japanese men changed the main hall into a sea cucumber depot for eight months before they disappeared with their smuggled goods. For lodging, ask the family of Natalia and Jorge Jaramillo, on the other side of the road. There are some *comedors* and food places in town (see map, page 247). To get to Isabela on your own, ask for '*la Lancha de Ingala*' (in Puerto Ayora, Santa Cruz Island), a ferryboat that goes to the inhabited islands once or twice a week, and which also transports mail and cargo.

Sierra Negra Volcano

The local bus leaves for Santo Tomas in the highlands, at 7 am and 2 pm, and returns to Puerto Villamil at 4 pm (cost = $1 or 2,000 sucres) Sierra Negra Volcano The village of Santa Tomas, 18 kilometres from Villamil in the highlands, used to be the departure point for the ascent of Sierra Negra volcano. It was founded by Don Antonio Gil at the end of the 19th century, and has a population of 300 people. Cattle breeding and agriculture—there are plantations of coffee, oranges, grapefruits, papayas, guavas and avocados—are the main activities.

The road from the lowlands was constructed 20 years ago. A minibus makes the daily trip to the *parte alta*, from Puerto Villamil, but the new road goes up directly to the rim of the crater.

Otherwise, it's a three-hour walk from Santo Tomas. It is possible to hire horses, at $20 for the day (see Sr. Antonio Gil, at Hotel San Vincente, in Puerto Villamil*).

Sierra Negra is a huge caldera, ten kilometres wide, the oldest on the island. During the garua season the summit of the volcano is covered in mist; be prepared for rain. On the rim, the trail divides in two: Towards the west, it heads to Volcan de Azufre, an old sulphur mine that was exploited by the first settlers (10 kilometres, or three to four hours' walk); towards the east, the trail leads to Volcan Chico on the external slope of Sierra Negra, which erupted in 1979. The weather is often clear and good, once you reach the northern side of the caldera. You'll get excellent views of the Perry Isthmus, Elizabeth Bay and Alcedo volcano.

The Galápagos hawk, short-eared owl, vermillion flycatcher and large-billed flycatcher are common to Sierra Negra. Wild horses are sometimes seen. Camping is allowed, but fire is forbidden. Do not get lost. For refreshment there is a small bar on the road, just under the rim of Sierra Negra.

Hotel San Vicente (Sr. Antonio Gil) cafeteria-bar, 4 rooms, at $3.50 with private bathrooms. Horses for hire.

FERNANDINA

land surface: 642 square km
elevation: 1,494 m

Fernandina has an impressive volcano, one of the most active on the planet. Even though it is the youngest in the Galápagos, at least 12 eruptions have been recorded in the last 150 years. The caldera is six kilometres wide, with a depth of 900 metres. The lake that was once in the crater in 1946 disappeared in 1958 after two lava flows inside the caldera. In 1964, there was a new lake, but in June 1968, a memorable explosion blew up the caldera floor, which fell 300 metres. The personnel of Skylab mentioned a small eruption in December 1973, and the lava flow on the southeastern slope, inside the crater. The most recent eruptions were recorded in 1977, 1978, 1984, September 1988, April 1991 and February 1995. This last eruption maintained regular activity for over a month. Lava flows ran into the ocean from parasitic cones on the southwest towards Cape Hammond, creating a new cape three to four kilometres north-west of the former one.

The vegetation on the slopes of Fernandina belongs to the arid zone. At an elevation of 1,200 metres, the flora is reduced to islets of ferns, surrounded by lava flows. On the top of the volcano, high grasses and scalesia bushes are dominant (see drawing, page 248).

PUNTA ESPINOSA

The only visitor's site on Fernandina is on the northeast of the island, facing Isabela Island on the Bolivar Channel. Galápagos penguins and flightless cormorants are established, but rare. Disturbed by man, they tend to move their nesting sites regularly. The pahoehoe lava flows are bedecked by lava cacti (*Brachycereus*), which form yellow or dark green tufts with white spines.

Tectonically uplifted in 1975, the site of Punta Espinosa is also the home of a colony of sea lions and a few colonies of marine iguanas. Red and turquoise-blue crabs, *zayapas*, are everywhere. Land iguanas that came down from the volcano were once present in the bushes, but they seem to have disappeared. They are still numerous on the rim of Fernandina, however, where they dig burrows and lay eggs in the volcanic sand. The Galápagos hawk is common to the site, where it preys on snakes and marine iguanas.

CABO DOUGLAS

This site is not yet open to visitors, but will attract many visitors due to the considerable natural beauty. On a black basaltic shore (uplifted), one may observe a small colony of marine iguanas, a few land iguanas, Galápagos hawks and a big nest of twigs on a lava promontory, a few nests of flightless cormorants and a colony of fur sea lions. There is also a colony of blue-footed boobies.

THE 'PEPINOS' AFFAIR

The scandal of the exploitation of *pepinos*, or sea cucumbers, a delicacy to Chinese and Japanese palates, broke in 1992. Local pirate camps, encouraged by Japanese fishing ships, were established on the coast of Fernandina to collect sea cucumbers along the shoreline. Families with women and children lived illegally in this 'no man's land' to catch pepinos, which they dried in the sun on the lava rocks. Then they packed the merchandise in bags and placed the goods to local boats in Villamil and Puerto Ayora, which in turn delivered them to the Japanese fishing boats.

The sea cucumbers (*Isostichopus fuscus*) move on the rocky bottom at a depth of between 2 and 20 metres. They are ecologically important because they help to clean seawater by recycling organic waste. The ban on the fishing on *pepinos*, declared by President Borja in June 1992, was contested one year later by the Galápagos fishermen, who recognized the amount of money at stake. The illicit fishing went on, and about 1,000 pounds of pepinos was seized by the Equadorian authorities in one of the pirate camps, in November 1993. Thirty million pepinos were fished, dried or cooked on the coast of Fernandina in 1992. In 1994, striking fisherman pressured the government of the new president, Sixto Duran Ballen, to suspend the 1992 decree. Somehow they succeeded, because, as of July 15, 1994, the Ministry of Industry and Fisheries (MIIP) allowed lobster fishing for three months (July 15-October15), then sea cucumber fishing for three months (October 15-January15), then even shark fishing (January15-April 15), which has always been forbidden. For the Galápagos Marine Reserve, this is definitely 'Apocalypse Now' (see photo, page 174).

According to recent sources (March 1995), the local fishermen of Isabela have also been fishing Pacific sea horses (*Caballitos del Mar*) to sell to the Chinese for aphrodisiac medicine.

CHAPTER FIVE

THE LANDINGS

Whether you take an organized tour with an Ecuadorian travel agency or you decide to charter a boat from Puerto Ayora or San Cristobal with a few friends, once in the islands you'll have to get familiar with some practical advice and some new words.

You drop anchor in a turquoise-blue cove or in a wild bay with foaming surf. Then the *panga* will take you to shore. The panga is a small boat, comparable to a dinghy, accommodating up to 12 people, which is conducted more or less skillfully by the *pangero*.

The landing can be fun or it can be hell, depending on the difficulty of disembarking, and this depends on the season or your luck. It could be on a fine sand beach or on sharp coral rubble, on dry or wet rocks (with the wave and surf behind) or on a safe rocky quay where a few sea lions bask (and, of course, like Charlie, the big peevish male on South Plaza, they do not want to be disturbed). Simply imagine the paradisiacal setting, and this is where you step in. You do not get into heaven for free.

In short, you may experience a dry landing or a wet landing. You should have your shoes on or in hand, with your pants rolled up to your knees. In the latter case, shorts are definitely the most practical. If you disembark on a beach, do not forget about the wave behind you; if you are not careful, it could make you lose your balance with all your belongings (imagine your camera equipment in a bath of salt water). Consequently, you should sit on the side of the *panga* and put both your feet in the water at the same time, not one foot after the other. You may smile, but if you do not follow these directions you will find out what happens by which time it will be too late. Plastic bags may be useful for wrapping your camera to protect it from spray. In any case, the guide is there to warn you.

LIST OF THE LANDINGS

Island	Site	Type of landing
Santa Cruz	Puerto Ayora	dry
	Itabaca	dry
	Las Bachas	wet
South Plaza		dry, sea lions on wharf
Mosquera Islet		wet

Island	Site	Type of Landing
Santa Fé		wet
Floreana	Punta Cormorant	wet
	Post Office Bay	wet
	Black Beach	dry
Española	Gardner bay	wet
	Punta Suarez	wet
San Cristobal	Puerto Baquerizo	dry
	Cerro Brujo	wet
	Punta Pitt	wet
Genovesa	Darwin Bay	wet, coral beach
	Prince Philip's Steps	dry, but slippery rocks
Rábida		wet
Sombrero Chino		wet
Bartolomé	volcano climb	dry, but slippery rocks
	beach	wet
Santiago	Puerto Egas	wet
	Espumilla	wet
	Buccaneer's Cove	wet, watch for surf
Isabela	Tagus Cove	dry, but slippery rocks
	Puerto Villamil	dry
	Punta Moreno	dry, on rocks
	Urvina Bay	wet, watch for waves
	Punta Albemarle	wet, watch for waves
	Alcedo	wet
Fernandina	Punta Espinosa	dry, but slippery rocks

CHAPTER SIX
SCUBA DIVING

The underwater fauna is very rich in the Galápagos, and unusual by comparison to traditional dive sites, such as the Caribbean, Maldives, Red Sea, Indian Ocean, Philippines and Southeast Asia, where the warm tropical seas abound with colorful coral reefs. In the Galápagos, one finds more than 400 species of shore fishes, 32 species of corals, and 600 species of mollusks. Diving in Galápagos is not to be undertaken lightly. Some sites have strong currents, lava rocks and underwater ridges may be sharp and dangerous, and caves make enticing traps. One should never dive alone.

The Galápagos are still new to the sport. Even though a presidential decree of May 13, 1986, declared the Galápagos archipelago a 'Reserve of Marine Resources', very few laws were defined and implemented governing their proper exploitation. Nevertheless, one thing is certain: it is impossible to dive without a local dive guide, licensed by the Galápagos National Park and by the Ecuadorian Merchant Marine, who will look after you underwater, but who is not responsible for you in case of an accident.

No facilities are offered for the safety of divers. The closest decompression chamber is 1,000 kilometres away, at the Ecuadorian naval base in Guayaquil. Divers are informed that they dive at their own risk. A liability waiver will have to be signed before the cruise begins. In any case, you will have to show proof of your diver's certification, your logbook and a medical certificate.

There are two dive clubs in Puerto Ayora. Recommended is Scuba Iguana at Hotel Galapagos, run by Mattias Espînosa and Jack Nelson who operate day trips with a fast dive boat. One-day, two-boat dives cost US$78–110 per person, depending on dive sites. Minimum of two or three divers.

WATER TEMPERATURE

Despite their equatorial position, the Galápagos are considered to be a cold-water environment. Three main marine currents bathe the archipelago: two are cold (coming from the west and southeast) and one is warm (coming from Panama in the northeast).

The water temperature is influenced by the season: cold from May to December, warm from December to May. The sea surface temperature varies from 17° C to 27° C, and drops to 15° C sometimes to the west of Isabela.

In the Galápagos, temperatures are warmer in the northern islands, cooler in the central and southern islands, and cold west of Isabela and Fernandina. The exception occurs during Niño years, when the sea surface temperature averages 25° C to 30° C. Therefore, it is necessary to have a 5-mm wetsuit any time of the year. (See Part One, Chapter 2, for more details on seasons and temperatures.)

Visibility

Water is generally clear during the cold season, but the sea surface is rough in August-September. In the warm season, water may be murky due to the presence of plankton on the surface, but it depends on the site.

Currents

Mainly from east to west, they can be very strong. Underwater navigation with a compass is often necessary, and it is important to be cautious at all times.

Dangers

There are no real dangers in the Galápagos; nevertheless, it is advised to avoid submarine caves. These can be long tunnels, sometimes labyrinthine, which can be rather dangerous because of the surf action.

Sharks are no real threat, and are not aggressive, as long as they are not provoked. An attitude of respect is recommended, and some distance has to be kept between the diver and the sharks. A refuge in the rocks or in the cliff should be nearby, just in case. Whitetips, grey reef or hammerhead sharks are usually inquisitive by nature. Although shy, they do not hesitate to come close to the diver, but at the last minute they turn at a right angle and disappear out of sight. Schools of Galápagos sharks, of up to 30 individuals, may circle you (eg Gordon Rocks). Fortunately, it doesn't mean that they have you in mind for a feast, for they usually vanish in a few minutes, with majesty and indifference.

If ever you notice a shark that wriggles or arches its back suddenly, then beware. This aggressive display is a warning preceding an attack. You should come up to the surface and leave the water quickly. There was a case in which a Galápagos shark bumped into a diver from the back (James Gribb, 1984)—not too nice. In March 1991, the guide Jonathan Green claimed he was attacked by a two-metre-long great white shark when he was skin diving at Playa Escondida, to the northeast of Pinzón Island. He kicked off the shark with his fins. The same year, again off Pinzón Island, a park guard was bitten in the thigh by a three-metre-long shark while in one metre of water.

Until now, sharks in the Galápagos have not attacked humans, for they have enough natural food to eat. This situation may change, triggering a series of accidents in the future.

There is one venomous snake on the islands. The yellow-bellied sea snake (*Pelamis platurus*, family Hydrophiidae), is dorsally black, ventrally yellow. About 85 cm long, this rare pelagic species appears in the warm season (especially during Niño years), when the sea surface temperature rises. It should not be approached, for its venom is more virulent than that of the cobra.

Among other pain-inflicting animals are the stingrays, which inhabit sandy bottoms in shallow water, and the scorpionfishes on the rocks. The long black spines of the crowned sea urchin can easily penetrate one's skin, and leave a numbness that may last or two or three days. The flower sea urchin (*Toxopneustes roseus*) should not be touched, for it is also venomous and may induce a high fever.

DIVING SITES

DEPTH

Classification: - Snorkelling   < 3   metres
            - Skin diving   < 10 metres
            - Scuba diving   + 10 metres

CENTRAL ISLANDS

Diving around Santa Cruz	Snorkelling	Skin diving	Scuba
Isla Coamano (Academy Bay)		x	x
Punta Estrada (Academy Bay)	x	x	x
South Plaza (lagoon and cliffs)	x	x	x
Gordon Rocks		x	x
Itabaca canal (south Baltra)	x	x	
Mosquera Islet (east coast)	x	x	x
Nord Seymour (south coast)	x	x	x
(northwest caves)			x
Daphné Mayor			x
Daphné Minor			x
Santa Fé (northeast bay)	x	x	x

Around Santiago			
Bartolomé (pinnacle,	x	x	x
Cousin's Rock			x
Bainbridge rocks			x
Sombrero Chino (lagoon)	x	x	
Beagle rocks	x	x	x
Rábida (beach and west cove)	x	x	
James Bay (Puerto Egas and 'grottos')	x	x	x
Buccaneer's cove (rocky point)	x	x	x
Sullivan Bay	x		

EAST	Snorkelling	Skin diving	Scuba
Around San Cristobal			
Frigatebird Hill			
(Cove, Puerto Baquerizo)	x		
Kicker's Rock (Stephens Bay)			x
Punta Pitt	x	x	x
Roca Ballena			x
NORTH			
Genovesa			
Darwin Bay (beach)	x		
Darwin Bay (west reef)	x	x	x
Prince Philip's steps		x	x
Marchena			
Punta Espejo	x		
Punta Mejia	x	x	x
Wolf			
East coast			x
North Cove			x
Isla de la Fresa			x
Northwest cliff			x
Darwin			
Northeast coast		x	x
The Arch			x
Tower rock (west cove)			x
WEST			
Around Isabela			
Crossman Islands			x
Isla Tortuga	x	x	
Punta Moreno	x	x	x
Elizabeth Bay	x	x	
Tagus Cove	x	x	x
Punta Vicente Roca	x	x	x
Roca Redonda			x
Punta Albemarle	x	x	x
Alcedo beach	x	x	

WEST	Snorkelling	Skin diving	Scuba
Fernandina			
Punta Espinosa	x	x	x
Cabo Douglas			x
SOUTH			
Around Floreana			
Punta Cormorant (beach and rocks)	x	x	
Devil's Crown	x	x	x
Champion Islet		x	x
Enderby Island			x
Caldwell Island			x
Around Española			
Punta Suarez	x	x	
Gardner Bay (rocks)	x	x	
Gardner Island			x
Xarifa Island		x	x
OTHER			
Hancock Bank			x
McGovern Bank			x
Guy Fawkes Island		x	x
Punta Bowditch (Conway Bay)	x	x	

PART FOUR

THE GALAPAGOS NATIONAL PARK

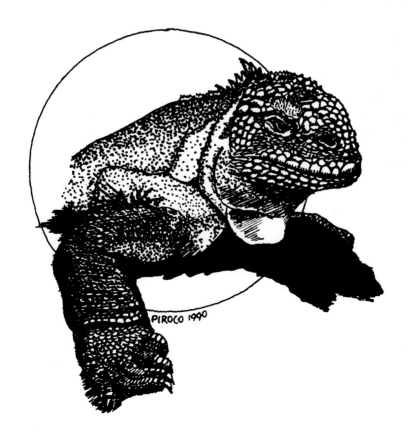

PIROCO 1990

CHAPTER ONE

ADMINISTRATION AND HISTORY

The Galápagos National Park is a public institution recognized by the Ecuadorian government. Its administration depends on INEFAN (1993), the Instituto Forrestal y Aereas Naturales, which in turn depends on MAG, the Ministerio de Agricultura y Ganaderia, the agriculture department based in Quito, capital of Ecuador.

There are about 15 national parks in Ecuador, which cover the Amazonian, Andean and coastal regions, but the Galápagos National Park is the first and most advanced in its administration, management and development. The first laws to protect the Galápagos were passed in 1934. Some islands were then declared reserves for a national park, with the exception of Santa Cruz, Floreana, Cristobal, the south of Isabela and Fernandina.

On July 4, 1959, all areas not colonized by man were declared a national park. The Charles Darwin Foundation was created in Brussels. The same year, to conserve and protect the unique Galápagos ecosystem and to promote scientific research. The Charles Darwin Research Station (CDRS) was established on Santa Cruz Island in 1960, with Raymond Lévêque as its first director.

The National Parks Department was created in 1968 within the Forestry Department. Two conservation officials were sent to the Galápagos and began the Ecuadorian administration. As the number of employees rose, it became necessary to construct the Galápagos National Park Service (SPNG) building.

In 1979, 60 park guards were on duty, supervised by five conservation officials. There were also an accountant and four university-trained professionals: the superintendent and his attendant, the chief of protection and the chief naturalist. The park staff is divided into two groups with specific functions. Four programs were introduced:

- eradication and control of animals and plants introduced by man.
- protection of the endangered native species.
- tourism management.
- education.

The budget of the Galápagos National Park comes directly from the Ecuadorian government, through the MAG. In 1978, it was estimated at $200,000, or six million sucres. The rest of the funds come from international organizations such as the WWF, the Frankfurt Zoological Society and private donations.

Use of the Park

Special Use Zones
On islands colonized by man, some areas of the National Park can be used by settlers and residents to extract products such as wood, sand and volcanic rocks. The hunting of introduced animals is also possible in some places, with a necessary permit.

Scientific Research
Scientists wanting to do research within the National Park must submit a detailed project to the director of INEFAN, to the park superintendent, to the director of the Darwin Station and to the secretary of the Darwin Foundation. The study has to deal with anything related to evolution or concerning conservation problems.

Tourism
Visitors to the National Park have to follow a number of rules made to protect the ecological integrity of the islands. Forty-eight visitor sites have been designed, with marked trails and open areas. Visitors are led by a guide, licensed by the Galápagos National Park, who will make sure the rules are respected.

These rules are set forth on decree 1306, published in 1971, which states the dos and don'ts. The entry fee to the National Park was of $6 in 1981, then $40 in 1989 and $80 for foreigners in 1993. The funds collected go to the management of tourism (30 per cent) and to INEFAN (70 per cent).

Mass tourism in the Galápagos started in 1969, with the arrival of the 58-passenger cruise boat *Lina-A*, of Metropolitan Touring. In the beginning of the 1970s, Ecuador became better known internationally, and the number of visitors increased in the following years: 1,200 in 1969, then 2,500 (1971), 3,000 (1972), 4,500 (1973), between 5,500 and 7,500 in 1974.

The *Lina-A* sank in 1975, without casualties, far off the coast of Ecuador. In 1977, two new cruise ships arrived in the archipelago: the M/N *Bucanero* of Gordon Tours and the M/N *Neptuno* of Macchiavello Tours. In 1980, Metropolitan Touring's M/N *Santa Cruz* replaced the *Lina-A*. The famous and unforgettable *Neptuno*, which, according to hearsay was under a curse and held together by paint alone, sank near Guayaquil in June 1984, drowning the unfortunate cook, who blew up with the kitchen.

It was replaced in 1987 by the M/N *Galápagos Explorer* of the Canodros agency (Guayaquil). The M/N *Bucanero* stopped operating in 1990. A new cruise ship arrived in the archipelago in September 1993: the M/N *Ambassador I*, with a capacity of 86 passengers, belongs to a Greek named Zacharias, of Islas Galápagos Turismo y Vapores (Quito).

Three big boats ply the Galápagos waters now, as well as another 100 smaller boats, yachts and sailboats. After being limited to 12,000 people (1973), then to 25,000 people (1981) by different Master Plans, the number of visitors to the Galápagos National Park is now out of control, and limits have become meaningless. The last Master Plan of Miguel Cifuentes (1985), former manager of the SPNG, forecast a new limit of 45,000 people per year. This limit was blown at the end of 1994, when the number of visitors exceeded 54,000 people. The economic pressure is such that the future looks hectic. Hotel construction has boomed in Puerto Ayora, Santa Cruz Island, for the last two years.

Annual flow of visitors to the Galápagos National Park (1974–1997)

Year	Total Visitors	Ecuadorians	Foreigners	% nationals	% foreigners
1974	7500				
1975	7000				
1976	6300	868	5432	13.78	86.22
1977	7788	1349	6439	17.32	82.68
1978	12299	1606	10693	13.06	86.94
1979	11765	2226	9539	18.92	81.08
1980	17445	3980	13465	22.81	77.19
1981	16265	4036	12229	24.81	75.19
1982	17123	6067	11056	35.43	64.57
1983	17656	7254	10402	41.09	58.91
1984	18858	7627	11231	40.44	59.56
1985	17840	6279	11561	35.20	64.80
1986	26023	12126	13897	46.60	53.40
1987	32593	17767	14826	54.51	45.49
1988	31248	14218	17030	45.50	54.50
1989	41899	15133	26766	36.12	63.88
1990	41192	15549	25643	37.75	62.25
1991	40746	14815	25931	36.36	63.64
1992	39510	12855	26655	32.54	67.46
1993	46818	10136	36682	21.65	78.35
1994	54000	12800	41200	23.70	76.30
1995	55782	15483	40303	27.75	72.25
1996	61895	16113	45782	26.03	73.97
1997	62809	13979	48830	22.26	77.74

(source: Servicio Parque Nacional Galápagos, 1997)

The rise of the numbers in 1978 is explained by the arrival of the *Bucanero* and the *Neptuno* (with a capacity of 90 passengers each); the same applies in 1980 to the *Santa Cruz*. In 1986, a renewed influx of visitors followed the big fire that burned part of Isabela Island in 1985 and brought publicity to the islands.

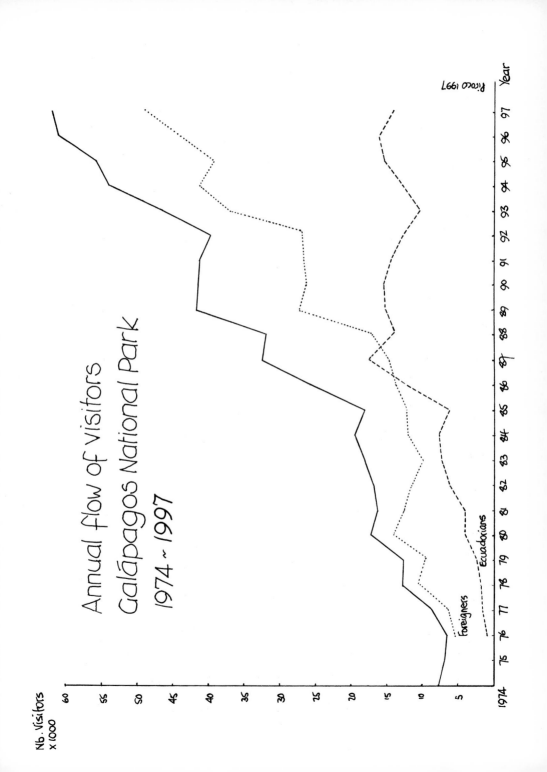

Nb. Visitors
x 1000

Annual flow of visitors
Galápagos National Park
1974 ~ 1997

Ricoco 1997   Year

Foreigners

Ecuadorians

About 3,000 to 5,000 people visit the Galápagos each month. In 1993, the heaviest months were January/February/March, then July/August and December.

As for Ecuadorian visitors, after their numbers peaked in 1987, when they accounted for 54.51 per cent of visitors, they have become gradually less interested in the islands, with only 12,000 people (27.50 per cent) visiting in 1993. The flow of foreigners, by contrast, is increasing, with 33,000 people in 1993, or about 72.50 per cent. By order and number of visitors, here are the 12 countries that send people to the Galápagos:

1	Ecuador
2	USA
3	Germany
4	Switzerland
5	Italy
6	Canada
7	South America
8	England
9	France
10	Holland
11	Israel
12	Japan

(source: SPNG and Carta Informativa CDRS, February 1988).

THE MASTER PLAN

Most of the natural and wildlife areas rapidly deteriorate if they are not managed properly. A number of objectives have been established for these natural areas, which includes designation as a national park. Consequently, the Galápagos Master Plan was divided in two parts, which sum up:

- the information concerning the resources of the area, culturally, historically, flora and fauna, and the human factor.
- procedures and goals of management, characteristics and qualities to preserve, not to mention the development of the local population.

The Master Plan for the protection and use of the Galápagos National Park was written in 1973 by a team of Ecuadorians and international experts. The Food and Agriculture Organization (FAO) already had 15 years' experience in South America. The plan, printed in 1974, is carried out by the park personnel and states seven main objectives:

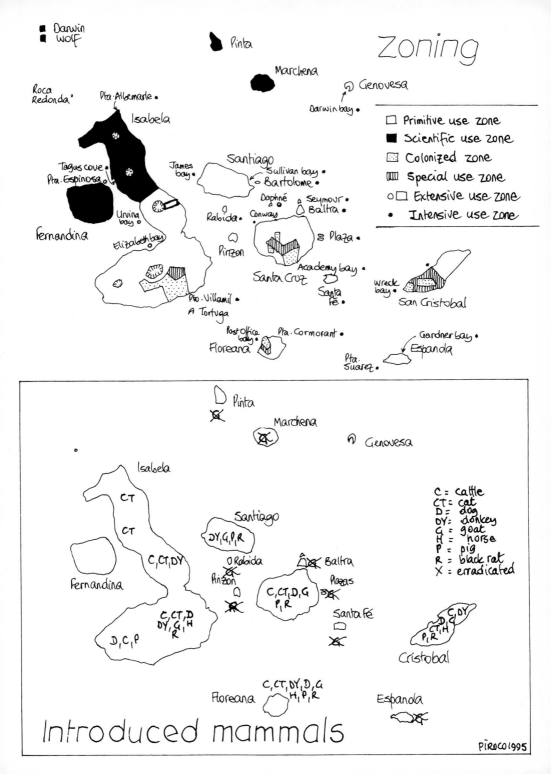

Zoning

- Darwin
- Wolf
- Pinta
- Marchena
- Genovesa
- Darwin bay
- Roca Redonda
- Pta. Albemarle
- Isabela
- Tagus cove
- Pta. Espinosa
- Fernandina
- Urvina bay
- Elizabeth bay
- James bay
- Santiago
- Sullivan bay
- Bartolome
- Daphné
- Rabida
- Conway
- Seymour
- Baltra
- Plaza
- Pirzon
- Academy bay
- Santa Cruz
- Santa fé
- Wreck bay
- San Cristobal
- Pto. Villamil
- A Tortuga
- Post Office bay
- Floreana
- Pta. Cormorant
- Pta. Suarez
- Gardner bay
- Espanda

Legend:
- ☐ Primitive use zone
- ■ Scientific use zone
- ▨ Colonized zone
- ▥ Special use zone
- o☐ Extensive use zone
- • Intensive use zone

Introduced mammals

- Pinta ⊠
- Marchena ⊠
- Genovesa
- Isabela — CT, CT, C,CT,DY
- Fernandina
- Santiago — DY,G,P,R
- Rabida ⊠
- Pinzon
- Baltra ⊠
- Plazas ⊠
- Santa fé ⊠
- C,CT,D,G P,R
- C,CT,D DY,G,H R
- D,C,P
- Cristobal — D,C,DY CT,H P,R
- Floreana — C,CT,DY,D,G H,P,R
- Espanda ⊠

Legend:
- C = cattle
- CT = cat
- D = dog
- DY = donkey
- G = goat
- H = horse
- P = pig
- R = black rat
- X = erradicated

PIROCO 1995

* Protection of the Galápagos ecosystem.
* Eradication or control of introduced species.
* Appropriate use for visitors.
* Providing information to visitors on what they can see.
* Educating for the local population.
* Encouraging economic development of the archipelago's residents
* Encouraging scientific research.

Another important point of the Master Plan is zoning. This technique allows division of the National Park into distinct zones for better management. Five zones were established (see map of Zoning, page 265):

Intensive Use Zones
There are about 25 of these particularly extraordinary touristic zones within the National Park. The plan recommends that a maximum of 90 people (four to five groups of 20 people with a guide) be authorized to disembark at the sites. Some of the areas are fragile, and control remains important.

Extensive Use Zones
There are about 16 of these zones, which are not as interesting as the intensive-use zones. A maximum number of 12 people may disembark on these sites. No large groups are allowed.

Primitive Use Zones
The majority of the land surface of the National Park. Sometimes affected by the presence of introduced species. These zones are nevertheless ecologically unique. A special permit is required.

Primitive Scientific Zones
These are kept for scientific research (eg Tower, Fernandina). No possible access to the casual visitor with no specialized interest.

Special Use Zones
Adjacent to colonized areas, these zones may be exploited by the residents, for wood, sand, volcanic rocks. Activity is nevertheless strictly controlled.

Among the numerous objectives of the park, as stipulated in the Master Plan, are the following:

* Eradication of introduced plants and animals; protection of the endangered species, touristic management. The transfer of organisms from island to island will be controlled and prevented.
* The park infrastructure will be more elaborate in the colonized areas, with construction of offices and staff quarters. A reception centre was built on Baltra for visitors, and a park guard station will be constructed in Puerto Egas (Santiago).
* A concession system will be established. Responsible tour operators may proceed with tourism within the archipelago, but they must comply with certain rules and pay a 10 per cent tax on their gross annual income. In exchange the SPNG will ensure the necessary protection to the tourism industry, and will supply ground services to the visitors.
* An area of two nautical miles will be added to the park's territory to ensure the protection of the marine environment. In this way, the interaction of the land and marine ecosystems will be protected. (The new Marine Reserve was established in 1986.)
* To enforce the Master Plan, the park personnel will be composed of 66 park guards, plus several technical advisers: carpenters and mechanics, six university-trained experts in education, protection and biology.

The aim of the Master Plan, however idealistic, is allow the people of the Galápagos to live in harmony with their environment, taking from nature only what they need, and disposing only of noncontaminating materials. Easy to say and hard to do.

All in all, man would not be a destructive organism (there are already too many in the islands) but, on the contrary, an introduced species that has found its place in the ecosystem of the Galápagos.

CHAPTER TWO

Introduced Mammals
Rules of Preservation for the Visitor
Role of the Guide

Introduced Animals

The history of introduced mammals goes back 450 years, to man's discovery of the archipelago. Since then, the islands have been populated with herbivores, carnivores (cats and dogs) and omnivores (rats, mice and pigs), which all turned feral after a time. Dogs, pigs, goats and rats were brought by pirates as early as the 16th century. One of the worst introduced animals is the fire ant, which destroys the vegetation (see map of Introduced mammal).

Nowadays, at least 14 species of introduced animals are found in the Galápagos: 11 mammals, two birds, and one insect (see map, page 265).

The 14 Introduced Species

English	Spanish
Cow	Ganado
Goat	Cabra, chivo
Guinea pig	Cuy, cobayo
Donkey	Burro
Horse	Caballo
Sheep	Oveja
Black rat	Rata negra
Mouse	Raton
Pig	Chancho
Dog	Perro
Cat	Gato
Rooster	Gallo
Pigeon	Paloma
Fire ant	Hormiga colorada

GOATS (*Chivos*)

Mainly on Floreana, Santiago and Isabela. These unstable animals live in groups and often move from the coast to the highlands in the dry season.

Goats reproduce once a year in April-May, and have one or two young. These fierce herbivores are a plague upon the vegetation, for they'll eat anything, with the exception of two plants, *Vallesia* and *Castela galapageia*. Their predators are Galápagos hawks, dogs and feral pigs.

CATTLE (*Ganado*)

Found mostly on Isabela, where the population is about 1,000 individuals. They are a threat to the vegetation, but are also of economic value for their meat. Exportation has been considered.

HORSES (*Caballos*)

The threat is not so important, and no serious ecological impact is involved. Horses are found in the highlands of Isabela, Santa Cruz, Cristobal and Floreana.

DOGS (*Perros*)

Dogs turned feral on Santa Cruz and Isabela, where their population is estimated at 200 to 500. They gather mainly to the west of Cerro Azul volcano, where they decimate marine iguanas on the coast, and also on the slopes of Alcedo volcano, where they arrived recently after crossing the Perry isthmus. This barrier of basaltic lava, eight to 10 kilometres wide, has until now controlled their progression toward the north. Generally of a white colour with black spots, feral dogs hunt in small groups of two to three individuals. They attack cattle in the highlands and marine iguanas on the coast. On Santa Cruz Island, they are a serious threat to the Hawaiian petrel, which nests in the tropical zone. Feral dogs have been eradicated from Floreana and San Cristobal.

RATS (*Ratas*)

Recorded on Santa Cruz and on Santiago, they were eradicated from Pinzón (known once as the 'Island of the Rats') by a campaign of the SPNG, from September to November 1989. *Rattus*, the black rat, lives in the arid zone as well as in the humid zone. It reproduces in the hot season, with a breeding cycle of 27 days. Vegetables, insects, fruits, grains, turtle eggs and fledglings are part of its diet. The black rat is responsible for the disappearance of the Galápagos endemic rats, *Oryzomis* and *Nesoryzomis*, because of its competitiveness, aggression and spreading of disease.

The two native predators of the rats are the short-eared owl and the Galápagos hawk. Introduced predators are cats and dog. The black rat was eradicated from Bartolomé in 1976 by traps and poison.

PIGS (*Chanchos*)

Mainly on Santiago, but also on Isabela, where they dig up the nests of marine turtles. They also dig up a number of native plants.

CATS (*Gatos*)

Found mostly on Isabela, where they attack finches, boobies, lava lizards and even marine iguanas (Cartago Bay).

DONKEYS (*Burros*)

In the arid zone and in the highlands of Santiago and Isabela. Their population is estimated at 700 on Alcedo volcano, and 300 to 500 on Sierra Negra volcano.

The major problem of the Galápagos National Park is after all the eradication of goats, which is not an easy task. With time and numerous campaigns, some islands have been cleared of this plague: South Plaza (1961), Rábida and Santa Fé (1971). After a new introduction, Rábida was again cleared (1975); 4,000 goats were eradicated on Marchena (1976), then definitively (1979), as well as on Española (1978).

RULES OF PRESERVATION FOR THE VISITOR

The archipelago of the Galápagos belongs to those few places in the world that remain relatively untouched by human exploitation. The preservation of the environment is everybody's problem. Everyone may take part in it, by following some simple rules which will help to maintain the archipelago's fragile ecosystem intact. The future depends on you.

1. Be careful not to transport any live material to the islands, or from island to island (insect, seeds). If you have a pet, do not bring it to the islands. It will not be allowed.
2. No plants, rocks, animals or their remains, such as bones, pieces of wood, corals, shells, or other natural objects should be removed or disturbed. You may damage the island's ecological conditions.
3. Animals should not be touched or handled. A sea lion pup will be abandoned by its mother, for example, if she smells the scent of man on its young. The same applies to chicks of birds.
4. Animals may not be fed. It may alter their life cycle, their social structure and affect their reproduction.
5. Do not disturb or chase any animal from its resting or nesting spot. This is especially true for birds such as boobies, cormorants, gulls and frigates. The nests

should be approached carefully, keeping a distance of 1 to 2 metres. If disturbed, the bird will flee and abandon its egg or chick, which could die under the strong sun within 30 minutes.

6. All groups which visit the National Park must be accompanied by a qualified guide approved by the National Park. The visitor should follow the trail, marked with small black-and-white posts, and never leave it. If you do so, you may destroy nests without being conscious of it (eg marine iguanas nests in the sand).

7. Follow the guide; stay with him for information and advice. He is responsible for you. If he behaves badly or does not follow the rules himself, report him to the National Park.

8. Litter of all types must be kept off the islands. Disposal at sea must be limited to certain types of garbage, only to be thrown overboard in selected areas. Keep all rubbish: film wrappers, cigarette butts, chewing gum, tin cans, bottles, etc., in a bag or pocket, to be disposed of on your boat. Do not throw anything on the islands or overboard. It could end up at the coast or the beach, or eaten by sea turtles or sea lions. A sea lion may play with a tin can found on the bottom and cut its sensitive muzzle. Sea turtles may die from swallowing a plastic bag.

9. Do not paint names or graffiti on rocks. It is against the law, and you will be fined for it.

10. Do not buy souvenirs or objects made from plants or animals of the islands (with the exception of articles made from wood). Among such articles are turtle shells, sea lion teeth, black coral. This is the best way to discourage such a trade.

11. To camp, you need a permit from the National Park Service (Santa Cruz, Cristobal, Isabela). Do not make fires, but use a gas stove instead. Park suggestions may be useful.

12. Do not hesitate to show your conservationist attitude. Explain these rules to others, and help to enforce them.

The Galápagos National Park thanks you for respecting these rules. Think about others who come after you; they'll be grateful to you for your conservationist attitude.

THE ROLE OF THE GUIDE

The guides are trained by the Galápagos National Park with the help of the Charles Darwin Research Station. For many years, until September 1992, there were two categories of guides in the Galápagos: naturalist guides and auxiliary guides. Some were foreigners, multilingual, and with a scientific background; others were Ecuadorians, natives of the islands without any specific background. Some did not get along; the jealousy of others changed to racism, and eventually there developed a cold war between the guides of the Asociación de Guias and of the Agrupacion de Guias Interpretes, hidden behind the big smiles shown to foreign visitors. But it was common practice to be mean to each other, to denounce a guide at the National Park office for real or imaginary professional mistakes.

As is often heard in Santa Cruz, 'Pueblo pequeño, infierno grande', ie 'Small village, big hell.' Just as in the animal world, the human world submits to fierce competition in a struggle for survival and to irreversible evolution, which forces each individual to make a quick adaptation to this environment. Otherwise, he has to leave the islands. 'The survival of the fittest...' said Darwin.

Moreover, the galloping immigration of the last 15 years has not helped much: 5,000 people in the archipelago in 1980 swelled to more than 20,000 in 1994, and the numbers are on the rise, to such an extent that the authorities are now concerned about the future of the Galápagos.

In 1992, decree number 0434 of the Ministerio de Agricultura y Ganaderia, the Ministry of Agriculture, decided to establish a single organization of naturalist guides, divided in three parts: 'Guias Naturalistas (Naturalist Guides) I, II, III'.

Guia Naturalista I

A native of the islands or resident of the archipelago for many years, with a high school diploma, who has a sound knowledge of the region and speaks English. He must pass the course of Guia Naturalista I, and can lead a group of 10 visitors maximum.

Guia Naturalista II (ex-auxiliary)

Ecuadorian by birth or by naturalization, who has achieved a high school education or has a university background in biology or related fields, or in tourism. He has to be fluent in English, French or German, and must pass the course of Guia Naturalista II. He can lead groups of up to 16 visitors.

Guia Naturalista III (ex-naturalist)

Ecuadorian by birth or by naturalization, and, in the case of a foreigner, must have legal working papers. He has to show proof of a degree in biology or related fields, or in tourism. He must be fluent in Spanish, English, then French or German. He must pass the course of Guia Naturalista III, and may lead a group of 16 (in reality: 20) visitors.

The naturalist guides course takes place each year in September, for a period of six weeks. Priority is given to Ecuadorian nationals and Galápagos residents in registering for the courses, while 20 per cent of foreigners may be accepted to take the course for Naturalist Guides III. The candidate must pass the final exam with an 80 per cent grade in order to receive the guide's license of the Galápagos National Park. The license is valid for two years; the future guide must show proof of at least 120 days worked per year in order to keep his guide's status and the right to continue working.

Guides are responsible in the eyes of the law, and have many essential functions:
- To inform and educate visitors on the richness of the protected area and the natural history of the Galápagos, competently and with diligence.
- To be responsible and to control actions committed by the visitors, within the Galápagos National Park.
- To keep in touch with the administrative authorities, to signal the his group's whereabouts and to receive instructions.
- To carry a guide's license and identity papers, and to wear a uniform, if necessary.
- To be vigilant of the application of technical and administrative measures in order to protect the natural resources and the visitors.
- To cooperate with the control and with the patrol of the region to ensure conservation and rational use of the resources.
- To participate in the activities of observations, involving the collection of data on the ecological impact and other environment aspects.
- To provide interpretation for special groups.
- To report to the legal and technico-administrative authorities whenever necessary.

In conclusion, and in the eyes of visitors, the guide must make sure the rules are respected. In the intensive use zones, he has to keep his group on the trail. In the extensive use zones or open areas, all decisions are his responsibility and must prevent harm to the ecosystem. The guide may also interfere with another group in cases of questionable behavior. The Galápagos National Park has the right to sanction or even take away the license of a guide if he is convicted of a serious offense, whether he deserves a warning or suspension from work.

CHAPTER THREE

THE CHARLES DARWIN RESEARCH STATION

In 1957, UNESCO, in cooperation with the New York Zoological Society, Time Incorporated, and the Ecuadorian government, sent a mission to the Galápagos Islands for the purpose of conducting a study on flora and fauna, and also to look for an appropriate site for building a biological research station.

Two years later, in 1959, the centenary of the Theory of Evolution drew the attention of the International Congress of Zoology. A Galápagos committee was created under the presidency of Sir Julian Huxley. Thus was founded the Charles Darwin Foundation in Brussels, intended to preserve the environment and to favor scientific research with an aim toward conservation. The construction of the Darwin Station in Puerto Ayora was undertaken in the beginning of 1960, facing Academy Bay, with funds from UNESCO and Ecuador. The station was in operation two years later, but was officially inaugurated in 1964.

In 1965, the Ecuadorian government passed decree number 525 thus defining the boundaries of the National Park, so as to protect the giant tortoises and eradicate all feral goats. The first protection programmes started in 1968, with the creation of the Servicio Parque Nacional Galápagos (SPNG). In 1973, the Galápagos became a province of Ecuador for the second time in order to help the development and promotion of the archipelago. The INGALA, or Instituto Nacional Galápagos, was created in 1980 with the aim of developing the islands touristically, economically and for the producing for major projects such as airports.

The Charles Darwin Research Station, which celebrated its 30th anniversary in 1994, hosted a dozen directors, all European or American scientists; Chantal Blanton, the current, American director, was nominated in May 1992, after the terms of Daniel Ewans (1989–92) and Gunther Reck (1984–89). The research station has four main functions:

- to provide scientific information.
- to obtain funds from international organizations for conservation purposes.
- to help the National Park with education programs.
- to educate Ecuadorian students.

In 1986, the budget of the Darwin Station was US$600,000. In 1994, it was US$2 million per year. Visiting scientists with research projects must pay an indemnity for their expeditions and outings. Twenty per cent of the budget of the station is supplied by the Ecuadorian government. Another important donor is the Smithsonian Institution, which provides 20-30 per cent of the budget. The WWF was a serious contributor in the past, but gradually retired. The San Diego Zoo supports the giant tortoises projects. Other well-known donors include the Frankfurt Zoological Society. Private European and American societies also contribute modest funds to the CDRS.

PRACTICAL INFORMATION

HOW TO GET TO THE GALÁPAGOS

By Plane
TAME (Transportes Aereos Militares Equatorianos)
      Avenida Amazonas y Avenida Colon
      Edificio Banco del Pichincha, 7mo piso
      P.O. Box 8736
      Quito, Ecuador
      Tel: 509392, 590375

It is also possible to make reservations through travel agencies in Quito and Guayaquil. Officially inaugurated on November 3, 1980, the Boeing 737 links Quito to Baltra Island in the Galápagos, Monday to Saturday. The flight stops over in Guayaquil—with or without a plane change—then proceeds to Baltra. The international return fare is US$378 (1998), US$328 for students with a student card. For Ecuadorians, the fare is 396,000 sucres return (US$203). For Galápagos residents, it's 201,000 sucres (US$103). A new low season fare has been offered by TAME at US$289 From January 16 to June 14 and from September 1 to November 30 (official since 1995).

		Quito	Baltra
UIO-GLPS	flight 191	9:30 am ..stopover Guayaquil 11:00 am.......	12:30 pm

		Baltra	Quito
GLPS-UIO	flight 190	12:30 am..........stopover Guayaquil...............	5:30 pm

Since January 1986, it has been possible to fly straight to San Cristobal with SAN (Servicios Aereos Nacionales), based in Guayaquil. Daily flights except on Sundays. The international price is the same as on TAME, including the 25 per cent student discount for persons under 26 years of age with a student card. Starting from Quito, the return flight costs $297, but it is only US$264 from Guayaquil.

SAN	Avenida Colon 535 - Quito	Ave. Arosemena Km. 2.5
	Tel: 561995 - 562024	P.O. Box 09-01-7138 - Guayaquil
		Tel: 201516

		Quito	San Cristobal
UIO-GYE	WB821/800	11:00 am.....stopover GYE 12:00 pm.............	1:30 pm GLPS
		San Cristobal	Quito
GLPS-UIO	WB 801/832	1:00 pm.....stopover GYE 4:00 pm................	4:30 pm

There is an hour's difference between the mainland and the archipelago.

Visas

British and American citizens do not require a visa to enter Ecuador, as is the case for citizens of most countries. Since July 1993, French visitors must obtain a visa.

Exchanging Money

The currency in Ecuador is the *sucre*. It has been fluctuating since 1980, quite alarmingly, in fact, if one considers that US$1 was worth 30 sucres back then. In 1989, $1 = 500 sucres, and in 1995, $1 = 2,350 sucres.

There are two banks in the Galápagos, both are in Puerto Ayora (Santa Cruz Island) and in Puerto Baquerizo Moreno (San Cristobal Island): the Banco del Pacifico and the Banco de Fomento. It's possible to change money there, as well as in souvenir shops. But you would do better to change your money at the Quito airport upon arrival, at the banks of Avenida Amazonas or at the Casa de cambio (Casa Paz). You can also change back sucres into dollars at the airport before leaving Ecuador.

Spoken Languages

Spanish is the national language, but English is usually well understood in the Galápagos. Guides may also speak German, French, Italian and Dutch.

Electricity

110 volts in Ecuador as well as in the Galápagos, with American-type plugs. Europeans may be advised to bring along a plug adapter. On the Galápagos boats, you may also plug into 220 volts, 12 or 24 volt system, and recharge the batteries of your video camera without any problems.

Sun

Being right on the equator, the sun is very strong. Do not forget your hat, sun protection, lip balm. Burns may occur rapidly for those who are not protected from the very first day. You are well advised to put sunblock cream on your neck, behind your knees, on your calves and on your feet.

Clothes & Footwear

Light clothing like shorts and T-shirts is sufficient. Bring along a light raincoat or a rainjacket for protection during the garua and the showers of the hot season. A sweatshirt or jumper will be necessary for cool and windy evenings on the boat, and for the high elevations of the Andes (Quito, 2,850 metres) and Ecuador. Sports shoes are the best for the islands, not to mention a pair of flip-flops (thongs) for walking in the shallow water or for disembarking on a coral beach.

Mosquitoes & Related Diseases

Mosquitoes are found in the hot season on the coast, in the mangroves of Puerto Ayora and in the islands. On the sea, where a breeze is always present, they are not a problem. There is no malaria in the Galápagos.

Besides seasickness, there are no risks of disease in the islands, even though some cases of cholera were reported after the 1992 epidemic in Ecuador. This bleak period is now over. Vaccinations against diphtheria and tetanus are recommended, however.

There is a small hospital and pharmacy in Puerto Ayora, as well as in Puerto Baquerizo Moreno (San Cristobal), and one dispensary is found in Puerto Villamil (Isabela). For any serious accident, returning to Quito or Guayaquil is strongly advised.

Photography

Kodak, Fuji and Sakura film are available, for slides or prints, in Puerto Ayora, Pto. Baquerizo and in Floreana (at Mrs Wittmer's place). Nevertheless, if you want to be sure of its freshness, it is better to bring your own supply from home, or, alternatively, from Quito or Guayaquil.

Hours of Sea Crossing

For small boats sailing at six or seven miles per hour.

		Nautical Miles	Hours
Puerto Ayora	-Punta Suarez (Española)	53	9
	-Puerto Baquerizo	40	7
	-South Plaza	17	3
	-Santa Fé		3
	-Bartolomé	45	8
	-James Bay (Santiago)	57	9
	-Puerto Villamil (Isabela)		8
	-Punta Espinosa (Fernandina)	140	22
South Plaza	-Bartolomé	33	5
Bartolomé	-James Bay	27	3-4
Bartolomé	-Genovesa	52	8-9
James Bay	-Rábida	16	2-3
James Bay	-Punta Espinosa	90	12-14
Punta Suarez	-Floreana	42	5-6

HISTORICAL INDEX

1535   Official discovery of the Galápagos, on March 10, by Fray Tomas de Berlanga, archbishop of Panama, on a boat that drifted off its course with the ocean currents. The first mass is celebrated on the islands.

1546   Arrival of Diego de Rivadeneira, who experiences the same trouble as Fray Tomas. He is the first to mention the Galápagos hawk and the flamingos.

1570   The Galápagos Islands appear for the first time on a world map, drawn by Abra ham Ortelius. They are called *Insulae de los Galopegoes*.

1593–   Pirates use the Galápagos as a refuge and as a base to look for water and to collect
1710   turtle and tortoise meat. From there, they attack the Peruvian and Ecuadorian ports. Goats seem to have been introduced at this time.

1684   The pirate and cartographer Ambrose Cowley draws one of the first navigation maps of the islands, as does William Dampier.

1685   The viceroy of Peru introduces dogs on some islands to eradicate goats, food of the pirates.

1790   The first scientific mission, led by the Sicilian captain Alexander Malaspina, sent by Charles V of Spain, lands on the island. The report of that expedition was lost.

1793   The British James Colnett makes a trip to the Galápagos to study the possibility of whale fishing. Start of the whaling industry, which will last until 1870. Some tortoise species are on the brink of extinction. James Colnett draws the first detailed map of the archipelago. The post office barrel is erected on Floreana by Colnett or Hathaway to facilitate communication with the United States and England.

1800–   Exploitation of the fur sea lions by North Americans and Europeans. The species
1900   comes close to extinction but some individual sea lions survive on Fernandina and Genovesa.

1801   The American captain Amasa Delano reports an eruption of Alcedo volcano or Darwin volcano when anchored at James Bay. He is the first to mention the lava lizard in the archipelago.

1807   Irishman Patrick Watkins is the first authentic settler in the Galápagos, being exiled on Floreana (unless he requested it). He grows vegetables, which he trades for whisky to the passing ships. Two years later, he steals a ship's boat and sails to the Ecuadorian coast.

1813   Arrival of the USS *Essex*. Darwin Porter, the captain, practically destroys the British whaling fleet in the archipelago. He makes many important observations on the natural history of the islands, but he is responsible for the introduction of goats to Santiago. He reports volcanic eruptions on Isabela and Fernandina.

1825   Captain Benjamin Morell of the *Tartar*, who came to look for sea lions in February, observes a volcanic eruption on Fernandina, from Banks Bay. Lava flows into the sea, heating up the water and air to such an extent that parts of the boat start melting. Two weeks later, the eruption was still not over.

1832   Ecuador, a young republic since 1830, takes official possession of the Galápagos Islands on February 12, and names them 'Archipelago del Ecuador'. The first colony—composed of soldiers exiled for having fomented a rebellion on the mainland—is founded on Floreana. General Villamil is the first governor. Domestic animals are brought to the island and turn feral when the colony is abandoned some years later. Thirty-one ships stop over in Floreana during the following three years.

1835   Visit of Captain Fitzroy's HMS *Beagle* for five weeks, from September 15 to October 20. The young naturalist Charles Darwin disembarks on San Cristobal, Santiago, Floreana and Isabela. His observation will lead him to publish *The Origin of Species* 24 years later. Captain Fitzroy draws very accurate maps, which will be used until WW II.

1841   The American writer Herman Melville visits the Galápagos and writes a poetic book on the *Enchanted Islands*.

1846   The French boat *Genie* reports three huts at the foot of Cerro Ballena, south of Conway Bay. A trail to the top of Santa Cruz Island starts from there.

1859   Publication of *The Origin of Species*.

1861   Ecuadorian president Garcia Moreno declares the Galápagos 'Provincia', with Floreana as capital.

1872   Scientific expedition of Professor Louis Agassiz of Harvard University.

1875   First visit of Theodore Wolf, with a few scientists of the Quito Polytechnic School. He will make another trip three years later, and will publish a monograph explaining that the islands are of volcanic origin and were never linked to the mainland. The highest volcano of Isabela (1,707 metres) bears his name.

1885   The Galápagos are linked to the province of Guayas. The new authorities move to Puerto Baquerizo Moreno (San Cristobal).

1886   First school in San Cristobal.

1888   Manuel Cobos founds the penal colony of El Progreso (San Cristobal) after a first failed attempt in 1869. A sugarcane industry is established.

1890   Volcanic activity in the southeast of Santiago. The lava flows of Sullivan Bay may be from that period.

1891   Visit of Georges Baur, an American scientist who claims that the islands were connected to the mainland. For him, there is no other way to explain the presence of so many species on the islands.

1892   The archipelago gets the official name of Archipelago de Colon, after Christopher Columbus. Spanish names are given to the islands.

1897   Antonio Gil starts the colonization of Isabela, with the port of Villamil and the village of Santo Tomas in the highlands.

1904   Manuel Cobos is murdered by a Colombian convict (Sanbal).

1905–   Under the presidency of Rollo Beck, scientists of the California Academy of Science
1906   conduct studies and make numerous samples for one year. They take away with them the greatest collection of plants and animals ever made in the Galápagos. The last giant tortoises were collected on Fernandina, as well as a few specimens found on Rábida Island (which has never been a distinct subspecies). The fur sea lions are almost extinct, according to their findings.

1923   Visit of the American William Beebe, with the *Arcturus* expedition. His book, *Galapagos World's End*, a worldwide success, stimulates many expeditions, among which is the Norwegian colony of 1926.

1924–   First commercial exploitation of the salt mine of Puerto Egas in James Bay (Santiago).
1930   A second exploitation will be undertaken from 1960 to 1968.

1926   A group of Norwegians lands in the Galápagos, with the aim of fishing and agriculture. The company fails, triggering the return of many settlers, although a few remain on Santa Cruz and San Cristobal.

1930–   Appearance of the fire ant in the Galápagos, on the Bellavista road (Santa Cruz).
1934
1932   Drama on Floreana, with Dr Ritter, Dore Strauch, the Wittmer family and the Baroness von Wagner de Bousquet, with her two lovers Lorenz and Philipson. Disappearances, poisoning, strange deaths.

1934   First laws aimed at protecting the fauna of the Galápagos. Some islands become re serves or natural park. Some land iguanas are brought from Baltra to Seymour by a team of Americans of the Hancock Foundation, to find out whether the habitat of Seymour is favourable to the reptiles. (Curiously, that will save the species of Baltra, eradicated after the Second World War. The first flight over the Galápagos is made by two Americans, who came to help a yacht captain suffering from appendicitis in Tagus Cove (Isabela).

1935   Expedition of Victor von Hagen, who commemorates the centenary of Charles Darwin's journey and deposits a bust in his memory.

1941   The American Air Force takes over the islands and builds an air base on Baltra. They are partly responsible for the eradication of the land iguanas on the island, and for the bombing of Pinnacle Rock on Bartolomé, a perfect target for shells.

1954   Uplift of a coral reef at Urvina Bay, in Isabela.

1957   The American scientists Eibl-Eibesfeldt and R Bowman are sent by a few institutions to report on conservation, and to choose a site for the future research station.

1959   On July 4, the Ecuadorian government declares the Galápagos a national park, with the exception of the colonized areas. The Darwin Foundation for the Galápagos Islands is created in Brussels, on July 23. Victor van Straelen is the first president. Upon the centenary of Darwin's book, the penitentiary of Isabela is closed and blown up.

1960   Beginning of lobster fishing. Raymond Lévèque is the first director of the Darwin Station. Funds from UNESCO help to finance the first buildings of the station. Hotel Galápagos, run by American Forrest Nelson, opens the same year in Puerto Ayora.

1961   Goats are eradicated on South Plaza. Frenchman André Brosset becomes the second director of the Darwin Station. The laboratory and the meteorological station are built the same year.

1963   David Snow becomes the third director of the Darwin Station.

1964   Grand opening of the Darwin Station on January 21, with many international personalities. In May, Miguel Castro becomes the first official in charge of conservation and protection of the tortoise population. Roger Perry becomes the fourth director of the station.

1965   Tortoise eggs from Pinzón Island are brought back to the station to be incubated and for the young giant tortoises to be bred in captivity.

1968   Juan Black and Jose Villa, conservation officials, are sent by the Ecuadorian govern-
        ment. They begin the administration of the Galápagos National Park, in October.
        During an intense period of activity, the caldera floor of Fernandina volcano drops
        down to 300 metres (small eruptions within the caldera will follow in 1972, 1977,
        1978, 1988 and 1991).

1969   Mass tourism starts in the Galápagos with the arrival of the *Lina-A* of Metropolitan
        Touring, which will build many landing sites in the islands.

1970   The first 20 baby tortoises bred in captivity are freed on Pinza, their native island.
        Peter Kramer becomes the fifth director of the Darwin Station.

1971   Scholarships are given to Ecuadorian students to study at the Darwin Station. The
        giant tortoise named Lonesome George is found on Pinta Island.

1972   The *Beagle III* is inaugurated in March; it is the first boat of the Darwin Station, offered
        by the WWF (World Wildlife Fund). Engineer Jaime Torres is the first superintendent
        of the National Park. The Japanese boat *Chicuzen Maru* captures hundreds of turtles
        in Galápagos waters. Construction of the Van Straelen Hall at the station.

1973   Construction of the Puerto Ayora-Baltra road. Once again the Galápagos become
        'Province of Ecuador'. National and international experts write the Master Plan for
        the protection and use of the National Park.

1974   Craig MacFarland becomes the sixth director of the Darwin Station. Publication of the
        Master Plan.

1975   Seventeen five-year-old tortoises, bred in captivity, are released on Española, bringing
        the total number of adults to 14 on that island. The feral dogs of Santa Cruz destroy
        the population of young tortoises of the reserve and hundreds of land iguanas of the
        northwest of the island. A breeding centre will be established at the station. The cruise
        ship *Floreana* (ex *Lina-A*) sinks 60 miles off the mainland, with no human losses.

1976   *Rattus rattus*, the black rat, is eradicated on Bartolomé, thanks to the experiments of
        the Darwin Station with traps and poison.

1977   Two new cruise ships arrive in the islands: M/N *Bucanero* and M/N *Neptuno*.

1978   The islands are declared a 'Patrimony of Humanity' by UNESCO.

1980   Arrival of the cruise ship M/N *Santa Cruz* (90 passengers) of Metropolitan Tour
        ing, and of the first B-727 of TAME Airline for the Quito-Baltra flight.

1982 Eruption of Wolf volcano, late August-early September, on Isabela. Unusual warming of the sea surface in the Galápagos. Dieter Plage and Friedmann Köster shoot a video for Survival Anglia Productions (English), for two consecutive years. First use of a ULM to fly over the archipelago.

1983 Memorable year of a disastrous Niño: nine months of rain until July. The Baltra road is flooded and cut off. Real streams appear and bridges are built in Bellavista. Sea surface temperature in Puerto Ayora reaches 30° C. The local population suffers from the humid heat, from colds and skin infections. Many couples divorce or separate. The number of sea lions, marine iguanas and sea birds is decimated.

1984 In April, volcanic eruption on Fernandina. In May, arson fire at the administrative building of the Darwin Station. On May 28, fire on the boat M/N *Neptuno* of Macchiavello Tours, sinks off Guayaquil with the death of the cook.

1985 Big fire in the south of Isabela (March-April), on the slopes of Sierra Negra volcano, in the agricultural zone of Valle Alemania and in the National Park. A trench 62 kilometres long and seven metres wide is dug by the Ecuadorian army. Tortoises are evacuated on men's backs. Two Canadairs are sent from Canada to extinguish the fire, which lasts for 50 days. Covered on TV and in the international press. At the same time, the fishing boat B/P *Intrepido* of Captain Miguel Andagana disappears on March 6 and drifts for 74 days before it reaches the coast of Coast Rica. The six crew-men survive on turtles, sharks and dolphinfish. In November: first course of Dituris, the Ecuadorian tourism office. Estimate of the number of visitors for 1985: 17,850 people (65 per cent foreigners).

1986 Opening on January 9 of the airport of San Cristobal by the vice-president. Creation of the Galápagos Marine Reserve by presidential decree on May 13, which extends 15 miles from the extreme points of the islands. In September: paving of Puerto Ayora. The new guides' hall of the National Park opens its gates for the naturalist guides course. The number of visitors to the Galápagos goes beyond 26,000.

1987 In October, arrival of the *Galápagos Explorer,* the new cruise ship of the company Canodros (SAN/SAETA), with a capacity to carry 90 passengers. New restrictions for the practice of scuba diving in the Galápagos. The dive guides must now have a diver's license from the Ecuadorian Merchant Marine. The number of visitors reaches 32,593.

1988 International Congress of Herpetology at the CDRS in May. It is decided to save the semen of Lonesome George, the last giant tortoise survivor of Pinta Island. The cargo boat *Iguana* (an old cruise ship) sinks in front of the CDRS in Academy Bay, in June. Around September 12-14, new eruption of Fernandina volcano: lava flows inside the caldera, displacement of the crater lake, fumaroles on the outer slope of the volcano. The number of visitors exceeds 31,200.

1989   The French cruise ship *Mermoz* (500 passengers) visits the archipelago twice, but the passengers cannot disembark on the islands of the National Park. Opening of the site of Punta Pitt on the eastern tip of San Cristobal. In May, the goats of southern Isabela cross the Perry Isthmus and climb up Alcedo volcano. A new Niño is preparing, with a noticeable change in life cycles. Gunther Reck resigns as director of the Darwin Station and is replaced by American Daniel Ewans. On July 4, the 30th anniversary of the Galápagos National Park is celebrated. In September and October, the blue-footed boobies abandon their chicks on a massive scale throughout the archipelago, but the albatrosses reproduce well. During the same month, black rats are eradicated on Pinzón Island. Illegal taking of shark fins by the Japanese becomes important. The number of visitors reaches 41,900.

1990   Creation of new trails on Santa Fé, Seymour and Rábida. Return of the cruiseship *Mermoz*. In March-April, the park guards of the Galápagos National Park go on strike for three months, asking for a salary raise. Disputes between the national guides of the Asociacion de Guias and those of the Agrupación de Guias Interpretes del PNG. Sergio Basan breaks the arm of Matthias Espinosa in Puerto Ayora with a club. In May-June, the French TV TF1 shoots two programs of 'Ushuaï a' with Nicolas Hulot and the author aboard the schooner *Cyprae*. Second use of the ULM to fly over the islands. Death of Marga Angermeyer, wife of Carl the painter and German pioneer. Foreigners cannot participate in naturalist guide's exam. In November: dramatic fire of the M/N *Bartolomé* at sea during the night. Five passengers and one crewmember sink with the boat and disappear. A wooden stairway is constructed at Tagus Cove by SPNG.

1991   A French team of XL Productions led by the author shoots two programmes: 'Les Animaux de Mon Coeur' ('Animals of My Heart') for French TV TF1, and 'Wildlife Sanctuaries', which will air on the Discovery Channel. In March, first report by Jonathan Green of an attack by a three-metre-long great white shark, at Playa Escondida (northeast Pinzón Island). March 21: earthquakes at Alcedo volcano, and in April, the eruption of Fernandina volcano. In June: 35 land iguanas are reintroduced to Baltra by the SPNG, after a 40-year absence. In July: opening of Banco del Pacifico in Puerto Ayora, on Santa Cruz Island. September 25: first historical eruption of Marchena Island, during the night, incandescent clouds and lava flows to the southwest. On October 19, Prince Henry of Luxembourg visits the islands. The Ecuadorian government extends for another 25 years the right of the Darwin Foundation to operate the Darwin Station. In December, Arturo Izurieta, former naturalist guide, becomes the new superintendent of the Galápagos National Park, after the scandal that ousted Fausto Cepeda. The telephone is connected in Puerto Ayora. The total number of visitors reaches 40,746.

1992   January: Daniel Ewans ends his term as director of the Darwin Station, and will be replaced by American Chantal Blanton in May. The Japanese commercial fishing boat *Kaiyo Maru*, with sophisticated electronic equipment, drops anchor at Academy Bay, in

Puerto Ayora. On February 10, the *Donai*, an Ecuadorian fishing boat from Manta, is seized by the Ecuadorian navy patrol boat off Pinta with a load of 50 hammerhead sharks. Impounded, the sharks are found two days later on February 12 at the house of Copiano in Puerto Ayora, where they are slaughtered for illicit commercial purposes. The affair is reported in the international press (Europe and the US). The scandal of the exploitation of pepinos follows, with pirate camps established on the coast of Fernandina. In June: President Borja declares a ban on sea cucumber fishing. New Niño year, with warming of the sea and considerable rains, landslides above Santa Rosa (Santa Cruz). Construction in Puerto Ayora of the Thomas Fisher Science and Education Building, near the Darwin Station. A new wooden stairway is built at Bartolomé Island to stop the erosion of the trail and of the slope by the visitors (August). In September, a new system for the naturalist guide's course. Number of visitors: 39,510.

1993 Lobster fishing is banned for seven years until 2000. The National Park fee goes up to $80 for foreigners, and the port tax to $6. Blue whales are reported for the first time, by the research sailboat *Odyssey* south of Isabela (May), Fernandina, Cape Berkeley, Roca Redonda (David Day, personal communication). Telephone connections are now possible between the islands and the mainland. In September, arrival of the cruise ship *Ambassador I*, of the company Islas Galápagos Turismo y Vapores, of Mr. Zacharias in Quito. Pressure from Galápagos fishermen on the government of Sixto Duran Ballen, to suspend the ban on the fishing of pepinos. The American photographer Doug Perrine, takes underwater photos of hammerhead sharks caught in drift nets at Wolf Island (a letter is sent to the president of Ecuador). The number of visitors to the Galápagos reaches 46,818.

1994 The Department of Industry and Fisheries (MIIP) re-opens lobster fishing for three months (July 15 to October 15), pepinos fishing for three months (October 15 to January15), and shark fishing for three months (January 15 to April 15). One hundred and forty Japanese fishing boats are authorized to fish for tuna west of Isabela during the whole month of October, but must pay $20,000 each for the permit. Press campaign in Quito and Ecuador for the protection of the Marine Reserve. The number of visitors to the Park reaches 53,825.

1995 February: Death of Bernhard Schreyer an old German settler and owner of the schooner *Tigress*. February-March: Eruption of Fernandina Volcano and lava flows towards Cape Hammond. July: arrival of SPNG's new boat 'Guadalupe River' to patrol the Marine Reserve. Goats found on top on Volcan Wolf. September: new tortoise centre at Villamil (Isabela) named after Arnoldo Tupiza. After new law project made by Eduardo Velez and veto by President Sixto Ballen Duran, Pto.Ayora and Pto.Baquerizo go on strike for three weeks; assault of SPNG and CDRS offices. Army comes in. Introduction of goats on Pinta. Illegal fishing of 'pepinos' and shark goes on. Eight boats from Manabi found at Roca

Redonda, where a diver is attacked by a hammerhead shark. A Izurieta leaves Galápagos as Park's intendant. Number of visitors: 55,782.

1996   Chantal Blanton leaves as director of CDRS, replaced by Robert Bensted Smith (GB). M/N Galápagos Explorer hits the rocks in San Cristóbal and is sunk offshore. Road Itabaca- Pto. Ayoras asphalted. New dive centres: 'Scuba Iguana' (Hotel Galápagos) and 'Nautidiving' (Red Mangrove Inn). New president Abdala Bucaram prepares a law for protection of Marine Reserve, which is declared a 'biological reserve' by INEFAN in November. Number of visitors up to 61,500. December: Pierre Constant missing at sea after a scuba dive at the entrance of Darwin Bay (Genovese Is.). Swims one hour, 15 minutes with fins and two underwater cameras to reach the shore at the northern side of Darwin Bay. Notices whale bones and other mammal vertebrae on the lava rocks.

1997   Following corruption scandal and escape from Ecuador of President Abdala, Galápagos deputy Eduardo Velez (Rinon) disappears. Fanny Uribe ('Pepinera aletera') becomes new deputy of the Galápagos with Alfredo Serrano. March: sea cucumber fishing boat cap tured by *Guadalupe River* on west Isabela and northwest Fernandina. Julio Lopez of SPNG wounded by bullet fire by one of 20 armed men processing sea cucumbers. A peaceful demonstration of 300 people marches to reject violence in Galápagos. June: Abnormal warming of sea temperatures; 28° C west of Isabela until December. A new Niño is preparing at planet level. 'Nautidiving' of Polo Navarro stops its diving operations after boat wreck in Tortuga Bay. Report of penguins nesting on the northwest coast of Floreana Island (Cerro Daylight and Piedra Dura).

1998   January: Arrival of the new passenger cruise boat *Galápagos Explorer II*. March 11: Pepe Salcedo, captain of the yacht *Sulidae* falls off the cliff at South Plaza Island and survives with only one broken rib. April: El Niño is still strong with hot temperatures, calm and clear seas, but little rain. UNESCO forces Ecuador to a law of 40 nautical miles for the Marine Reserve but otherwise draws support and the title of World Heritage Site. April 20: Pepe Salcedo dies of a cardiac arrest.

Lexicon of the Fauna of the Galápagos

English	French	Spanish
SEABIRDS		
Common egret	Aigrette	Garza blanca
Waved Albatross	Albatros des Galápagos	Albatros de Galápagos
White-cheeked pintail	Canard Bahama	Patillo, pato
Flightless cormorant	Cormoran aptère	Cormoran no volador
Blue-footed booby	Fou à pattes bleues	Piquero patas azules
Red-footed booby	Fou à pattes rouges	Piquero patas rojas
Masked booby	Fou masqué	Piquero enmascarado
Magnificent frigatebird	Frégate magnifique	Fragata, tijereta
Great frigatebird	Grande frégate	Fragata comun
Great blue heron	Grand héron bleu	Garza azul
Lava heron	Héron des laves	Garza de lava
Yellow-crowned night heron	Héron de nuit	Garza nocturna
Oystercatcher	Huitrier	Ostrero, cangrejero
Galápagos penguin	Manchot des Galápagos	Pinguino de Galápagos
Swallowtail gull	Mouette à queue d'aronde	Gaviota colabifurcada
Lava gull	Mouette des laves	Gaviota de lava
Brown pelican	Pélican brun	Pelicano
Storm petrel	Pétrel des tempêtes	Golondrinas del mar
Hawaiian petrel	Pétrel hawaïen	Pata pegada
Redbill tropicbird	Phaéton, paille en queue	Rabijunco, pajaro tropical
Semipalmated plover	Pluvier semi-palm	
Audubon shearwater	Puffin d'Audubon	Pufino
Brown noddi	Noddi	Gaviotin
Sooty Tern	Sterne fuligineuse	Gaviotin
Royal Tern	Sterne royale	
Ruddy turnstone	Tourne pierres à collier	Vuelvepiedras
Whimbrel	Courlis	Zarapito
Common stilt	Echasse	Tero real
Flamingo	Flamant rose	Flamingo
Wandering tattler	Chevalier errant	
Sanderling	Becasseau sanderling	
Northern phalarope	Phalarope hyperboren	Falaropo
LAND BIRDS		
Smoothed-bill ani	Ani à bec doux	Garapatero
Galápagos hawk	Buse des Galápagos	Gavilan de Galápagos
Dark-billed cuckoo	Coulicou	Cuclillo, aguatero

ENGLISH	FRENCH	SPANISH
Barn owl	Effraie	Lechuza blanca
Yellow warbler	Fauvette jaune	Canario, maria
Short-eared owl	Hibou brachiotte	Lechuza de campo
Galápagos martin	Hirondelle des Galápagos	Golondrina
Galápagos mockingbird	Moqueur des Galápagos	Cucuve de Galápagos
Galápagos rail	Râle des Galápagos	Pachay
Painted-bill crake	Râle à bec rouge et jaune	Pachay
Galápagos dove	Tourterelle des Galápagos	Paloma de Galápagos
Large-billed flycatcher	Tyran à poitrine jaune	Papamoscas
Vermillion flycatcher	Tyran rouge	Brujo
Finches	Pinsons	Pinzones
Sharpbill Ground finch	Pinson à bec aiguisé	Pinzón de pico agudo
Carpenter finch	Pinson carpentier	Pinzón artesano
Warbler finch	Pinson chanteur	Pinzón cantor
Tree finch	Pinson des arbres	Pinzón arboreo
Small tree finch	- à petit bec	Pequeño pinzon arboreo
Medium tree finch	- à bec moyen	Mediano pinzon arboreo
Large tree finch	- à gros bec	Gran pinzon arboreo
Cactus finch	Pinson des cactus	Pinzón de tuna
Large cactus finch	Grand pinson des cactus	Gran pinzon de tuna
Mangrove finch	Pinson des paltuviers	Pinzón de manglar
Ground finch	Pinson de terre	Pinzón de tierra
Small ground finch	- à petit bec	Pequeno pinzon de tierra
Medium ground finch	- à bec moyen	Mediano pinzon de tierra
Large ground finch	- à gros bec	Gran pinzon de tierra
Common gallinule	Gallinule, poule d'eau	Gallinula comun
Purple gallinule	Gallinule violace	

REPTILES

Galápagos snake	Couloeuvre des Galápagos	Culebra
Gecko	Gecko	Salamanquesa
Marine iguana	Iguane marin	Iguana marina
Lang iguana	Iguane terrestre	Iguana terrestre
Lava lizard	Lézard des laves	Lagartija de lava
Black turtle	Tortue noire	Tortuga negra
Giant tortoise	Tortue géante	Galapago

MAMMALS

Feral donkey	Ane	Burro
Feral Cat	Chat	Gato salvage
Bat	Chauve-souris	Murcielago

ENGLISH	*FRENCH*	*SPANISH*
Wild horses	Chevaux sauvages	Caballos salvages
Feral goat	Chèvre sauvage	Chivo
Wild dog	Chien sauvage	Perro salvage
Fur sea lion	Otarie à fourrure	Lobo de dos pelos
Galápagos sea lion	Otarie des Galápagos	Lobo marino de Galápagos
Feral pig	Porc sauvage	Chancho
Galápagos rice rat	Rat de riz des Galápagos	Rata endemica
Black rat	Rat noir	Rata negra

FISHES AND MARINE LIFE

Galápagos garden eel	Anguille de jardin	Anguila de jardin
Yellow grouper	Bacalao, mérou jaune	Bacalao
Barracuda	Barracuda	Barracuda
Whale	Baleine	Ballena
Pacific amberjack	Carangue du Pacifique	Palometa
Slipper lobster	Cigale de mer	Langostino
Black coral	Corail noir	Coral negro
Shells	Coquillages	Conchas
Shrimp	Crevette	Camaron
Crab	Crabe	Cangrejo
Dolphin	Dauphin	Delfin
Blue lobster	Langouste bleue	Langosta azul
Red spiny lobster	Langouste rouge	Langosta roja
Green moray	Murène verte	Morena verde
Sea urchin	Oursin	Erizo de mar
Stingray	Raie à aiguillon	Raya de aguijon
Golden cownose ray	Raie dorée	Raya dorada
White spotted	Raie léopard	Raya aguila
Manta ray	Raie manta	Manta
Hornshark	Requin à cornes	Tiburon gato
White tip reef shark	Requin à pointes blanches	Tintorera
Blacktip shark	Requin à pointes noires	Tiburon aleta negra
Whale shark	Requin baleine	Tiburon ballena
Galápagos shark	Requin des Galápagos	Tiburon de Galápagos
Grey reef shark	Requin gris de récif	Tiburon gris
Hammerhead shark	Requin marteau	Tiburon martillo
Smooth hammerhead	Requin marteau lisse	Martillo
Scalloped hammerhead	Requin marteau à festons	Martillo
Tiger shark	Requin tigre	Tiburon tigre
Sea snake	Serpent marin	Culebra de mar
Tuna	Thon	Atun

APPENDICES

OCEANIC RESEARCH AND 'HOT SPOTS' IN THE GALÁPAGOS

Studies were conducted in the eastern Pacific Ocean, off the North American, Mexican and South American coasts, to explore the east Pacific mid-oceanic ridge and the transformation faults located along the ridge. During the summer of 1977, the American scientific submarine *Alvin* dived on the ridge at the latitude of the Galápagos islands. The fault is an extension of the southeast Pacific ridge, almost parallel to the equator, and separates the oceanic Cocos Plate (to the north) from the Nazca Plate (to the south). This is the tectonic hinge of the Central America/South America system. Westward and beyond the East Pacific Rise is the Pacific Plate.

Given these facts, we may conclude that the Galápagos archipelago is located on an important tectonic joint, which explains not only its volcanic nature, but also the fact that it is a hot spot, with quasi-permanent seismic and volcanic activity.

In the Galápagos rift, the spread of the plates is about eight to ten centimetres per year, while it is only 6.2 centimetres at the tip of Baja California, but 13.7 centimetres per year north of the equator and 17.5 centimetres per year at the latitude of Easter Island. That is to say that the Pacific Ocean opens up toward the south.

The dive of *Alvin* has observed hot springs, sulphur deposits and a very intense and localized life. The interest in the *Cyamex* dives, at a depth of 2,600 to 2,800 metres, mainly concerned with geological features, was then doubled. The scientists noted a biological and geological analogy with the dive of RITA (Riviera-Tamayo), which was made in 1979 in the rift (on the ridge) at the southern tip of Baja California. The geological conditions are the same, ie a rift spreading at an average of six to ten centimetres a year. The physical conditions and bathymetry are identical, and the temperature of the water is 2° C. Here, too, extremely hot springs, more or less active, bring about profuse sea life. Twenty new species have been reported, but in the Galápagos, a unique mussel was discovered which does not exist in the RITA zone.

These hot springs are not so frequent in the Atlantic, where if present, they are weak. This is due to the fact that the Atlantic mid-oceanic ridge has reached old age, which is evidenced by reduced activity, a slow speed of expansion, a thermic flux which is not so high and a more conspicuous hydrothermal metamorphism.

In contrast, proof of volcanic activity is spectacular in the Pacific. The French oceanographic ship *Jean Charcot* conducted a survey in March and April of 1980 between Ecuador and Easter Island, at 115° west longitude, where very localized gas emanations could portend a powerful submarine eruption. Such a deep-sea eruption was observed in 1991, 10° north of the equator, off the coast of Mexico, by the submersible *Alvin*.

Hot springs, loaded with black material, create true chimneys, with deposits of sulphur and other minerals. These fragile pipes are two or three metres high and made of sulfides of iron, tin, copper, lead, silver and gold. The temperature of the hydrothermal vents reaches 360-380° C. Basaltic landscapes of pillow lava and basalt columns were also observed.

The Americans found important thermal activity in the zone of the Galápagos. This prolific life is a real 'oasis of the deep', where giant tube worms of the species *Riftia pachyptila* (three metres long, and two to three centimetres wide) swarm, and where bacteria may survive at temperature up to 402° C.

All actual and recent volcanic zones are closely associated with seismic zones, which does not mean that one phenomenon is the cause of the other, but that both arise from a common origin. The latter resides in the movement of the lithospheric plates. The main volcanic and seismic zones coincide perfectly with the mobile joints of these plates.

Oceanic Ridges

Seismologic and oceanographic studies show that these are distension zones from which the expansion of the oceanic floor is made. These are characterized by a mean thermic flux (1.82 micro cal/cm2) which is superior to the mean thermic flux of the earth (1.5 micro cal/cm2) and which can reach up to 8 micro cal/cm2 in some areas called 'hot spots', the most active areas of the globe.

From the petrochemical point of view, it seems that in the stage of intense activity (fast expansion and high thermic flux) corresponds tholetic lava flows (subalkaline basalts), poorly or not at all affected by hydrothermal metamorphism of the oceanic floor. This is the case of the southeast Pacific.

Oceanic Archipelagoes

These are a chain of islands or submarine volcanoes, which are only active at one of their extremities. The volcanic formations getting older towards the other end. This is the case in the Galápagos. Some create a single chain from a 'hot spot' located far away from any ridge. Others are placed symmetrically on each side of a hot spot located on a ridge, eg Tuamotu-Easter Island, in the southeast Pacific (see map of the Hot Spots, page 15).

An abnormally high thermic flux creates a 'plume'. This magmatic plume is right on the hot spot, at least at the emerging ones. When such a plume hits a lithospheric plate, it pierces it like a laser beam. If the plate moves on the asthenosphere, the plume will leave its track on it, ie a chain of islands or a chain of submarine volcanoes. The farther they are from the point of origin, the older they are.

Distribution of the Land Birds According to Vegetation Zones

Mangrove Zone

Common
Herons
Yellow warbler
Small ground finch
Mockingbird

Present
Mangrove finch
Medium ground finch
Dark billed cuckoo
Small tree finch
Dark-billed cuckoo
Large-billed flycatcher
Short-eared owl

Arid Coastal Zone

Small ground finch
Medium ground finch
Cactus finch
Galápagos dove
Mockingbirds
Yellow warbler
Vegetarian finch

Large ground finch
Vegetarian finch
Carpenter finch
Large-billed flycatcher
Galápagos martin
Barn owl

Transition Zone Common

Small ground finch
Medium ground finch
Cactus finch
Small tree finch
Yellow warbler
Galápagos dove

Large ground finch
Carpenter finch
Warbler finch
Dark-billed cuckoo
Vermillion flycatcher
Short-eared owl

Tropical Humid Zone

Common
Warbler finch
Tree finches
Large-billed flycatcher
Vermillion flycatcher
Dark-billed cuckoo
Yellow warbler
Short-eared owl

Present
Small ground and medium ground finches
Mockingbirds
Carpenter finch
Barn owl

Herbs and Fern Zone

Galápagos rail
Galápagos martin

Small ground and medium ground finches
Short-eared owl

Appendix 3

Human Population of the Galápagos

In 1980, the resident population of the Galápagos was about 5,000 people. Ten years later, it had doubled. In 1995, it was estimated that the population had reached 20,000. Most immigration from the mainland is made up of Ecuadorian Indians and *mestizos* (mixed blood) who consider the Galápagos the new El Dorado, a touristic paradise where it seems easy to make money. But there is no such heaven, and problems become more apparent as time goes by and new settlers arrive: water and electricity problems (the power plant cannot meet the demands), problems of garbage disposal and pollution, poor medical and surgical facilities, disrespect for the rules of the National Park and abuses of all kinds, illegal fishing in the Reserve of Marine Resources, economic pressure, and so on.

Inhabited Islands in 1986

Number of Inhabitants

Santa Cruz	Baltra	San Cristobal	Isabela	Floreana
3,632	50	2,752	729	65
7 primary school 1 high school	air and naval base	8 primary schools 1 high school	3 primary schools 1 college	1 high school

At this time migration from the continent comprised 54 per cent men between 20 and 35 years, looking for work, and 15 per cent women. On San Cristobal, 66 per cent of the population is not native to the Galápagos; on Isabela, it is 50 per cent; and on Santa Cruz, 90 per cent. The number of cars in the islands increased from 88 in 1980 to 186 in 1986.

The population of Santa Cruz Island was around 10,000 people in 1994, and Cristobal's around 8,000 people.

TABLE OF MAPS AND ILLUSTRATIONS

" Flightless
cormorant "

PIROCO 1981

296

INDEX

"Great Frigates"

GLOSSARY

Andesitic .... From the name Andes. This type of volcanic material is found in the volcanoes of the South American mainland, above the subduction zone of the eastern Pacific, and due to a mix of granitic and basaltic materials. Grey in colour with small white crystals.

Caldera .... Huge craterlike depression formed by the subsidence of the upper part of a volcano following a series of dramatic collapses.

Dimorphism .... Two distinct forms of the same species.

Hornito or .... Pocket of gas escaping from the still-molten lava. When the flow
driblet cones encounters a pocket of moisture, the water is turned into steam and bubbles up through the flow. Patches of lava are flung into the air and pile up to form small chimneys less than one metres high.

Medio-oceanic ...... A chain of undersea mountains found at a depth of 2,500
ridge or mid metres below the ocean surface, resulting from the opening of the
-oceanic ridge oceanic crust, and from where magma expands constantly, pushing oceanic plates toward the continents. Known as the East Pacific Rise in the eastern Pacific Ocean.

Orthogonal .... Parallel fractures lines at right angles in a crisscross design.
fractures

Oviparous .... Egg-laying, as opposed to giving birth to live young.

Ovoviviparous ...... Giving birth to live young hatching from eggs held inside the body without receiving nutrients from the mother.

Pelagic .... Organisms living in open ocean waters, rather than close to the shore.

Plate tectonics ...... A theory that was initiated by Alfred Wegener in 1929, and then known as the 'drifting of the continents'. Later on perfected by the French Prof. Xavier Le Pichon in 1969, who renamed it 'plate tectonics'.

Scoria cones .... Or cinder cones. Explosive ejection of large amounts of solid volcanic rock thrown into the air, which deposit as tephra.

Subduction .... When the sea floor is forced under the continent, the oceanic plate goes under the continental plate in the subduction zone.

Tephra .... Solid fragments of different sizes from explosive volcanic eruptions.

Thermic flux .... A flow of temperature due to the 'magmatic soup' which circulates under the oceanic crust (creating convection currents), and which can be high, medium or low, according to its intensity. A hot spot is the result of a high thermic flux. It is calculated in micro calories per square centimetre.

Transformation .... A type of plate boundary that occurs where two plates are moving
fault past one another, with little or no destruction of plate material. Occurs along the mid-oceanic ridge and the Galápagos rift.

Viviparous .... Bearing live young, which have received nutrient from the mother.

BIBLIOGRAPHY

ANGERMEYER, Johanna. *My Father's Island,* Viking Penguin, 1989, London.

BOYCE, Barry. *Traveler's Guide to the Galápagos,* California.

COLLIN-DELAVAUD, Anne. *Guide de l'Equateur et des les Galápagos,* Ed. La Manufacture, 1993, Paris.

CONSTANT, Pierre. Notes des 'Cours de Guide Naturaliste 1980-82-86',Galápagos National Park Service, Puerto Ayora.

CONSTANT, Pierre. *Marine Life of the Galápagos—a guide to the fishes, whales, dolphins and other marine animals,* Paris, 1992. Ed Pierre Constant. (Distributed in the USA by Sea Challengers, 4 Sommerset Rise, Monterey, California.)

DARWIN, Charles. *Voyage d'un Naturaliste de la Terre de Feu aux îles Galápagos,* Ed Maspero, 1979, Paris.

GRANT, Peter. *Ecology and Evolution of Darwin's finches,* Princeton University Press, 1986.

HARRIS, Michael. *A Field Guide to the Birds of Galápagos,* Collins, London/Taiplinger, New York, 1974.

HICKMAN, John. *The Enchanted Island: the Galápagos Discovered,* Anthony Nelson, 1985, England.

JACKSON, Michael. *Galápagos, a Natural History Guide,* University of Calgary Press, 1995, Canada.

LA TORRE, Octavia. *La Maldicción de la Tortuga,* Quito, 1992, Ecuador.

MACBIRNEY
and WILLIAMS. *Geology and Petrology of the Galápagos Islands,* Geological Society of America, 1969.

MOORE, Tuy de Roy. *Galápagos, Islands Lost in Time,* Viking Press, 1980, New York.

MOORE, Tuy and Alan. *Guia del Parque Nacional Galápagos,* SPNG, 1980.

PERRY, Roger. *Galápagos, Key Environments,* Oxford, Pergamon, 1984.

STRAUCH, Dore. *Satan Came to Eden,* New York and London, 1935.

THORNTON, Ian. *Darwin's Islands: a Natural History of the Galápagos Islands* Natural History Press, Garden City, New York, 1971.

TREHERN, John. *The Galápagos Affair,* Jonathan Cape, 1983, London.

VONNEGUT, Kurt. *Galápagos,* Dell Publishing, Doubleday, 1985, New York.

WITTMER, Margret. *Floreana, Poste Restante,* Anthony Nelson, 1989, London.

ABOUT THE AUTHOR

Pierre Constant was born on December 3, 1954, in Boulogne sur Seine (near Paris), France. A student at the University of Pierre and Marie Curie - Paris VI, he earned a DEUG degree in biology-geology in 1975, then a master's in geology from Grenoble and Paris (1977-79). At the same time, he followed courses at the School of Anthropology in Paris (1977-78). Nevertheless, an unquenchable thirst for travelling has held him since 1974. The US, India, Central and South America, Pakistan and Nepal were his first travel experiences, followed later by the Philippines, Thailand, Japan, Malaysia, Papua New Guinea, Taiwan, Namibia and Madagascar.

The mirage of the Galápagos struck him in 1980. Having been selected by an English marine consultant (Julian Fitter), he signed a contract with an Ecuadorian company (represented in England), and was sent to Ecuador, where he attended the naturalist guide's course for the Galápagos National Park on Santa Cruz Island. He then worked in Ecuador for two years, in the Galápagos Islands and the Amazon jungle. Back in France, he published his first book, *L'Archipel des Galápagos* in 1983, and has become the French specialist on the Galápagos Islands for the last 13 years.

He organized expeditions and cruises for the agency Explorator, based in Paris (1984-86), then on his own ever since. Invited to radio and television programs in France and Switzerland (1983-84), he has also been a lecturer in different settings, including the 500-passenger French cruise ship *Mermoz* of the Compagnie Française des Croisières Paquet (1989), sailing from the Caribbean to the Galápagos. Constant organized two television programs of 'Ushuaïa' for the French TV TF1, leading Nicolas Hulot to the Galápagos (1990); he then organized the shooting of two video programmes: 'Animals of My Heart' (TF1) and 'Wildlife Sanctuaries' in the Galápagos, for XL Productions (1991), which aired on the Discovery Channel around the world. In 1992, he led a group of students of the Ushuaïa Foundation for a discovery and scientific mission in the islands.

Immersed in the underwater world of the Galápagos since 1984, Pierre Constant took up underwater photography and produced a new book (in English), *Marine Life of the Galápagos, a guide to the fishes, whales, dolphins and other marine animals (1992)*, in Hong Kong. The following year, he published a 1994 calendar of Galápagos marine life.

As a photojournalist, Pierre Constant has also published articles and reports on various countries, in travel and diving magazines, such as *Les Nouveaux Aventuriers, Iles Magazine, Voyager Magazine, Grands Reportages, Oceanorama, Apnea* and *Subaqua*, as well as in the American magazine *Ocean Realm,*and the Hong Kong-based magazine *Action Asia*.

Any person interested in the organization of trips and cruises in the Galápagos Islands, diving trips, filming trips or any other relevant subject may write to the author at the following address:

Pierre Constant   8 rue Erlanger, 75016 Paris - France
Phone: (331) 4224 8983 or (331) 4761 9329   Fax: (331) 4621 7736

The Man Who Planted Trees

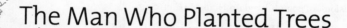

The Man Who Planted Trees

**A STORY OF LOST GROVES,
THE SCIENCE OF TREES, AND
A PLAN TO SAVE THE PLANET**

Jim Robbins

Random House

NEW YORK

Published in the United States by Random House,
an imprint and division of Penguin Random House LLC,
New York.

RANDOM HOUSE and the HOUSE colophon are
registered trademarks of Penguin Random House LLC.

Originally published in hardcover in the United States
by Spiegel & Grau, an imprint of Random House,
a division of Penguin Random House LLC, in 2012.

LIBRARY OF CONGRESS CATALOGING-IN-PUBLICATION DATA
Robbins, Jim.
The man who planted trees : a story of lost groves, the science
of trees, and a plan to save the planet / Jim Robbins.
p. cm.
ISBN 978-0-8129-8129-2
eBook ISBN 978-1-58836-999-4
1. Forest germplasm resources conservation.
2. Forest conservation. 3. Tree planting. I. Title.
SD399.7.R63 2012
333.75'16—dc23   2011040738

This book was printed in the United States of America
on Rolland Enviro™ 100 Book, which is manufactured
using FSC-certified 100% postconsumer fiber
and meets permanent paper standards.

randomhousebooks.com

9 8 7 6

Book design by Debbie Glasserman

Without the following people this book would not have been possible, and to them it is dedicated: To David, who showed up with his wild stories, changed everything, and let me tell his story. To my editor, Cindy Spiegel, and bless her Job-like patience. For Chere, whom I love. For Matthew Robbins and Annika Robbins, who will inherit the future we leave. For Leslie Lee, Diana Beresford-Kroeger, Bill Libby, Bill Werner, Meryl Marsh, Kerry Milarch, Jared Milarch, Jake Milarch, Michael Taylor, Marybeth Eckhout, Chris Kroeger, Andrew St. Ledger, and all those who are trying to make the world a better place. Thanks to Stuart Bernstein, my agent, who believed in this book, and Donna Dell Dowden, for the beautiful drawings. Hannah Berglund, thanks for your help and the crepes. And thank you, especially, to the trees, who do so much and ask for so little.

A fool sees not the same tree that a wise man sees.

WILLIAM BLAKE

Trees are the earth's endless effort to speak to the listening heaven.

RABINDRANATH TAGORE, *FIREFLIES,* 1928

A fool sees not the same tree that a wise man sees.

WILLIAM BLAKE

Trees are the earth's endless effort to speak to the listening heaven.

RABINDRANATH TAGORE, *FIREFLIES,* 1928

Preface

In 1993 my wife, Chere, and I bought fifteen acres of land on the outskirts of Helena, Montana. The property was tangled with a dense ponderosa pine forest so thick it's called dog hair, and some of the stubborn old trees had lived well there for centuries, in rocky terrain, marginal soil, and cold temperatures. We installed a Finnish woodstove called a *tulikivi*, a mammoth dark gray soapstone box about six feet tall, in the middle of the living room of our new house. Tulikivis are highly efficient because the soft, dense stone mass around the firebox soaks up heat from a roaring fire and holds the warmth for 24 hours. Heat from the stone is radiant, softer and more pleasant than the heat from a burning fire. It's also clean—woodstove pollution comes from damping down a fire so that it burns slowly, which gives off a dense cloud of smoke. This stove burns hot.

Our forest and stove were the perfect marriage—we planned to thin the trees gradually and feed the fire with what we cut. We had more than enough wood, I figured, to last not only my lifetime, but my children's and grandchildren's. We were fireproofing our home as well, reducing the fuel in the woods around us in case a wildfire should blow up. Thinning would help open the dense forest for the wildlife that occasionally appeared. A moose ran through the yard one day, a black bear turned over the barbecue, a bobcat sauntered by. The eerie ululating howls of coyotes echoed at night and sent chills down my dog's neck, and she wailed from her bed in the front hall.

One day in 2003, as I was hiking through the woods to town, I saw my first "fader." A fader is a tree that has been attacked and killed by insects and is slowly fading from green to a reddish brown. In this case the perpetrator was the mountain pine beetle, a small dark insect that burrows beneath the bark and lays its eggs. Larvae hatch and eat the *phloem,* a thin, moist membrane under the bark that is a life support system for the tree. As the grubs gobble their way around the trunk, they cut the crown of the tree off from its source of water and from nutrients in the soil; the life in the tree ebbs, and it fades slowly from life to death. Alarmed at the outbreak, I quickly chainsawed down the red tree and stripped off the bark to expose the insects to the cold. But I noticed several other large trees that, while still green, had been infected. Having finished this one off, the bugs had flown to other nearby trees to begin again.

The appearance and efflorescence of these bugs paralleled a series of warmer winters the West has experienced in the last few decades. In the 1970s and 1980s, winter usually meant two or three weeks or more of temperatures 20, 30, or 40 degrees Fahrenheit below zero. Since the 1980s the temperature has dipped into 30 below territory only a handful of times and never for a long period, and it has never fallen anywhere near the record of 70 below set in 1954. The warmer wintertime minimum temperatures make a huge difference to the bugs. The larvae are well adapted and manufacture their own supply of glycol—the same chemical found in automobile antifreeze—as they head into winter. They easily survive temperatures of 20 and 30 below.

Bark beetles such as the mountain pine beetle are highly evolved and ruthlessly efficient—the beetle's Latin genus name, *Dendroctonus*, means tree killer. They carry a blue fungus from tree to tree in pouches under their legs, a super-rich food source that they plant in the host tree. As it grows, they feed it to their young. After the larvae feast, they turn into adults, each the size of a letter on this page, and hatch from the host tree by the thousands. Swarming to a nearby uninfected tree, they tunnel through the bark, and once ensconced, they send out a chemical mist called a *pheromone*, a scented request for reinforcements. They need to overwhelm the tree quickly in order to kill it. When their numbers are large enough, they send out a follow-up pheromone message that says the tree is full. Each infected tree produces enough new insects to infect five to eight other trees.

The telltale signs of an infected tree are ivory-colored, nickel-sized plugs that look like candle wax plastered on the trunks, which mean the tree is pumping out resin to try to drown a drilling bug. Sometimes a tree wins by entombing a beetle; far more often these days, the tree loses to the mob assault. The stress caused by warmer temperatures and drought makes it harder for the trees to muster enough resin to resist attacks.

A year after I saw the first fader, a dozen trees in our backyard forest were dead. Then things went exponential. A dozen dead trees turned to thirty, which turned to 150, dying far faster than I could cut them down and turn them into firewood. Finally, five years after the first infected tree, virtually all of our trees were dead. We threw in the towel and hired loggers to come in and cut our trees down.

Enormous machinery rumbled into our woods on tank treads. A piece of equipment called an "excadozer" grabbed a tree, cut it off at the base, and stripped the branches in less than a minute. I watched trees falling around the house, heard the angry hornet whine of chain saws, and looked below to see our forest piled up like Lincoln logs ready to be turned into paste. The tang of pine scent hung thickly in the air.

It's eerie when the tree reaper comes to claim your forest and renders the once living world around you stone dead. When the forest is gone and the sky opens up, it's disorienting, as if someone has removed a wall of your house. Broken branches, smashed limbs, and slivered stumps were all that was left; tank tread marks scarred the exposed forest floor. "It's like open-heart surgery," said my "personal logger," Levi. "You don't want to watch while it's going on, but in the end it's a good thing."

The loggers hauled the logs off on trucks and loaded them onto a freight train headed for Missoula, Montana, where they were sold to a paper plant, which chipped them and turned them into an oatmeal-like slurry to become cardboard boxes. It cost us about a thousand dollars an acre to cut and ship out our dead trees. They have little value as lumber because of the blue stain from the fungus the beetles inject. And there are so many dead trees in Montana these days that it's a buyer's market. The landscape looks postapocalyptic in many places.

The once forested hill behind our house is now a meadow. A perch on a grassy hilltop a short hike from my house reveals an entire mountain valley draped with trees, nearly all of which are dead and dying. All around Helena, in fact, the forests are mostly dead, a jumble of rust-red dead trees.

Trees and forests come and go all the time. Like fire, beetles are agents of the natural cycle of life and death; they break down trees so their nutrients can be absorbed into the soil and used by the next generation of trees. But the boundaries between what is natural and what is unnatural have broken down—and this outbreak and others in the West appear to be unnatural. Climate change, experts say, is partly a human artifact and has elevated the beetles into a much larger destructive role than they might otherwise play. Freed from their usual boundary of cold temperatures, they have broadened their range and claimed more territory, going higher in altitude and pushing farther north than ever. They used to hatch from their tree and fly to a new host during two weeks in July; now they fly all summer and part of the fall. They used to attack only trees over five inches in diameter; now they are eating trees no bigger around than my thumb. Although the growing season for forests is two weeks or more longer than it used to be, the amount of precipitation is the same, and so the trees must go longer with the same amount of water, which has stressed them and reduced their defenses.

As I researched and wrote stories for *The New York Times*

and other publications about this massive change in the woods, it dawned on me—I mean really dawned on me—that North America's cordillera, the mountains that extend from Alaska to northern New Mexico, and that include my patch of forest, were ground zero for the largest die-off of forests in recorded history. "A continental-scale phenomenon," said one shocked scientist. Suddenly climate change hit home.

Imagine a world without trees.

It was no longer an abstract question for me. The forests on my property, in the valley where I live, in my region, and in much of my state are dying. The speed and thoroughness of the die-off is stunning.

Take a minute to imagine if every tree around your home, your city, your state were to wither and die. What would the world be like? And it promises to become much worse if even the most conservative climate predictions come to pass. Few people are thinking about the future of forests and trees.

Credit where credit is due. This book began a decade ago with vital questions that I never heard asked until they were posed by a third-generation shade tree farmer who claimed he had died and gone to heaven and then returned. He was worried about the future of the global forest and told me that the trees that make up most of the world's forests are the genetic runts—the scraps left after the last few centuries of orgiastic clear-cutting, which selected out the biggest, straightest, and healthiest trees. There is a strong, urgent case to be made that this is true, that we are witnessing a kind of evolution in reverse, and that genetically our forests are a shadow of what they once were and may not be strong enough to survive on a rapidly warming planet.

For a long time I doubted that this farmer, a recovering alcoholic, former competitive arm wrestler, and street brawler who claimed a fantastic ride out of his body and back, really knew what was going on with the world's trees. And then forests in my backyard and state and region and continent started dying; not just a few trees, but trees by the millions. They are still dying. His ideas seem more valid every day.

Aldo Leopold wrote that "to keep every cog and wheel is the first precaution of intelligent tinkering." It's unimpeachable common sense that we have ignored. When it comes to our ancient forests, we have nearly wiped them out—more than 90 percent of America's old-growth forest is gone and is still being cut, and some 80 percent of the world's has vanished. Yet we have only begun—*only begun*—to understand the ecological role these forests play or what secrets might be locked away in their genes.

Forests hold the natural world together. They have cradled the existence of our species since we first appeared—trees and forests are the highest-functioning members of ecological society, irreplaceable players at the apex of the complex ecological web around us. They are ecosystem engineers that create the conditions for other forms of life to exist, on every level. As I worked on this book the Gulf oil spill occurred, and was widely covered as the black tarry substance fouled beaches and killed wildlife. The loss of our trees and forests, our ecological infrastructure, isn't nearly as dramatic; it's a quiet crisis. But the impacts are far greater.

·   ·   ·

THIS BOOK IS about several things. It is first and foremost about David Milarch, the aforementioned tree farmer and an interesting guy if there ever was one. It is about the longtime human love affair with trees and forests, a love affair that has ebbed and flowed but has been ongoing since the dawn of humans, since our ancestors first climbed into them to escape predators. It is a book about the science of trees and of forests, and about the unappreciated roles they play in sustaining life on the planet.

Trees are responsible for half the photosynthesis on land, taking in the energy from sunlight and transforming it to leaves, where that energy is usable by insects and mammals and birds. They are highly evolved water management specialists; a forest is a soft carpet on the landscape that allows a downpour to reach the ground gently rather than in a torrent, so that it can be absorbed rather than run off and can recharge groundwater. Trees feed oxygen and minerals into the ocean; create rain; render mercury, nitrates, and other toxic wastes in the soil harmless; gather and neutralize sulfur dioxide, ozone, carbon dioxide, and other harmful air pollutants in their tissue; create homes and building materials; offer shade; provide medicine; and produce a wide variety of nuts and fruits. They sustain all manner of wildlife, birds, and insects with an array of food and shelter. They are the planet's heat shield, slowing the evaporation of water and cooling the earth. They generate vast clouds of chemicals that are vital to myriad aspects of the earth's ecosystems and likely vital to our health and well-being. They are natural reservoirs—as much as a hundred gallons of water can be stored in the crown of a large tree. The water they release is part of a largely unrecognized water cycle.

Even viewed conservatively, trees are worth far more than they cost to plant and maintain. The U.S. Forest Service's Center for Urban Forest Research found a ten-degree difference between the cool of a shaded park in Tucson and the open Sonoran desert. A tree planted in the right place, the center estimates, reduces the demand for air conditioning and can save 100 kilowatt hours in annual electrical use, about 2 to 8 percent of total use. Strategically planted trees can also shelter homes from wind, and in cold weather they can reduce heating fuel costs by 10 to 12 percent. A million strategically planted trees, the center figures, can save $10 million in energy costs. And trees increase property values, as much as 1 percent for each mature tree. These savings are offset somewhat by the cost of planting and maintaining trees, but on balance, if we had to pay for the services that trees provide, we couldn't afford them. Because trees offer their services in silence, and for free, we take them for granted.

This book also delves into the long history of the sacred aspects of trees, a worship that has been around for as long as people have. There is a view among many to this day that trees were a gift from the creator, placed here to provide for our basic food and shelter needs. Across cultures and across time, trees have been revered as sacred, as living antennae conducting divine energies. "The groves were God's first temples," wrote William Cullen Bryant in his 1824 poem "A Forest Hymn."

Science has not, as we like to think, conquered every realm. And one of the places it has a great deal of work to do is with the trees. What an irony it is that these living beings whose shade we sit in, whose fruit we eat, whose limbs we climb, whose roots

we water, to whom most of us rarely give a second thought, are
so poorly understood. We need to come, as soon as possible, to a
profound understanding and appreciation for trees and forests
and the vital roles that they play, for they are among our best
allies in the uncertain future that is unfolding.

Contents

The Man Who Planted Trees

CHAPTER I

Champion Tree

THE ORIGINAL BOOK TITLED *The Man Who Planted Trees* is a slim volume, just four thousand words; in fact, it was first published as a story in *Vogue* magazine in 1954. That book was written as a fable by a Frenchman named Jean Giono and has tapped a deep well in the human imagination, and since its publication in book form, it has sold close to half a million copies. Speaking in the first person, its unnamed narrator describes hiking through the French Alps in 1910, enjoying the wilderness. As he passes through a desolate, parched mountain valley where crumbling buildings testify to a vanished settlement, he comes across a middle-aged shepherd taking his flock out to pasture. The shepherd has one hundred acorns with him, and he plants them as he cares for his sheep. It turns out that the shepherd has planted more than a hundred thousand trees on this barren, wind-ravaged landscape.

Six years later, after surviving the front lines of World War I, the narrator returns to the shepherd's hut. He is surprised to see small trees "spread out as far as the eye could reach. Creation seemed to have come about in a sort of chain reaction. . . . I saw water flowing in brooks that had been dry since the memory of man. . . . The wind, too, scattered seeds. As the water reappeared so too there reappeared willows, rushes, meadows, gardens, flowers and a certain purpose in being alive."

As the years go by, the trees grow taller and the forest in the valley grows thicker, and a dying ecosystem is transformed into a thriving one. When the narrator returns for a third time, toward the end of the story, more than ten thousand people are living in the flourishing valley.

> Everything was changed. Even the air. Instead of the harsh dry winds that used to attack me, a gentle breeze was blowing, laden with scents. A sound like water came from the mountains: it was the wind in the forest. Most amazing of all, I saw that a fountain had been built, that it flowed freely and—what touched me most—that someone had planted a linden beside it, a linden that must have been four years old, already in full leaf, the incontestable symbol of resurrection.

Some experts say *The Man Who Planted Trees* is wishful thinking, that reforestation cannot effect the kind of transformation imagined in the book, bringing a barren landscape back to life and bringing harmony to the people who live there. Planting trees, I myself thought for a long time, was a feel-good thing, a nice but feeble response to our litany of modern-day environmental problems. In the last few years, though, as I have read many dozens of articles and books and interviewed scientists here and abroad, my thinking has changed. Planting trees may be the single most important ecotechnology that we have to put the broken pieces of our planet back together.

Take the growing number of emerging infectious diseases. Their connection to the natural world is one of the most revelatory things I discovered about how little we understand the role of forests. I learned that there is a surprising single cause that connects a range of viral diseases including hantavirus, HIV, Ebola, SARS, swine flu, and West Nile virus with bacterial diseases including malaria and Lyme disease. Rather than just being a health issue, these deadly diseases are, at root, an ecological problem.

To put it in a nutshell, the teams of scientists researching the origins of disease say that pathogens don't just mysteriously appear and find their way into human populations; they are the direct result of the damage people have done, and continue to do, to the natural world, and they are preventable. "Any emerging disease in the last thirty or forty years has come about as a result of encroachment into forest," says Dr. Peter Daszak, director of EcoHealth Alliance, a New York–based international NGO that is pioneering the field of conservation medicine. "Three hundred and thirty new diseases have emerged since 1940, and it's a big problem." Most of these diseases are zoonotic, which means they originate in wildlife, whether in bats or deer or ticks, which then infect people who live near the forest. It's believed, for example, that the human immunodeficiency (HIV) virus crossed the species barrier from monkeys to humans when a bushmeat hunter killed a chimpanzee, caught the virus from the animal, and brought the disease out of the jungle and into the world of humans. Fragmenting forests by building subdivisons in the oak forests of Long Island or logging in the mahogany forests of Brazil degrades the ecosystems and exacerbates disease transmission to humans.

SO THIS BOOK is not just about planting trees. It is about the state and the likely fate of the world's forests as the planet journeys into a possibly disastrous century of soaring temperatures. Precisely what such rapid warming is doing, and will do, to the forests is unknown, but more virulent pests and diseases, drought, climate extremes, high winds, and an increase in solar radiation will likely take a steep toll on the forests.

We are beyond known limits, and traveling farther beyond them every day.

What will happen to the trees and forests? There is no formal predictive model because trees and forests have been poorly studied; there are no long-term data, and the world's forests are extremely varied and complicated. Despite the lack of data, it doesn't take an ecologist to imagine what could happen. Apparently, though, it takes a journey into another realm to come up with an idea about what might be done to save our oldest trees in the event the changes become catastrophic.

My journey into the world of trees started in 2001, when I

read an article about an organization called the Champion Tree Project. At the time, the group's goal was to clone the champion of each of the 826 species of trees in the United States, make hundreds or thousands of copies, and plant the offspring in "living archival libraries" around the country to preserve the trees' DNA. A "champion" is a tree that has the highest combined score of three measurements: height, crown size, and diameter at breast height. The project's cofounder, David Milarch, a shade tree nurseryman from Copemish, Michigan, a village near Traverse City, said he eventually hoped to both sell and give away the baby trees cloned from the giants. "Clones," in this case, are human-assisted copies of trees made by taking cuttings of a tree and growing them—an old and widely used horticultural technique for growing plants. Unlike a seedling, which may have only 50 percent of the genetics of its parent, a clone of a tree is a 100 percent genetic duplicate of its parent.

I have always been drawn to big old trees, and the idea of making new trees with the genes of champions was compelling. I proposed a story to *The New York Times* science section about the idea, got the assignment, and drove to Big Timber, Montana, not far from my home, to visit Martin Flanagan, a lanky working cowboy and tree lover who helped gather materials for Milarch's Champion Tree Project in the West. On a bluebird day in May, Flanagan drove me down along the Yellowstone River, bank-full and the color of chocolate milk, as the spring sun melted snow in the mountains. He showed me several large trees, including a towering narrow-leaf cottonwood. "This is the one I plan to nominate for state champ," he said excitedly, spanking the tree with his hand. "It's a beauty, isn't it?"

There wasn't much to the Champion Tree organization, I found out. It was mostly a good idea with a tiny budget, with Milarch and occasionally one of his teenage sons working out of his home in Michigan; Flanagan working part time in Montana, driving around in a beat-up pickup truck gathering cuttings; and Terry Mock, from Palm Beach, Florida, who was the director.

Over the next week I interviewed Milarch several times by phone, and he talked to me about the need to clone champion trees. "The genetics of the biggest trees is disappearing. Someone's got to clone them and keep a record. No one knows what they mean. Let's protect them so they can be studied in case they are important. A tree that lives a thousand years might know something about survival." I also interviewed several scientists who agreed that researchers don't know the role that genetics plays in the longevity and survivability of trees; it simply hasn't been assessed. Environmental conditions, including soil and moisture, are obviously critical as well. Two identical clones planted twenty feet apart might grow far differently. Almost all of them said, however, that in the absence of study, it's Botany 101 that genetics is a critical part of what's essential to a long-lived tree. If you want to plant a tree and walk away and have it live, it makes sense to plant a tree that is the genetically fittest you can find. The big old-timers have proven their genetic mettle; they are survivors. Or as General George Cates, former chairman of the National Tree Trust, put it to me, "You can bet Wilt Chamberlain's parents weren't five foot one and five foot two."

Dr. Frank Gouin, a plant physiologist and the retired chairman of the horticulture department at the University of Maryland, is a friend of the project and spoke to me in support of the notion of cloning. He had cloned a big tree himself, the legendary 460-year-old Wye Oak on Maryland's eastern shore. "These trees are like people who have smoked all their lives and drank all their lives and are still kicking," Gouin said. "Let's study them." And the way to perpetuate and study them, he said, is just the way Champion Tree proposes.

My story about Champion Tree ran on the front of the *Science Times* section on July 10, 2001, with several color photographs of various champions, and over the next few days other media picked up the story. After a flurry of interviews, including eleven minutes on the *Today* show, Milarch, flabbergasted at the reach of the *Times*, called me. "It put us on the map, big time," he said. "I can't thank you enough." He said he wanted to come to Montana to meet me and give me a gift of a champion green ash tree as a thank-you. Though I loved the idea of a champion of my own, professional ethics prevented me from accepting the gift. "Let's plant one on the Montana capitol grounds instead," he suggested.

Fine, I said, a gift to the state.

With the attacks of 9/11, the tree planting wouldn't come until the following year. On a warm, sunny June day, David Milarch came to my office in downtown Helena and introduced himself with a big hand. He is a jovial bear of a man, six foot three with broad shoulders and big arms. He looks like a lumberjack and was dressed like a farmer, in a short-sleeved snap-button shirt, jeans, and a plastic foam farm cap that said OLYMPICS 2002, and he carried a hard-shelled briefcase. There is a bit of Viking in him, not only in his outgoing personality and swagger but in his ruddy complexion, though the hair that is left is white. A small strip of wispy white beard didn't cover his ample chin. A belly spilled over his belt.

Milarch has the charm gene, and I liked him right away. A born storyteller, he laughs loudly and frequently, and he has a flair for the dramatic and a fondness for announcing things rather than just saying them. He is an expert in the use of compliments, but pours it on a little too thick sometimes. As we talked he flipped open his briefcase and pulled out a crumpled pack of Marlboro Lights, put one in his mouth, and, in a practiced move, lit a cigarette with one hand by leaving the match attached to the book, folding it over, and lighting it with his thumb.

Over lunch, I expected a chat about the science of big tree genetics. I was wrong. As we sat down at a local restaurant, Milarch began a story. In 1991, he told me, he died and went to heaven. Literally. A serious drinker, he had quit cold turkey. The sudden withdrawal of alcohol caused kidney and liver failure, and a friend had to carry him to the emergency room, where a doctor managed to stabilize him. The next night, his wife and his mother beside him, he felt himself rise. Not his body, he said, but his awareness—he could look down from the top of the room and see himself lying there. It was a full-blown near-death experience, a phenomenon also known as disambiguation, something; at the time, I'd never heard of. His consciousness, he said, left the room and soon passed through brilliant white light—"It was like a goddamn blowtorch!" he told me. On the "other side" he was told it wasn't his time, that he still had work to do on earth, and he needed to go back. When his awareness returned to his body, he sat up in bed, shocking his wife and mother, who thought he was dead.

The experience changed him—afterward he felt more alive and more present—and he understood, for the first time, he said, the importance of unconditional love. He appreciated his children and family more, and had a deeper connection to music and art. He felt more intuitive and more spiritual, even more electric, so charged that he couldn't wear a wristwatch or use a computer—they were affected by his body's electrical properties, which had been enhanced somehow. He wasn't perfect; there was still some of the old David there. But it existed along with this new part of him.

Months later, still adjusting to this new life, he was visited in the early morning hours by light beings, who roused him. The big trees were dying, they told him, it was going to get much worse, and they had an assignment for him.

In the morning he told his kids that the family had a mission—to begin a project to clone the champion of every tree species in the country and plant them far and wide. They were a farm family in the middle of what many call nowhere, a world away from environmental groups and fund-raising and politics and science. But the Milarchs were hopeful, naïvely so, and unaware of the obstacles that confronted them.

Lunch came and I was quietly incredulous. Was I really hearing this? I thought he was joking or spinning a yarn, but he said it all with a straight face. It was, to say the least, the most unusual origin of a science story I'd ever heard. I'd had no inkling of any of it during phone interviews. It didn't diminish the science, as far as I was concerned, because all the scientists I'd interviewed for the story said cloning trees to save genetics is a scientifically sound idea. Where people sourced their inspiration didn't matter if the science passed the test. Still, it was curious. And this chain-smoking tree farmer who liberally deployed the F-bomb didn't fit the mold of the typical New Ager.

During his visit over the next couple of days, Milarch laid out his take on what humans have done to the world's forests, based on his peculiar blend of science and intuition, and how the Champion Tree Project wanted to change that. "People should be awestruck, outraged, overwhelmed," he said. "A tree that is five, six, eight, or fifteen feet across, the champions we are cloning, is what the size of all the trees in our forests once was, that all of America was covered with, not just one lone, last soldier standing. When we look at the trees around us, we're looking at the runts, the leftovers. The whole country should be forested coast to coast with these giants, not with the puny, scraggly, miserable mess we call our forests. We don't realize what we've lost."

"The champions are in harm's way," he told me. "They do their best in communities that are hundreds or thousands of acres. They're struggling in little pockets to hang on. We either get on it and get it done, or in twenty years they'll be gone. If man doesn't take them out, Mother Nature will. We're in the fifty-ninth minute of the last hour."

"Why do these light beings care about trees?" I asked.

"They are concerned about the survival of the planet. Call them light beings, plant *devas,* earth spirits, or angels, they are real, and there are some in charge of the trees. Americans are about the only ones who don't believe in such things, but they are out there and a lot of people can hear them, including me. We treat the earth like it's dead, which allows us to do what we want, but it's not dead." Genetics is critical to the survival of the forests, they told him, and one day science will be able to prove it.

He has taken his lumps from critics, including from some scientists who say he doesn't know about science, and that it's not known if genetics is what make these trees survivors. They say it could be just plain luck that these trees have survived. It's not a bad idea to clone the trees, they say, just not necessary. Others have said that it is impossible to clone a two-thousand-year-old tree—that it's akin to asking a ninety-year-old woman to give birth.

"They can criticize all they want. But these are the supertrees, and they have stood the test of time," said Milarch. "Until we started cloning the nation's largest and oldest trees, they were allowed to tip over, and their genes to disappear. Is that good science? If you saw the last dinosaur egg, would you pick it up and save it for study or let it disappear?"

What we have lost by mowing down the forests around the world, he insists, is far more than big trees. We've squandered the genetic fitness of future forests. With humans high grading, cutting down the best trees time and again, the great irreplaceable trove of DNA that had been shaped and strengthened over millennia by surviving drought, disease, pestilence, heat, and cold—the genetic memory—was also gone. The DNA that may be best suited for the tree's journey into an uncertain future on a warming planet has all but vanished, just when we need it most. By making copies of the cream of the big tree crop and planting

thousands or tens of thousands of the 100 percent genetic copies of these "last soldiers standing" all over the country or the
world, Milarch wants to ensure that they will live on. They may
well not turn out to be better, but if they do turn out to have superior traits, then their genetic traits have been saved—"money in
the bank," Milarch says. When it comes to trees, proven survivor status is all we have to go on. Trees cradle human existence
in ways known and many more ways unknown, he said. "And if
we lose the trees, we're in a world of hurt."

There are myriad other reasons to plant trees, of course. It's a
way to address climate change by soaking up carbon dioxide. Los
Angeles, for example, has a campaign to plant a million trees;
if it reaches its goal, because each tree will store two hundred
pounds of carbon annually, that will be the equivalent of taking seven thousand cars off the road every year. Trees also filter
air pollution, water pollution, and toxic waste in the soil. Flooding, though often thought of as a natural catastrophe, is more
often than not man-made, caused when water is unleashed
from the natural storage and regulation of forests and marshes,
exacerbated by deforestation. A one-hundred-year flood event
becomes a one-in-five-year event when deforested land cover is
a quarter of the total. The floods caused by deforestation also
last longer—4 to 8 percent longer for each 10 percent of the forest that is lost. And the floods are more severe than when forests
are intact. Ninety percent of the natural disasters in the United
States involve flooding, and floods have become far more frequent, largely because of deforestation. Recent unprecedented
floods in Pakistan may have been in large part the results of a
warmer planet—2010 was the warmest year on record, and a

warmer atmosphere holds more moisture. But Pakistan also has one of the highest rates of deforestation in the world. Between 1990 and 2005 it lost a quarter of its natural forest cover. An irony is at work here: as the climate grows warmer, the atmosphere will carry even more precipitation. Already, scientists say, rainstorms and snowfall have become more extreme. The increased precipitation around the globe in the coming years will occur when the landscape is least equipped to handle it.

"It seems hopeless," Milarch said. "The planet is warming and we hear this bad news all the time. We decided to do something. With no money and no staff. Some of the experts told us it couldn't be done. But we couldn't just sit here and watch the ship go down. And we are doing it. And we hope it's an example to other families." Someday, Milarch went on, he envisioned a movement, people planting clones of a global collection of thousands of the world's great trees, from the cedars of Lebanon to the ancient oaks of Scotland, Ireland, and England—not only to restore forests, but to create functioning old-growth forests in cities and suburbs around the world. Living among them, we would be able to take advantage of their ecosystem services, their ability to cool hot asphalt, to protect us from ultraviolet radiation, to cleanse the soil and air of pollutants, to grow nuts and fruits, to calm us and beautify our surroundings.

It was such big talk for a farmer who had no funding, even if he had died and gone to heaven. He wanted me to write a book about his inspiration, but I couldn't see it. There's a saying in Montana: Big hat, no cattle. How would he ever bring his fascinating idea to fruition with no funding? Besides, I'm a science reporter, and I had trouble coming to terms with a wild story about out-of-body travel to heavenly realms and back. He was asking me to believe in a magical universe, and it was a big step to take over lunch.

While I didn't see a book in his tale, Milarch certainly had my attention and started me thinking. There was something in what he said, and the way he said it, that I couldn't dismiss. This was in 2001, before my own forest had started to die. Could he be right about forest die-off? Are the world's trees in big trouble? Is old-growth genetics important? I had written a great deal about forests in my thirty years as a journalist, but never with these ideas in mind.

Not long after David's visit, I joined classes from a local high school in a small ceremony on the front lawn of Montana's capitol. As we planted a champion green ash tree that the Champion Tree Project had sent by truck, the marching band played the theme from *Mission: Impossible*.

CHAPTER 2
White Oak

IN 1996, DAVID MILARCH called Frank Gouin to see if the Champion Tree Project could obtain a clone of the venerable Wye Oak, the country's oldest and largest white oak tree, named for the nearby town of Wye Mills, on Maryland's eastern shore. At the time, it was just under 32 feet in circumference, nearly 7 feet in diameter, and 96 feet tall, and the crown of the tree covered a third of an acre.

Dating to the sixteenth century, the Wye Oak witnessed the changes of history. The Choptank Trail alongside it grew from an Indian footpath through the woods to a wagon road to a highway. Because of its size, the tree was a local landmark as far back as the mid-nineteenth century. The Wye Oak got official recognition in 1909, when Maryland's state forester, Fred Besley—who also created the Champion Tree measurement formula and the first list of champions in 1925—measured and photographed it and later named it one of the first champions on his list.

Visitors started coming by to see it. In 1939, the Maryland General Assembly, recognizing the tree's historic and champion status, purchased one acre of ground around it to create a park. As the old oak started to decline, foresters for the state of Maryland made a valiant effort to keep the tree alive. Its base was hollow, and they dropped cyanide pellets into the cavity to kill termites and carpenter ants; they supported the branches with long strands of thick steel cable to keep them from breaking. "Man, it was a big tree," said Gouin. "Four guys could sit around a table and play cards in the cavity of that tree."

As a horticulturalist and tree lover, Gouin took note as state foresters tried repeatedly to clone the Wye Oak. "Nurserymen have always had a tough time grafting oak trees because they are so slow-growing," said Gouin, referring to the way that the cells on the tip and root stock combine slowly. "The state had spent some twenty-seven years trying to clone the Wye with grafting and budding and tissue culture. They were not able to, though they had tried everything."

But Gouin, with a thick shock of white hair and an Amish-style beard, is a master gardener who grows Christmas trees, persimmons, and peaches, and when Milarch called he was moved by Milarch's notion of cloning each of the champions. He also felt there was something special about the Wye Oak, and that those traits were likely stored in the genes. "A lot of white oaks get blight, but I have never seen blight on this tree," he said. "No oak wilt and no gypsy moths, either."

Trees are most often cloned by taking a six-inch or so cutting of the newest growth. A small opening is scraped into the cambium layer at the base of the cutting. It's then immersed in a mix of soil and hormones, and if the procedure is successful, new roots emerge from the small scrape. But Gouin had a different idea. Over a period of three years, he took three hundred cuttings of scion wood from the tree each spring. Scion wood is part of a branch that has several buds on it, and Gouin grafted those cuttings onto the roots of seedlings from the Wye Oak, which had been grown from acorns and so had inherited at least 50 percent of their genetics from the parent Wye and 50 percent from another tree, through pollination. Using such closely related root stock, Gouin figured, would be comparable to a bone marrow transplant among family members and would reduce the possibility of rejection. He used a tight rubber band to join the roots and the tips together. Getting the graft to retain moisture long enough for the slow-growing oak tips to successfully connect with the root was critical, so he wrapped them in tape and then buried them in soil.

The first year, just two cuttings of the three hundred taken were successfully grafted. The second year, he took fresh cuttings and nine clones survived. The third year, in 2002, Gouin visited the clones more often, making the 140-mile round trip to the nursery once a week to ensure that the soil was kept consistently wet and cool, and thirty clones of the Wye Oak grew. "I finally figured out what I was doing," said Gouin. Subsequent years, he felt, would produce even more clones. On June 6 of that year, however, a violent thunderstorm roared across the eastern shore and toppled the Wye Oak. Gouin drove straight to the fallen tree to take more fresh cuttings before the branches perished, but it was the wrong time of year. "We couldn't get any more good budwood," he said, "and none of them took."

After the oak fell, thousands of people from around the region went to pay their last respects to the fallen champion, mournfully taking pictures and gathering pieces of the tree. "We all kind of hoped the Wye Oak would never fall down," said Maureen Brooks, coordinator of the Maryland Big Tree Program.

Two of the Wye Oak clones were given to Mount Vernon for an Arbor Day planting, and they now grow there on George Washington's estate. Another clone is planted inside the stump of the old Wye Oak and is producing acorns. The other clones are in a seed orchard operated by the State of Maryland Department of Forestry and are sexually mature. "The clones are already producing acorns," said Gouin, "and you can buy a seedling from the state of Maryland."

The Wye Oak may be gone, but its genetic heirs live on.

CHAPTER 3

Forests on a Warmer Planet

IN 1982, A controversial and cryptic visionary named John Allen, along with his followers, built a $200 million structure called Biosphere 2 in the saguaro-studded Sonoran desert north of Tucson. The glass-and-steel-tube dome and other buildings, the size of two and a half football fields, are a contradiction in terms: a man-made natural environment that includes a mini-savanna, desert, ocean, coral reef, and tropical rain forest. The vivarium, as the complex of buildings is known, was meant to be a self-sustaining mini–Planet Earth that would function like the real Earth, with no external input.

Biosphere 2 was a pilot project for the day Allen and his followers hoped they could fly the pieces of the vivarium to Mars, assemble it there, and allow the group to "terra-form" the planet to create a human habitat. One by one, they thought, biospheres flown to Mars could be used to create a reservoir of trees, flowers, and other forms of plant life until one day the planet would be covered in vegetation and would sustain life as Earth does. The project collapsed, however, and the University of Arizona took over Biosphere 2.

While it didn't colonize the red planet, Biosphere 2 has proven nifty for studying planet Earth because it allows researchers to control variables and play out different scenarios in a way that can't be done in the real world. In 2009, two researchers, Henry Adams of the University of Arizona's ecology and evolutionary biology department and his professor David D. Breshears of the University of Arizona's School of Natural Resources, moved twenty mature piñon pine trees, five to six feet tall, into the dome and split them into two groups of ten. One group was placed in a chamber where conditions were equal to what they are today, and the other group was placed in conditions some seven degrees Fahrenheit warmer than it is now—roughly equal to the high end of the temperature rise scientists predict for the next century. Once the trees established themselves, researchers deprived both populations of water.

The human-induced drought killed the trees in the warmer chamber 28 percent faster than the trees in the chamber with normal temperatures. The message from the mini-Earth, researchers say, is that forest die-offs could increase by a factor of five if the climate warms seven degrees as predicted over the next century. "Droughts can kill trees faster when the temperatures are warmer," Breshears said. "Instead of one die-off in one hundred years, that number could increase by a factor of five. That's the take-home message. When I saw that in the data I went 'wow' and 'yikes.' This looks like a big deal, and it's based on temperature alone."

Based on temperature alone. That means the study looked only at the effect of warmer temperatures on trees, and not at the effect of warmer temperatures on disease and insects as well, which in concert with water stress kill many more trees than drought alone. And it makes the very conservative assumption that the increase in forest die-offs as temperatures increase will be linear rather than curvilinear. "Curvilinear means it gets a little warmer and it will kill a few more trees," said Breshears. "Then a little warmer, only this time it kills a lot more trees and perhaps a lot more species of tree."

The most recent forecast for the mean global temperature rise by the end of the century is 6.3 degrees Fahrenheit. That's a huge change in a very short period of time. Since the last ice age, twelve thousand years ago, the average global temperature has stayed fairly steady. If the global average increases as forecast, the changes will be wrenching, and the climate won't just get warmer. James Hansen, who heads the NASA Goddard Institute for Space Studies, writes in his book *Storms of My Grandchildren* that under present predictions, the earth is on track to see 20 percent of its species become extinct or be on their way to extinction by the end of the century, and to see droughts, heat waves, and forest fires of unprecedented ferocity, rapidly rising sea levels, and more storms with hurricane-force winds. E. O. Wilson, the distinguished professor of biology at Harvard, believes that by 2100, *half* of all plant and animal species could be extinct. Some leading scientists think we are in the beginning stages of a new mass extinction, one of six in

Earth's history. This one is different from the others, they say, because it is brought on by humans through the fragmentation of the natural landscape, the introduction of exotic species and new pathogens, the alteration of the climate, and unsustainable exploitation of plant and animal species.

Here's one of the ways warmer temperatures impact trees. A critical part of a tree is a cell found in its leaves and needles, called a *stoma*. Each of these pores is surrounded by two guard cells that act as a kind of valve, opening and closing the stoma according to changes in light, humidity, and the concentration of carbon dioxide. The tree takes water up from the ground through its roots and transpires it—that is, it releases water vapor into the atmosphere—through the stomata. As the water makes its way up to the canopy, it supplies not only moisture but also minerals to the entire tree.

But along with releasing water, the stomata also take in carbon dioxide for photosynthesis. So when they open, it is at the cost of releasing the tree's water stores. The death of the trees in Biosphere 2 was due to something called *carbon starvation*—at least, that's the hypothesis, because precisely how an individual tree dies is not clear. Researchers do know that when a drought hits, a hormone released by the tree tells the stomata to close in order to preserve the dwindling water supply in the air spaces of the leaf. With its stomata closed, though, the tree can no longer take in carbon dioxide, and so photosynthesis stops, and it must use its carbon stores, the food stashed in its pantry. When those stores are gone, the tree perishes. What Breshears and Adams hypothesize is that warmer temperatures cause trees to use up their carbon stores faster. "The tree says, 'I am going to close my stomata and ride this out,' " Breshears explained. " 'I am not going to do anything until I get more water.' But you are paying a cost every day, and at some point you collapse because you run out of juice."

THERE'S A STORY about a drunk searching for his car keys under a streetlight. Another man walks by and asks him what he is doing. The first man says he is looking for his car keys, and the second asks where he dropped them. "Over there," the first man says, gesturing toward the dark. "But there's more light here."

It's an apt metaphor for science. Many important subjects are difficult to study, or generate little profit, or aren't popular, and so they are largely ignored. So we assume implicitly they are not important. Much about trees and forests, it turns out, falls outside the ring of light.

Virtually every scientist I interviewed for this book said the same thing: we are hamstrung in assessing the health and risks to forests by an overwhelming lack of data and knowledge. So if we are waiting for a team of distinguished scientists to issue a report warning that the world's forests are in crisis and recommending a ten-point plan to fix them, forget it. The future of the world's forests is a black box and no one can reliably predict what is going to happen on a stable planet, let alone on one as unstable as ours is forecast to become. And the impact to the world's forests may already be well under way.

The giant forest die-offs in the Rocky Mountain West that my small forest tract is part of exemplify the secondary impact of warmer temperatures that Breshears referenced—in my case, bark beetles—and those secondary aspects may be far more deadly and unpredictable than heat and drought alone. In the last half century, the two-degree rise that has occurred in the West has already begun to turn ecosystems inside out, and the anomalous behavior of insects is one of those changes.

Dr. Diana L. Six is an entomologist at the University of Montana, and she knows well the biological amplification warmer temperatures bring. As we toured a beetle-killed forest, buzzing along dirt logging roads in the Blackfoot Valley, a half hour's drive out of Missoula, she explained how things have changed in her neck of the woods. "I used to plan my field season for the same two or three weeks in July," she said, which is when her quarry, tiny black mountain pine beetles, hatched from the tree they had just killed and swarmed to a new one. "Now everything is different. Instead of just two weeks, the beetles fly constantly from May until October, attacking trees, burrowing in, and laying their eggs for fully half the year." There are other anomalies. The beetles rarely used to attack immature trees, and now they do so all the time. And there's evidence that the beetles are switching to other species of tree, which has been unheard of. In some high places where the beetles had a two-year life cycle because of cold temperatures, it's changed to a one-year cycle, which means that their populations can increase more rapidly during warm droughts when their host trees are most stressed, resulting in more beetles doing a lot more damage.

In some ways, Dr. Six allowed, it's an exciting time to be an entomologist as the field's textbooks get rewritten. But it's also deeply unsettling. Large-scale die-off sometimes happens in a forest, she knows, but this magnitude is surreal. "A couple of degrees warmer could create multiple generations of beetles a year," she told me as she chopped a piece of bark off a dead lodgepole pine to show me the galleries of burrowing larvae, shallow squiggly channels in the wood. Trees here are the standing dead, varying shades of gray and brown, their bark drying and falling to the ground in jigsaw-puzzle pieces. "If that happens, I expect it would be a disaster for all of our pine populations." She looked around for a minute, more than a little aghast at how the ordered world of her science has been upended. "The whole ecosystem is changing," she said. "I've never seen anything like it."

As of 2010, across Colorado, Wyoming, Idaho, and Montana, about eight million acres of lodgepole and ponderosa pine had been killed. That's small change compared to what has happened recently in the Canadian province of British Columbia. The second largest known die-off occurred there in the 1980s and claimed a million and a half acres. The latest has claimed 43 million acres. By the time the outbreak ends, British Columbia may lose 80 percent of its old-growth lodgepole pine trees. Moreover, a freak wind event a few years ago blew the insects across the Continental Divide for the first time in history, and, freed from the bitterly cold temperatures that once kept them in check, they could, Canadian officials fear, munch their way across Canada's boreal forest, which forms a crescent across the northern half of the country, all the way to the Atlantic Ocean. This insect damage to Canada's forest comes on top of the devastation of the mature forests of British Columbia by logging. The only thing harder on trees than beetles, it seems, is people.

Dr. Craig D. Allen is a forest ecologist with Jemez Mountains

Field Station, part of the U.S. Geological Survey, the federal agency that studies the earth's natural systems. He's one of the scientists at the center of the study of climate-related forest changes and is a core member of the USGS Western Mountain Initiative, a coalition of six federal agency scientists and numerous university colleagues who are studying mountain ecosystems across the western United States and how these unique ecosystems are responding to a warming climate. He also works on forest die-offs in other parts of the world. Wiry and intense, with short graying hair and glasses, Allen has memorized a global list of troubling die-offs, and he hits the highlights as we walk through the Ancestral Pueblo ruins near his office in Bandelier National Monument. In 2005, for example, a one-year climate event in the Amazon, an El Niño drought accompanied by high winds, killed large numbers of trees. This event is well documented because so many researchers had study plots on the ground for other research projects. Moreover, during the drought, a violent storm swept through the region, and according to experts from NASA and Tulane University, that single storm killed a whopping half a billion trees in forty-eight hours. That year, the Amazon Basin went from being a carbon sink to being a source of carbon to the atmosphere. In 2010 another, even more severe drought struck.

But to see part of one of the worst cases of forest die-off ever documented, Allen needed look no farther than out his office window. In crystalline sunshine, as only the Southwest can do it, we walked across a mesa-top of dead, gray needleless piñons. This is the southern end of the sprawling patchwork of die-off that stretches from here, a couple of hundred miles north of the

Mexican border, all the way to Alaska—and includes the trees in my backyard forest. Former secretary of the interior Ken Salazar has called the die-off in the Rocky Mountains the West's version of Hurricane Katrina.

The die-off around the Southwest is attributed to a five-year drought that struck in 2000 and killed 90 percent of the trees in some areas, with widespread mortality across millions of acres. Populations of many species of bark beetles exploded (the Arizona pine engraver, pinyon ips beetle, and the Southwest pine beetle among them) and attacked many different tree species, presumably because the forests were stressed by drought, although this is one of the many things that researchers don't know for sure. And it's a conundrum that gets to the heart of attempts to assess forest die-offs.

It would seem a no-brainer to say that this die-off is caused by a warmer climate. In the last half century the average temperature in the Rocky Mountain West has gone up some two degrees, but the wintertime minimum temperatures—the really cold below-zero temperatures that kill overwintering beetles—have soared fifteen to twenty degrees, allowing more insects to survive. But there are so many other factors—fire suppression that has resulted in too many trees, for example, and a lack of research in key areas—that scientists can't say for certain that there's a direct link. "There are huge information gaps and uncertainties," Allen told me. "Huge. We don't even know for sure exactly how a tree dies. Not only can we not predict mortality, we can't even tell you for sure if forest mortality is increasing globally in recent years, as there hasn't been consistent long-term monitoring." If scientists could predict die-offs in the same way that climate forecasters can forecast rising sea levels, land managers could take preemptive action, such as mechanically thinning dense forest, or prescribing fires to reduce tree numbers. With fewer trees, moisture goes further, which increases the vigor of stressed forests, and it might allow them to fend off insects and disease. Even those actions, though, may just buy time as temperatures warm.

A dying forest is problem enough, but when large landscapes die they become contributors to a warming climate, a cycle called a *positive feedback loop*. One of the most important things forests do for life on the planet is to capture carbon dioxide from the atmosphere and store it as plant tissue; trees contain half of the terrestrial stores, more than any other single source on land. Otherwise the carbon dioxide would still be in the atmosphere, causing more warming. When forests die or are cut down, they release that stored carbon dioxide into the atmosphere; in fact those sources comprise 20 percent of annual carbon emissions. So much forest has died in British Columbia that, just as in the Amazon, the province went from being a net carbon sink—it sequestered more carbon than it emitted—to a carbon source in 2008. More global forest die-offs and their carbon releases compound warming, which can cause more forests to die, and around it goes.

Another example of a cycle that is changing weather patterns to create drier conditions involves heavy isotopes found in water. Mature trees take up as much as four hundred gallons of water per day, more than they need, and release much of it into the atmosphere, and the moist exhalation of the forests

moves with the prevailing winds. Without this forest phenomenon, much of the interior of countries would be desert. It's
difficult to research, but some new studies shed some light on
how coastal forests create optimum growing conditions for forests a great distance away. In the Amazon, researchers found
that not all water is created equal. One in every 500 molecules
of water they examined had a heavier than normal hydrogen
atom, and one in every 6,500 water molecules had a heavy version of the oxygen atom. While the heavier molecules are much
slower to evaporate from surface water, the researchers found
that these molecules were readily pumped into the atmosphere
through transpiration, the release of moisture into the atmosphere through the leaves of trees. Forests, in other words, are
key to keeping these heavy molecules moving through the water
cycle. Research shows that in the last few decades, the number
of heavy molecules has significantly declined, because so much
of the forest has been cut down. "With many trees now gone
and the forest degraded, the moisture that reaches the Andes
has clearly lost the heavy isotopes that used to be recycled so
effectively," scientists reported. That has markedly reduced the
amount of rainfall.

Trees are also home to an unusual microorganism that may
be a major contributor to rainfall, something scientists are just
beginning to understand. Dr. David Sands, a researcher at Montana State University, and several colleagues have identified bacteria called *Pseudomonas syringae* that make their home on the
leaves of most vegetation. The research team believes that as
these bacteria are swept into the atmosphere and absorbed into

clouds, a protein in them forms the nucleus for rain. When they fall to earth in rain and snow, they find their way back onto the leaves, where they multiply and start the cycle over again.

IN SPITE OF the lack of data and research, many scientists, Six and Allen among them, believe something unprecedented is happening to the world's forests. In Colorado, for example, not only have the mature lodgepole pines nearly been wiped out, but the quaking aspen, a deciduous tree famous for turning the mountain slopes a brilliant yellow in the fall, is also in danger. In 2005, researchers noticed that the aspens were dying in large numbers; thirty thousand acres perished that year. A hundred fifty thousand died the next year, and the number soared to more than half a million acres out of a total of about five million acres the following year. Not only are mature aspen stems dying, but the root mass underground, the source of all the trees aboveground, is dying. The rapid decline slowed in 2010, but experts say it was probably because of a couple of wet winters, and they fear the die-off could return.

In November 2012 the front pages of British newspapers erupted with the alarming news that a fungal disease had begun to infect the country's iconic ash trees. The disease, called ash dieback, likely came from continental Europe, where it has already killed millions of trees. Experts say that Britain's ash population could be devastated in the coming decades, as happened in Denmark in 2003, where 90 percent of the trees were killed.

Diana Six told me that she suspects that hotter, drier weather and a shift in rainfall patterns are responsible for unusual mortality rates in other places where she works. "Whole hillsides are suddenly dropping dead in South Africa," she told me. "It's happening so fast people are in shock. It's a tragedy." The dying species include the quiver tree—so named because it's fashioned by tribesmen into quivers to carry arrows—the camel thorn, and the giant euphorbia, a beautiful, weirdly shaped thirty-foot-tall succulent that looks like something out of a Dr. Seuss book.

"The feeling about forest die-off," said Allen, who is in touch with researchers around the globe, "is that there's a lot of it and it's flying under the radar." He can make that statement as a person who knows a lot about trees and forests, but as a scientist armed with nailed-down, bulletproof fact, he cannot. It's a painful situation to believe that there's a climate change crisis in the forests and not to be able to sound the alarm. "These recent die-offs we are seeing are before we put two to four degrees centigrade of warming into the system," said Allen, referring to the prediction for the rest of this century. "We don't know how much stress the forests of the world can take."

CHAPTER 4
Bristlecone

BRISTLECONE PINE FORESTS are found on mountaintops in Colorado, Utah, Nevada, California, and New Mexico. The oldest of the bristlecones, named for the bristlelike spine on their cones, are nearly five thousand years old, almost twice the age of redwoods and sequoias, yet a fraction of their size. The tallest specimen rises to just sixty feet, and most are much shorter. Not only are they the oldest trees in the world, they are among the world's oldest living organisms.*

The Great Basin bristlecone pines that grow in Great Basin

---

* Bristlecones are the oldest trees, but there are root masses below ground, or "clonal colonies," from which much younger trees grow on the surface. The known oldest of these is Pando, or the "Trembling Giant," an eighty-thousand-year-old aspen root mass in Utah and, at 6,600 tons, the world's heaviest organism. Although some might consider Pando the oldest living tree, when discussing trees I am referring to those lone trees that suffer the slings and arrows of the aboveground environment.

National Park in eastern Nevada are one of three species of the tree. The Wheeler Peak Grove there, in a mountain cirque, is one of my favorite groves of any species. The trees are gnomish, twisted into bizarre shapes like sculptures or giant bonsai trees, an adaptation to life in this harsh part of the world. The soil is rocky and alkaline, with few nutrients, and the winters are ten months long. The trees are exposed to high winds in this aerie, and their crowns often lean way over, while others hug the ground, a response called *wind training*. The bristlecone has survived in this unforgiving environment with an unusual strategy: as a main root dies, the section of trunk above it dies as well. But the tree keeps a small strip of living tissue alive. Until the climate started warming, the ability to adapt to extreme weather was its greatest strength, a strategy its enemies could not match.

Wheeler Peak is the grove where Prometheus fell, a bristlecone tree named by a group of local researchers and tree enthusiasts in the 1950s. It was "stooped as under a burden, with roots like claws grasping the ground, a magnificent monster standing alone," wrote a local author named Darwin Lambert, who helped name it, in a piece for *Audubon* magazine. "Four spans of my outstretched arms, six feet to the reach, were needed to encircle the misshapen trunk." They named it after the Greek demigod who was immortal and chained to a mountain crest by Zeus for aiding humans with the gifts of fire and art.

In 1964, a graduate student in geography from the University of North Carolina at Chapel Hill, Donald Rusk Currey, came to Wheeler Peak to study climate records in tree rings. Because bristlecones are so long-lived, they harbor an unparalleled record in their thousands of rings. There are conflicting accounts about what happened next, but apparently Currey drilled into Prometheus—whose name he did not know and whom he called WPN-114, for it was the 114th tree he sampled—to withdraw a core sample, thinking it was very old and held a long record of climate. Unfortunately his drill got stuck. Without it, he couldn't continue his research, so he cut down the bristlecone to retrieve the tool. Currey carried a slice of the bristlecone back to his motel and sat outside in the desert sun to count its rings. He finished at 4,844, but he believed the tree to be even older because the section wasn't from the bottom of the tree, which contained additional rings. Prometheus, he estimated, was at least 4,900 years old, perhaps 5,000, when he abruptly ended its life. Others believe it was 5,100 years old. It was the oldest known tree in the world.

Lambert was heartsick when he read Currey's paper in the journal *Ecology* and realized what the scientist had done. "The wounds open every time—to this day—when the memories of that ancient tree surface," he wrote later. Prometheus became a martyr to the cause of bristlecone protection. Lambert used the story of the destruction of the tree to campaign for national park status for the grove, and in 1986, Great Basin National Park was established.

Now, almost five decades later, and after five millennia dwelling at the roof of the world, all of the bristlecone pines may soon meet their match—though the threat is not the chain saw. The study of tree rings from the ancient trees shows that in the last fifty years, temperatures in the lair of the bristlecone are warmer than they have been in any other fifty-year period in the last 3,700 years. And that means the frigid temperatures that once protected the trees by killing off threatening insects are disappearing and the trees are becoming more defenseless.

Compounding the attack of the bark beetles is blister rust, a fungal disease that came to the West Coast from Asia, via Europe, on a shipment of white pine seedlings in 1900, spread across the West, and a hundred years later has reached the most remote and inaccessible mountaintops—probably because the climate has warmed. Because blister rust kills young trees quickly, and the pine beetle kills older trees, which produce seeds, the future of the bristlecone appears grim—in fact, over the coming decades, scientists say, all of the ancient bristlecones in the West will likely die out. So scientists are searching for trees that are resistant to the rust and planting seeds from those trees to grow new bristlecones, which they say offers the best chance for survival of the species. The case of the bristlecone illustrates the importance of preserving a range of genetics in a changing world. But while a new crop of the resistant pines will carry on the species, the oldest trees in the world will most likely not survive.

The loss of the bristlecone might represent more than the loss of a single species; it could be a loss to the entire ecosystem. The bristlecones and other mountaintop pines are what are known as *foundation species*—they create conditions that allow other species to gain a foothold, by providing habitat, food, and shelter. They build small pockets of soil in between their roots where other trees can grow, and they slow the melting of snow with their shade, which causes a slower release of spring runoff.

The bristlecones are also a window into longevity. They are members of an exclusive club of organisms on the planet that defy senescence—they don't appear to age, or to age very much. Even at several thousand years old they reproduce as if they were still teenagers. No one knows why or how they live so long. The question, sadly, is whether they will live long enough for us to find out.

CHAPTER 5

Great Unknowns

DAVID MILARCH WAS born in Detroit on October 5, 1949. His great-grandparents had emigrated from Germany and Ireland to Michigan, where they cleared forty acres near Copemish to grow food for a family of ten. After World War II there was more money to be made in the city, so the family decamped for suburban Detroit. His father, Edward, owned E. L. Milarch Nursery, where he grew shade trees and ran a construction company. It was here that Milarch learned the nursery business, working long, backbreaking days. "From the time I was eight or nine I worked in the nursery," he told me. "I dug and balled trees, dug holes to plant them in frozen ground, hoed, and did all kinds of things like that. My father was a driven man. He had the old-school German philosophy that every day every man earns his salt. He was stern and harsh to the extreme and taught me the discipline of hard work from a young age. There was never any margin. He would probably go to jail today for how I was raised as a child and how I was punished."

Milarch vowed that things would be different in his own family. He is a firm believer in what he calls "mind power," and he tried to instill in his sons the power of positive thinking. "I'd have the kids say these things over and over again: 'The impossible just takes longer.' 'If you think you can't, you're right.' 'Our enemies hold our greatest messages and opportunities.' 'What other people think of you is none of your business.' 'Firmly believe in something, or you will fall for anything.' 'The true measure of a man is not how he falls, it's how he gets back up.'

" 'Boys, what are the limits?,' I'd ask them. 'There aren't any,' they were taught to answer back. 'What can you have?' 'Anything!' Starting when they were two years old, I recorded these sayings on cassette and played them over and over again, overdubbing all the negative things in the world. Hearing positive self-talk is valuable for kids."

In the summer of 1992, several months after he had his near-death experience and his vision, David and his twelve-year-old son Jared gathered the first big tree DNA. Jared had been moved by his father's vision. "When that idea came to him he woke me, and it was like a lightning bolt," Jared Milarch says. "I said 'Yeah, we have to do this.' He always had ideas, and we were always looking for something that had passion in it, but he'd never come up with something like this."

Kerry Milarch was not that surprised by the turn of events. "It was like 'Okay, whatever,' " she says. "He's never been conventional in any way. He seemed to really believe it, but I also thought, 'Maybe he's off his rocker.' "

The younger Milarch thought cloning the champions was good for another reason. "We noticed that the trees on the farm that used to thrive twenty or thirty years ago just weren't growing as well. We thought a lot of the problem was because of warmer temperatures, but some of it was poor plant stock. The shade tree industry has grown the same trees for fifty years, and has not done much improvement in the genetics. When my dad told me about his idea of cloning the champions I thought it might help us grow a better shade tree." For the first few years they sent off cuttings from wild sugar maple saplings. Milarch's father had dug thousands of young trees in the woods on his property over the years to sell at his nursery business, and of those he found some that were extremely fast-growing and cold-hardy from surviving Michigan winters. If they could clone and reproduce those trees, they thought, they could sell a line of Michigan sugar maples. They called the two lines Chippewa Fire and Camp Fire, and they sold them for a while, but more important, the experience taught them how to clone trees.

They collected champion genetics here and there, but it wasn't until the summer of 1994 that they made their first major foray. A bankruptcy had left them with very little, and they had to borrow a pickup truck, pruner, and aluminum ladder from Milarch's father. They obtained a list of the state and national champions from Elwood "Woody" Ehrle, a professor of biology at Western Michigan University and keeper of the state register of big trees, and they drove to Antrim County, Michigan, to a house with the national champion green ash in the front yard, one of fifty-one national champions in the state.

The elder Milarch knocked on the door. "It's a beautiful tree you got there," he told the owner, and he asked permission to take a few cuttings. Jared climbed up the low-hanging limbs with the pruner and brought back a baggie full of new growth snipped from the very end of the branches. Then they took photos of themselves standing by the giant. "If it works," Milarch told the homeowner as they left, "we'll send you a copy." The Milarchs had bagged their first tree. Over the next two days they collected material from four other trees. They shipped the buds to Schmidt's, a large commercial nursery in Oregon that had volunteered to do the cloning for free if they could keep some of the clones.

The discovery and cloning of the Buckley Elm in 1997 created the first national press for Champion Tree. Evelyn Sika, the postmistress at Milarch's rural post office, knew he was working on champion trees and for months had bent his ear about the big tree in the middle of a cornfield south of Traverse City, Michigan, not far from his shade tree farm. And every time Milarch picked up his mail he would agree to go see it, but he never got around to it. One day, Sika made Milarch promise to visit the tree. "You've got to go see the big tree I played under every day as a girl," she said. "You've got to." It was raining that particular day, so Milarch thought, why not today. As his pickup truck approached the field where the tree stood, he was floored. "From a mile away I could see that thing, and I could see how big it was. My God, the crown on it towered over all the other trees. It looked like King Kong. It was eleven stories high and the trunk was eight feet across, a wall of wood. When I got up to it I was at a loss for words."

Moreover, the tree appeared to be an elm. Nearly all of America's elms had died from Dutch elm disease, and here was a giant living specimen. Milarch sent some leaves and bark to Woody Ehrle. It was indeed an elm, and more than four hundred years old. Ehrle couldn't believe it either. It must have survived, he thought, because of its remoteness.

Milarch had heard stories about the big hardwood forests that had stood here in his great-grandfather's time, and finally seeing one of the biggest trees for himself was like a window into the past. The reigning champion elm, near Louisville, Kansas, had just been blown up with a pipe bomb and killed, by a vandal or terrorist of some kind, and Milarch helped nominate this tree, which became the new national champion.

The Traverse City newspaper, the *Record-Eagle,* ran a front-page story about the giant "lost" elm, centering on the Milarch family and Champion Tree; then the *Chicago Tribune* wrote a front-page story describing it as so big that two ranch houses could fit beneath its crown. The radio broadcaster Paul Harvey mentioned it on his show. The owners put a kitchen chair out in front of the tree with a Tupperware container that held a notebook and asked people who came to see it to write their name and their thoughts. More than a thousand people signed in.

The Buckley Elm died in 2002, of Dutch elm disease, perhaps weakened by the fact that its roots were damaged from plowing in the cornfield around it. Fortunately Milarch and his son Jared, with the help of Dow Botanical Gardens, made three clones before it died, and they planted them in three places, including at the Interlochen Center for the Arts.

When the first stories about Champion Tree came out—in

December 1996, their project was the subject of a cover story in the national nursery trade publication *American Nurseryman,* with color photos spread across five pages—the family started to get occasional unannounced visits from Native Americans. "They call them grandfather trees, and they wanted to know what we were doing," Milarch said. "Because we were messing with their fifteen-thousand-year-old drugstores, and we were messing with the spiritual home of their ancestors, because some Native Americans believe their ancestors live in those trees. But when they heard that the project was helping the trees live on, they were okay with that."

Something that struck Milarch as odd was the fact that no one had thought of cloning these big old trees before. Cloning in itself was not difficult; any nursery could clone a fruit tree. Cloning shade trees was more difficult; only a few nurseries were doing it. No one had ever succeeded in cloning the ancient trees; it was thought to be nearly impossible. But everyone knew that genetics could be critical to a tree's health and longevity. Here he was, a nurseryman with little formal schooling, and some of the country's top tree experts were agreeing with his idea to clone trees to preserve their genetic record. What other simple things weren't known or imagined about trees, he wondered.

In the early 2000s, Kerry Milarch bought a book called *Arboretum America: A Philosophy of the Forest* by a botanist, medical biochemist, and author named Diana Beresford-Kroeger. Beresford-Kroeger's message is that the role of forests in maintaining the health of the natural world is far more extensive, and far more critical, than is generally appreciated. We know that trees filter water and air, and that they provide habitats for all manner of insects, which are the first level of the food chain. What is generally overlooked, though, she argues, is the role of the chemicals emitted by trees in the maintenance of the biosphere. "Kerry handed it to me and said, 'You have to read this book.' I was flabbergasted when I read it," Milarch says. "She was the first person who saw the big picture, the global role that trees play. She knew about the medicine in trees, the aerosols, the critical environmental role they play in the world, and the same mysteries of trees that I knew. I found her number and called her, and we bonded immediately and knew we had the same task." The task, he said, was to reforest the planet.

Beresford-Kroeger had emigrated to Canada from Ireland in 1969. Her research ranges from scanning microscopy on trees to foundation cardiovascular research for heart transplants and artificial blood at the University of Ottawa School of Medicine. For the last thirty years she has conducted research in her 160-acre garden and arboretum, funding the work herself. Her books have attracted the attention of some well-known scientists. E. O. Wilson told me he finds her work fascinating. "Her ideas are a rare, if not entirely new approach to natural history," he said. In a foreword to one of her books he referred to her as part Druid and part scientist and wrote, "Beresford-Kroeger speaks for the trees as well as it has ever been done." Dame Miriam Rothschild, a distinguished naturalist, has raved about Beresford-Kroeger's notion of bioplanning—a sustainability system that includes planting trees and other plants according to where their aerosols will do the most good.

"When you peel an orange and get a cloud of mist in the air, that's an aerosol," Beresford-Kroeger explained to me when

I visited her rural home near Ottawa, Canada. She pointed to a towering wafer ash tree. "It's a chemical factory," she said, and the aerosols the tree emits are part of a sophisticated survival strategy. When the showy, creamy, greenish white flowers bloom in the spring, they broadcast terpene oils into the air, which repel mammals that might feed on the tree. But the ash needs to attract pollinators, and so the flowers also have a powerful lactone fragrance that appeals to large butterflies and honeybees. The chemicals in the flowers in turn provide protection for the butterflies from preying birds, because they have a bitter taste. The trees emit medicinal compounds as well. Fox, deer, and other wildlife rub against trees and shrubs, while birds, bats, and honeybees feed and fly among the leaves, and all of them are showered by a range of antifungal, antibacterial, antiviral, and anticancer compounds that protect them from disease and infection. Beresford-Kroeger also believes that the clouds of aerosols emitted by forests are scrubbers that disinfect the air. "A forest of pines acts as an air sweep, cleansing and soporifying the atmosphere anywhere they grow in the global garden. Other trees do likewise. In fact the global forests exert an antiviral and antibacterial action on moving air masses, in general." While a few scientists over the years have done some research into these ideas, Beresford-Kroeger's work has gone a long way to promote a little-studied field.

ON A WARM day in 1970, Dr. A. Kukowka, a professor of medicine in Greiz, Germany, had spent a couple of hours puttering in his garden beneath the crown of four massive yew trees. As he described the incident later in a paper in a German medical journal, he was suddenly overcome by nausea, headache, and dizziness. He felt disoriented and lost all sense of time. Visions of vampires, vipers, and other "diabolical" images played in his mind's eye. His limbs became weak and he broke out in a cold sweat. Then the experience shifted and he felt as if he were under a large dome with angelic music playing. He saw visions of a paradise and felt "indescribably happy."

Dr. Kukowka's doctor found no obvious explanation, such as dehydration, for the bizarre sensations. Kukowka said he was able to replicate the experience beneath his yew trees, but he wrote that subsequent journeys troubled him and he stopped his experimentation. Dr. Kukowka hadn't ingested anything from the yew; he had only stood beneath its crown. The active ingredient that had caused the powerful effect upon him, he presumed, came from a chemical in the tree, likely a terpene, aerosolized by the warmth of a summer day.

Terrestrial, as opposed to atmospheric, aerosols are released from the leaves of trees and other plants, sprayed out of something called *glandular trichomes*—microscopic structures on a leaf that look like the onion domes of Russian cathedrals, thousands of which grow at the end of a slender stalk. These biogenic volatile organic compounds include an array of alcohols, esters, ethers, carbonyls, terpenes, acids, and other compounds, and they have a lifespan of anywhere from minutes to months. The abundance of the chemicals depends on a range of factors, from the amount of sunlight to ambient temperature to the genetics of the tree and the species. Their role in the life of the tree, the forest, the earth's ecosystems, and the atmosphere is poorly understood largely because they are difficult to study and they have been considered unimportant. That's begun to change as microanalytical techniques have improved.

In California's Sierra Nevada, researchers took samples from the air just above a remote forest, away from the contaminating effects of urban areas, and found that the air contained a hundred twenty chemical substances, though only seventy could be identified. In French Guiana, researchers sampled compounds emitted after they damaged leaves and bark in the rain forest, and they were surprised to discover 264 different volatile organic compounds in 55 tropical tree species—an average of 37 per species.

Some aerosols rise into the atmosphere and travel hundreds of miles. Others affect the immediate area of the tree, repelling threats or encouraging useful organisms. Some roots emit a volatile substance that attracts useful fungi. Black walnut trees emit a chemical aerosol called juglone as an aerosol, which repels competitive nearby plants by inhibiting respiration and repels some insects as well. The release of these chemicals varies from hour to hour, day to day, month to month, even year to year. The chemicals act in the environment on their own and also combine with other volatiles from other sources, and shower the earth with their essence.

Isoprene is the most abundant forest aerosol, with forty thousand different chemicals. More than half a billion tons of isoprene are emitted annually by the forests of the world, and one of its key atmospheric roles is to protect the trees from solar radiation—in other words, it acts as a natural sunscreen for the planet. Terpenes are the most abundant isoprenes. The world's evergreen forests emit two trillion pounds of dozens of different terpenes each year. Among other things, terpenes are a natural pesticide.

Studies of the boreal forest, the great shield of forest that stretches across the northern latitudes of North America and Europe, show that the emissions of terpene aerosols from the forest into the atmosphere double the cloud condensation nuclei, the microscopic particles that cause the formation of clouds. Because this forest-generated cloud cover keeps sunlight from reaching the earth's surface, the study's authors argue that one role of forest aerosols emitted across the planet is to act as key regulators of a balanced climate: in the northern latitudes, with the onset of the cold of winter, aerosols from conifers diminish and allow more sunlight to reach and warm the planet; when spring arrives and temperatures warm, the trees emit more of these volatile aerosols, which rise into the atmosphere, create more cloud formation, and moderate the heat.

These aerosols play a micro role as well. How plants interact chemically with other plants has intrigued gardeners and researchers since the time of the Greeks and Romans, who noticed that some plants emitted chemicals that "sickened" the soil. The field of aerosol study was formalized in 1937 by a distinguished Austrian plant researcher, Dr. Hans Molisch, a chemist and botanist who would become president of the University of Vienna. He noticed in some simple lab experiments that ethylene, a gas released by early-ripening apples and pears, induced nearby late-ripening apple varieties to ripen earlier. He coined the term *allelopathy* for this new field of study, which, derived from Greek, means "mutual harm."

In the 1920s and '30s, research on these plant substances became popular, and much of the work centered on one type of aerosol, the *phytoncides*. The name "phytoncide," which means "exterminated by the plant," was coined in 1937 by Boris P. Tokin, a Russian biochemist at Leningrad State University. Tokin found thousands of these substances in the air around trees and other plants and hypothesized that these chemicals helped the plants maintain their health and ward off attackers. He also believed that phytoncides influenced everything from microorganisms to higher order mammals, including humans, scrubbing the air of a range of disease-causing organisms. To this day the role of phytoncides is widely recognized in Europe and Asia, where Tokin's work is well known, but his papers and the work of others were never translated into English.

In the West these substances are known as *allelochemicals*. They were studied as a possible source of medicines in the 1960s, but have since fallen out of favor, although lately there is renewed interest in the chemical ecology of trees. "There are three hundred thousand different plant species," said Dr. Gary Strobel, a veteran plant researcher at Montana State University. "Only a tiny fraction of them have been explored thoroughly to see if they are applicable to human ailments."

In the early 1980s an ecologist at the University of Washington, David Rhoades, proposed that a tree attacked by insects signaled its brethren when it was under siege, telling them to take appropriate countermeasures—the release of a chemical that upsets the digestion of the attacking bugs. Rhoades thought the trees communicated chemically through their root systems, but his colleagues Ian Baldwin and Jack Schultz were able to show that it was actually airborne hormones that warned other trees of the attack. The popular media, including *People* magazine, picked up on the story and wrote of the scientists who studied "talking trees." The popularization caused some critical colleagues to sharpen their knives. In 1985 a review of the existing science was published in *The American Naturalist* that concluded that there was nothing to the notion of signaling between plants. Rhoades left his career and bought a bed and breakfast.

"That was the end of this field for fifteen years," says Rick Karban, a professor of ecology at the University of California, Davis, one of those who recently picked up where Rhoades and the others left off. Critics were wrong, though, says Karban, for trees and other plants are far savvier than is generally believed, and are much more than sticks of wood with leaves. "Trees have been poorly studied because it's hard to get to the canopy, where a lot of the action takes place, and they're slow-growing. But trees and all plants are up to a lot more than we're aware."

Sophisticated chemical communication is one of the things trees are up to. Karban has studied this phenomenon in sagebrush in the steppes near Truckee, California, and above Mammoth Lake, because sagebrush contains a key hormone at levels hundreds of times higher than that of any other tree. Sagebrush plants recognize themselves as distinct individuals, he says, and moreover can also recognize their cloned relations.

When sagebrush is attacked by grasshoppers, which eat leaves, the plant releases a hormone called methyl jasmonate, which communicates to other parts of itself, and to neighboring plants, that it's time to produce something called *phytoalexin,* which can kill or seriously damage the intestinal tract of a feeding insect. "Other plants respond to these chemical cues and become more resistant, so they don't get eaten," Karban says. "Getting eaten is a drag, so over millions of years those plants that can defend themselves do better."

Methyl jasmonate is a fairly recent discovery, only twenty years old, and the handful of scientists in the field have just begun to tease out some of its properties. "Every year the list of the things it does gets longer," Karban says. "And it's active at ridiculously small concentrations." Studies conducted on plant aerosols to date have detected about fifteen different compounds in sagebrush. Newer technologies have begun to show that there are many more hormones, and that the situation is far more complex than anyone suspected. "We're measuring things in the highest concentrations, which are the easiest to measure, but they are not necessarily key," Karban explains. "Fancier toys can detect far more of these, an order of magnitude more. Moreover the chemical milieu is so important that if you take these substances and isolate them you get bogus results." In other words, the synergy among these regulating chemical mists is vital, yet they have only been studied in isolation.

While the study of chemical interaction between trees and other plants is a very small field, there is virtually no study of how the aerosols from trees interact with humans in the environment. There has been a great deal of study of the chemicals that trees broadcast into the environment, however, and this wide array of compounds is being used or studied for healing. One of the sharp, pungent smells in the air during a walk through a pine forest on a warm day is *pinene,* a monoterpene that has been shown to relieve asthma, perhaps by reducing lung inflammation caused by ozone trapped in the lungs. Another aerosolized monoterpene is *limonene,* which, along with *perillyl alcohol,* a limonene derivative, has been widely studied and has demonstrated a range of positive health effects, among them the ability to dissolve cholesterol and gallstones and to prevent asthma. Most significant, though, is its role in cancer—in animal studies it has a robust impact on cancer at all stages. "As a chemopreventative, limonene is very, very good," Dr. Michael Gould told me. Gould is a professor of oncology at the University of Wisconsin and researches the anticancer properties of limonene and perillyl alcohol. In one study he found that limonene in the food of rats prevented chemically induced breast cancer. "There's no question about its role in preventing cancer in animals, and there is evidence it's a cancer preventative in humans," he said. Perillyl alcohol has also shown anecdotal success in treating breast cancer, though, as Gould told me, "it takes a lot more of a dose to treat cancer than it takes to prevent cancer." It has performed quite well in early stage clinical trials for colorectal cancer, leukemia, and pancreatic cancer. One study showed that limonene fed to rats as part of their diet caused "complete regression in the majority of advanced rat mammary cancer." In another study it was shown to reduce the stress response in rats, which may be one reason people feel good among the trees. Other terpenes have similar properties.

Oral administration of perillyl alcohol didn't perform as well in humans as it did in animals, so Gould and others are looking at alternatives—a cream for skin cancer, for example. Clovis O. Fonseca, a Brazilian medical doctor and professor of neuro-oncology, uses inhalation therapy with perillyl alcohol to treat brain tumors that don't respond to surgery or chemotherapy, and his attempts show great promise.

Researchers in the Far East take seriously the notion that forests hold a chemical secret to health. In Japan, Russia, Korea, and elsewhere in the world the positive effect of forests on human health is widely accepted. *Shinrun-yoku*—"forest bathing" or "wood-air bathing"—is a bona fide field of study aimed at understanding what's at work in the moist, fragrant air of an old-growth forest.

In 2000, for example, researchers at the Nippon Medical School took twelve healthy men, from thirty-five to fifty-six years of age, out of Tokyo and into the forest. For three days they followed a regimen: the first day they walked among the trees for two hours, the second day for four hours, and on day three they offered blood and urine samples and filled out a questionnaire. They were sampled a week and a month after the trips as well, and these results were compared to samples taken after walks on normal working days in Tokyo, in areas without trees.

Analysis from the samples taken after the hikes in the forest showed significant increases in "natural killer," or NK, cells, which prevent the formation of tumors; an increase in anticancer proteins in the cells; and a reduction in the concentration of adrenaline in urine, effects that lasted a week after the trips. Alpha and beta pinene were found in the air in the forest, but not in the city, and the researchers assume phytoncides to be the active ingredient in the health effects. Other studies of people who have spent time among trees have shown lower concentrations of the stress chemical cortisol, lower pulse rates, lower blood pressure, greater parasympathetic nervous system activity, and less sympathetic activity, which means that people are more relaxed.

Methyl jasmonate, the plant hormone in Karban's sagebrush studies, which is present in many other trees and plants, has also been found to be a highly effective chemopreventative and chemotherapy agent and is sold for use as an inhalant in natural medicine circles. Remember Karban's statement: "It's active at ridiculously small concentrations." He was talking about its effect on the plant and insect world. But could it be that it is active at ridiculously small concentrations in humans as well?

The big question about the possible role of using forest aerosols as medicine is dosage. Do these substances enter the lungs and bloodstream in large enough quantities to have an effect? Some scientists say the quantities in the air are likely too low for clinical effects compared to the dosage that comes from a pill. Of course no one has measured how much of the substances is getting into the blood from breathing in the aerosols. But if breathing microscopic amounts of pollutants can give us lung or other cancers, or ingesting the microscopic amounts of chemicals called endocrine disruptors can cause problems for us, isn't it possible that tiny amounts of other chemicals might make or keep us well? As Karban said with regard to hormones as messengers between plants, the chemical milieu—the mix of chemicals that travel together—may have a robust synergistic effect that we aren't aware of. Or there may be a chemical in the human body that activates these substances because we have, as a species, coevolved in close proximity to trees and other plants. This is another subject that falls outside the ring of light, and the way to answer these important questions is with more research.

But some of the beneficial effects of trees and vegetation on humans may also arise from simply being around trees, since even the experience of seeing trees through a window seems to have a positive effect on health. Dr. Frances Kuo is one of the associates at the Landscape and Human Health Laboratory at the University of Illinois at Urbana-Champaign. Kuo and her colleagues are also on the trail of why trees and other vegetation make us feel good.

Kuo and her colleague, University of Illinois landscape architecture professor William Sullivan, undertook two studies in Chicago's notorious crime-ridden housing projects, the since demolished Robert Taylor Homes and the Ida B. Wells Housing Project. In the first study, published in 2001, they found that people who lived in housing units with access to, and a view of, natural landscape settings that were otherwise identical to housing units where a natural view was missing had substantially fewer aggressive conflicts with family members. Fourteen percent of residents living in buildings without trees threatened violence against their family with a knife or gun, while just 3 percent did so in buildings surrounded by trees and other greenery. The other study found that the highest crime statistics for residences at Ida B. Wells correlated with places where there was no view of, or access to, nature.

Kuo and her colleagues have also studied the effects of green space on children with attention deficit hyperactivity disorder. In one case they looked at the ability of children to concentrate before and after a walk in the woods, and before and after a walk through urban Chicago. The kids, scored by people who did not know where they had been, were substantially better able to concentrate after a walk in the woods. Another study found that girls in a housing project with a view of trees had better self-discipline—they could concentrate better, inhibit impulsive behaviors, and delay gratification, which meant better grades and better life decisions.

Researchers in Europe and Japan and in other parts of the United States have made similar findings. In a very large study, of 345,000 people, Dutch scientists found the amount and proximity of green space to a person's home was a reliable predictor for generally improved mental and physical health. People who lived within a kilometer of 10 percent green space had anxiety disorders at the rate of 26 per thousand, for example, while for those living within a kilometer of 90 percent green space, the rate of anxiety disorders was 18 per thousand. Depression rates were similarly reduced. Green spaces, the researchers wrote, create a halo of improved health around them.

And one 2013 study found that where trees are disappearing there is a decline in human health. It's estimated that 100 million ash trees have been lost to an insect pest called the emerald ash borer. A thorough study by the U.S. Forest Service's Pacific Northwest Research Station found that in regions of the country impacted by the emerald ash borer there were fifteen thousand additional deaths from cardiovascular disease and six thousand more from respiratory diseases than in places not affected by beetles. "There's a natural tendency to see our findings and conclude that, surely, the higher mortality rates are because of some confounding variables, like income or education, and not the loss of trees," said lead researcher Geoffrey Donovan. "But we saw the same pattern repeated over and over in counties with very different demographic make-ups." Researchers did not look at why the loss of trees would cause more deaths, simply the correlation.

Kuo believes the evidence for the human need for trees is strong but says the subject needs more study. Personally, however, she has no doubt that the lack of trees is a cause of some of society's biggest ills. "A disappearing urban forest leads to a psychological, physical, and social breakdown," she says. "Just as animals in unfit environments develop certain behavioral and functional pathologies, we may see more child abuse or crime or other problems when people live in unfit environments."

The mechanism for these effects is not known. Some researchers speculate that natural settings such as parks mean more chance for social interactions, or it might be because trees clean the air, so there are fewer pollutants and less stress on the human body. A leading theory, though, is that a human-made environment of objects—cars, buildings, or other structures—requires high-frequency processing in the brain. A landscaped environment doesn't require concentration on one or a series of objects, but allows the observer to relax his or her attention, which then has systemwide effects, from reduced muscle tension to lower heart rate and a generally less stressful physiology. It's called Attention Restoration Theory.

It may be that there is something else at work altogether, or a combination of things. We can dissect the elements that appeal to us about going to visit our mother, for example: the smell of our childhood home, the look of Mom's face, how relaxed we feel in her presence. Have we really explained love, though? E. O. Wilson coined the term *biophilia hypothesis* to propose that humans have an instinctual and deep emotional relationship with nature that it is part of our subconscious. Love may be what is at work in a forest.

For Diana Beresford-Kroeger, there is no doubt that trees help maintain human health, and the health of the rest of the natural world, as they constantly shower healing chemical mists into the air and over the land and water. "These substances are at the heart of connectivity in nature," she says. "In a walk through old-growth forest, there are thousands, if not millions, of chemicals, and they play an untold number of roles. What trees do chemically in the environment is something we're only beginning to understand. And what's happening in the natural world with this web of chemical relationships is something that we ignore at our peril." It's no wonder that when David Milarch contacted Diana Beresford-Kroeger after reading her work, she took to Milarch's big idea and offered to help him.

CHAPTER 6
Willow

THERE ARE BETWEEN three hundred and four hundred different species of willow, from ground-hugging shrubs like the two-inch-high dwarf willow to the weeping willow, the champion specimen of which is over a hundred feet tall.

The willow is one of the most useful trees in the history of mankind. Tribes across North America used its strong, light wood for crafting things as diverse as baskets, cradles, furniture, fish traps, bows and arrows, sweat lodges, wands, whistles, and travois. More recently the willow has been used to make artificial limbs, brooms, cricket bats, and apple crates.

The medicinal properties of the willow are robust and varied, and can be traced to an abundant chemical produced by the plant called *salicylic acid,* which can be used as a mild antibiotic, analgesic, fever reducer, and anti-inflammatory. The use of the willow as a remedy goes back to the time of the Egyptians, when it was a staple in the indigenous medicine cabinet—papyri describe willow leaves as a cure for fever. In Alaska, in the spring, native tribes eat the tender shoots of willows mixed with seal oil as a source of vitamin C. The Cheyenne used it as a poultice for bleeding cuts, and the Cree used its shredded bark as a sanitary napkin "to heal a woman's insides." Fevers, body aches, headaches, and a range of other problems were all addressed by drinking willow teas, applying willow poultices, or chewing willow sticks.

In 1763, a British vicar and pioneering scientist named Edward Stone, suffering from ague, an illness with symptoms that include fever, fatigue, and pain, walked through a meadow near his home at Chipping Norton in England's Cotswold Hills searching for a possible remedy. Stone believed in the "doctrine of signatures"—the idea that where a plant grows provides a clue to its applications. Because willows were abundant in swamps, he reasoned, they might be a treatment for fever, which also often occurs in swampy regions. He tasted a piece of bark; it was bitter and astringent, like the Peruvian cinchona tree, which is the source of quinine, used to treat malarial fever in South America. Stone gathered and dried out a pound of willow bark to make a powder. For the next five years he tried out the drug on fifty feverish people, and it worked quite well. "It's a powerful astringent and very efficacious in curing agues and intermitting disorders," he wrote.

In 1828, German researchers isolated a bitter yellowish crystal from willow bark, which they named *salicin*. A decade later, French chemists created a synthetic substance based on salicin called salicylic acid. Physicians administered the acid to patients with rheumatic fever, and the symptoms subsided. In 1899, chemists at the drug company Bayer in Germany created another derivative, acetylsalicylic acid, a buffered form of the acid, which had fewer side effects—in particular, it didn't cause gastrointestinal irritation. They called it *aspirin*. Acetylsalicylic acid inhibits the production of fatty acids called *prostaglandins*, which are created during the body's fight against fever and other infection and cause pain when they appear around wounds and in muscles. Prostaglandins also appear in the brain's hypothalamus, which regulates the body's temperature, and those fatty acids trigger the fever. When the world was struck by the flu pandemic in 1918, the new wonder drug proved its mettle. Now eighty million aspirin tablets are taken each day worldwide.

Aspirin remains something of a miracle drug. Beyond head and body aches, taken regularly in small amounts it can prevent heart attacks and strokes. Studies show that aspirin can also play a powerful role in preventing mortality from lung, colon, breast, prostate, rectum, and esophageal cancer. And one study showed that people who use aspirin and other anti-inflammatory medication on a regular basis have a substantially lower risk of Alzheimer's disease. Its only drawback is that it can cause serious gastrointestinal bleeding in some people.

Diana Beresford-Kroeger believes that the compounds from the willow are nature's way of caring for creatures that live in and around the waterways. The different species of willows along a creek are, she writes in her book *Arboretum Borealis: A Lifeline of the Planet,* "united to produce salicylate aerosols as antibiotic, antifungal, and aseptic air cleansers. . . . They are highly water soluble, and are added by atmospheric pressure to solubilize into water surfaces. They dissolve into the chemistry of the fresh water as protectants of fish, waterfowl, and underwater life."

Beresford-Kroeger believes that the lack of the dense blanket of forest and other vegetation that once covered the country is the cause of many seemingly unrelated problems, from the disappearance of honeybees to human illness. In her opinion, there just aren't enough trees still standing to produce these important medicinal molecules.

CHAPTER 7
David's Tale

THERE IS ONLY ONE native coast redwood forest in the world, in a heavy fog belt 30 miles wide and 450 miles long, between the California shore and the Sierra Nevada to the east and from south of Monterey to just across the Oregon border. In 2007, David Milarch called to tell me that he had received a small grant for a new Champion Tree project: cloning the largest redwoods. His plan was to use climbers to take cuttings from a few trees; eventually he wanted to take cuttings from a hundred redwood trees across their range to clone, move, and protect the old-growth genes. The new trees with old-growth genetics would be planted in "living archival libraries," like the other trees, and he also talked of wanting to use the clones to recreate an old-growth redwood forest near Golden Gate Park and to plant them in other countries with hospitable climes to protect the old-growth genetics should something destroy the only population of redwoods in California. In October I flew to San Francisco to meet him there and to write a piece for the *Times* about cloning the redwoods.

It's not unthinkable that a disaster could befall the redwoods. Sudden oak death is a fungal disease that showed up in tanoak trees in 1995, a species that grows in the redwood ecosystem. It has killed more than a million trees. What if a similar disease or pest were to decimate or destroy the redwoods? Redwoods are famously disease resistant, but in fact the fungus *Phytophtora ramorum* has affected them—along with Douglas fir, maple, and other oak species—though it only makes them ill; it doesn't, as a rule, kill them. Could it, though, evolve to become more potent and kill the big trees as the planet warms?

DAVID MET ME at the airport. I hadn't seen him in a few years, and he was a little heavier and his hair a little whiter. He looked every bit, as his son Jake describes him, like a cross between Kenny Rogers and Santa Claus. We drove for two hours up the coast, along the black rock cliffs above a frothy sea to an old-growth redwood grove. When we walked into the cool, dark cathedral of giant redwood trees, we stepped into another world. A dead, decaying redwood, a crumbling tapestry of maroons, wines, and russets, lay on the ground like a beached whale, the top of it well above my head. The living trees soared straight up and out of sight, taller than a football field is long. The odor of damp earth filled my lungs. In some places the dense canopy woven by the crowns of the trees all but blocked out the sun, and a velvety carpet of moss on the forest floor was bathed in a dark emerald half-light. A single brilliant shaft of butter-colored light spilled into a pool on the forest floor, illuminating a clump of sword-shaped ferns, like an epiphany from above.

Every tree can be thought of as an ecosystem, as having a complex, evolving relationship with thousands of other living organisms around them, both above and below ground. Because of its size, a redwood is an incredibly large, diverse ecosystem. Tannin, which is found throughout the redwood—in the bark, the wood, and the cones—repels insects, bacteria, and disease, and volatile oils in the wood keep the tree resistant to rot in this temperate rainforest. Tannin also plays a critical role in slowing the cycling of nutrients in the soil. Branches in the canopy fuse to other trees, which helps keep them stable during storms. There are centuries-old five-hundred-pound wet fern mats in the branches of the trees, more than two hundred feet up, essentially small lakes, where huckleberries, ferns, and even other trees thrive. Salamanders and tiny crustaceans called *copepods* live in these worlds above the world, and researchers think they climb up the bark of the massive trees during rain. The marbled murrelet, a small black-and-white seabird with webbed feet that feeds in the ocean, nests here as well.

As we sat and took in the forest, Milarch had a smoke and began to tell me the long version of his near-death experience. I hadn't heard about it since he'd visited me in Montana. He told me that after his experience, he continued to receive ongoing guidance from a range of sources, from archangels to spirit guides, and that the assistance he receives is largely how he navigates. Sometimes the guidance was about small things—

a storm coming that meant he should think about postponing a trip. I was with him once when he said, "I keep hearing the word 'tires.' " We checked the pressure in the car tires, and it was drastically low, though not visibly so. Sometimes it was about big things. He would hear someone's name and have a strong sense he had to meet them, that somehow they would help with the tree project. He had become psychic, he said, and could sometimes intuit what people were feeling. It wasn't like a radio you could turn on—the messages weren't always clear, they didn't always come when he was looking for help, and they weren't always right. On balance, though, they were very useful—to him and to others. While he was waiting in a veterinarian's office near his home one day he noticed a young woman waiting there as well, whom he described as having a dark halo around her that only he could see. "She was about twenty-five," he said. "I don't usually say anything when I see something like that. You're not supposed to intervene. But I saw how pretty she was, and how happy, and I walked up and said, 'You don't know me, but I have to talk to you.' " After explaining his near-death experience, he continued, "I know your boyfriend likes to drink, and I know you are going to a wedding. Please don't ride to the wedding with him." A month later the phone rang and it was the young woman. She had tracked him down to tell him that she and her boyfriend had broken up the day of the wedding. He had gone alone, had gotten drunk, and was killed when his car hit a guardrail. She wept as she told David the story.

The advice and knowing touched various parts of his life, but the tree project was always the main focus of the help he received. Still, the help didn't mean that he would always meet with success. In 2001, for example, Milarch traveled to California to scout for big trees and stopped at Mission Ranch, part of Clint Eastwood's empire in Carmel, to see the champion blue-gum eucalyptus tree that stands on the property and that has since been dethroned. Eastwood had posed on the cover of *American Forests* magazine next to the huge tree, and Milarch had a sense that Eastwood, who is one of his heroes, would like the project. He mentioned to the property manager his desire to clone the tree. Clint Eastwood himself called back and gave his permission. The next time David returned to California, Eastwood met Milarch and his son Jared, and the actor told them how much he admired the project. The Milarchs took cuttings and sent them to a nursery for propagation. A few weeks later the nursery called—all of the blue-gum clones had died. Eastwood's tree was never successfully copied. Even with guidance, projects still sometimes failed.

I didn't dismiss Milarch's claims about intuition and guidance. In the 1990s, I'd written a piece about George McMullen, a remote viewer, or psychic, who worked for many years with Dr. Norman Emerson, one of Canada's leading anthropologists, to find archaeological sites for excavation. Dr. Emerson was an eminent anthropologist, a professor at the University of Toronto, and a founding vice president of the Canadian Archaeological Association. In a paper he presented at a conference to his peers, he described how McMullen's abilities had helped him locate new Iroquois village sites at a level of detail that would have been impossible without psychic abilities. For my article, I'd interviewed a dozen or so police detectives and archaeologists, and they had all insisted that these skills were very real; they all agreed that while psychics weren't necessarily always right, when they were right, it was often to such a deep and detailed degree that it defied guesswork. So when Milarch described his process of locating donors or figuring out the next step in the Champion project, I was more intrigued than skeptical.

Milarch's beliefs are all experientially based; he had no interest in anything remotely spiritual before his encounter with death. Though as a child he attended a Lutheran grade school for eight years, his spirituality has no relationship to any church. His beliefs in karma and reincarnation, for example, come from an intuitive feeling that he has lived before, not from a reading of texts. The conversations I had with friends and family who knew him before and after his near-death experience confirmed his otherworldly journey as transformative. Yet the more I learned about him, the more unlikely Milarch's path to a modern-day mystic seemed—imagine Ken Kesey's *One Flew Over the Cuckoo's Nest* protagonist Randle Patrick McMurphy as Johnny Appleseed.

Milarch had a difficult childhood working on the family farm. And yet the hard labor had its benefits. "When you work sunup to sundown on a farm, you get strong hands and arms," he told me. "By the time I was twelve I had grown from five foot nine to six foot three. When you are in a man's world, doing man's work, and have a slave driver for a dad and you are the son and have to try and outdo everyone, you have a man's body at an early age. If you put on the harness of hard physical labor, and stay in the harness, it has its rewards."

With Popeye arms and oak-strong hands, wrists, and fingers,

Milarch found that in junior high school his strength was vastly superior to that of the other kids, most of whom were just coming into their bodies. He took full advantage. "Hand wrestling was big back then. In ninth grade there were very few kids, if any, I couldn't rip in hand wrestling, where you lock fingers and bend them back. I not only bent 'em back, I'd put 'em down, and it was painful. They started crawling right up the wall." Not fond of academics, Milarch found his calling more in physical contests. "As kids got older and tougher, and more mean, and there were tougher kids from other schools, I used to break fingers and things," he said. "Not intentionally. But it was nose to nose, and they'd break mine if I wasn't careful."

He created what he calls an "arm wrestling machine" out of boards and old inner tubes and spent hours in the garage building up his arms with resistance training, pulling back an old shovel handle attached to a heavy black rubber strap. In high school, he started drinking and hanging out in bars, arm wrestling for beer money. "It was something I was really good at, and you enjoy anything that you're good at, whether it's chess or crossword puzzles or spelling. I just had a predisposition for arm wrestling and bare-knuckle fighting and things along those lines."

Milarch and a few friends started a gang called the Blatz Gang, named after beer brewed by the Valentin Blatz Brewing Company. Members had tattoos and a uniform of sorts—black T-shirts, black Levis, steel-toed boots, and a chrome chain bracelet welded shut, which they couldn't remove. "We were kids with bad attitudes, a lot of anger, emotional problems, things to prove. We'd pull in the parking lot at a drive-in restaurant and our gang would take on other gangs from other parts of Detroit. It was acceptable then. The Jets and the Sharks and James Dean and all that stuff." Things are different now, he said, and he sounded almost nostalgic for that era, with its own kind of dark chivalry. "Now it's no longer a contest of strength or fighting ability, it's who has the most guns."

Bare-knuckle fighting was also part of the gang wars, and with his strong hands and arms, he was the one the Blatz Gang put up against other comers. "It was usually for money, but sometimes we'd do it for fun at drive-ins or after school. Then there started being real fiscal wagers. Their buddies and your buddies would lay money on the ground with a stone on it and then I would start fighting someone from their side, and whoever lasted the longest and got over there to pick it up was the winner. It wasn't pretty, even if you won it wasn't pretty. Let's just say there weren't a lot of referees around." He retired from gang warfare when he was eighteen, in 1968. "I got shot at, stabbed in the shoulder, and beat up bad with a rumble chain all in one year, and I realized there was not much of a future in it," he said. His sister Kathy was a nurse in the ER in Redford, Michigan, and she alone stitched him up eleven times over the course of his fighting career.

After high school he did a year of college at Ferris State but dropped out when he realized it wasn't for him. He took off and hitchhiked around the country, partaking freely in the 1960s and 1970s carnival of excess. "I arm-wrestled my way from Key West with shrimp fishermen all the way to San Francisco, across the country, wrestling cowboys and loggers and all. People who do this aren't always the nicest people you meet, but I had fun doing it." He laughed, started to say something, and thought better of it. "Let's just say I had a lot of colorful experiences and met a lot of colorful people." With his long wavy red hair, his leather jacket, and a penchant for mind-altering substances, he fit in well with the crowd in Haight-Ashbury, where he stayed for a while. He saw his first grove of old-growth redwoods on this trip and was deeply impressed. But he was dismayed to find that the old-growth giants were still being logged. "They were cutting them down as fast as they could," he said.

In 1970, when Milarch was twenty-one, he drove his chocolate-brown 650 Triumph north from Detroit to the Milarch family farm at Copemish, near Traverse City. His father and others in the family had once lived there, but now the place was empty. For three months he camped out beneath the oaks on the nearby shore of Lake Michigan, near the Interlochen Center for the Arts. Smitten by the beauty of Traverse City, he never went back to Detroit. He dug out a basement on the family property, laid boards over it, and lived there for a while. In the summer of 1976 he met the future Kerry Milarch, who worked at Interlochen. They met at a bar called the Fireplace Inn and their rapport was instant. Two weeks later they sold their belongings and hitch-hiked across the country, not returning for a year. They married in 1977, and not long after that David and Kerry built a home on the family land, on a beautiful spot on a hilltop overlooking a broad valley. They built it themselves with lumber from logs that David's father said he could have if he logged them from the swamp on family land. To reach them, they had to wait until the water in the swamp was frozen, so in January, in below-zero weather, they cut down the trees. A friend with a team of horses pulled them out and loaded them on a wagon. Kerry, pregnant at the time, drove the truck to haul out the wagon. The logs were sent to a sawmill and cut into lumber.

While family life brought out a softer side of him, Milarch still loved drinking and arm wrestling—and collecting good stories, which he has a gift for telling. For instance, he told me of traveling to Whitewater, Wisconsin, in 1980 for a family wedding, where Kerry's uncle asked him if he wanted to head down to the saloon for a couple of beers. "Sure," he said. "Always up for that."

"There was a woman at the bar," Milarch recalled. "She was five eight, weighed maybe two hundred sixty pounds. She was two axe handles and a wedge wide. She had on a pair of coveralls and looked every bit like a Wisconsin farm woman, a good-sized one." Kerry's uncle and the rest of the family challenged Milarch to arm-wrestle her. Milarch scoffed, "I don't arm-wrestle women." After more beers were drunk they called him a chicken and made *bawk, bawk, bawk* sounds, until finally Milarch relented. He sat down across from the woman and they locked hands. Someone slapped the counter, the signal to start the contest. "Well, it wasn't three seconds and my arm was on that counter and she damn near threw me off the chair. This couldn't have happened, I thought. Did my arm fail me or am I dreaming, or have I drunk too much? I just got beat by a woman! A farm woman!

"They said, 'Come on, two out of three.' I said to myself, 'Okay, I better get serious.' I really dug in and I was giving her everything I had and I got beat again! I was almost laughed out of that bar." He was laughing hard, shaking his head as he told me the story.

On the way back to the house, his in-laws revealed their little joke: the ample "farm woman" was the national women's arm wrestling champ, who lived in Whitewater. His uncle laughed so hard, tears ran down his cheeks. "They set me up and it was probably one of the most perfect humblings, which I needed and deserved," Milarch said. "If I knew who she was I'd send her a thank-you card for helping to end all of that ego and silliness. It was a gift, it really was."

The Milarchs were back-to-the-landers, living on a 150-acre farm in a small house with kerosene lamps and a woodstove for heat, raising goats and corn and other crops. David helped start a natural food co-op in Traverse City called Oryana. And there were always the trees. He started growing a shade tree farmer's bread and butter: Norway maples, crimson king, sunburst maples, locusts, and birches. His parents also returned to the farm in the late 1970s. In 1979 his first son, Jared, was born, and in 1981 his second son, Jake. The shade tree farm has always been a struggle, and the family bartered honey and firewood with the doctor for the cost of the deliveries.

In 1982 he had his last arm wrestle with a young man from the hockey team at a nearby college. Milarch beat him handily, to the point where the young man fell off his chair. The man was ashamed that he had capitulated so easily. A week later the hockey player died in a hunting accident, and Milarch was crushed that he had humiliated him so soon before his tragic death. Kerry asked him to quit his pastime, and he has not arm-wrestled since.

Though family was important, Milarch couldn't set aside the bottle. "Drinking was my hobby, pastime, and sport," he said. In June of 1991, when he was forty-three, he disappeared for a few days on a bender. When he reappeared it was at one of his kids' T-ball games. He stumbled out of the car, tripped at the top of a small hill, and rolled down to the first base line in the middle of the game. "The kids thought, 'Oh shit, Dad's here,'" Milarch recalled. After that incident, Milarch told his boys he would quit drinking for good. "I told the kids I would never embarrass them again."

He asked his family to leave him alone for a few days while he quit, cold turkey. He placed a bottle of vodka and a six-pack of beer outside of the bedroom door, closed it, and shut himself in. That way, instead of hiding from the bottle, he said, he would beat it. "There is only one of two ways I'm coming out of this room," he told Kerry. "Dead or sober." After three days with no food or alcohol, with only water, his kidneys and liver started to fail, probably due to cirrhosis. He became extremely weak and sick. A drinking buddy, Larry Roundtree, came by to see him. When Milarch let him into the bedroom, Roundtree knew something was very wrong. He carried David, who was in great pain and having trouble breathing, to his car and drove him to the emergency room in Frankfort, Michigan. Doctors discovered that fluid that his kidneys could no longer process was filling the lower thoracic cavity and pressing against his lungs and his heart. They performed a thoracentesis—the withdrawal of fluid from his chest—and the attending physician told Milarch he would need to go on dialysis.

"Dialysis? I don't think I am going on dialysis," Milarch said.

"You've got to go on dialysis," the doctor responded, "or you won't make it twenty-four hours."

But Milarch could breathe again, and he had made up his mind. Roundtree helped him to the car and took him home to bed. His family returned home to care for him.

The next night, as his wife and mother sat at his bedside, Milarch remembers taking a sip of water and then experiencing a strange sensation. "I knew I was dying," he said, "and I was frightened and full of sorrow, but I was so sick I didn't care. I remember lifting up out of my body. It was so painful and smelled so bad, I was glad to be out of it. I remember thinking I was sorrowful to miss the boys, they were only in grade school. Then an angel came alongside me and said, 'Don't be afraid, we know you're afraid, but we're with you.'

"They were with me as I went through the tunnel of white light. Not pure white—it had a pink and blue ribbon, like a DNA helix. Everything went so fast, it was like getting shot out of a rocket. But the angel stayed with me, and I'm glad because I was really afraid. I started to decelerate, and then I arrived on the other side. I stepped out onto a vista. It was like the most beautiful sunrise you ever saw times a hundred, and there was beautiful music. But the best thing was unconditional love. I felt like when you are handed your firstborn child and hold it for the first time—it was like that times a hundred. There were people in spirit form I thought I knew, and light beings, and it was really overwhelming." If this be death, he thought, it was okay.

Then he described a large male angel with a voice like thunder, who seemed to be the boss of the other angels. The angel approached him and told him he couldn't stay; he had to return to his body.

"I said 'Whoa, wait a minute, wait a minute. Why?'

" 'You have work to do.'

"So they sent me back. And you really don't want to leave that situation, let me tell you. But I had to return to the tunnel of light, and *whoosh,* a thousand miles an hour again. When I returned I remember hovering over the bedroom ceiling and looking down at my body. After renal failure for four or five days it looked and smelled pretty painful. But *bang,* back I went. When I got back to my body, I sat up. It scared the hell out of my mom and Kerry, who were sure I had died. I haven't had a desire to drink since then."

For six weeks he lay in bed, unable to walk. The nerves in his feet had died and they had turned a dark color, a necrosis. He finally went to the doctor, who suggested his feet be amputated. "I said, 'No, that doesn't sound like a good idea,' " Milarch recalled. "They hurt like hell, and they don't look too good, but I've grown attached to them. I think they're staying on." Instead, he soaked them in five-gallon buckets of ice water every day to numb the pain. Now, two decades later, his feet still hurt. "To this day that pain is a reminder," he said. "When I'm traveling and people are having cocktails, sometimes for a minute I think it sounds like a good idea. But my feet are there to remind me that maybe it isn't such a good idea."

After three months of recovery he could walk again, though he was frail and had lost weight, dropping from 220 to 159 pounds.

"I looked like a newborn robin that had fallen out of the nest."
Weak as he was, every day he'd go to the local saloon—and have
a soda pop, "because I said I am not going through life running from this thing, from wanting a drink. For two or three
months, I walked into town and had a pop and stared the urge
down. I looked the devil in the eye, all those bottles behind the
bar, and said, 'Not me, not today.' " He started lifting weights,
five pounds in each hand at first. He placed a sign in his garage
with an affirmation that read, "No Man Should Be Shaped like
a Pear." After a year and a half of workouts he was squatting
hundreds of pounds.

   In the early morning hours one winter night in 1992, a few
months after his dying experience, his bedroom lit up, waking
him. "It was like three or four cars were shining their lights in
the window, and it scared the starch out of me," Milarch told me.
"I don't know how Kerry didn't wake up. I put my hands over
my eyes and heard a female voice say, 'Get a pad and pen and
go to your leather chair and write this down.' So I said, 'If you
turn the lights down I'll do whatever you want.' They dimmed
the lights and I got a pad and pen and sat in my recliner. I don't
remember anything after that until six, when I got up to wake
the kids for school. And there on the pad were ten pages of an
outline. I'd never written an outline in my life. I hadn't written
too much at all. I guess that's how music comes through when
people write music. That's how this project was born." When
Milarch showed his wife the pages she was dumbfounded. "You
didn't write this," she said, though it looked like his printing.
"You couldn't have written this, there aren't any spelling mistakes and you can't spell."

"I'm pretty sure what I saw on the other side three months earlier was an archangel," Milarch said. "And when they call on you, they need something done, and you're gonna do it because they ask with positive attention and love. You don't forget it right away, either." Again, a belly laugh. "That's what I know."

WHEN I LOOKED into the subject of near-death experiences, I was surprised to find a large body of science and writings about a phenomenon I had never heard of. The first written record of an NDE was authored by Plato, who transcribed the story of a soldier named Er who died in battle and returned to consciousness when the bodies of the dead were collected ten days later. He told a tale of ascending to a celestial realm where he saw a brilliant rainbow shaft in the meadows of heaven and watched as other souls chose a new life in which to be reborn. Cheyenne chief Black Elk, psychologist Carl Jung, pilot Eddie Rickenbacker, and actors Peter Sellers and Elizabeth Taylor are a few who have said their lives were deeply transformed by an experience of dying and then returning. "It seemed to me I was high up in space," Jung wrote of his transformative experience. "Far below I saw the globe of the earth bathed in gloriously blue light. . . . The sight of the earth from this height was one of the most glorious I have ever seen."

A 1992 Gallup poll estimates that eight to thirteen million people in the United States have had NDEs—the feeling they have died, left their body, and embarked, as pure consciousness, on a journey to another place—though Dr. Kenneth Ring, a professor emeritus of psychology at the University of Connecticut, believes the figure is smaller, about three million. Like David Milarch, many who have had the experience say it has brought on a deep and long-lasting spiritual transformation. And the experiences happen similarly in all cultures, and across all religions, even among atheists.

While some skeptics dismiss these experiences as sophisticated hallucinations, possibly the products of a neurobiological system convulsed by the shock of death, there are a number of researchers around the world who take NDEs as a journey out of the body seriously. Though Ring retired in 1996 and has not been involved in the field of NDEs since 2000, I found his work interesting because he had worked on the subjective side of the NDE phenomenon, which was germane to Milarch's experience. Ring's research is based on self-reporting; he has interviewed nearly a thousand people who have claimed to have had near-death experiences and has studied the reports of hundreds more gathered by other researchers. When we talked, I expressed some concern about venturing, as a science writer, into the realm of reports of heaven and angels. He laughed. "I wouldn't worry about it," he said. He told me that near-death experiences are almost a mainstream topic these days among serious scientists. Ring cited Dr. Oliver Sacks, whose book *Musicophilia* begins with an account of a physician's NDE, and Dr. Pim van Lommel, the respected Dutch cardiologist and author of the book *Consciousness Beyond Life,* who has studied the phenomenon and whose groundbreaking thirteen-year study of NDEs was published in the scientific journal *The Lancet.* And in 2012, Dr. Eben Alexander, M.D., a neurosurgeon and neuroscientist on the staff at Harvard Medical School, published *Proof of Heaven,* an account of his NDE and journey to the imaginal realm and back. As a result of his experience, he and Dr. Edgar Mitchell, one of the astronauts who walked on the moon during the Apollo 14 mission, helped found an organization called Eternea to help support the scientific study of consciousness and spiritually transformative experiences, and to encourage positive global change.

I described to Ring the NDE that Milarch experienced, his messianic conversion to environmentalism, and his mission to clone the biggest trees in the world ahead of a planetary catastrophe. Ring called it a classic. "One of the common thematic aspects of an NDE is a heightened ecological sensitivity," he said. "NDEers often come back with a sense of mission, and it's not uncommon for these missions to be, or sound, grandiose. There's a feeling among many NDEers that the planet is in peril and unless people move en masse toward a solution and do something about it, we're all going to go down." One example is Dannion Brinkley, who, Ring explained, was told on the "other side" that his mission was to help the terminally ill die in a more compassionate way by providing hospice volunteers. After his experience, Brinkley set up the Twilight Brigade, an international nonprofit with thousands of volunteers that offers hospice care to dying military veterans.

In his books and papers Ring describes a realm beyond this life where the light beings Milarch speaks of dwell, something he refers to as an *imaginal realm,* a term coined by the French scholar and mystic Henry Corbin. "It's a distinct realm, not physical, but quasiphysical, imaginal, but not imaginary, not at all," Ring said. "These light beings are nonphysical intelligences that can communicate information to human beings in deeply altered states—in NDEs or other states of extremis." Some believe that this realm is the source of the visions experienced by everyone from saints to shamans to mystics and poets.

Though Milarch says he encountered angels on his journey, Ring doesn't think of them that way. "I don't know how to describe these otherworldly intelligences. I wouldn't use the term angel, I just don't feel comfortable with that because it has religious connotations that are best to avoid. 'Light beings' is a better term and is used fairly commonly by people who've had NDEs." In Ring's opinion these beings are very real and are working for the good of the planet. "They are higher intelligences that have an interest in the earth and are worried about the future," he said. "Since they cannot directly intervene in human affairs, all they can do is try to influence sensitive and gifted souls and get them to act on their behalf. It's almost like they are spiritual custodians or stewards of the planet, and they need hired help. People like Milarch are recruits. They are in service to an ecological imperative." Milarch describes it as a "noninterference policy." The beings must allow humans to exercise free will, but they can try to influence some who will choose the right path.

While NDEers are transformed and become more spiritually oriented and compassionate after their experience, Ring emphasized that they are still human beings, with real-world motives and desires in addition to their spiritual agendas. They are so possessed with their vision that they can at times be manipulative in order to accomplish their goal. "They read people really well, but they don't always work with passionate selflessness," he said. "They can exploit people," he adds, though they view it as working for the greater good. I asked Ring about the fact that even though Milarch has had this enlightened experience, he sometimes does things that could be described as unenlightened. It's common, he said. "They usually return from their NDE enlightened in some ways, but with their ego intact"—the ego they had before their experience. "Milarch is certainly not unique in that respect.

"As far as the nature spirits, or *devas*"—a Sanskrit word that literally means "intelligent agent" but commonly refers to a nature spirit—"many NDEers report sensing the same," Ring told me. These spirits are widely perceived by indigenous cultures, by Buddhists, Native Americans, other sensitive souls, and even by some scientists who have struggled to incorporate them into the model. From this frame of reference there is nothing preposterous about what Milarch is saying. It's just that our culture, and our normal science, do not operate out of this paradigm. As a result, people like Milarch are often regarded as flakes. They're not flakes, though—they're on to something.

"We do indeed live in a magical universe," Ring said.

All of this doesn't necessarily mean that cloning champion trees is somehow fated, he explained. "I have known a fair smattering of NDEers who have dreamt these big dreams and have had grand plans that make sense from the point of view of an NDE—the vision they were shown—and nothing comes from it. To have a sense of mission, to act on it, does not necessarily mean it will be fulfilled."

Is David Milarch's story true? After much doubt, and after talking with others who have had near-death experiences, I came to believe him. And I believe his claim to be in touch and guided by his higher self, which Carl Jung describes as a guiding intelligence, and perhaps by other spirit beings. I understood, though, that I didn't need to believe that Milarch's deus ex machina is real. I have not found any scientist who says that protecting the genetics of the world's biggest trees in advance of a possible catastrophe on a rapidly warming planet is not a good idea. In fact, with the recent large-scale earthquakes, hurricanes, and tsunamis we've seen, and world leaders who have abdicated their responsibility to deal with climate change, it seems smarter every day.

Milarch, for his part, remains moved by his experience; now, many years after it occurred, it continues to fire his optimism. "When you have a project and you find yourself in a crunch situation and you absolutely have to get it done and it's overwhelming, and you have half enough help and half enough money, your best bet is to find a farmer," he told me, "because those are the circumstances most farmers operate under. It's the situation Champion Tree found itself in from the very beginning. We went from a family project, to a local, regional, state, to a national project, and now we have several countries asking us to come over and do their trees. We don't have near enough money, but we will have enough. I know it. These trees need to be archived, the sooner the better, and the universe wants it, so we'll get it done. The impossible just takes a little longer."

CHAPTER 8
Redwood

CALIFORNIA WAS SPANISH territory in the 1830s when an illegal immigrant from England named Bill Smith jumped ship and walked ashore, disappearing into the fog-shrouded forest of virgin redwoods. He was joined by two brothers, and together they became the first commercial redwood loggers, probably using a whipsaw mill, in which a large tree was laid on a wooden framework above a pit. One man would stand on top of the log and the other in the pit below, and in tandem they would work a two-man saw to form rough planks. It was the beginning of a massive industry that would cut the heart out of the world's greatest forest.

Lumber from old-growth redwoods is among the best in the world. It has rich, beautiful colors, is lightweight yet strong, is straight-grained, and is resistant to rot, termites, warping, water, and fire. Its most valuable attribute is something called *dimensional stability*—the ability of wood to retain its shape over time. It holds nails fast, for example, a hundred years after they were pounded in, even in a wet coastal environment.

Dismantling a towering redwood with nineteenth-century tools required innovation and gumption; loggers had never dealt with trees that size. The wood at the bottom of old-growth redwood trees is extremely dense, forming a strong base to keep the rest of the massive tree upright. Instead of attempting the impossible task of cutting through the base, tree fallers would cut through softer wood ten to fifteen feet above the ground. They did this by driving a board with a metal cleat on one end into the tree. On this diving-board-like platform, which bounced up and down as they worked, they swung their oversized axes and pulled and pushed enormous two-man saws. If a tree fell too hard, it could shatter and become worthless, and so loggers often made a bed of small trees and branches to cushion the fall. Or the giants were dropped uphill to create the shortest fall path. It could take a week for a crew to fell a single tree.

Waste was rampant. Once dropped, the tree was sawn where its diameter was small enough to get a saw through, as high as two hundred feet above the stump. The rest was often left, or loggers drilled holes, packed them with black powder, and blew the trunks apart, destroying much of the wood in the process. Bull, ox, horse, and mule teams pulled pieces of logs out of the forest on log skid roads. Eventually the huge logs were carried out on special wide-gauge railways built into the woods. Trees were peeled and cut into lengths and shipped out on the rail cars; some logs were so big that only a single one would fit in a car. Single-log trucks were also built to carry giants.

In the early days some redwoods, such as those near San Francisco, were close to harbors and relatively easy to load onto freighters. Other parts of the West Coast forest, though, were rugged with no harbor access. Timber companies designed a complex system of chutes and cables on scaffolding that shuttled wood from the hills out to small specially built schooners that could maneuver in small coves called "dog holes" and pick up the logs.

The early cutting of California redwoods was accelerated by the U.S. Timber and Stone Act of 1878, which allowed federal lands with old-growth redwood forests to be sold to private companies at the bargain rate of $2.50 an acre, with timber value per acre at the time at $1,300. The low price was meant to help small-scale loggers, but most of the land, and with it the timber, went to the corporate syndicates. It was a giant transfer of public wealth to private companies. Still, the logging would go on for a long time before the primeval forest of giant redwoods came close to disappearing. In 1854 there were just nine sawmills on California's North Coast; toward the end of the century there were four hundred. In spite of nearly a century of unbridled, unregulated cutting, only a third of California's unique old-growth redwood forest had been felled.

After World War II, with a housing boom to accommodate returning GIs, a soaring California economy, and improved technology, logging efforts were redoubled. In 1953, a billion feet of redwood lumber were produced—triple the yield of any other year prior to 1950. That level remained stable until the 1970s, when it began to decline, falling to half a billion by the late 1990s.

Despite the massive size of the redwood forest, just small bits and pieces were protected before they were cut. Some 95 percent of the ancient forest was logged, and of the 5 percent of old-growth forest that remains—about 106,000 acres—around 82 percent is protected. That tiny fraction of the original old growth is split among forty-eight redwood forest preserves in California, ranging from the 295-acre Muir Woods National Monument to the largest contiguous old-growth redwood forest, the ten-thousand-acre Rockefeller Forest in Humboldt Redwoods State Park. The size of these preserves was determined by cost and availability, not by whether they were large enough to be sustainable into the future. There are real questions about whether these isolated pieces of forest will survive, even without climate change.

The real problem lies in the fact that what remain are fragments, which are far less resilient than large-scale, intact old-growth forests. *Resilience* is the ability of a forest to suffer droughts, windstorms, insect outbreaks, diseases, and fire and to self-repair, to keep functioning as a forest. Small patches of forest often can't recover from large-scale natural events, many of which are predicted to intensify as the climate changes.

Because trees have a cooling effect, for example, the temperature in the interior of a large landscape forest is often a few degrees lower than at the edges, so while the margins may die, the rest of the forest can carry on. Small tracts, on the other hand, suffer from something known as the *edge effect*. When a new edge of a forest is created by logging or road building in an adjacent forest, sun and wind are able to penetrate the remaining forest. Exposure brings changes as far as a quarter mile from the new edge, causing the forest and soil to dry out and allowing invasive plants to find their way in. Many small forest fragments are all edge and will likely die as the climate warms.

And of course the issue Milarch has raised about genetics is a big question mark. What does two centuries of selecting out most of the oldest, biggest, and healthiest trees from the population mean to the future of the redwood forest? "If we lose genetic diversity, we make it less likely that species can adapt to change," says Reed Noss, a conservation biologist at the University of Central Florida, who has studied the redwoods, referring to the dangers of eliminating large acreages of old-growth trees. "Some species are evolving quite rapidly in response to climate change, so less diversity means less possibility for adaptation. Genetic variability is the raw material that evolution works from. With many genotypes [variety of genes in an individual] the chances for survival are greater."

The great decline in genetic diversity in the redwoods is the result of their range being reduced so dramatically. The loss of so many big trees also means a marked reduction in diversity. "The big old trees in many cases probably had superior genes to those that never got so big," Noss says, "and were probably less inbred." Trees also become more diverse as they age, through mutations.

Another factor in the survivability of forests is forest migration. Trees move, though slowly. As the climate gets warmer, seeds that spread to the north might do well, while trees to the hotter and drier south will die out. Scientists estimate that eastern hardwoods are migrating north at the rate of sixty-two miles per century. But forest migration to more favorable habitat as

the climate changes is thwarted by development and other barriers.

The problem of forest fragmentation is not limited to the
redwoods. The great hardwood forests of the East Coast are
in even worse shape. When the Europeans landed, the forests
were so thick it's often been said that a squirrel could travel
from the Atlantic coast to the Mississippi River without touch-
ing the ground. Squirrels can't make that journey anymore. Dr.
Doug Tallamy, who heads the Center for Managed Ecosystems
at the University of Delaware in Newark, lists figures in his
book *Bringing Nature Home* that cut to the heart of the problem.
Seventy percent of the forests along the Eastern Seaboard are
gone. In the lower 48 states, 43,500 square miles are paved with
asphalt—an area five times the size of New Jersey—and 62,500
square miles are covered with sterile, nature-free lawns—an
area eight times the size of New Jersey. "We've turned fifty-four
percent of the lower forty-eight into a suburban matrix"—
homes, roads, malls—"and forty-one percent more into various
forms of agriculture." And each year sprawl gobbles up two million more acres of wild land—an area the size of Yellowstone
National Park. Large-scale forests are extremely rare; most are
highly fragmented, shot through with roads, and riddled with
exotic species. According to U.S. Forest Service Research, half
of the existing eastern forest is subject to edge effects. But more
relevant is the fact that most of the edge effect exists where
people live—and that's where the ecosystem services that trees
offer, such as cooling and cleansing, are most in demand, and
will be even more so as temperatures warm.

CHAPTER 9
Cloning Redwoods

THE MORNING AFTER our visit to the redwood grove where I learned more about David Milarch's near-death experience, David Licata, a filmmaker who was documenting Milarch's work, and I drove to a 306-acre Marin County park called Roy's Redwoods, a few miles out of Mill Valley, where Milarch planned to take his first redwood cuttings. It was a cold, damp Bay Area morning, with a low ceiling of fog engulfing the tops of the trees.

James and Thomas Roy were brothers who were given this land in 1877 by Adolph Mailliard as settlement for a $20,000 debt. Mailliard was the grandson of Joseph Bonaparte, the older brother of Emperor Napoleon Bonaparte and king of Spain and Naples. The property changed hands a couple more times, was slated to be developed for a subdivision, but then was purchased in 1978 for a county park. For a while, hippies lived in some of the giant hollowed-out tree trunks. In 1984, George Lucas filmed scenes from *The Ewok Adventure* here. The three red-woods Milarch planned to clone are four and five centuries old and between two and three hundred feet tall, with a circumfer-ence of up to thirty-eight feet. They are named Gramma, Twin Stem, and Old Blue. It's a verdant spot, with a large meadow where weddings and other celebrations are staged.

The best chance for successful cloning lies in using the "sun needles," the new growth in the tips of the branches, which are most vital; they reach up to the sun vertically, and some-times look like small Christmas trees. The first branches on a redwood, though, are often a hundred feet or more above the ground. (Milarch had arranged with Bartlett Tree Experts, one of the nation's largest tree service companies, to send two tree climbers to Roy's Redwoods.)

Climbers use ropes and harnesses to scale these big trees, similar to the equipment used by a rock climber. When the arborists arrived they cordoned off a circle around the bottom of one of the trees with yellow warning tape. Wearing yellow climb-ing hard hats and harnesses, they used an eight-foot-tall line launcher—a slingshot on the end of a long metal handle—to fire a weighted throw bag tied to fishing line over a branch where the sun needles grow, and then used the small line to haul up a heavier line. Once the climbing rope was in place, the climbers pulled themselves up the single strand, using both their feet and hands. When they reached the branches they sought, they swung out to the end to remove ten-inch-long cuttings with a saw. Some of this action was captured in a "helmet-cam" that one of the climbers wore.

Milarch had some high-caliber scientific help on the trip. He had invited Dr. William Libby, a professor emeritus of forestry and genetics at the University of California, Berkeley, and a board member of the Save the Redwoods League. They hadn't met before, but after Libby talked to Milarch on the phone, he became intrigued with the idea and offered to bring his considerable expertise to support the cloning efforts.

Libby has written four books on genetics and clonal forestry and has published more than two hundred papers on dendrology (the formal name for the study of trees), forest genetics, genetic conservation, clonal forestry, and biodiversity. He has practiced his own assisted migration, planting California redwoods in New Zealand, where he lived for several years, and taking twenty thousand sequoia seeds to Turkey to establish a population of sequoias in the Taurus Mountains there. He has a collection of several unusual redwoods growing in his suburban yard from clones of the trees he has studied, and one grown from a redwood seed that orbited the moon.

"Glad you could come, Bill," David said when we were gathered, putting on the charm. "When I started making calls to do this, someone told me when it comes to redwoods, you're god with a small g."

"Don't feel like you need to use a small g," Libby joked.

What, I asked Libby, as we stood next to Gramma the redwood, did he think of the plan to protect the genetics of the oldest redwoods in a living archive? "He's picked a bunch of interesting trees," said Libby. "He's gotten trees that have done well for a long time, that have done well in various environments. But a whole lot of things go into living longer, not just genetics. No one can be sure these bigger trees are better trees, though some of them likely are." Libby's opinion was similar to that of Frank Gouin, who had cloned the Wye Oak. We can't prove they are better trees, but like a racehorse or a champion show dog, it's common sense that genetics plays a large role in those traits. And protecting these champions for study in case they disappear could well be useful. "Set aside the guys who really got old so we can study them, absolutely, it's a good idea. It's going to be very nice, if we are able to keep civilization going thirty years from now, that scientists can go out to where clones of these trees are growing in accessible archives and study the genetics with techniques we don't even have yet. If we archive them, future scientists won't have to go throughout the range and get individual permission for each tree, which could keep a project of this scale from happening. And cloning gives you a reliability and level of control over the genetics that you don't have with seedlings."

An authenticated clone of a tree is critical to archiving its genetics—that's the idea at the heart of Champion Tree. "You have to archive the known genetics and know what the attributes of the tree are, the known age and other knowns," says Milarch. "You can only do that with a clone. Even if it's a seedling growing under the tree, you don't know. Did a squirrel carry that one in?" But Libby had doubts about whether trees this old, or older, could be cloned. He had cloned redwoods but was unable to get trees much over 120 years to take, presumably because they are so mature. Cloning the champion tree of every species is therefore picking one of the most difficult trees of each species to clone.

"It's really embarrassing how little we know," Libby said, speaking not just about tree genetics but about trees in general, echoing things I had heard from others. "There're lots of questions for a researcher to ask. Why, for example, is a redwood a youngster at four hundred years of age, while a Monterey pine has generally checked out before it's a hundred? One of the things we know the least about is what is going on underground, the microflora and microfauna that live in the soil around the roots, for example. We don't even have good lists of what is living there yet, let alone what functions they have. They are very important and are likely to be more sensitive to climate change than the trees themselves."

Libby was talking about a tree's *rhizosphere*—the vast complex root system and the soil and the microorganisms affecting, and affected by, the roots. It's a large ecosystem unto itself and is far more complex than the tree aboveground. Roots are vital to the tree's search for nutrients, and its many miles of roots reach into every nook and cranny, working symbiotically with soil, microbes, fungi, and fauna such as nematodes, mites, and spiders to bring sustenance to the tree. Roots feed bacteria in the soil with a range of energy-rich exudates derived from photosynthesis by the tree's leaves, for example, and the bacteria, in turn, process nutrients with the help of fungi on the roots. Until the 1990s the realm of the rhizosphere was largely an unexplored frontier, though in the last decade some gains in understanding have been made. There's an international rhizosphere conference each year that draws hundreds of root researchers, who are fond of quoting Leonardo da Vinci's "We know better the mechanics of celestial bodies than the functioning of the soil beneath our feet."

The global tree canopy is a similar story. Researchers have only recently begun to ferret out what is going on in the canopy of trees because it has been so difficult to access. Steve Sillett's work in the redwood tree canopy is a first for the redwood forest, and researchers have been working in other canopies around the world as well. They have discovered that canopies are an astoundingly rich and complex world—the highest biodiversity on the planet lives in the canopy of tropical rainforests, more than thirty million species—and they have barely scratched the surface. It's the part of the forest that feeds wildlife—a "gigantic food factory on stilts," according to one researcher.

ONE OF THE most important reasons for cloning the old redwoods, or any long-lived tree, is that they may well have a memory for survival encoded in their genes. This idea is based on something called *epigenetics*—the word means "over the DNA," since the changes don't affect the DNA itself but its expression— a field that in the last decade has quietly revolutionized the understanding of genetics. In 2000, Randy Jirtle, a professor of radiation oncology at Duke University, performed an experiment with a type of mouse that carried the agouti gene, which makes the mice appear yellow in color and susceptible to cancer and diabetes. Just before conception and throughout their pregnancies, the mice were fed onions and other foods rich in methyl donors, chemicals that prevent the expression of harmful genes. The pregnant mice didn't give birth to sickly mice—in fact, their offspring were not only more robust, they showed no evidence of their parents' susceptibility to disease, demonstrating that the epigenetic signals that come from the environment can be passed on from generation to generation. Once thought to be an unchanging code containing the instructions for life that was passed from one generation to the next, DNA is now believed to be mutable, affected by adjoining chemical switches that play a regulating role in how those instructions are expressed. Those chemical switches are altered by the experiences in an organism's life. In the case of the mice, it was diet. Other factors that could change the epigenetics include family experience, stress, or environment. These changes are not necessarily passed on through sexual reproduction, but are passed on when trees are cloned.

In the case of a tree, available nutrients, extreme temperatures, drought, or response to a pest or disease could play a part in a tree's epigenetics. It is not overstatement to say that a tree has some type of memory, and this memory may be a big part of what helps the champion trees survive. "We've seen it with insect attacks," said Libby of epigenetic responses. "A tree once attacked by insects is sometimes able to set up some kind of defense against them the next time around. And there's even evidence that they put out some kind of pheromone that helps the trees around them, and those trees become resistant to the insect as well."

There's something similar at work with disease, called *systemic acquired resistance,* a phenomenon in plants roughly equivalent to a mammal's immune system. In the 1980s, California's Monterey pines, which grow in the southern end of the redwood belt, became afflicted with a disease called pitch canker. Scientists, in an effort to preserve the forest, inoculated some of the trees with the disease to find out which were susceptible to it. The resistant ones were then cloned and the survivors planted. When the trees that survived were inoculated a second and third time, each time they were better able to withstand the disease.

A case can be made that the DNA of old-growth trees contains a library of knowledge vital to survival of the species, and the older the tree and the more traumas it has survived, the bigger the library. The tree has gone to school on pests, climate swings, and diseases, and if those hardships don't kill it, as the saying goes, they make it stronger, and it can pass the benefits of its experience on to its cloned offspring. Are these attributes the key that will get these trees through the gauntlet of climate change? Only time and more research will answer that question. But it's one strong argument for relying on protecting proven survivors for the possibility of afforestation.

Or the answer may lie not in clones of the big trees that get planted, but in the clones of their offspring. Bill Libby, for example, has planted sequoia seeds gathered from a grove in Converse Basin, near Bakersfield, California. These sequoias are only three centuries old, offspring of nearly two-millennia-old parent trees. Libby hypothesizes that the younger trees produce better seeds than seeds from their parents—they grow faster and are much more vigorous, and they could be better suited for planting on a warming planet. Libby explains that the old sequoias came of age and survived stresses from long ago, whereas the younger trees survived pollution and other modern insults from the onset of the industrial age but missed other things. It could be that the younger trees have less "epigenetic loading" and so might respond better to modern stresses.

As we chatted, Libby said he thought there was an important nonbiological reason for cloning the redwoods: their tremendous iconic status. They are arguably the world's most loved tree, and cloning them could bring attention to the plight of the world's forests and the effort to assist the trees in their migration to other parts of California and the world. "There's no other tree that has the reverence that exists for coastal redwoods," said Libby. "They have a powerful presence, you could even say they are magical. I've seen European foresters cry when they've stood at the foot of some of the trees for the first time."

By the end of the day Bartlett's tree climbers had taken dozens of cuttings from the three trees at Roy's Redwoods, dropping pieces of green foliage to the ground as they worked. Milarch and others gathered the pieces of future forest into a plastic ice chest. It was an unusual trip for them, the climbers said. While they had climbed many trees in their careers, they had never climbed a redwood to create a clone.

The sampling from Gramma, Old Blue, and Twin Stem was well covered by the media, a testament to the fame of the redwoods and the novel idea of cloning them. By now Milarch knew the media well and could provide them with the sound bites and the drama they were looking for. "Okay, we made a huge mistake and stole our children and grandchildren's heritage," he tells the handful of assembled reporters and later repeats on film for Licata. "We've sawn down ninety-seven percent of all old-growth redwoods. There's three percent left. Of that three percent left, only ten percent is protected. Ninety percent of it could fall to the axe or chain saw. So three-tenths of one percent is left of a forest that was here for ten thousand years. Now if you were down to three-tenths of one percent of gasoline for your car, or three-tenths of one percent of your life savings, wouldn't it be time to do something?" In light of recent sophisticated imaging work, Libby says Milarch's comment overstates the threat to the redwood forest. But old growth is still rare, and from the Associated Press to the BBC to my story in *The New York Times*, people heard a message about the cloning of the California redwoods.

MILARCH TOOK THE cooler that contained the redwood cuttings and drove them to an office supply store in Mill Valley, where he packed them in a cardboard box and overnighted them to nurseries, including that of Bill Werner, who has long cloned the West Coast champions for Milarch. Werner is passionate about his role as a steward for rare plants, both as a vocation and an avocation. A devout Christian, he often meets with a small men's group to ask for help from the Creator in growing roots on the cuttings from ancient trees.

"It's money in the bank, and it's a savings account our grandchildren will thank us for," Milarch said after he sent off the package and opened a new pack of Marlboro Lights. A few months later, Milarch got word from Werner that there were now two hundred clonal copies of each of the three trees. "Pretty soon we can start reforesting with them," he said. "We'll have old-growth forest trees, and I'd like to put the first one in downtown San Francisco, in Golden Gate Park. It might seem odd, but that was old-growth forest for thousands of years, and it's only been a couple of hundred years that it's been a city. Why not? We can build old-growth forests around the world."

Again, it seemed wildly unrealistic for Milarch to believe he was going to accomplish all this on the budget of Champion Tree. It would take a great deal of funding to collect a random assortment of DNA from big trees across their range—Milarch's hope was to sample a hundred redwoods from their entire 450-mile range—using climbers to take cuttings from branches, along with the cost of travel and shipping, not to mention the cloning and growing of hundreds and thousands of copies. But Milarch had come a lot further, and lasted a lot longer, than I had expected. Just like the old trees, he had learned a lot by surviving this long.

CHAPTER 10
Dawn Redwood

WHILE THE NOTION of moving trees to protect them might sound novel, it has been done before, and in one memorable project, with a relative of the coastal redwoods. In 1949, Dr. Ralph Chaney, a paleobotanist at UC Berkeley, brought a handful of dawn redwood trees to the United States from China and went on to establish a population of the nearly extinct tree across the globe, a move that assured the species's survival.

The coastal redwood, *Sequoia sempervirens,* and the giant sequoia, *Sequoiadendron giganteum,* closely related members of the Taxodiaceae family, are conifers. While redwoods top out at just below four hundred feet and the giant sequoias reach their maximum height at under three hundred feet, the third member of the Taxodiaceae family, the dawn redwood, *Metasequoia glyptostroboides,* has the muscular redwood trunk of the redwood and sequoia but is the shortest of the three, with the height of the tallest trees just over one hundred feet. Unlike the others it is deciduous, and its feathery leaves give it a shimmery, ghostly appearance. When they drop in the fall, the tree is often mistaken for dead.

Like the others, *Metasequoia* was widespread across the world for millions of years, though unlike its relatives it did quite well in cold temperatures. Botanists thought it had long gone extinct; the most recent fossil was millions of years old. So the scientific world was rocked when, in the 1940s, the trees were found in an isolated valley in south central China. They were given to Dr. Hu Hsen-hsu in Beijing, who, in 1944, sent some specimens to a mentor, Dr. E. D. Merrill at Harvard's Arnold Arboretum, who in turn sent them to Chaney, saying that, unless he missed his guess, these were a living version of a *Metasequoia.* Chaney didn't believe it. How could he? The whole world thought they had disappeared millions of years ago. When Chaney received a packet with green samples from the tree, however, which he had seen only in fossil form, he was overcome. Martin Silverman, a *San Francisco Chronicle* reporter present when he opened the envelope, said Chaney fainted at the sight of evidence that the ancient redwood still lived.

Beside himself with excitement, Chaney, in 1948, arranged a Save the Redwoods League–funded expedition to the remote and often hostile Sichuan province in central China, along the Yangtze. He asked Silverman to accompany him. Silverman talked it over with his editor, who liked the idea but said the tree, then known as the Type tree, needed a catchy name. How about "dawn redwood," because it's been around since the dawn of time? he asked.

In China, the men and their party sailed on a steamer up the Yangzte River to the ancient city of Wanxian. Hiking and sometimes carried in a sedan chair, they spent three days covering rough, mountainous terrain. Bandits prowled the region, and on the return trip one of the expedition's guards shot and killed one. Chaney himself very nearly died, though not from bandits or an exotic disease. For three nights he suffered the wheezing and gasping of asthma attacks, because one of his Chinese guards had accidentally stepped on and smashed a small vial of his medication. Still they pushed on to the village of Modaqi. There, from a ridge a half mile away, Chaney saw his first dawn redwood. It was massive—112 feet tall and nearly 8 feet in diameter. It had no needles, and Chaney realized, for the first time, that the dawn redwood was deciduous—that was why it had thrived in extreme cold while the sequoia and coastal redwood did not. Moving closer, the party could see that a shrine had been built at the base of the tree. Chaney was told that the villagers believed a god inhabited the tree, which they called a water fir, and they prayed to it for healing and abundant rice crops.

There were only three dawn redwoods in the village, and Chaney wanted to push on and see the forest of *Metasequoia* he had heard about near a village called Shushiba. He was still laboring to breathe, and Silverman, who was worried about him, suggested turning back. Their guide made the case to keep going. Whether they continued on or returned, he said, Chaney could die. "If the professor sees the forest, and then dies, will he not die with great happiness?" he asked, and Silverman agreed.

Near the remote village the party reached its goal: several thousand dawn redwoods growing in a natural mixed-species forest in a narrow side canyon. Once widespread, these trees, and the few at the shrine, were all that remained of the dawn redwoods. They had survived because of their remoteness.

Chaney and Silverman returned home with thousands of dawn redwood seeds and seedlings. A photo of the balding scientist holding a seedling appeared on the front page of the *Chronicle* with a caption that read BACK TO AMERICA—AFTER A 25,000,000-YEAR ABSENCE.

"Finding a living dawn redwood is at least as remarkable as discovering a living dinosaur," Chaney was quoted as saying proudly. In an early example of what is now called *assisted migration* or *managed relocation*—moving a species to a new home that it can't move to on its own in order to enhance its chance for survival—Chaney sent seeds from the Chinese valley across the world. The dawn redwood now grows in many places, as far north as Alaska, and is a popular ornamental landscape tree.

CHAPTER II

A Light Shines Down

IN 2008, NEARLY eight years after I first met David Milarch, few people were thinking about how climate change might affect them, or whether trees and forests could be prepared for the journey into uncertain times. That fall I went to Traverse City to talk to Milarch again. He wanted to introduce me to a woman he called a real-life angel who would ensure the fate of his project. The day I arrived, amid a swirl of cigarette smoke, a Joe Cocker CD blasting, Milarch drove me around his farm in a pounding summer rain, pointing out the rows of different shade trees, some of them the champion clones. One reason for his persistence with the project, he told me as we drove, is that when he went through the tunnel of light, he was shown, by his spirit helpers, the tough times that lie ahead on the planet—not just hotter and drier conditions, but a landscape of extreme cold, more violent wind, tornadoes, earthquakes, flooding. There was a deep need, he said, to keep the old-growth DNA alive.

"There isn't the science to say this," he reiterated. "Not yet. But I know it's true. We are not smart enough yet to read DNA. I can only imagine what our computing and science and genetic knowledge will be in a hundred years, and I know in my heart that the information in that DNA will be invaluable. The key is that we are preserving a known lineage, unadulterated, all the way back in the history of that tree. We're not guessing, and future generations won't have to guess."

It is impossible to overestimate the deep and abiding passion that many people have for big old trees. Almost as soon as the story about making copies of the giants ran in *American Nursery-man*, Milarch knew Champion Tree had struck a deep, resonant chord. Along with an inpouring of letters and even money, a call came from the governor of Michigan. He and several state officials had read the story and wanted to meet with the Milarchs. David, Jared, and Jim Olsen, a friend and attorney, drove to Lansing, where Milarch thought they might receive praise and help for the project. It was quite the opposite: state officials did not take kindly to Champion Tree. "It was a set-up," Milarch told me. "For four hours they unloaded on us. 'It won't work,' or 'The trees are too old to clone,' or 'A lot of those trees are on state land, and you can't clone those.' And they questioned what we would do with the money from selling trees."

Milarch was crushed, and he expressed his feelings to his son on the long drive back to Copemish. Maybe the project wasn't such a good idea after all, if the governor's office was opposed to it. "Hey Dad, remember all of those things you taught me when

I was a boy?" Jared asked. "Remember the poster of the pelican with the frog in its mouth that said 'Never ever, ever give up,' even if you are like that frog? Here you are, giving up." Milarch appreciated the wisdom of his son's words, and though he had no organization behind him, no lawyers on staff to advise him, no cash, no membership list, no cloning facility, not much of anything, it turned out that he was a fast learner. "The next day we filed to become a nonprofit," he told me. "All of the royalties would go into environmental education for kids."

But as much as David Milarch did to make Champion Tree a success, many more things seemed to happen of their own accord. In December of 1996, he flew to Florida to spend time in a second home the extended Milarch family owned in Venice. One afternoon, as he visited the orchids at the Selby Botanical Garden, the director of the garden stopped him: "You're the Champion Tree guy, the one who's cloning trees, aren't you?" She had recognized him from the story on the cover of *American Nurseryman*. She asked if he would return the following day to talk to their botanist about the project and discuss how Florida might clone some champions. When Milarch arrived, a surprise awaited—four television trucks and other local press. He figured they were there for some visiting dignitary but soon realized they had come to interview him, the man who was going to clone Florida's champions. Speaking before the glaring klieg lights and a swarm of microphones rattled him, and he describes those first interviews as among the hardest things he has ever done.

"They say you have a Florida Champion Tree project," a reporter said. It was the first Milarch had heard of it. "Yes, I do," he responded. It was part of his style—bluff your way to the next level and then figure out how to accomplish the task at hand. During the presentation he agreed to clone two trees, and the story went out across the state the next day, including on the front page of the *Sarasota Herald-Tribune*. "I had no idea how many people read newspapers," he told me. "I never subscribed to a newspaper and I don't watch TV. I'd never heard of a wire service, and I quickly learned what those are." Florida's trees, however, were not cloned successfully. "Both of them did not work," he said. "I did not know what I was doing back then."

On the afternoon of the day the stories ran, the phone at his vacation home rang. A woman told him she had read about him in the local paper and that someone named Bobby Billie wanted to meet him. When Milarch asked who Bobby Billie was, the woman explained that he was the chief and the medicine man of the Seminoles, a Florida Native American tribe, and she asked Milarch if he would meet them at Bok Tower Gardens, a fifty-three-acre historic garden and bell tower atop a mound sacred to the Seminole people.

Milarch knew that trees were very important to Native Americans, and so the next morning he set out on the two-and-a-half hour drive to meet them, stopping thirty miles from Bok Tower Gardens to fill his gas tank. When he went inside to pay, he saw, standing by the counter, a Native American man with waist-length black hair and a white woman, both with big smiles. "David, it's good to see you," the woman said.

"How in the world did you know I was going to be here?" Milarch asked.

"There are a lot of things Bobby knows," she said.

They drove to Bok Tower Gardens in their separate cars. Milarch has broken his back twice and the drive had caused back pain. As they sat beneath an oak tree on a grassy spot near the parking lot, Bobby Billie asked if he wanted help with his sore back. Sure, Milarch said. "Within a minute or two a giant gray squirrel came out of the tree, ran behind me, and rubbed against my back," he recalled. "I stood up and there was no longer any pain in my lower back. Then Bobby Billie said he knew that one of my favorite birds was a red-tailed hawk, and five minutes later a red-tailed hawk circled over us and landed on my arm." Before they left, Bobby thanked Milarch for coming. "I wanted to meet the 'great white bear of the north' my grandfather said would come and work with the grandfather trees," Milarch recounted him as saying. He laughed remembering the incident. "Welcome to the world of Champion Tree." He then mimicked the theme from *The Twilight Zone*: "Doo-doo-doo-doo, doo-doo-doo-doo."

Not long after, when Milarch was back in Michigan, a man named Terry Mock from West Palm Beach, who had also read the newspaper story, called and asked Milarch to return to Palm Beach Island in Florida to clone the national champion green buttonwood tree. Buttonwoods are a tropical tree and have been widely used for landscaping in south Florida. Milarch felt honored and made the trip. Again the media turned out in force. "This time the story of cloning champion trees went national, and I saw, for the first time really, what power this idea had," Milarch said. "It was Jared and me and some friends creating a group with no funding and no infrastructure, but it was going strong. It's always had a life of its own, like a runaway locomotive. And in Florida was the first time I heard the word 'noble,' that it was a 'noble project.' "

Mock, who would become the executive director of the Champion Tree Project, led it to some of its big early break-throughs. He and Milarch helped clone a different buttonwood, the national champion silver buttonwood, in Key West, none too soon. In 1998 it was nearly killed by Hurricane George, and in 1999 it was mortally wounded by Hurricane Irene. Fortunately the clones took. In 2001, one of the tree's clones was planted in the same spot at the Key West Golf Course where the mother tree had stood for a century.

During the first four years of the project, until 1999, the Milarchs funded the project themselves, largely through Kerry's job as an English teacher at a local college and their meager shade tree income. Milarch had made a fair amount of money for a few years building log cabins, but he lost it all when a worker without insurance was injured and he was forced to declare bankruptcy. "Neighbors chipped in and bought the kids coats and tennis shoes one winter," Kerry Milarch told me. At one point, early on, Milarch decided to look for funding and went to Washington, D.C., to talk to American Forests, a non-profit organization that promotes tree planting and healthy forests. They are the keepers of the National Register of Big Trees, the list of the 826 species that Milarch hoped to clone. They said they weren't interested. Later, as the idea started to gain a star-tling amount of traction in the media, and perhaps because they viewed Champion Tree as competition to their own project, they went on the attack. They criticized the science and published an article in their magazine arguing against the importance of tree genetics. A "fundamental mistake would be to assume that so-called 'champion' trees are somehow genetically superior to their counterparts. In some cases, in fact, just the opposite is true," wrote the organization's forester, Gary Moll. And in an interview, their executive director told me she believed Milarch had stolen their idea. "He reinvented our program, basically," said Deborah Gangloff, who has since left the organization.

I thought both claims were disingenuous. Milarch and his advisers weren't saying that champion tree genes were superior— just that they might be. And though he had used the public register to look for the champions, no one at American Forests was cloning them. What Milarch had said was true: the champion trees were disappearing until Champion Tree came along. Later, American Forests filed a lawsuit to stop Milarch from using the name Champion Tree. The suit was dropped, but it cost precious resources.

Terry Mock, savvy about navigating the world of nonprofits and high-end donors, brought some valuable connections to Champion Tree that helped to keep the struggling organization alive. In 2000, Milarch and Mock went to Washington, D.C., to plant a champion ash tree at the Marjorie Merriweather estate. General George Cates, a retired Marine general, had been lobbied by Mock, and after the planting he stepped out of the crowd to propose that Champion Tree partner with the National Tree Trust, a foundation created in 1990 by President George H. W. Bush and endowed with $20 million, whose purpose was to educate people on caring for America's urban forests. They in turn funded Champion Tree with $280,000 a year for three years, allowing the organization to carry out its mission. "It was a third of what we needed, but it allowed us to go national," Milarch said, "and to travel more widely looking for trees to clone."

In 2002, Champion Tree was asked by aides to U.S. senator Carl Levin, one of Milarch's home state senators, who had taken a shine to the project, to provide champion red ash clones for a living memorial to the victims of the terrorist attacks on 9/11. On September 10, 2002, Milarch arrived at the Pentagon to plant the trees. Surrounded by batteries of Stinger antiaircraft missiles and vigilant soldiers prepared to respond in the event of another terrorist attack, Milarch stood on the emerald green lawn of the Pentagon and spoke to a knot of misty-eyed people whose relatives had been killed a year earlier. Next to him were Paul Wolfowitz, deputy secretary of defense, and Carl Levin, the ranking Democrat on the Senate Armed Services Committee. Groundskeepers had used a backhoe to dig large holes in the sod, and as the prayers and invocations ended, Milarch and his son Jared pushed the trees—offspring of the cuttings Milarch and his son had collected on their early foray for champion DNA—into the holes and began shoveling moist black earth onto the balled roots. Milarch asked if anyone in the crowd wanted to take part, and dozens of mourning family members waited in 95-degree heat to help with the planting. "It was so sad," Milarch told me. "It was all we could do to stand there without our knees buckling." Milarch remembers a five-year-old girl in a blue dress. Her father was crying but the girl wasn't. "Can I use the shovel?" she asked. "I want to throw some dirt on for my mom." "When I heard that," Milarch said, "I don't know how I remained standing."

When they were done, many in the crowd broke into tears.

"They offer hope for the future," General Cates said of the memorial trees. "We're going through a very trying time in this country right now. We hope these champions that have survived all these other things will give hope to the American people, saying, 'We've seen it all, we've come through it, and we're going to do it again.'"

That same day, at lunch, Milarch learned that the Tree Trust was being dismantled and its funding would be discontinued after that year.

Interest in the Champion Tree Project, fed by high-profile events like these, continued to grow. Through contacts at the National Tree Trust, the Milarchs planted a living "memorial treeway" at the Firemen's Memorial at Calvary Cemetery in Queens, New York, across the river from the twin towers, to commemorate the firemen who had died in the attack. "That was a tough one," said Milarch. "Seeing all those fresh graves with the pictures of the firemen next to them and the moms and dads and wives and kids, that tore me in half." They cloned a collection of thirteen trees, all that remained out of thousands that had been planted under George Washington's direction at Mount Vernon, including white ash and tulip poplars. Milarch then donated fifty copies of each back to Mount Vernon. They also gave a collection of one each of the thirteen clones to Edsel Ford II and Henry Ford, Jr., to plant at the Eleanor and Edsel Ford Estate on the shore of Lake St. Clair in Grosse Point, Michigan. In an Arbor Day ceremony in 2003, Milarch planted a clone of one of Washington's ash trees on the grounds of the U.S. Capitol as dozens of members of Congress watched. They cloned European copper beeches planted by Teddy Roosevelt on his estate in Cove Neck, Long Island, and Thomas Jefferson's oaks at Monticello. The plan is that all of these historic clones will become part of a presidential tree collection called the Mount Rushmore Collection, to be planted someday on the grounds of the U.S. Capitol. Milarch still has to clone elm trees at Abraham Lincoln's home in Springfield to complete the collection.

In 2003, in one of the high points of his career, Jared Milarch and his team set out to clone Methuselah, a bristlecone pine that, at over 4,800 years old, is the oldest measured living tree in the world. John Louth, the manager of the Ancient Bristlecone Pine Forest, had asked Jared and David Milarch to promise not to publish any full frontal pictures of the tree. Fewer than fifty people know its whereabouts, and the U.S. Forest Service, which manages the public land on which it grows in the White Mountains of eastern California, wants to keep it that way, for fear that vandals might damage or kill it. While Jared took cuttings and picked up some pinecones, others stood lookout in case hikers appeared. Louth feared that Milarch's activity might give away the tree's location, and the plan was to scatter and act nonchalant if anyone approached. In another location, meanwhile, Terry Mock took cuttings from the Patriarch, a young bristlecone at 1,500 years old but the national champion because of its size.

The team drove back down the steep, rutted dirt road and overnighted the cuttings to the University of California, Davis, where a propagator attempted to clone them. The clones didn't take, but Bill Werner coaxed seeds that Jared Milarch had gathered. They weren't clones, of course, but because bristlecone pines pollinate themselves, something many trees do, there is a chance that they are 100 percent genetic copies, although no one will know until further study. *The Washington Post* and *The New York Times* both ran feature stories about the attempted cloning of Methuselah.

In 2006, the 3M Corporation, a technology company, called with a request. They had seen the articles about Methuselah and wished to have a copy of a bristlecone pine for the renowned five-hundred-year-old arboretum at Charles University in Prague. Would it be possible to get a seedling? The company's employees held a fund-raiser to raise money to fly David and Kerry to the Czech Republic to deliver it. The Czechs nicknamed the seedling Methuselah Jr., and Milarch was overjoyed. "Einstein went there!" he exclaimed of the university.

THERE ARE FEW things in this world that can compare with the satisfaction of giving a gift of a seedling from a nearly five-thousand-year-old tree to one of the most renowned arboretums in the world. And when Clint Eastwood puts his hand on your shoulder and asks, "Mr. Milarch, how *do* you clone those trees?" you feel you are doing something right. The project was featured in a television special about DNA, and PBS came to interview the Milarchs. David and Jared chatted with Katie Couric on the *Today* show when they did a segment on the Milarchs' efforts to clone George Washington's tulip tree. They were named heroes for the planet by *Biography* magazine.

Still, striking a deep chord is one thing and striking pay dirt is another. It was deeply frustrating for Milarch that while the tree planting idea had brought him in touch with leading figures, it was nevertheless a titanic struggle to find long-term funding to continue the work of Champion Tree. The Tree Trust had been a godsend, but funding was going to run out and the project would be in financial straits again.

Over the years, many things broke Milarch's way. Besides the Tree Trust funding, he received a small grant here, a little money there. But he couldn't, as he said, "drag the big buffalo back into camp" and provide for the project and his family. I watched a number of potential funding sources come his way, show interest, and then disappear. Part of the problem, it has to be said, is Milarch himself; his blunt, working-class style is sometimes a square peg in the round hole of the white-collar world of nonprofit organizations and garden clubs. It was sometimes difficult for this farmer from Detroit—one who had been a bare-knuckle street brawler and a founder of the Blatz Gang, no less—to rein in the rough-hewn, alpha male part of him and move carefully in the cultivated world of high-end donors.

There have been times when it appeared things were going to finally work out, and then, at the last minute, they collapsed in a heap. That was the case with Patagonia, the outdoor clothing company. David and Jared went to Ventura, the company's headquarters, to talk about a line of T-shirts with champion trees on them. Founder Yvon Chouinard toured them around the compound and they discussed the idea of offsetting Chouinard's "paper debt" by planting trees. The company would figure out how many trees had been cut down to make the paper to operate the company and then commit to planting that many new trees. Everything was agreeable. Then the Milarchs and a few of the company officials went to lunch. Afterward David was told that the deal was off. Someone at lunch had been offended by an off-color joke he had told, and she had the authority to call off the arrangement. "To tell you the truth, I don't even remember the joke, but I think it was something about big breasts," said Milarch. "It was just casual. But it constituted the downfall of the deal." He shrugged. "I think she had a chip on her shoulder. I'd probably tell the same joke again."

Milarch often told me that this kind of adversity energized him. "Storms drive the oak's roots deeper," his grandma Duell used to tell him. One might reasonably ask why, if Milarch had the ear of earth spirits and light beings, the task of carrying out the cloning of the champion trees was so obstacle-strewn. "Maybe they tried to help," he said in answer to my question, "but it was human resistance on my part. I am sure that I have been my own biggest enemy every step of the way. I think I needed to learn a lot about being humble. I have more faults and more weaknesses than most people. So part of the process is for me to learn, and they had me work on a lot of my shortcomings."

Still, I was always amazed at the project's resilience. Over and over again, when it seemed as if Champion Tree had run into a blind alley, that the project was on the verge of tipping over and disappearing just like one of the dead champions, David would meet someone who loved what he was doing and who would pony up just enough money to keep things going. Or he would get a call out of the blue—a garden club would invite him to speak, and out would come the sports coat and off he would go to California or Detroit or New York and his mission would be recharged. In 2002, the Garden Club of America gave him its National Garden Clubs of America Distinguished Service Award, and later its Award of Excellence for Conservation and the Garden Clubs of America Zone X Highest Award for Conservation.

In 2008, the clouds finally parted for Champion Tree. Milarch called me with the news that he had found a real-life angel to fund his dream. "It's time to gather the trees to put in the archive," he said. "It's going to be the biggest damn scavenger hunt in the world. We're going to fill up the ark." As he told me about Leslie Lee, a philanthropist and businesswoman who was ready to do all she could to help the project succeed, I was almost as incredulous as when I heard the tale of the roller-coaster out-of-body trip through the tunnel of light. Milarch doesn't always let the facts get in the way of a good story, and I thought that might be happening here. "Leslie said she'll send the jet for you," he said. "You can come here and see for yourself what's going on." The next thing I knew I was headed to the airport, to the fixed-based operations where private jets land. Two pilots greeted me and ushered me onto a small white jet. My first meeting with Leslie Lee, a determined environmentalist, convinced me that in spite of the odds, the grandiose dream to clone and archive not only the country's but many of the world's grandfather trees was going to become a reality.

LESLIE LEE HAD been following the exploits of David Milarch and the Champion Tree Project in the pages of her local newspaper. She had called the project more than once during that time and left messages about the possibility that her giant walnut tree was a champion, but she hadn't heard back. Had he realized who she was, Milarch might have found time to return the calls. In the 1980s, with her then husband Casey Cowell, Lee had helped build a struggling company called U.S. Robotics. Just when computers were taking off, a handful of computer geeks from the University of Chicago developed a new and much improved modem that connected PCs to the rest of the tech world. It made all of its founders extremely wealthy. Lee and Cowell eventually divorced, and she moved to northern Michigan to raise her kids and become a full-time philanthropist.

In August, her landscaper, Russ Clark, a friend of Milarch's, asked him to assess a three-century-old black walnut tree near Eastport, Michigan. Clark told Milarch that he thought it was a champion. "Christ," said Milarch, "I have had ten thousand people calling me to tell me they think they have a champion in their backyard. If I responded to everyone who thought they had a champion that's all I would have time to do." Clark insisted, and Milarch agreed to take a look.

When they arrived, Milarch was greeted by one of the largest black walnut trees he had ever seen, not quite a champion but a behemoth nonetheless. Clark introduced him to Lee, who immediately blurted out, "You don't return phone calls very well! I've been trying to call you for ten years!"

He was taken aback. "I was busy," he said.

"Nobody's that busy!"

"Well, I'm here now," he said. "Let's take a look at this walnut." The tree was healthy, though in precarious shape because of rotting in some places. Milarch suggested she call a local tree service, who brought in a bucket truck and cabled it with a half-inch steel cable to keep the branches from breaking off the trunk and ground-wired it to protect it from lightning strikes. They took cuttings and cloned the tree.

There was a powerful rapport between Milarch and Lee. Both have a playful sense of humor, and Lee shared David's concern for the fate of the natural world. As he told her about the Champion Tree Project, she fell in love with the vision of cloning and reforesting the world with the genes of champions. The source of the deep connection between them, she believed, was based on their mutual journey to the threshold of death's door and back. Lee had had her own near-death experience many years before, and though the circumstances were different, the effects endured in her as well. "Since that experience I've always been able to go to a place inside and align myself with it, and with what I wanted to do," she told me when we met. "That's a connection I have with David. I love old trees, and with this project there's a promise of excitement and adventure." Clean fresh water is also a funding priority for her—all of the rooms in her mansion on Lake Michigan are named after the world's largest lakes, and she knows how important trees are to keeping lakes clean.

"What's it going to take to do this project?" she asked.

"A million, million and a half," he said.

"Done," she responded. She bought the whole dream, not just cloning and archiving, but also establishing a way to create sustainable forests in cities and towns. Lee established a corporation, though later it would become two nonprofit organizations—Archangel Reforestation and Archangel Ancient

Tree Archive, with offices in Traverse City and Copemish. The latter would gather the genetics of the old trees and archive them, while Archangel Reforestation would use those genetics to replant and reforest around the world. She hired her cofounder as marketing director, and for the first time in his life, Milarch had a job with health insurance and a six-figure salary. Later she hired his son Jared as nursery manager and his son Jake as a climber and propagator. As a gift, Milarch gave Lee a clone of the Hippocrates Tree, an Oriental plane tree beneath which the father of medicine had taught his students. When the tree is seven or eight feet tall in a few years, Lee plans to donate it to the hospital where her father was treated for leukemia, and where, his clinical options exhausted, he allowed doctors to use experimental treatments on him.

The day after I met Lee, Milarch drove me to the Milarch Brothers Nursery. We walked behind a grassy hill, a half mile or so from the road, to a few old-growth white pine and cedar trees missed by the Michigan loggers, who didn't miss very much. They made the other trees around them look scrawny. "All we know is what we experience in our lifetime," Milarch told me. "But what was here for ten thousand years after the glaciers left? When you go to these remnant old-growth areas you see cedars like this, three feet across, and pines five feet across, and you realize you should be seeing these across the whole ecosystem, that these are what was normal for thousands of years. Our natural systems aren't working because what we perceive as normal in our lifetime is way, way off the mark of what should be here. What we have left is the junk of the junk of the junk, after three or four clear-cuts and taking the best of everything. We have genetically inferior trees with genetically inferior immune systems and an inferior filter system for the land. It doesn't matter if the whales are disappearing, or there are elevated carbon levels, or any other environmental problem—trace them back far enough, and the answer is always more trees. But when you go to the tree store or look in the tree catalog, you realize the trees that are there aren't going to save us. The people who sell trees never looked at the genetics of drought resistance, or resistance to warming, and never did the studies to know what trees hold the most carbon."

Milarch had reached a big milestone—he could now stop searching for the money to make his dream a reality and devote his energy to finding the biggest trees in the world, cloning them, growing them, and moving them to living libraries around the world.

CHAPTER 12
Stinking Cedar

THE BARELY EXTANT Florida torreya, or stinking cedar, is the antithesis of the redwood, sorely lacking in anything close to big-tree charisma. Most of the thousand or so individuals that remain look a lot like Charlie Brown's sad little Christmas tree, small and spindly and just a few feet tall. When the seeds rot, they smell to high heaven, like vomit, of all things, an unendearing attribute that earned *Torreya taxifolia* its nickname.

They were once abundant in this part of the world, and as tall as fifty feet. Their fine-grained yellow wood is rot resistant, and the species was decimated by people for fenceposts, Christmas trees, shingles, and firewood. Over the years the few seedlings that sprouted were trampled or eaten by feral pigs, voles, deer, and other wild animals. A fungus took the lives of many. The stinking cedar appears close to blinking out.

The biggest problem of all, though, is that these cedars thrive in cool mountain habitats. During the last ice age they flourished here in Florida, but now it's too warm and they are stuck. In the past, cedars mostly migrated in one way—gopher tortoises would eat the walnut-sized seeds and travel with them in their gut, then deposit them at some distant site more hospitable to both the tree and the tortoise. But the tortoise is now rare here, and the trees can no longer migrate long distances because of man-made barriers.

Perhaps it was the underdog phenomenon, but when Connie Barlow met these puny, smelly, and exceedingly rare little runts, it was love at first sight. In 1999 she stopped along the banks of the Apalachicola River in north Florida at Torreya State Park and came upon the trees. Barlow asked park officials if she could see some torreya seeds, and they brought out two, on a branch, in a jar of preservative. A botanist passionately interested in biodiversity and deeply concerned about its rapid disappearance, Barlow said she looked at the pitiful offering and thought, "Here was the state park named after the tree, and this was the best they could do?"

Months later, unable to forget the struggling tree, she returned to the park and lay down beneath one for a while. "In my magical, mythical way, even though I am an atheist, I asked the tree what it wanted." She divined that the tree wanted a new home in cooler climes before it disappeared. "I made a commitment to that tree that I would do everything in my power to move it." She would become its new animal partner, she decided, and formed a group called Torreya Guardian. But she couldn't move the trees because they had stopped producing seeds. She vowed to find others, and in 2005, she found Woodlanders Nursery in Aiken, South Carolina. Nurserymen there had taken cuttings from the national champion torreya, growing in someone's yard, and another big old torreya, and cloned them. The seedlings came from the offspring.

Though torreyas are *dioecious*—that is, each individual is one sex and needs a sexually complementary tree to reproduce through pollination—it's believed, perhaps in response to the stress of near extinction, that these two old trees had evolved to become *monoecious*—that is, they grew male and female reproductive parts on the same tree, and self-reproduced—"just like the dinosaurs in *Jurassic Park*," said Barlow.

In 2008, *Torreya taxifolia* was rewilded—Barlow and other volunteers planted thirty-one three-foot-high trees in the mountains of North Carolina, in an undisclosed location, fulfilling Barlow's promise. The species *Torreya taxifolia* is on the short list of trees that may have been saved by human-assisted migration, or at least given their best chance for survival.

CHAPTER 13

The Planet's Filters and Other Ecosystem Services

AFTER WE LEFT the farm, David and I drove to the outskirts of Traverse City and stopped in front of a motel, whose name must be withheld to protect the giant black willow tree that grows in front of it. The ridges of the rough bark are as thick as bridge cable, and the trunk is so fat that, were it hollow, several people could stand inside. Milarch walked up to it, grabbed a handful of branch, pulled it down toward us, and showed me the tips, a glistening vibrant green. He clipped the branches, put them in a plastic bag, and placed them in the back of his truck. Milarch believes this is the national champion. "No one knows it because I haven't nominated it," he said. "But I've taken hundreds of cuttings from it and propagated them." It's not the only big black willow he's taken cuttings from; the Michigan state champion willow is also near Traverse City, and he and officials from the Chippewa Indian tribe have taken cuttings from that one, too.

Milarch has a fondness for willows, which grow in abundance here along Lake Michigan. He showed me two willow houses—circles of willow trees planted as whips, or young trees, and tied together at the top; as they grow they become a dense wall of trees and a great fort for kids to hide and hang out in. One of them stands behind the library in Traverse City. In 2008, Milarch and a friend, Hank Bailey, the natural resource director for the Chippewa tribe, cut about a thousand eighteen-inch-long willow pieces, each about the diameter of a pencil. That year, on Earth Day, they took several dozen schoolchildren out to the mouth of the Boardman River, where it empties into Lake Michigan near downtown Traverse City. There they stuck the thousand cuttings into the black soil on the muddy flats. The next Earth Day they planted three thousand cuttings. "The year after that we had requests for ten thousand, and there aren't that many sticks on the tree," Milarch told me. Now Archangel is propagating black willows in a large nursery facility near his home using cuttings from the national champion.

Milarch said that one of the first trees he had ever wanted to clone was the willow, which has one of the largest natural ranges of any tree, growing from north Florida to Canada and as far west as Texas. Milarch felt that every river and stream should have them, since they are an effective way to clean our waterways. "Imagine a beautiful aquarium," he said, "with green plants swaying in sparkling water, and colorful fish swimming around. Now what would happen if someone unplugged the filter? What would it look like a week later? Would the water still be clear or would it be cloudy? Would the fish still be alive, gasping for the last remaining oxygen? What about the plants? That's what we have done by removing all of the willows along streams and lakes and rivers, and all the other trees. We've unplugged the earth's filter system." Willow trees, which are often found on the banks of rivers, may indeed be a way of cleaning up some of this nation's worst toxic waste sites. Buried in the muck along the Boardman are decades of chemical waste, from machine shop oil to cleaning solvent to chemicals used for timber processing, and Milarch hopes that these plantings will begin to remove some of it.

Many people cite the fact that trees create oxygen, the stuff we all need to live. But some researchers say the oxygen created by the world's forests is minuscule compared to the vast amount of oxygen created by the green mass of microscopic creatures called *phytoplankton* that inhabit the world's oceans. Some 20 percent of the earth's atmosphere is oxygen, and 90 percent of that comes from the seas. In cleaning the water and providing essential nutrients for aquatic life, trees also help the phytoplankton thrive. But in addition to cleaning up the water, trees are remarkably good at sweeping large amounts of pollutants out of the atmosphere. American urban forests alone sequester nearly half a billion dollars' worth of carbon and remove air pollutants that would cost nearly $4 billion to clean up in other ways, including some very toxic ones, from lung-cancer-causing particulates to benzene, ozone, sulfur dioxide, nitrogen oxides, and lead—all of them health hazards. Trees also mitigate some obstructive lung diseases. The leading cause of admission to hospitals in New York City for children under fifteen, for example, is asthma, which causes the network of bronchial tubes in the lungs to close up, making it difficult to draw a breath. It's an increasing problem—the rate of asthma among children soared by 50 percent between 1980 and 2000, with rates particularly high in poor neighborhoods. Air pollution exacerbates the disease. Researchers at Columbia University compared admissions to hospitals around the city for asthma and found that admission rates in a given area fell by 25 percent or so when the number of trees there increased by 343 per square kilometer.

Treating water pollution may be the single most critical service that trees offer to the world. One case study is the relationship between New York City and the rolling forests in the Catskill Mountains to the north of the city that form a catchment and filter for the water New Yorkers drink. Concerned that cryptosporidium, a microscopic intestinal parasite, and other waterborne pathogens might find their way into New Yorkers' water supply, in 1989 the federal Environmental Protection Agency ordered the city to build a new water treatment plant at a cost of $8 billion. After much political debate, and the threat of a lawsuit by the environmentalist Robert Kennedy, Jr., officials instead decided that the cheaper and better option was to protect the two-thousand-square-mile forested watershed that naturally filters water flowing into the city, at a cost of about $1.5 billion. The money was spent on such things as buying buffers of natural landscape around reservoirs as filters and crafting agreements with upstate cities and towns to limit development in watershed areas. While the clean water from the forest alone made economic sense, the intact native forest also provides a host of other ecosystem services, including wildlife habitat, recreation, and carbon dioxide sequestration.

The move to preserve the Catskill forest filter is an exception. Far more common are the hard lessons learned after forests have been removed. One of the most egregious examples is that of the Chesapeake Bay in eastern Maryland, the largest of 130 estuaries in the United States. Once teeming with life, it was home to blue crabs, shad, swarms of anchovies, and schools of striped bass. "Baltimore lay very near the immense protein factory of Chesapeake Bay," wrote the *Baltimore Sun* newspaper columnist H. L. Mencken in 1940. "Out of the bay it ate divinely." This nearly two-hundred-mile-long, forty-two-square-mile shallow mix of fresh and salt waters is now a great American ecological tragedy, a shadow of what it once was. Numbers of blue crab, the signature seafood of Maryland, have dropped precipitously. Oyster fishermen once harvested twenty-five million bushels out of the bay each year; now the take is around two hundred thousand. Diseases such as mycobacteriosis and Pfiesteria, from agricultural runoff, are rampant and cause widespread fish kills. The bay recently experienced its largest dead zone ever, which stretched for eighty-three miles. Nothing lives in this oxygen-poor water caused by fertilizer runoff.

Deforestation is one of the largest causes of the myriad problems in the bay. Where fresh water once fell and was filtered and slowly released back into the bay there are now farm fields, construction sites, lawns, and parking lots that pour polluted sediment into the bay. Farms are particularly bad culprits in this scenario—research shows that river basins with the greatest amount of farmland produce the most sediment, while river valleys with the most forest cover produce the least. Nitrogen and phosphorus from agricultural fertilizers and poultry waste feed the proliferation of bacteria that consume dissolved oxygen, and the low levels of oxygen create massive dead zones that cannot support aquatic life.

Deforestation along tributaries to the bay means there are no woodlands to hold back the water, and so more water flows faster. That increases erosion, which causes streams to deepen and narrow. Faster flowing streams reduce the number and array of ecosystem services a waterway can provide. The Chesapeake drains thousands of miles of more than 150 major streams and rivers from six states and the District of Columbia, a massive catchment of 64,000 square miles. Broader forested streams flow more slowly than those without streamside forests, allowing more time for contaminants to settle out and be taken up and neutralized by microbes. A study of sixteen tributaries to the rivers that flow into the Chesapeake found that forested streams are significantly better, as much as ten times better, at removing ammonium and nitrogen, and much more effective at breaking down toxic organic pesticides.

Reforestation can help reverse these kinds of problems. In fact, trees could be utilized to remedy a lot of modern-day water pollution problems, including some of the worst kind of human-created chemical waste: dioxin, ammonia, dry cleaning solvents, oil and gas spills, ammunition waste, polyaromatic hydrocarbons, PCBs, and other industrial waste, even the explosive trinitrotoluene, or TNT. The trees take up waterborne toxic waste and neutralize, metabolize, or aerosolize it. *Phytoremediation*, the cleaning up of toxic waste with trees, is a robust

ecotechnology. Instead of digging up waste with heavy equipment, and trucking it to a hazardous waste site, the task can often
be accomplished by planting willows and poplar forests atop the
site. These species are preferred because they grow more roots
than other species; when the trees are buried deep—eight feet
or so—they grow a large, tangled, robust mass of roots, and the
rhizosphere, with its multitudes of fungi and bacteria, is where
most of the magic happens.

Lou Licht is the founder and president of an Iowa-based
company called Ecolotree that installs fields of poplar and willow trees to remediate toxic waste. He uses tough, fast-growing
hybrids, thirsty trees that suck a lot of water out of the ground,
and he plants only male trees, so there is no reproduction and
therefore no little trees to remove. He sets up an irrigation system to water the trees. "Lots of water is necessary," Licht says,
"because water carries the waste around." One willow can process fifteen gallons of waste a day, and a field of a thousand trees
on an acre can treat ten gallons of toxic water per minute.

Just before the water reaches the trees' roots, it hits a zone
around the root as thick as a finger. "The microbial population
is a hundredfold greater here, because it's fed by the root exudates," Licht explains. Exudates are organic sugars and other
compounds, much sought after by the microbes, that precipitate out of the tree through the roots. Licht calls this finger-wide
halo the "root zone reactor," a critical quarter or half inch of
microbial stew that does the lion's share of the work. "The waste
is often broken down right there, or turned into a precipitate.
The microbial jungle under there just rips the stuff apart."

Licht estimates that a willow sewage treatment "plant" costs

25 or 30 percent as much as a conventional sewage treatment facility. It also has lower maintenance and energy costs and is far easier to operate. But not only is phytoremediation far cheaper, the strategic planting of willows and aspen often does things standard methods of toxic cleanup cannot. The natural filters scrub out pollutants that can't be extracted by conventional methods—pharmaceuticals, flame retardants, chemicals from plastic, and other endocrine disruptors. The hardest part of a conventional toxic waste cleanup is often getting rid of the last few percent of waste, and tree roots can often reach and handle that. In 1984 a tanker truck skidded on an icy road near Medford, Oregon, and spilled 111 trichloroethane, a carcinogen used to preserve lumber, which leaked into the groundwater. For years the carcinogen was removed from groundwater by the usual method of pumping out the contaminated water, but the process was only partially successful. In 1997 a phytoremediation firm from Washington State planted eight hundred hybrid poplars, which pulled the rest of the waste out of the groundwater.

There are some trees and other plants that specialize in taking up extraordinarily high levels of metal—called "hyper-accumulator" plants—and they are starting to be tapped for cleanup at toxic waste sites. Silver birch, for example, take up high levels of zinc in industrial areas. A small tree discovered in the Philippines called *Rinorea niccolifera* can take into its stem and leaves one hundred to one thousand times the amount of nickel that normal trees take up, without being harmed. The tree is used for cleaning up toxic waste and can even be used for phytomining, the commercial harvest of metals using plants that collect them. Unfortunately, the tree is endangered.

Still, man-made phytoremediation forests can't take care of everything. Mercury and plutonium can find their way into leaves and become airborne, causing air pollution, so annual plants that can be harvested and burned in an incinerator, such as sunflowers, are safer on such sites. And the technology can be oversold. If the waste is too deep, or the site too wet, or the water too salty, phytoremediation might not work.

Enköping is a prosperous farming town in central Sweden near the shore of Lake Mälaren. Sewage sludge here used to be dewatered in a conventional sewage treatment plant, but in recent years the city has replaced the plant with a willow field. The wastewater, which contains high levels of nitrogen, is pumped onto about 190 acres of coppiced willows—willows whose main trunks have been cut off, allowing dozens of basal sprouts, or suckers, to grow. This field of dense willow forest takes up and neutralizes the waste. The system treats about eleven tons of nitrogen a year, the production of the entire city, and some phosphorus, which the trees turn into fertilizer. Then the willow coppices are harvested, chipped into small pieces, and used as a biofuel to generate electricity for Enköping.

The Swedish approach, says Licht, is the beginning of the next generation of phytoremediation, something he calls "function-rich"—serving more than a single use. "The question is, how can we make phytoremediation prettier, make it produce food, use it to save endangered species? We already capture greenhouse gases. Can we increase that? How can we grow something with market value, such as fuels or fiber?"

A critical application for strategically placed fields of poplar and willow trees is the scrubbing of urban and rural runoff that washes into rivers, streams, and oceans when rain falls across a landscape. In cities and suburbs, rain falls on pavement, construction sites, and other impervious surfaces that carry oil, lawn chemicals, pet waste, and industrial waste into waterways. Storm water and leaking sewage from aged and broken sewer lines carry viruses, bacteria, and protozoa that cause diseases that can kill and contaminate shellfish, fish, and other sea life. Sea otters, for example, are plagued by a brain parasite that comes from ingesting cat feces. In farm country similar problems are caused by herbicides, pesticides, and fertilizers. Because this runoff water comes from wide-ranging sources, it's difficult to capture and treat in a sewage treatment plant. "You can't catch all of that storm water and treat it conventionally, it's too expensive," says Licht. "The only way to get streams and oceans cleaned up is to tree-farm our way through it." The water that runs off 80 percent of the soluble soils in farm country is funneled through a very small portion of the total watershed, or drainage, which means that strategically placed willow and poplar farms could be planted in these areas to capture tainted water on which the trees could work their root zone magic.

Along those lines, Licht has just finished a seven-acre willow installation in Seattle to catch urban runoff that flows into Puget Sound. The water Licht is treating flows into a swale and percolates through the roots of a large grove of willows. When a hundred thousand gallons of water are stored, a drain is opened and the water is released into Puget Sound. "Every drop of water passes within an inch of the roots, and the root zone reactor cleans it," says Licht. In farm country, Ecolotree has used a field of trees to reduce 45 milligrams per gallon of the organic waste nitrate nitrogen—more than four times the federal drinking water standard—to less than one milligram. "It's excess fertilizer in water washing off of a cornfield, going through fields, and entering a stream," says Licht. The trees not only neutralize the waste, they use it for their own growth. "The trees love it and grow enormous." So why aren't these organic systems more widely used? "Engineers who design waste treatment are botanically challenged," Licht tells me.

Phyto fields might also be a solution for dying regions of the ocean. In the 1960s there were 49 hypoxic zones in the world's oceans, and that number has doubled every decade since. Dead zones are caused by nitrogen and phosphorus, largely from agricultural fertilizers. As the nutrients run off farm fields and make their way into the ocean, they fertilize the blooms of naturally occurring algae. When the algae naturally die and sink to the bottom of the sea, bacteria feed on them and consume the dissolved oxygen that is needed to sustain fish and other life. As the bacteria continue to eat, the level of dissolved oxygen declines to the point where the ocean in that region is no longer able to support life. The most infamous of dead zones, extending over 8,500 square miles—bigger than the state of New Jersey—is in the Gulf of Mexico, fed by nutrient runoff from large-scale agriculture along the length of the Mississippi River.

PHYTOPLANKTON ARE TOO small to be seen with the naked eye, yet they are vital to all life on the planet. They are abundant in the world's oceans and, through their process of photosynthesis, they are tasked with the job of turning sunlight into food for other sea-dwelling creatures. Experiments have proven that their numbers are greatly enhanced when iron is added to the ocean.

The importance of iron led one path-breaking scientist to make a unique connection. The Erimo Peninsula on the north coast of Japan saw its forests clear-cut and its hills turned into pasture long ago. The change drove off the schools of fish that once teemed there, and caused a decline in oyster populations. Katsuhiko Matsunaga, a Japanese marine chemist, spent years studying the relationship between forests and oceans. His key finding is that even where iron is abundant in parts of the ocean, it is oxygenated, which means it is not readily available for the tiny creatures. What *can* make iron available to phytoplankton to perform photosynthesis, however, is fulvic acid, one of several humic acids that comes from the decay of leaves and other organic matter. The ongoing, natural decomposition of centuries of tree leaves and other material on the forest floor, and the leaking, leaching, and washing of this chemical stew into the ocean, is vital to increasing coastal phytoplankton, and thus the things that eat them, and those that eat them, from oysters all the way to whales. The award-winning chemist spent much of his life working with fishermen in coastal communities to reforest the coast and the banks of rivers and streams to increase fish stocks, and he wrote about it, in Japanese, in one of his papers, "When Forests Disappear the Sea Dies."

Not only oceans benefit from trees. A study at Ontario's Daisy Lake, near Sudbury, looked at fish that lived in two distinct regions in the large body of freshwater—one where trees on shore were absent and the other where forests were robust. Fish from areas where there were forests along the shore were dramatically "fatter" and "larger and stronger," according to researcher Andrew Tanentzap of Cambridge University. Perch pulled from nonforested areas were "much smaller, and consequently much less likely to survive and breed." Organic materials from the forests around Daisy Lake are consumed by bacteria, which are eaten by one-celled animals called zooplankton, which are in turn eaten by fish.

These are the understated and poorly researched roles that trees and forests play in maintaining and enhancing the biosphere that earns them the term "ecotechnology." Nothing that the human enterprise does can come anywhere near the elegance and efficiency of a robust global forest.

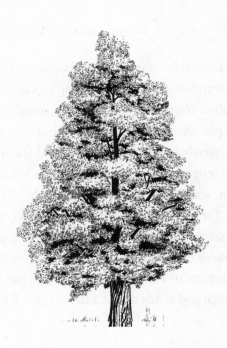

CHAPTER 14
Ulmo

THE ULMO TREE grows in Chile and Argentina, and is similar to the elm. It is deciduous, elegant in appearance, with a stout trunk, broad green leaves, and beautiful white flowers whose nectar is gathered by bees to make a creamy, highly-prized honey. The dense, hard, decay-resistant wood is also prized for making fences and firewood, and so the tree is in trouble.

There may be yet another reason to value the tree. For the last forty-five years, Gary Strobel, a plant pathologist at Montana State University, has scoured far-flung forests around the world for what he calls the "jewels of the jungle." He doesn't look for compounds in the leaves or the bark of the tree, as most bio-prospectors do; Strobel is looking for fungi with unusual properties in the microscopic crevices between the cells of the new leaf stems. Fungi and other microbes that grow in these spaces are called *endophytes,* a scientific term that means "in the plant." The trees he is examining are those that have grown in the same place for millions of years, which means that the fungus and the tree have had a long time to coevolve. The Ulmo is one of them.

Strobel made headlines in 1987 when he injected elm trees on the Montana State University campus with a genetically engineered bacterium he created from bacteria he found in between the cells of wheat, which he believed would protect the trees from Dutch elm disease. The injections violated EPA rules on the release of genetically engineered organisms, and when a story about the rogue experiment appeared on the front page of *The New York Times,* Strobel was required to cut down all of the inoculated trees.

Some of the compounds Strobel has found in trees have led to patents, including for several different kinds of antibiotics as well as a new type of immunosuppressant drug that is gentler than the ones currently used. He recently found an antibiotic in Bolivia that kills drug-resistant staph, E. coli, and salmonella but is safe to use as a mouthwash. But his most surprising discoveries to date are the properties found in a fungus he named *Gliocladium roseum.* This fungus gives off eight compounds associated with diesel fuel, including octane and heptanes, yet it does not contain some of the polluting compounds found in diesel such as naphthalene. Through a microscope in his campus laboratory he showed me the fungus, which looks like a red, long-stemmed flower. He calls the compounds "survival microbes"; he believes they help the trees ward off disease and insects in exchange for a place to live.

While any possible fuel production from the fungus is still

a long way off, the fact that such an organism even exists is the real discovery. "There is no other creature on the planet we know that can create diesel without refining," he told me. Fungi are known to emit hydrocarbons, but they need processing. This fungus is different—it emits diesel compounds into the atmosphere around it. Pure diesel in its natural state does not need refining from crude oil, and Strobel's fungi can be grown in vats on wood chips or crop waste and produce what the scientist calls "mycodiesel." "The main value of the discovery may turn out to be the genes controlling the production of hydrocarbons and the potential for being able to genetically engineer them into other microbes, such as yeast, which grows faster and could carry out the process more efficiently," Strobel notes.

Strobel's work is yet another argument for archiving rare trees whose properties we do not yet understand. While fungi are commonly researched for their beneficial properties, the fungi that grow in the spaces between the cells of leaf stems are especially interesting because they compete in an environment with far fewer microbes, and less competition means they develop more unusual properties to live compatibly with their host plant. The diesel emissions are likely a kind of natural antibiotic that helps the tree ward off infections. According to Strobel, "There's an untold plethora of unidentified species out there, and they are useful products. Not just for medical uses or for fuel, but for a whole range of things." Perhaps the most precious jewels of the jungle are yet to found.

ONCE LESLIE LEE agreed to create the Ancient Forest Archive, the resources were available to launch the project on the scale Milarch had always hoped for. He and Lee decided that the first country outside the United States they would try to clone in would be Ireland. The native Irish old-growth forests, almost completely mowed down and never replanted, are in even worse shape than those in the United States. Only about 1 percent of Ireland's native woodlands remains, the least of any European country. The forest fragments are so small and vulnerable that protecting them as soon as possible is critical.

With polar ice rapidly melting as a result of climate change, and an increasing amount of freshwater pouring into the oceans, much of northern Europe could be at serious risk. Experts say it's very possible that the Gulf Stream, the conveyor belt of warm water that flows from the south and keeps northern Europe warm, could become so diluted with heavier freshwater that it will sink into the ocean. That could plunge Europe into a deep freeze, which could in turn mean widespread forest death.

Or, as is already occurring in the United States, more, or more virulent, diseases could wipe out stressed forests. In 2010, officials from Britain's leading tree groups, Woodland Trust and Woodland Heritage, sounded the alarm about the discovery of a new disease called acute oak decline that has infected both of the United Kingdom's two species of native oak, the sessile and pedunculate oaks. The fungus causes a canker on the tree, which oozes fluid—something known as "bleeding." Then it causes the dieback of the branches, starting at the tips, which finally leads to death, within three to five years. "This is our most iconic tree, it totally dominates our landscape, and here we have a potentially new disease that leads to a rapid decline of the tree," says Andy Sharkey, the Woodland Trust's head of woodland management. Acute oak decline also kills beech, larch, and ash.

One of the first things David Milarch and Leslie Lee did after they formed their partnership was to bring Diana Beresford-Kroeger for a visit to Michigan, first as a consultant and later as senior science adviser. Bill Libby was also hired as a consultant. One of Beresford-Kroeger's first tasks was to choose the first one hundred trees from the global forest to be cloned, the most important trees to have archived in case of a catastrophe. The crew also made a trip to Bill Libby's home in Orinda, California, to talk about the ethics of collecting trees and the ethics of assisting trees in a migration to other parts of the world.

They decided that species would be grown and planted in suitable places where they are native, or moved to places where they had already proved to be uninvasive. Redwoods and sequoias, for example, grow around the world with almost no invasive properties. Meanwhile, the risk of importing disease on trees would not be a problem if cloning was done in certified nurseries, since trees that are shipped between countries from these facilities must have bare roots and be certified as disease free. In the absence of proof that some tree genetics are better than others, proven survivors are arguably the best bet. "If you want to plant a tree and walk away," Milarch said, "where will you get your genetics? From trees that have survived." Moreover, it's not just old trees but old-growth forest that may be critical, and plantings will include native soil, soil microorganisms, and understory species—as much of the forest as possible.

David Milarch, Leslie Lee, Diana Beresford-Kroeger, and her husband, Chris, would go to Ireland for two weeks in early December to begin the European collection, and I was invited to join them. The morning after our arrival, we were met by our driver, Dermot Buckley, who guided us through the small villages and rolling farm fields in the countryside of southwest Ireland. December in Ireland is a damp, dark affair, with nickel-gray clouds hanging low and a sun that comes up late and goes down early. The heart of a North Atlantic winter, though, is the time to take cuttings from the trees, when the buds are dormant and the branches will survive being cut and transported.

Climax oak forests covered more than two-thirds of the country until the sixteenth century, and as a result Ireland was one of the great forest civilizations of Europe. The worship of trees goes back thousands of years in Ireland, to the Druids, the high priests of the Celts, who taught that sacred springs, stones, and groves were a way to connect with the divine. Brehon law, an ancient Irish code of conduct, was centered on the protection of the forest. Each of the original twenty letters of the Ogham, the alphabet of the native Irish, was named after a tree or another plant of the native forest. Trees were sources of food and medicine and inspiration, and were often where teachers assembled their students for lectures. The forest and the native culture were so inseparable that in the early sixth century, Caesarius of Arles, a Catholic leader seeking to convert Ireland, forbade tree worship and urged the faithful to burn up and chop down the "sacrilegious" trees to their very roots. Another Catholic leader, Martin of Tours, found out just how sacred trees were. A crowd of worshippers stood by as he demolished a pagan shrine but mobbed him when he tried to cut down a sacred tree. Centuries later, after the British subjugated Ireland and banned the old ways, the Irish formed outdoor "hedgerow schools" to teach children about their native history, language, and faith. So critical were the forests to the Irish way of life that one of the planks in the Sinn Féin platform was the replanting of the native forests.

In the 1500s, when the Tudors arrived from England to conquer, they started to mine the vast oak woods, caring nothing for proper forestry. "Trees are an excrescence provided by nature for the payment of debts," said the landowner Sir Jonah Barrington in the late eighteenth century, characterizing the prevailing attitude toward the great Irish deforestation. Large trees were taken to be used for ship and house beams, branches were used for barrel staves, which the English used to ship their goods around the world, and the remainder of the tree was used for charcoal to fire iron and glass furnaces. There was also a side benefit for the English—stripping the country bare deprived the Irish rebels of their hiding places.

Today, native trees in Ireland are usually solitary, growing in the middle of a farm field or in a town. The only forests most visitors see are the commercial, monoculture stands of Sitka spruce, a conifer native to North America, planted by Coilite, the Irish forest agency. These exotic forests are planted solely for timber, not for the ecological benefits of a forest or for recreation.

OUR FIRST STOP to collect old-growth DNA was Mount Congreve, a carefully tended English-style garden overlooking the River Suir, where the trees are three and four hundred years old. Mount Congreve is the epitome of the English garden, from the time when Britain's ships ruled the world and brought species to the United Kingdom from all over. The seventy-acre property was owned by Ambrose Congreve, who married into a family of industrialists, the Glasgows, who have cared for these gardens since the 1700s. Congreve, who was 102 when we visited and living in the Bahamas, had given us permission to take cuttings.* Even in the damp gloom, the garden was an idyllic landscape. Diana Beresford-Kroeger clipped several samples of new growth from the branches of two yews that had been planted by the Glasgow family in the 1700s. All of Ireland's yew trees

*Ambrose Congreve died in May 2011, at the age of 104.

are descended from just two yews that were brought here from England in the sixteenth century. It's a good thing we came to this garden when we did; there is talk of "developing" this glorious piece of real estate.

As we drove to our next stop we discovered the persistence of the old ways of the forest. On Ireland's most modern motorway, Buckley pointed out a single small, scraggly tree growing in an ocean of grass along the road. "It's the Latoon fairy tree," he announced. In 1996, when the motorway was under construction, a traditional Irish storyteller named Eddie Lenihan called the local press. A hawthorn tree that lay in the path of the road being built, Lenihan claimed, was where the fairies once did battle. A farmer had told Lenihan of driving his cows there one morning and seeing the fairy blood on the ground. Unlike the gentle fairies in Disney movies, Lenihan explained, Irish fairies are fierce, and the blood was likely from battle. "Immediately, he knew that the fairies had been fighting the night before and had dragged back their wounded and dead after the battle," Lenihan told the paper. When construction workers read the story, they refused to cut down the tree. Hawthorn trees are said to have a powerful guardian spirit that becomes angry if the tree is not cared for. At night, however, someone sneaked over to the construction site with a saw and reduced the hawthorn to a stump. Shortly afterward, in what seemed a miracle to the locals, the tree sprouted new leaves and branches. Contractors finally agreed to leave the tree in place.

Ireland is a small country, and by sheer coincidence, Buckley's cousin Andrew St. Ledger was a member of the Woodland League, a group whose motto is "Dedicated to restoring the relationship between people and their native woodlands." St. Ledger is also a craftsman who fashions fine furniture and sculptures out of wood. For years he and his colleagues have fought the Irish forest policy of planting monoculture timber farms and have asked the government to begin to restore native woodland across the country. Buckley says St. Ledger has grown hundreds of oaks from acorns and has worked on a plan with others in his group to harness the energy of schoolchildren to restore Ireland's woodlands. Joining us for lunch at a local pub, St. Ledger listened as Milarch explained the project to clone the largest trees, starting with his near-death experience and ending at the Congreve gardens. "We're here to help Ireland save the last of its old growth," Milarch told him. "The cavalry just came over the hill."

Hearing David's words, Andrew became overwhelmed, to the point where his eyes grew misty. He offered to take us to some of the old-tree genetics that remain in Ireland. We all got into Buckley's van and motored off to what Andrew called the Brian Boru tree. As a fine rain fell, we climbed carefully over an electric fence and splashed in inch-deep water across a farm meadow, where a large, lone bull eyed us warily. When we reached the tree, its crown spread over us, offering shelter from the steady drizzle. One large branch had grown to the ground, like a giant elbow, to stabilize the tree. This lone sessile oak dates to at least the tenth century and is named after Brian Boru, the last high king of Ireland. The border between fact and fiction is often permeable in Ireland, but the story goes that Boru rallied his men here, beneath the spreading crown of the tree, and then headed to Clontarf, where in a bloody battle he and his men beat the Vikings. That night as Boru prayed in his tent, an enemy penetrated the camp, entered Boru's tent, and ran a sword through him.

Many trees in Ireland have a story to tell.

Despite the rain and slippery bark, St. Ledger climbed the tree and inched his way out onto a muddy branch to take cuttings for us. We had expected that the collection would come from these big old solitary trees, so we were surprised when he then took us to an eighty-acre privately owned fragment of Ireland's forest past called Raheen Woods. A previous owner had logged most of a large tract of forest to farm but had protected this patch as a hunting preserve—a wild wood, as the Irish call it. The noise of whizzing traffic died as we walked into the growth of trees, and the forest hush took over.

Beneath towering moss-coated oaks, on a path carpeted with glistening wet oak leaves, we made our way into a forest cathedral of gnarly trees, a breathtaking remnant of Ireland's forest past. It was a walk through time as well as space, and a treasure trove of ancient forest genetics. Not only are the oak trees here old growth, but the entire ecosystem is as well. Just like oaks in North America, the oaks of the British Isles are a critical source of native biodiversity, home to more moths, butterflies, and other insects than any other tree. More than three hundred species of lichen alone grow on oaks in Britain and Ireland. "There's been oak cover here for eight thousand years," St. Ledger told us. "The forest is a three-dimensional maze of recycling nutrients—passing from plant to animal to bird back to plants again. It's a rare example of the authentic rainforest landscape of Ireland. There's common oak, hazel, holly, alder, willow, mountain ash, cherry, black thorn and white thorn, and an amazing variety of ferns, ground ivy, tree ivy, and brambles. I've seen badgers, pine marten, fox, voles, red squirrels, and deer. It's a symphony of sorts, each playing its part."

St. Ledger was pleased as punch to show us this secret garden, and we were all pleasantly shocked to see something akin to a living dinosaur. We walked around in wonder. Diana Beresford-Kroeger in particular was agog. "I know of no other place like this in Ireland," she said in amazement, "nowhere." St. Ledger had permission from the landowner for gathering, so Milarch and Lee leaned a stepladder up against the trees, took cuttings, put them in baggies, and stored them in an ice chest.

While Ireland's native forests may be Europe's most deci-mated, native forests across the Continent have similarly been destroyed. They once covered as much as 90 percent of mainland Europe; now they cover about 30 percent and are in fragmented condition. Ireland has the smallest amount of old-growth forest while Finland has the most, with 72 percent. If old-growth genetics are indeed critical to rebuilding forests to survive a changing world, the last chance for Europe is hanging on by a thread in many places. And even these small pieces are not safe. Only a popular uprising in England in 2011 averted the sale of much of the country's public woodlands to private land-owners who might well have cut them down.

Toward the end of our stay we drove on to Killarney National Park. We could not take cuttings here but came to look at some of the great old trees of Ireland. We walked along the Lakes of Killarney, past massive trees. But as beautiful as the Killarney woods are, they are mostly parkland and not a wild forest. The park does contain some slivers of old growth, though. One of Ireland's largest old-growth yew forests is found here, its mossy green floor carpeted with red yew berries. We were surprised to see a giant redwood tree lying prone on the ground in the park, planted a century ago and felled recently because of disease.

Killarney includes Muckross Abbey, an ivy-covered fifteenth-century stone structure with a cemetery in front. Major sections of wall and roof are missing, and as we approached, a crew of workmen were toiling, laying new stone floors and rebuilding the two-foot-thick abbey walls. The foreman agreed to show us around, and we climbed construction ladders to the top of the structure. The highlight, when we arrived there, was the view of a giant yew tree planted in the courtyard, its sharp conifer fragrance filling the air atop the church. The yew was planted here in 1448 and is among the oldest trees in Ireland. Churches and monasteries throughout Ireland were often built on sites sacred to the pagans, so that people who came to visit the sacred yew might also visit the church and be converted. Whether the visitor was pagan or Christian, the tree was viewed as a portal to divinity, a place where a seeker could go and have his or her soul lifted to the heavens.

CHAPTER 16
Yew

IN 1974 A YOUNG British man named Allen Meredith went to visit a churchyard in Broadwell, a village in southwest England, to give a talk about bird watching. On a tour before his talk, the guide pointed out a two-hundred-year-old yew tree. As recounted in the book *The Sacred Yew*, Meredith suddenly knew intuitively that the tree was far older. A year or so later he had a dream about a group of elders wearing gowns that brushed the ground and hoods that hid their faces. He was told by the elders to look for the Tree of the Cross, which he understood to mean that the tree was so long-lived that it held secrets to immortality. "I knew right away it was the yew tree," Meredith told the authors of the book. Dream upon similar dream followed, and they brought to mind the strong connection with the yew he had experienced in the churchyard. The dreams spilled into his waking life, and he became obsessed with efforts to find out more about the yew. He pedaled his bicycle around the English countryside visiting the ancient yews to try to figure out their age, and to find out how many listed in old records were still standing. What he found worried him.

Yews grow very slowly, and their wood is very dense. They are nearly impossible to date because, much like a bristlecone pine, they grow in peculiar ways. As part of their aging and self-renewal process, they will sacrifice their heartwood, the denser center of the tree, or other parts, to a wood-digesting fungus and yet keep growing, and as a result, much of a living tree may appear to be dead. Furthermore, the yew's ability to *branch layer*—to grow its lower branches toward the ground and root—can turn a single tree over many centuries into a grove. Because the trees sometimes seemingly stop growing, people think they are dead and cut them down. Meredith discovered that hundreds of ancient yews had mistakenly been cut down this way.

Meredith's dreams and intuitions were insistently telling him that the yews were far older than commonly thought and, furthermore, that they were sacred. Realizing that operating on intuition alone would brand him as a kook and he might never get his message about the true age of the yew trees heard, he set out to school himself in dendrochronology—the aging of trees—and spent months reading in libraries, scouring church records, and writing to experts around the country, even as he continued to visit yews to study and measure them.

In 1980 Meredith met Alan Mitchell, one of the leading tree experts in Britain and the founder of the Tree Register of the

British Isles, which contains records of tens of thousands of
Britain's Heritage Trees, the oldest, widest, rarest, and most historic specimens. Meredith told him of his passion for yews and
of his visions and showed him his records and research. Deeply
skeptical at first, Mitchell eventually came around to Meredith's
point of view: that the yews could be thousands of years old.
"In fact there appears to be no theoretical end to this tree, no
reason for it to die," Mitchell concluded. Many of Britain's tree
experts came to believe yew trees were ancient because of this
self-taught tree expert. It led to a new appreciation for the tree,
and to redoubled efforts to study, catalogue, and protect it.
Meredith disappeared from the tree scene many years ago and
became a recluse, but the work he began to reappraise the age
and importance of the yew is being carried on by others.

Some people believe the yew is the most sacred tree in the
world. "The yew is found on every continent in the northern
hemisphere and has a spiritual aspect in every country it is
found in," writes Fred Hageneder, author of the exhaustive *Yew:
A History* and founding member of the Ancient Yew Group,
which continues to catalogue and protect the ancient yews of
England, some two thousand of which are in their registry.
The yew has been worshipped across the world, from Europe
to Japan to the Pacific Northwest of the United States. Nature
spirits of the Shinto religion of Japan, called *kami,* are said to
sometimes take up residency in certain trees, and one of these
revered trees, called the Hakusan Jinja yew tree, some forty feet
tall and twenty feet around, was declared a god in 1673 because
it was believed to harbor *kami.* In the Pacific Northwest the Tlin-
git tribe used yew wood for death masks and spirit whistles. In

the British Isles the oldest yew trees are often next to Christian churches, in graveyards, and in other venerated places such as Muckross Abbey. The yew tree was believed to be a portal to the underworld, and a sprig or branch of yew was often laid in burial shrouds or coffins.

The yew has more earthly attributes as well. With the exception of the bright red *aril*, the fleshy pulp around the seed, the tree is extremely poisonous. A yew concoction was carried as a poison pill by the Celts and others in case they were captured by the enemy. Celtic warriors covered their arrowheads with the sap to increase its lethality. Surprisingly, the yew's healing properties are also more profound than those of any other tree. The Pacific yew in North America provided the natural molecule that has since been synthesized and is, under the brand name Taxol, a powerful chemotherapeutic used to treat breast, prostate, lung, stomach, head, and neck cancers.

The yew has also been praised for its lethal properties as a weapon. The military advantage in the thirteenth to sixteenth centuries lay in longbow proficiency. At the battle of Crécy during the Hundred Years' War, for example, the outnumbered English won, thanks to something called an "arrow-storm"— seven thousand archers firing seventy thousand arrows per minute, "as thick as snow, with a terrible noise, like a tempestuous wind preceding a tempest," wrote one witness. Deeply impressed, the English ordered every able-bodied man to learn to use a longbow, and to own two of them.

The best wood for a longbow was the yew. Bow wood was cut where the sapwood—or outer wood on the tree—and the heartwood meet. Because these two types of wood have complementary properties, when cut as one piece to form a single bow, a de facto composite, its power was unprecedented. The heartwood side, which compresses well, faced the archer, while the sapwood side was best at stretching and lengthening when the bowstring was pulled. The yew gave the bow a draw weight of 120 pounds compared with the 100 pounds of lesser wood, while some had a draw weight of 150 or more, and a range of up to a thousand feet. Neither solid oak nor armor could stop the metal-tipped arrows fired from a yew bow. The Gwent archers of Wales were known for their skill at nailing enemies on horseback to their mount by driving an arrow through the armor, the leg, the leather saddle, and deep into the horse with the power of the yew bow. "The strength inherent in a longbow, combined with the qualities of the 'composite' yew, forged the most effective killing device known to mankind at that time," Hageneder writes.

By 1470, English yew forests were nearly exhausted, and the British government realized a need for new sources of yew wood. They solved that problem in 1472 with a yew tax. Every ship that unloaded in any English harbor was required to bring four "bowestaffs" for every tun-tight, or large cask, of wine they imported. The rush across Europe for centuries-old yew trees was on. By the early sixteenth century, the yews of Europe were decimated. To this day they have not recovered, and most of the yews are solitary trees. One of the largest and most beautiful exceptions is Kingley Vale, a wildwood yew forest preserve near the city of Chichester in southern England, with thousands of trees, some of them up to two thousand years old.

CHAPTER 17

Mystics and Freethinkers

DAVID MILARCH ISN'T alone in arguing for a more expansive view of trees. For fifty years Lawrence Edwards, a geometry teacher who lived in the small, tidy village of Strontian on the west coast of Scotland, went to the park near his home and, through his thick glasses, painstakingly measured the new buds on the oak, beech, ash, elm, birch, and cherry trees there. He meticulously gathered more than a hundred thousand data points, quantifying changes in the shape of the buds, determining how sharpened or flattened they were. Over the decades he found that leaf buds have a subtle yet unmistakable pulse in the fall and winter, growing flatter in shape and then sharpening. His findings were especially unusual because even though trees stop their metabolism in the winter, this pulse continues.

A careful scientist, Edwards, who died in 2004 at the age

of ninety-two, found conclusively that each species of tree had a two-week shape-shifting rhythm geared to the alignment of the earth, the moon, and one of the planets. "When the moon passes through the line of Mars and Earth, all of the oaks do their little dance for a day or two," Graham Calderwood told me. Calderwood worked with Edwards for twenty years and now carries on his research. "When the moon passes through the line of Earth and Venus, the birches do *their* little dance." Edwards saw these kinds of changes in all species of tree he examined except one, a knapweed tree that was situated under the town's only power line. Edwards and Calderwood believe the electromagnetic field created by the power line may block the tree's link with the planets.

Edwards identified another cycle. As the fourteen-day cycle slips a bit in duration over the years, a seven-year cycle, reflected in the alignment of planets, seems to reset the clock, and the fourteen-day cycle becomes fourteen days again. The calculations are sophisticated and precise, says Dr. Jay Kappraff, a mathematics professor at the New Jersey Institute of Technology in Newark, who has studied and written papers about Edwards's work.

But what does it all mean? Edwards didn't advance a theory to explain his findings. A teacher of upper-level mathematics at the Edinburgh Rudolf Steiner School, he was an adherent of the teachings of the Austrian mystic Rudolf Steiner, who claimed to see an etheric field around all living things, a kind of geometric matrix that guides their growth. While the planets and trees would seem to be unrelated, they are, Steiner intuited, connected through this matrix that is invisible to most. Steiner believed that other plants, cells, embryos, even the human heart were connected to this sacred matrix, which could be understood and utilized for great benefit if it were unlocked by a geometric formula.

Edwards's and Calderwood's thorough work is among a great deal of unusual research into trees and forests that hints at how little we know about these beings on yet another level. The physicist Walter Heisenberg wrote that "what we observe is not nature itself, but nature that responds to our method of questioning." As we look into the world of trees, we begin to realize that there are many important questions that haven't been asked by scientists.

Other scholars have noted a link between trees and the cosmos, though it is hard to say what it means. In the mid-1970s, Russian scientists from the Botanical Institute of the Russian Academy of Sciences examined the growth rings of an 807-year-old juniper tree growing on a mountaintop more than 11,000 feet in altitude. The width of the rings showed a substantial slowing of tree growth during the fifteen years following known supernovas—in 1604, 1770, and 1952.

A few years ago, researchers at the University of Edinburgh in Scotland found that the single biggest predictor of tree-ring growth in fifty-three-year-old Sitka spruce trees wasn't precipitation or temperature, as one might expect, but *galactic cosmic rays*, or GCRs. In the years when the most galactic cosmic rays were bombarding the earth, the trees grew fastest, and the connection held up under scrutiny. There is a "consistent and statistically significant relationship between growth of the trees and the flux density of galactic cosmic radiation," the researchers wrote. Galactic cosmic rays are atomic nuclei that have had their electrons stripped away. They originate from outside the solar system, but from within our galaxy. The authors hypothesized about why this might be: the cosmic rays produce nuclei that cause cloud condensation, which diffuses the solar radiation reaching the earth, which may, the authors speculate, increase photosynthesis.

David Milarch, informed, he says, by his imaginal realm sources, also believes trees are connected to the stars. "Trees are solar collectors. Most people equate that with the sun's energy. But the sun is only one star, and there are billions of stars that influence Earth with their radiation—it's called starlight. Trees photosynthesize the energy from the stars just as they do from the sun. I also believe energies inside the earth are transmuted and transmitted into the cosmos by the trees, so the trees are like antennas, senders and receivers of earth energies and stellar energies. I don't know what the energy does, or where it goes, but I think in a hundred years science will be able to measure those energies and quantify them."

Rupert Sheldrake, a Cambridge-trained biologist, plant physiologist, and scientific heretic, hypothesized something similar to the idea of an intelligent matrix in his controversial theory of *morphic field resonance*. In his 1981 book *A New Science of Life*, Dr. Sheldrake proposed that there is an invisible field of intelligent information within and around a living organism—say, a redwood tree. The field contains information that organizes the structure and pattern of activity of the redwood, while the tree in turn feeds information learned from the environment back into the field of information for other, and future generations of, redwoods. The tree's DNA, rather than contain-ing the information itself, is instead more of a bioantenna that sends and receives information to and from the field. In other words, "believing in genes," said Fred Hageneder, a scholar of the mythology, ethnobotany, and mythological aspects of trees who accepts Sheldrake's idea, "is a little like believing the post-man created all your mail."

Many ancient cultures have had their own version of an intel-ligence, or field of intelligence, responsible for different king-doms on the planet. Buddhists call them *lahs;* in Sanskrit they are called *devas;* to the ancient Greeks they were dryads; Celts and Native Americans also had nature spirits. At Findhorn, the mystical garden in Scotland, communicating with *devas* is a rou-tine part of the farming. "I had never set out to learn to talk with angels, nor had I ever imagined that such contact could be possible or useful," wrote cofounder Dorothy Maclean in her book *To Hear the Angels Sing,* which equates angels with *devas.* "Yet when this communication began to occur, it did so in a way that I could not dispute." Is it possible that Steiner's matrix and Sheldrake's morphic fields are related to *devas* and *lahs?*

When Sheldrake's ideas were published they caused outrage among some in the scientific world. Sir John Maddox, editor of the prestigious magazine *Nature,* called the book "the best candidate for burning" to come along in a while. "Sheldrake is putting forward magic instead of science, and that can be condemned in exactly the language that the Pope used to con-demn Galileo, and for the same reason. It is heresy," he said in an interview televised on the BBC in 1994. Sir John's very unscientific condemnation earned him a great deal of criticism, even from people who agreed with him. And it may not have been the best analogy, for in the end Galileo was right.

Few people have written as much about the spirit and speculative science of trees as Fred Hageneder. Born in Hamburg, Germany—another country with a long relationship with trees and forests—Hageneder, fifty, now lives near the scenic harbor town of Swansea in Wales. He has written four books on trees, including his book on the yew. Like many people who have a reverence for trees, Hageneder believes they were vital to the spiritually inclined, not just as objects of veneration but as the source of some kind of native energy. His efforts have been focused on trying to explain that relationship in a way that isn't too far out. "In tree literature we have a huge chasm," he told me. "On one side are ecologists, botanists, and others who wouldn't touch anything spiritual with a beanstick, out of fear that the media as well as academia would ridicule them. On the other side are those neopagan believers, modern druids, or witches who write ever so passionately about spirits and fairies and messages from angels that you sooner or later think, Goodness, get real!" Hageneder tries to bridge the gap and find a middle ground between the two in his work.

He told me about a team in England who studied subtle energy grids across Britain and wrote a book about it, *The Sun and the Serpent*. "They dowsed a few trees in churchyards, and what they found is that each tree is collecting some type of life force from the universe, and as it gathers this energy it appears to spread it out. They found a star shape of lines going out into the land, and a star shape going out from the bottom of the tree. The tree serves as an irrigation system, but not for water, for this life force."

In his book *The Spirit of Trees*, Hageneder gathers together information from a number of sources to show some of the thinking about the myriad roles of trees in the world. How can we presume to know the full role of a forest, he asks, when science doesn't know all of the properties of so basic a substance as water? Water's physical properties are extraordinarily complex and a subject of disagreement among scientists. In the 1990s, Paul Caro, the head of the French National Scientific Research Center, wrote in his book *Water*, "We can measure the varied properties of water over a wide range of temperatures, yet the measurements reveal that water acts like a strange subject that defies logic." Water forms complex and stable clusters, for example, whose structure is more akin to crystals. And there is some research that shows that water, in defiance of the laws of modern physics, has a memory. When chemical substances were placed in water, and the water was then diluted until not a single molecule of them was left, somehow the water maintained the properties of the substances. Many mainstream scientists pooh-pooh this idea because it's outside the known model of the natural world, but the few studies there have been show that something might well be going on. Luc Montagnier, the French virologist who won a Nobel Prize in 2008 for discovering the link between HIV and AIDS, not only thinks the phenomenon is real but has developed a theory. He believes bacterial DNA emits low frequency radio waves that arrange water molecules into nanostructures.

Hageneder also writes about the electrical properties of trees. In the 1920s, a well-respected Yale neuroanatomist, Harold Saxton Burr, who studied the electrodynamics of trees for decades, released his findings: that trees have a steady but fluctuating electrical potential field ranging from 0 to 500 millivolts. In his research, the voltage was at its lowest in the morning and peaked in the afternoon. Burr also noted seasonal variations, with potentials peaking in September on the day of the equinox and hitting their nadir during the spring equinox. He found that light and darkness, the earth's magnetic field, moon and sun cycles, and other factors also impact the electrical field of trees. Five hundred millivolts is a little less than half the voltage of an AA battery. In 2009, researchers at the University of Washington created a device to harness this small, though not insignificant, amount of power. With something called a boost converter, they dialed up the tree's power to create 1.1 volts, enough to run a sensor that can remotely detect forest fires.

Hageneder describes a Czech scientist, Vladimir Rajda, who in 1989 found that the electrical activity of a tree is tied to its biochemical metabolism—in other words, the tree's chemical processes generate an electrical voltage, and the voltage in turn affects the chemistry, in a "soup-and-spark" process similar to the biochemical electrical activity of the human brain. The electrically active part of the tree is the thin membrane of xylem and phloem, layers just under the bark. Rajda also found that the tree's electrical activity is tied to atmospheric electricity, the daily changes of the planet's atmospheric electromagnetic network, and the movement of the sun and moon. Rajda believes that each species is different in its generation of voltage, and that trees can self-regulate this biophysical field.

There's Russian research from the 1970s that shows that light, moisture, nutrition, and photosynthesis are not the only keys to plant growth—an electrical charge in the air also plays an important role. Because the surface of the planet is negatively charged and the ionosphere is positively charged, the Russians believe that trees are "continually discharging electrical tension voltage between the earth and the ionosphere."

These electrical properties, Hageneder posits, may make trees a player in the global atmospheric electrical circuit. While the electrical field of lone trees is small, a German physics teacher named Rainer Fischer proposed that the electromagnetic fields of trees are amplified when they are gathered together in large forests. As their sap ebbs and flows, so does their electrical charge, and thus their magnetic field. A big question is what sets the planet's electrical currents in motion. "Many theories have been developed to answer this question. But the simplest, the electromagnetic effect of countless parallel vegetable electrical conductors, has been overlooked completely," Fischer said, referring to the forests. "The strength of Earth's magnetic field is dependent on the density of vegetation. When the vegetation retreats, the magnetic field strength of the earth decreases. Today, exactly this is revealing itself to a high degree." Widespread deforestation, in other words, may have reduced the force of the planet's magnetic shield against radiation from the sun and cosmos.

There is yet another realm to the study of the hidden lives of trees: some scientists believe that plants can both feel and respond physiologically to human emotion. Many of these ideas were taken up in the 1973 classic *The Secret Life of Plants*. One prominent subject of the book was Cleve Backster, a preeminent expert in lie detection who was an interrogation specialist with the CIA and chairman of the Research and Instrument Committee of the Academy for Scientific Investigation. At age eighty-seven, Backster still runs his own polygraph school, the Backster School of Lie Detection in San Diego. In a 1960s experiment, Backster hooked a polygraph to the leaves of plants. He found that if a leaf was harmed, or even if someone intended to harm it, the polygraph displayed a spike in electrical resistance similar to the response of a suspect who is emotionally distraught when lying. Backster called the phenomenon of plant communication *primary perception*.

More recently a new, scientifically grounded field to study plant intelligence has emerged. The International Society for Plant Neurobiology was founded in 2005 (and has since been renamed the Society for Plant Signaling and Behavior), comprising researchers who believe plants are far more sophisticated and intelligent species than we know—and that they even have brains of sorts. This notion was first proposed by none other than Charles Darwin, who after his career as the godfather of the theory of evolution conducted numerous experiments on plants and wrote several books about them with his son Francis. The Darwins believed a plant's "brain" is in the very ends of the roots, the radicle—a theory known as the "root brain hypothesis." "We believe that there is no structure in plants more wonderful, as far as its functions are concerned, than the tip of the radicle," they wrote.

The idea is that these tips explore the world, scanning the soil for the things the tree needs to live. The Darwins were ridiculed by scientists of the time, but in the last decade some researchers have come around to their point of view: Trees are not passive at all. They have intelligence and senses; they make decisions and can communicate and solve problems. They just go about it very differently than we do. "Plants are as sophisticated in behavior as animals but this potential has been masked effectively because [plants] operate on time scales many orders of magnitude slower than in animals," says a statement from the Society for Plant Signaling and Behavior.

A leader of research in this area is Daniel Chamovitz, director of the Manna Center for Plant Biosciences at Tel Aviv University and the author of the book *What a Plant Knows.* "People have to realize that plants are complex organisms that live rich, sensual lives," Chamovitz said in an interview with *Scientific American.* "Loads of research support the idea that plants see, smell, taste, and feel." Much of a plant's abilities, he says, comes as a response to its rootedness. "It means that plants can't escape a bad environment, can't migrate in the search of food or a mate. So plants had to develop incredibly sensitive and complex sensory mechanisms that would let them survive in ever changing environments.

"Plants are immobile. They need to see where their food is. They need to feel the weather, and they need to smell danger. And then they need to be able to integrate all of this very dynamic and changing information. Just because we don't see plants moving doesn't mean that there's not a very rich and dynamic world going on inside the plant."

Is there more communication going on in the woods than we know? Likely a great deal. Suzanne Simard, a professor of forestry at the University of British Columbia, believes there are "mother trees" in a forest, which care for the younger trees. "They are trying to help each other, shuffling carbon and nitrogen back and forth," Simard said. Is there some kind of electrical wave through which plants communicate with one another? An Oregon physicist named O. E. Wagner set up his detection equipment in Oregon's ponderosa pine forest. When he pounded a nail into the trunk of a tree he detected a slow-moving wave that traveled from one tree to others, signaling some kind of distress. He coined the term *W-wave* for the slow wave, which travels at three feet per second. "The tree with the nail put out a tremendous cry of alarm," he told the Associated Press in 1989. "The adjacent trees put out smaller ones." The W-waves "travel much too slowly for electrical waves," Wagner reported. "They seem to be an altogether different entity. That's what makes them so intriguing. They don't seem to be electromagnetic waves at all."

Some of these ideas are far from being scientifically established, and some are certainly fringe. Still, they ought to pique our curiosity about the kinds of questions we have asked about trees, and the kinds we might be asking.

CHAPTER 18
Sitka Spruce

ONCE UPON A TIME, on the banks of the Yakoun River in British Columbia's Queen Charlotte Islands, a sacred three-hundred-year-old Sitka spruce grew in the midst of an old-growth forest. It was a big tree, more than 160 feet tall and six feet in diameter, but it wasn't its size that made it special. The spruce had a genetic mutation that caused its chlorophyll to break down under UV rays, which in turn caused its needles to turn gold. It stood out in a forest of dark green, and some said it seemed to glow from within. In John Vaillant's 2002 *New Yorker* article about the tree, one woman described how, as the sun emerged on a cloudy day, she came upon the tree, and "suddenly there it was in its golden brilliance. We called it the ooh-aah tree, because that's what it made us all say."

The Haida tribe, the aboriginal people who live on the island, believe the sacred tree was a person, one of their ancestors, and they called it K'iid K'iyass, or Old Tree. According to legend, long ago an old man and a young boy were running away from their village, which the Creator had buried in snow as a punishment for the wicked people who lived there. The old man told the boy not to look back at the village, but he did and was turned into the unusual tree.

The Haida are one of myriad cultures across the world and throughout time who have revered a tree as sacred. In ancient Egypt the god Osiris in his earliest expression was believed to inhabit trees, while the Persians believed both good and evil spirits lived inside trees. In Oaxaca, Mexico, a massive cypress, El Arbol de Tule, or the Tule Tree, is venerated, decorated with locks of hair and ribbons, and Native Americans pay homage to many sacred trees with tobacco and other offerings. In Montana's Bitterroot Valley, a massive medicine tree was venerated for generations by Salish, Nez Perce, and other tribes, until someone poisoned and killed it because it stood in the way of a road widening project. "People use places like the Medicine Tree to pray because it reaches up and brings them nearest to the Creator," a tribal elder wrote about it. Siberian shamans believe trees mediate between Earth and Sky and are antennae for cosmic energy, a belief that resonates with Lawrence Edwards's and David Milarch's ideas. Perhaps these galactic energies were the source of the Buddha's enlightenment beneath the sacred fig tree known as the Bodhi tree. "There is little doubt that most if not all races, at some period of their development, have regarded the tree as the home, haunt, or embodiment of a spiritual essence," wrote J. H. Philpot in *The Sacred Tree*. "The god inhabited the tree . . . not in the sense in which a man inhabits a house, but in the sense in which his soul inhabits his body."

Many cultures also believed in a form of the Cosmic Tree, a symbolic tree that grew through all the realms of the world and symbolized the unity between the divine realm, the human realm, and the underground. The Norse people called it Ygg-drasil, an ash tree, which formed the axis of the three levels of the nine worlds of the Norse cosmogony; in Indian cultures the Asvatha is the Cosmic Tree. The Tree of Life is another symbol that appears in numerous cultures and speaks to the bounty of life on the planet, food, shelter, and other gifts for human-kind. It appears in the Garden of Eden, along with the Tree of Knowledge, and in esoteric Judaism it is a symbol for a pathway to God. For the Teutons, Celts, and Druids the oak was a symbol for the Tree of Life, because it often remained alive after it was struck by lightning and was believed to be favored by the gods.

As for the golden spruce, in 1997 a troubled unemployed Canadian forest engineer named Grant Hadwin swam across the frigid Yakoun River to where the sacred Sitka spruce stood and took a chainsaw to it, claiming he was doing so in protest of the industrial-scale logging that has ravaged much of British Columbia. The people in the nearby town of Port Clements were devastated. "It was like a drive-by shooting in a small town," one resident reported. The Haida mourned it as they would an ancestor.

Fortunately the tree was felled in the winter and was dor-mant, which meant it remained viable for a longer time than it would have had it been cut down in other seasons. The cuttings were grafted to the roots of normal spruce seedlings by experts

at the British Columbia Forest Service Research Station at Mesa-
chie Lake, and some are still growing at the nursery there. In
a private ceremony conducted by Haida spiritual leaders, one
of the saplings was planted next to the stump of K'iid K'iyass,
or the ooh-aah tree. One can't help but wonder, though: while
clones of a tree contain the biological properties of a tree, does
its sacred nature live on in its genetic duplicates?

CHAPTER 19

Lost Groves and Wonder Stumps

THE COASTAL REDWOODS are the tallest trees in the world, the tallest of them, Hyperion, topping out at 379.1 feet. As big as they are now, there were, just a century or so ago, much bigger redwoods that were cut down for lumber. Though these supertrees are gone, dozens of their stumps are scattered across parts of Northern California, and in these giant reminders of destruction are the seeds of a unique rebirth.

The redwood plan that David Milarch began when he cloned Gramma, Twin Stem, and Old Blue fell apart after he was told he couldn't use their DNA. Even though the Ancient Forest Archive is a nonprofit organization, federal, state, and other government agencies do not license rights to their properties. That meant that the biggest of all trees—the Stratosphere Giant coastal redwood and the General Sherman sequoia and other champion trees in federal parks and on other public property—were off-limits. It seemed for a while that the plan to clone the biggest redwoods and sequoias had been thwarted.

Then in 2008, Bill Werner found a brand-new website that belonged to a fellow named Michael Taylor. Taylor is a tree savant. Tall, thin, and much younger-looking than his forty-five years, Taylor eats, sleeps, and dreams big trees. He was featured in Richard Preston's book *The Wild Trees* because he and a friend, Chris Atkins, discovered Hyperion, the tallest of the redwoods, and he helped redwood researcher Steve Sillett locate other towering redwoods in California for research purposes. Jake Milarch followed up with Taylor, sending him pictures of a giant blue oak and a white oak he had taken on a trip to California. "You're the first hit on my website," Taylor wrote back. "If you are ever in California, I'll show you where the big trees are."

There are "extreme tree" hunters all over the world, people who love big trees with a deep and abiding passion, and they scour the wild—and often not so wild—places on the planet for them, measuring, recording, and sometimes nominating them for champion status. Taylor is considered one of the best, bushwhacking and hiking his way across the mountains of big tree country in California with his laser range finder, a $3,000 Impulse 200 LR, which is accurate in assessing tree height to within an inch. He lists all of the detailed data, photos, and other information on his website, Landmarktrees.net.

Taylor's father, James Searcy Taylor, chairman and CEO of a private real estate investment company called American Capital Group, which owns land in California, calls his son enigmatic; he doesn't care about money, as long as he has enough to live on.

Michael went to school in Arcata, California, and there became a full-time big tree hunter, hiking through the temperate rainforest of California looking for trees. He has found dozens of giant redwoods and, as is his right, he has named them—his finds include Thunderbolt (which had been hit by lightning), Bamboozle, Paradox, and Crossroads. David Milarch calls him the "rain man of trees" because of his brilliance with tree data and his uncanny knack for finding the big ones.

Taylor no longer looks for redwoods—the tallest have all been found he says, with LIDAR (Light Detection and Ranging), an airborne remote sensing technology using lasers that generates incredibly detailed topographic maps. That technology has found two hundred redwoods over 350 feet tall. "The frontier of the redwood is over," Taylor told me. "I've moved on to other tree species." He now searches the forests for trees that can be members of the "eighty-meter club," about 260 feet. He is looking hard for the first known hundred-meter tree (about 328 feet), which seems to be a threshold that few besides the redwoods can crack. He has found a 99.7-meter Douglas fir in Oregon, though the top is dead; and there is a eucalyptus tree in Tasmania that is 99.6 meters that has a live top and will, he says, break the hundred-meter barrier as it grows.

Taylor, who lives in a remote village of some 250 souls called Hyampom, in the redwood country of northern California, finds his trees in two ways. The first is by looking for places where there is water and protection from wind, the two most critical elements for a tree to attain extreme tree status. The second way is by intuition, something he remembers having since he collected snakes as a boy. "The most difficult snake to find was a king snake," he explained. One night, on his way home from an ice cream stop with his parents, he had a clear vision, "like a movie, playing over and over in my head," of a king snake crawling across his driveway. "Ten minutes later, there it was in the driveway." He was so shocked, though, that he didn't react in time to catch it. Now he uses the same sense to find trees. "A lot of the trees I find are through intuition," he said. "It's not psychic, really, but a knowing. I had a powerful dream about Hyperion and then a month later I found it. It's not been found, but I know where the tallest sequoia is, I just know. It's a knowing. The same with a sugar pine. The eighty-meter sugar pine is about to be found." The knowing might be coming from the trees themselves, he allowed. "Trees give off a detectable energy, and they also serve as a grounding for the energy coming down from the stars. I can feel it. It's something that you cannot explain with words."

Archangel had stumbled upon someone who knew more about the big trees of California than anyone else, and who shared their feelings about ancient trees.

ON THEIR NEXT trip to California, Jake Milarch and another grower for Archangel, Tom Broadhagen from Empire, Michigan, met up with Bill Werner and visited Taylor. They in turn introduced him to David Milarch, who began a friendship with Taylor centered on their shared fascination with big trees. The Milarchs told Taylor about the problem they faced because they couldn't collect on government ground. Did he know of any privately owned champion redwoods? Or did he know of any large stumps?

"I know the biggest stump *ever*," Taylor replied, referring to the Fieldbrook Stump. As was the case with cloning champion trees, it seems that no one had ever thought of taking clones from a huge stump. But that, too, made a lot of sense. Taylor was signed on as a consultant.

Jake Milarch, Michael Taylor, Bill Werner, and Tom Broadhagen successfully cloned the Fieldbrook Stump, the remains of the largest coastal redwood that ever lived and one of the five largest stumps in the world. Two weeks later, David returned to California with Jake and Michael Taylor to continue the search for the largest stumps that had ever lived, from trees that had been cut down in the 1890s. For the three men, spending twenty-one days combing Northern California for stumps thirty feet and bigger in diameter was a dream treasure hunt. Taylor stayed up late poring over maps and searching the Internet, looking for places where the crew was likely to find large redwoods or stumps on private land, often just outside redwood parks. When they set out in the morning, he turned on his internal compass. "When I travel with David Milarch, we really find trees," said Taylor. "It's beyond coincidence. I've experienced it again and again. We're driving down the road and we suddenly come upon the crown of a giant tree. It's like there's some kind of internal compass guiding us. It spins around and around, and then locks on. That's how we found them." When they came to a big tree or stump on private land, they would stop. David, in his customary role, would knock on the door of the house on the property, give a hearty hello, ask to take cuttings, have the owner sign a release, and offer to bring the family a cloned tree to plant next to the original. On that trip they found and successfully cloned thirteen giant coast redwood stumps, trees that had been much larger than any coast redwoods alive today.

A year later, on a sunny day in early September, Milarch and Meryl Marsh, the global field operations coordinator for Archangel Ancient Tree Archive, drove a few miles out of Arcata, California, not far from Jedediah Smith Redwood State Park, to show me the Fieldbrook Stump. Marsh is one of the world's few female big tree climbers. A marathon runner raised in Hartland, Michigan, she had in 2009 just quit her job working for a pharmaceutical company and was living in Belgium when she came back to Michigan for a visit and was introduced to Leslie Lee. Lee thought Meryl would be helpful in organizing European projects for Archangel and suggested she go to Copemish to see the grow operation and meet Milarch.

When Milarch met Meryl, he immediately thought her athleticism might figure into a role at the foundation. He showed her a video of climbers on the big redwoods and extolled the big tree project. As Marsh recounts it, the excitement of watching people scale the big trees made her forget about sales—she wanted to climb. Milarch was a step ahead of her. He had already arranged for Rip Tompkins, a former world champion tree climber, to come to Michigan to teach her and Jake to climb trees. "You start working with a climbing instructor next week," he told her, to her delight.

There was no climbing needed for the Fieldbrook Stump, however. It sits in the backyard of a house in the woods, and as we entered the property and headed to the yard, a man's impish face peered out from behind a thick growth of trees and berry bushes. Bill Daley, the owner of the property, was standing on the Fieldbrook Stump, which was overgrown with a tangle of blackberry bushes and small trees. The Fieldbrook Stump, cut down by loggers in 1900, is all that remains of one of the largest coast redwoods that ever lived. It's almost thirty-three feet across at a little above breast height, without the bark, which would have added another two feet to the width. The diameter of the largest living coast redwood is about twenty-five feet with the bark, depending on where it's measured. Crudely hewn steps are still visible on the stump where loggers carved them so they could climb up the tree and pound in springboards, which they stood on as they wielded axes and pushed and pulled the massive two-man saw that was needed to fell the giant.

The Fieldbrook Stump is a local celebrity. There is a black-and-white group photo, taken not long after it was cut down, with eighteen serious-looking schoolchildren in their Sunday best sitting and standing on the stump. Dances were held on it, nuptials exchanged, and children conceived on it. "It was the party place," Daley told us. "Young people brought beer kegs and sat on the stump and carved their initials." These days people who used to live in this region, known as the Redwood Coast, bring their children by to pose for photographs on it, and Daley accommodates them. "My daughter and I counted the rings about twenty years ago for a school science project," said Daley. "The best we could do, because there were sections of the stump missing, is that it was between two thousand and three thousand years old."

There is a two-foot-diameter redwood tree, some thirty feet high, growing out of the base of the stump. It's a sucker, or, technically, a *basal sprout*. Most trees, including redwoods, clone themselves by sending up shoots from the roots of the stump below ground. They become trees in their own right and have the same genetics as the tree that was cut down, but because they are not rooted in the ground and have no root system of their own, they are not as sturdy as the original tree and in heavy storms can be blown away. These sprouts are what Marsh and Milarch were after. And once the clones were viable, they would have their own root systems.

Marsh took a few additional cuttings of the Fieldbrook Stump that day. After she shot a GPS location for the tree and took photos and videos, she pulled out a bag with pruners, sponges, and other gear. She cut about twenty foot- to foot-and-a-half-long needle-covered branches from the base of the enormous sucker and stuffed them in a plastic trash bag. She tossed in some sponges and sprinkled in some water from a bottle, to keep the cuttings moist. The next day she would overnight them to Bill Werner in Monterey, where they would be treated with hormones, placed in rooting medium, and set on mist benches. If all went well and tiny root hairs could be coaxed from the cuttings, in three to four months the cuttings would be cloned and become hundreds of baby redwood trees with the exact same genetics as one of the largest trees that ever lived, one that had been given up for dead. Eventually, through advanced cloning techniques, thousands of copies could be made. "The Fieldbrook Stump is in a class by itself and will live again around the world in the clones we make," David Milarch pronounced. "People have studied it, partied on it, copulated on it, and some probably wept, but we're the first ones who came to help it live on. We can use this tree as a symbol of the reforestation of the world, because we will use its descendants to begin that process. This tree is a symbol that it's time to put things back the way they were." He promised Daley that he would bring him one of the offspring so he could plant it. "We're going to plant super groves of redwoods in England, Ireland, France, Australia, Chile, New Zealand, and of course California," Milarch told me. "We're going to plant four or five thousand seedlings, and for every hundred seedlings we're going to plant one clone of the Fieldbrook Stump and other big trees, so those old-growth genetics can begin to mingle with the other trees. Then we will walk away and leave them alone and let nature do her thing. That will be Archangel's gift to the world. This stump is back from the dead, same as I am. We're both playing the same role. It's a resurrection. This is where we ask the world to help heal itself. We won't read the end of the book, but our grandchildren and great-grandchildren will."

Just a few miles out of Crescent City is Wonder Stump Road, named after the Del Norte County Wonder Stump. We drove along it, keeping our eyes out for a large stump, and we asked the locals where it was, but no one seemed to know. Later, at the Crescent City library, we found an old, faded black-and-white photo of a man in a cowboy hat holding a rifle and sitting on top of a large redwood stump, which is in turn on top of a prone stump beneath it. After some searching we found the Del Norte Wonder Stump on a private piece of ground, covered by small trees and brush, unmarked. The Wonder Stump, it seems, is actually two redwood stumps—a thousand-year-old tree stump whose giant, clawlike roots have grown over a fallen fifteen-hundred-year-old redwood. From its name we had thought it might be larger than most, but it wasn't nearly as large as the thirteen stumps Archangel had already cloned a year earlier. David and Meryl weren't interested in taking cuttings of it.

Throughout the forest here, people have built homes amid the surreal ruins of the world's most dramatic big tree logging. Many homes have giant stumps shaped like the Devil's Tower monument in their front or back yard. Some stumps are covered with vegetation. Others have been incorporated into landscaping, made into playhouses, or decorated with lawn ornaments. After Meryl and David collected more redwood DNA from various stumps, they headed south to rendezvous with Michael Taylor, who, following his intuition, had found a little-known grove of old-growth sequoias on private property. The next day David called to tell me he'd hit the mother lode. They were going to take some samples and return in a month; he asked me to join the follow-up expedition to see some of the biggest trees in the world.

In October 2010 I flew into Fresno and met up with Milarch. The other members of the team were already at the sequoia grove, and he and I set out to join them in a rented SUV. Getting to the Lost Grove, as Milarch dubbed it, was an adventure. We drove through farm country and then climbed a serpentine road into the boulder-studded Sierra Nevada, a wild part of California. In the hills, armed Mexican drug cartels grow marijuana and rattlesnakes live under rocks. At lunch our waitress told us that a mountain lion had been prowling around her house and that she had just secured permission to shoot it. Later we saw a black bear on its hind legs taking apples off a tree in a backyard in Sequoia Crest, one of the most unusual rural subdivisions in the world.

Sequoia Crest, south of Sequoia National Park, was once a 670-acre logging operation owned by the Rouch family. Claud Rouch bought this land in the early 1940s, set up a sawmill, and started logging big trees. The business grew, and at one point there were twenty loggers and seventy-five workers at the mill cutting out the virgin pine, fir, and cedar to build homes in Los Angeles. Incredibly, in spite of their value, the Rouches never touched a sequoia. When I asked Claud's son Sonny, now a vigorous ninety-three years old, why they never cut down the valuable trees, he just smiled and said he didn't know. The property is now a subdivision with a hundred homes, most of them second homes, scattered across a mountainside pell-mell beneath a canopy of giant trees. The Rouch family still owns over five hundred acres of the land, though, including a man-made lake that Sonny built himself and what David Milarch referred to as the Lost Grove of giant sequoias, which is right where it shouldn't be, not below the tree line but at the very top of the mountain. Sonny told us that the grove was considered sacred by Native Americans, and it is here that Sonny wants his ashes scattered.

This Lost Grove is one of the sixty-eight or so groves in the mountains of central California, where the altitude, moisture, and soil come together perfectly to create these big trees. It is the only place in the world they are native.* And Sonny Rouch's trees aren't encumbered by federal or other regulations that

---

*The number of sequoia groves varies according to who is counting and depends on what defines a discrete grove. Sequoias cover about 35,000 acres, and there is a total of perhaps ten thousand trees.

would prohibit the collection of DNA. When Milarch proposed the cloning, Rouch was eager to have it done.

This grove is critical to the Ancient Tree Archive mission. "Sequoias like moist feet," says Milarch, "but these trees are high and dry. They have adapted to dry conditions without much moisture and at the southern edge of their range." In other words, they could be a critical genotype for life on a hotter and drier planet.

Milarch and his crew drove a four-wheel ATV up the mountain to the grove. There they would take cuttings from as high as they could climb on the sun-exposed side of the tree. To reach those branches, they would access the tree on the lowest branches, at around a hundred feet in the air, and then move up into the crown to take the cuttings. Jake Milarch had rigged up a bow and arrow with a fishing reel and line attached, a contraption he made after he saw big-tree climbers using something like it on the Internet. If an arrow with fishing line tied to it was shot over a branch but missed, it could be reeled in, and he could make another attempt. If the shot was successful, the fishing line would be used to haul up a heavier climbing rope. Here the climbing was different than it was at Roy's Redwoods. The climbers, wearing harnesses and helmets, used ascenders, tools for both the feet and hands, which allowed them to pull themselves up more quickly and with much less effort than the method used with the redwoods.

It takes a certain constitution to stand on a branch at a height that would induce vertigo in most people and reach out and take cuttings, even with a harness. The branches, though over a foot thick, are brittle and can break at any time. Still, Marsh said the height doesn't bother her. "At first I was a little nervous. But I started focusing on what I had to do, and as soon as I did, it wasn't an issue. And I love it. You get an exclusive view that almost no one else gets, just you and the birds. You get to leave everybody on the ground and leave behind whatever drama is going on down there. It's serene and peaceful, and as far as I am concerned, it's the best place to be."

Later the crew drove down a rutted two-track logging road on another part of the property to the Waterfall Tree. This is the largest-diameter single-stem tree in the world—57 feet across and 155 feet in circumference—and the fifth-largest sequoia tree by volume. It grows on top of a steep ravine, near a small waterfall. The thick base of the tree is obscured now because dirt was pushed up around the base when a road was built.

Over the course of a few days, Jake and Meryl took numerous cuttings from the trees, which were then driven down the mountain to be overnighted to Archangel. Like the redwoods, these ancient trees would be a challenge to clone. Old trees don't have the vitality of younger trees. Bill Werner has an 80 percent success rate when he clones a young redwood tree; with the old redwoods he had a success rate of between 4 and 7 percent. Bill Libby was unable to clone sequoias more than eighty years old.

Once Werner received the plant material he followed the usual procedure of disinfecting, selecting, and trimming cuttings to size and wounding the base of each cutting by removing a thin slice of bark to expose the cambium. The cuttings were dipped in a rooting hormone solution and inserted in propagation flats containing a mixture of peat moss and perlite, a growing medium made from volcanic material that increases aeration and drainage. The cuttings must be placed at just the right depth in the soil. "Too deep and you're toast because you get stem rot," Werner explained. The cutting flats are placed on benches with intermittent mist in a temperature- and light-controlled greenhouse. Every twenty minutes, a timed sprayer comes on with a hiss and mists the plants. Werner continually adjusts the hormone ratio in a range from one thousand to eight thousand parts per million, to see which concentration will work. "It comes down to a lot of trial and error, a lot of record keeping," he told me. Once the plant is treated with hormones and set in flats, said Werner, "You wait and pray and water."

Bill Werner and David Milarch have very different spiritual approaches to horticulture. Milarch says he works with a nour-ishing light—he asks the plant *devas* for pure white light to sur-round the top of the plant, and he asks for emerald green light from the earth to be held around the roots. "That's where some real magic can happen," says Milarch. Werner's men's Bible study group gathers and prays for, among other things, the plants to grow new roots. The ancient Stagg and Waterfall trees were the subjects of frequent prayer. "I have a certain amount of skill, but I ask for God's favor, whether for healing or a scientific break-through," Werner told me. "That includes cloning the Stagg and Waterfall trees." As for Milarch's approach, Werner says, "He acts upon his conviction, that's what's important." Both Milarch and Werner believe that the divine energies they invoke are behind their unusual success in cloning the world's oldest trees.

After three months of mist and prayer, the clones of the ancient sequoias finally sprouted. Milarch called, sounding like a proud father. "We've got roots on the cuttings from the three-thousand-year-old Waterfall Tree!" Then he emailed a photo of the cuttings with the long white beansprout-like roots dangling off the end. Emails of other sequoia and redwood clones followed. No one was more amazed at the cloning success than Bill Libby. "I had to eat crow on the giant sequoias," he said, "because I was convinced it would be very hard to root cuttings over a hundred years old. But Bill Werner has done it to enough of them with a high enough frequency that I had to go swallow that bird."

Clones of the trees are now growing and will soon be copied. In the next year, Milarch says, it will be time to farm out the babies to other countries and begin the creation of supergroves.

CHAPTER 20
Sequoia

FOR CENTURIES CALIFORNIA has had an aura of the fantastic. The state's name comes from the sixteenth-century novel *The Exploits of Esplandián* by Garci Rodríguez de Montalvo, which describes a mythical island adjacent to the gates of a terrestrial paradise. California was rumored to be the site of El Dorado, the fabled city of gold where tribes of Amazon women were said to wander the land. There were tall tales about waterfalls that flowed uphill and a buried core of solid gold, the mother lode. One fantastic story that was true, however, was the tale of the giant trees that grew in the wilderness.

The first known white man to see them was a miner, Augustus Dowd, in 1852. When he returned to camp with his tale of big trees, no one believed him. Later he named the first tree he spied the Discovery Tree, and people started to make pilgrimages to see it. The grandiosity of the trees pierced the hearts of even grizzled frontiersmen. In the 1850s an army surgeon named Lafayette Bunnell rode into a grove of sequoias and later wrote down his thoughts: "It seemed to me I had entered God's holiest temple, where that assembled all that was most divine in material creation."

Some were moved for mercenary reasons. In 1853, when Captain W. H. Hanford, John Kimball, and Ephraim Cutting, all principals in the Union Water Company, finished building a canal, they swung their attention to a grove of sequoias, especially a breathtaking grove with ninety-two big trees, which they saw as a ticket to a career in show business. Their ambitious plan was to drop one of the giants, strip off its bark, wrestle it onto a wagon, take it to San Francisco, put it aboard a schooner, and sail it around the Cape of Good Hope and up to New York City, where they would charge a fee for visitors to see a part of a now dead wonder of nature. The men set their sights on Dowd's Discovery Tree, twenty-four feet in diameter and more than twelve hundred years old.

The Discovery Tree was not, by a long shot, the biggest of the sequoias. Nearby lay a prostrate Father of the Forest, for example, which had died a natural death and fallen sometime before the white men arrived; it was 400 feet tall and 110 feet around, and the first branch was two hundred feet above the base. A fire had hollowed it out, and an early travel writer, James Mason Hutchings, wrote that a man sitting erect on horseback could ride from the bottom into the tree for ninety feet. "At the end of the burnt cavity within, is a never-failing spring of deliciously cool water," he wrote. After a hard rain, a pond formed on the trunk big enough to hold a steamboat.

The gung-ho crew of former canal builders set about their attack on one of the most massive creatures on the planet. They stripped fifty feet of foot-and-a-half-thick bark off the Discovery Tree in ten-foot sections. To fell the tree they drilled three-inch-diameter holes all the way around it into the base with a pump auger, a device they had used to drill out the center of much smaller trees for wooden flumes. They then used saws to connect the drill holes. It took more than three weeks to complete the cut through the trunk. However, when the sawyers finally finished, the tree refused to fall. The men pounded large steel wedges into the cuts in the tree, but it still didn't budge. Two days later, however, a storm rose up and the tree began to "groan and sway in the storm like an expiring giant," according to one witness, until it fell, burying itself twelve feet into the ground and creating a sound like thunder that could be heard fifteen miles away.

The tree was shown briefly in San Francisco, where a local newspaper reported that "thirty two couples waltzed within its enclosure." Then it was placed on a ship bound for New York. Unfortunately for the entrepreneurs, P. T. Barnum turned down the tree, and their ambitions were dashed.

The killing of the Discovery Tree sparked outrage over such crimes against nature. Newspapers carried long, florid descriptions about the felling of the giants. The image of revelers prancing on the remains of the once grand sequoia so angered the conservationist John Muir that he wrote an article titled "The Vandals Then Danced Upon the Stump!"

The outrage helped propel the creation of Yosemite, first as a state park, even though the Calaveras Groves, where the tree had been cut, were, ironically, left out of the park. (In 1931, though, the Calaveras North Grove became Calaveras Big Trees State Park.) But the big tree brouhaha didn't deter another entrepreneur from trying to make his fortune from another giant in the same grove. In 1854, George D. Trask brought in a crew to cut down the Mother of the Forest, a tree 363 feet tall, 31 feet in diameter, and more than 2,200 years old. It was perfectly round and straight as far up as anyone could see.

Trask's approach was to take only the bark, although that would of course kill the tree. His crew set up elaborate scaffolding and peeled sixty tons of bark, in two-foot-wide by eight-foot tall sections, up to one hundred sixteen feet. They numbered the sections of two-foot-thick bark precisely, so the tree could be pieced back together when it went on display.

The *New York Tribune* publisher, Horace Greeley, bought the massive bark and dubbed the tree that remained the "Tree Mastodon." He had it reassembled in New York and London, and it played to sold-out crowds. Mother's naked carcass still stands in the Calaveras Big Trees State Park, with the scaffolding marks visible. News stories about the trees resulted in large numbers of people journeying to see the forest of giants for themselves. Another big tree would not be cut; ecotourism would save the rest.

The giant sequoia, *Sequoiadendron giganteum*, like its relatives the coastal redwood and the dawn redwood, is an ancient species. Its family of trees, Taxodiaceae, dates back 200 to 230 million years to a time of the other giants, the dinosaurs. The range of the sequoias was greatly diminished about a million years ago by climate, leaving it only on the west side of the Sierra Nevada. The groves are widely scattered, which may be the result of the fact that they grew between tongues of a glacier during the Wisconsin period, which began 110,000 years ago and ended 10,000 years ago.

There is concern about the effect of climate change on these goliaths. I asked Nate Stephenson, an ecologist with the U.S. Geological Survey who studies the sequoias, what should be done to protect them. "That's the grand debate, and it is profoundly complex, socially and philosophically," Stephenson said. "Some people say hands off. Some people say assist migration, and some say water them. My hunch is that it will come down to all three. They are all on the table."

CHAPTER 21
A Bioplan

When is the best time to plant a tree? Twenty years ago. The second best time? Today.

CHINESE PROVERB

UNDER A GUNMETAL sky, David Milarch walked around the site where the train station once stood in Copemish. Copemish is an Ojibwe word for "place with the big beech tree," but the big beech, where Milarch's great-grandfather once traded with the tribe, is gone. The village of around two hundred inhabitants is now a melancholy place, and many of the homes are dilapidated. Six generations of Milarchs have lived here.

David showed me the trees he has been planting here, near the converted warehouse that houses the grow operation for the trees—stout six-inch-caliper trees with ninety-inch root balls, maples, white pine, and other natives. The planting is heavy on top of the old train depot, to help remediate the oil-, coal-, and diesel-contaminated soil. "We will rebuild the filter system, clean the air and water and the pollution, and make it habitable for people and for wildlife with these trees," he said. The forest of new trees will connect two fragments of existing hardwood forest, which will provide better cover for deer and coyotes and other wildlife to create a corridor to forests on either side of the road. "It's hotter than Dutch love in the summertime here, and we can cool it with these trees," Milarch said.

A few years ago the town sold dozens of the old maple trees in the city park for $4,000 to someone who wanted to buy them for lumber, and Milarch is replacing those. "They sold trees from the park!" he exclaimed. "That was the straw that broke the camel's back, and I am the camel. I have been all over doing projects to reforest the planet, and I said, 'the next one starts at home.'" He is changing minds, he hopes, as much as the landscape. "Copemish has always been the wrong side of the tracks, but I think people are thinking differently about this place." After seven semi loads of trash were taken from the once decrepit potato warehouse and it was remodeled, it is now bustling with people who are cloning, growing, and shipping trees, and at the other end of the building there is a company that makes solar and wind generators. There are ten or twelve well-paying new jobs in Copemish, people coming and going, and an all-too-rare feeling of prosperity.

Milarch gave me a tour of the grow facility, proud that his longtime dream has come to pass. Giant brilliant lights, bright enough for night baseball, hang from the ceiling illuminating thousands of plants a dozen different shades of green. "At night this place is lit up like a UFO," he laughed. He introduced me to the office manager of Archangel, Marybeth Eckhout, a longtime Michigander who loves her job at Archangel. Marybeth told me that in order to get things done she has to keep Milarch away from the office equipment because of the apparent changes in his electrical nature caused by his NDE. "Good God, he locks everything up," she said. "I've had every electrical piece of equipment—computer, scanners, fax machine—seize up when he's around. Not always—it's worse when he's upset. I have to tell him to calm down."

Collections of big tree genetics have now taken place across the United States and in Ireland, including cuttings there from the Charleville Forest, a private estate that has the massive Charleville King oak on its property, a tree featured in the book *Meetings with Remarkable Trees*. Seventeen of the fifty largest oaks in Ireland grow in Charleville, and Marsh has taken samples from most of them. In the coming year, Bill Libby, David Milarch, Meryl Marsh, and others plan to take genetic samples from the cedars of Lebanon, the massive kauri trees in New Zealand, and a range of other big old trees around the world to create what Milarch calls "the global collection," clones of a hundred of the planet's biggest and oldest trees. While the trees Archangel Ancient Tree Archive has cloned have been done largely by propagating cuttings—setting cuttings in growing medium to root—that method is time-consuming, and the multiplication rates are slow compared to the copy machine of tissue culture, or *micropropagation*. Tissue culture will be key to Archangel's reforestation plans as production ramps up. Once a dozen or two dozen copies of each champion are grown from cuttings, additional copies will be mass-produced by tissue culture.

I toured a fruit tree propagation facility in Canada to see how tissue culture is done. In a brightly lit lab, two workers took a shoot tip containing a tiny meristem from a single tree and dropped it into a jar containing an inch or so of clear gel with growth hormone. A *meristem* is a group of undifferentiated cells at the growing point of a shoot that is capable of developing into various organs or tissues, such as a new branch. The meristem often has a great deal of vigor. After a few days in the hormones it sprouts into five new green shoots, each of which resembles an alfalfa sprout. A technician pulls the emerald green shoots apart with tweezers and puts each one into another hormone-filled jar. In a few weeks each shoot makes several more, and they are pulled apart and placed in their growth-medium-filled jars, and the number of trees—technically called *plantlets*—grows exponentially. When the plantlets are about an inch long they are transplanted to soil in tiny shells and taken to a heat-and-humidity-controlled greenhouse. Within a year, they will be about six inches tall and ready to be planted in a special soil mixture. In a year's time, tens of thousands of genetically identical trees can be grown from a single meristem from a single tree.

Back in the Copemish growhouse there have been pitfalls along the way, in spite of the good fortune. In 2009, as they were growing the first crop of champions, a black mold called *mucor* infected the warehouse, spreading across the wall and ceiling in clouds of tiny black speckles. "Sixteen thousand rooted cuttings of thirty varieties all died in a month's time," said Milarch. "There was nothing we could do to stop it." It was a huge blow, and Milarch said he almost threw in the towel. They rebuilt, however, cleaning the mold with bleach solution, tearing out walls and relining them with special mold-resistant paneling.

More than seventy species of trees have been propagated under the lights here, among them balm of Gilead, dogwood, willow, and birch. In the back of the warehouse and stored on various other properties there are thousands of cloned champion saplings, ten feet tall or more, waiting to be planted. In California, Bill Werner has hundreds of redwoods, sequoias, Monterey cypresses, and other trees growing around his property, some of them now three or four feet tall. The Brian Boru oak and nearly all of the other oaks from Ireland have been successfully cloned and are between two and three feet tall.

The advice of Diana Beresford-Kroeger, Archangel's science adviser, led the group to focus the first production run on the black willow, one of what they call the waterway trees. These trees will be part of an effort to restore native vegetation to the banks of rivers, lakes, and streams, which will help clean up toxic waste and begin to introduce champion genetics and restore a more appropriate diversity. They hope the genes of the cloned champions will augment the variation present in the wild willows. "They are vital because they are the guardians of our fresh water," Beresford-Kroeger says. "Black willow is the first tree to produce pollen in the spring, which bees bring back to the nest to feed their young, and it has antibiotics and important nutrition to strengthen the brood. The salicylic acid and its daughter compounds, which willows release into rivers and streams, help fish fight infection."

Trees are vital as a drugstore for creatures that self-medicate, especially bees. Marla Spivak, a researcher at the University of Minnesota, has found that bees use aspen and willow resins, which are antifungal, antimicrobial, and antiviral, to line the insides of their nests and fight infection and disease. "Bees scrape off the resins from the leaves, which is kind of awesome, stick them on their back legs, and take them home," she told me in an interview for a piece on the decline of pollinators that I wrote for *The New York Times*.

The black willows will be produced and planted with a companion species, the red osier dogwood, with cold-hardy clones from dogwoods near Yellowstone National Park. Dogwood berries are an important source of food for a range of birds, from ruffed grouse to woodpeckers to a variety of songbirds, and the plants also offer cover and nesting sites. Dogwood flowers are a critical source of pollen for honeybees, while squirrels, chipmunks, and snowshoe hares eat the twigs. And they can also help clean the water. "If schoolchildren planted millions of dogwoods and willows in our waterways we could start to clean up some of the pollution out there," David Milarch says.

The biggest environmental problem of all is the increase of CO_2 and other greenhouse gases that trap heat in the atmosphere, causing climate change. While the world needs to quickly phase out the largest sources of carbon dioxide, perhaps the second most important thing we can do right now is plant trees. Just before this book went to press, a new study by the Carnegie Institution for Science's Global Ecology was published. Water that transpires from forests, scientists found, has a robust cooling effect on the planet, not only where the trees and forests are located, but on the entire global system.

If the right tree—one that will last fifty to a hundred years and reaches thirty inches in diameter—is planted in the right place, it will store four to five thousand pounds of carbon over its life. More important, says Dave Nowak, an expert on the ecosystem services provided by trees who works for the U.S. Forest Service in Syracuse, New York, if that tree is planted near a building, its cooling effect can reduce heating by up to 25 percent. That means that another 16,000 to 20,000 pounds of carbon is kept from the atmosphere over the life of the tree because fossil fuels aren't burned. "If I was going to plant one tree in this country it would be near a building to reduce energy use, to get both carbon sequestration from the tree and reduction in energy use," says Nowak. Placement and type of tree are so critical, though, that Nowak and his colleagues have created a software program called i-Tree, in which homeowners can type in their address and find out energy effects and other services provided when they plant trees on their property.

Perhaps the next biggest environmental problem the world faces is the shattering of nature into bits and pieces, which reduces resilience and greatly challenges nature's ability to sustain itself, especially in the face of warming temperatures and other stresses. Again, there's a troubling inverse relationship at work as well: the lack of trees and the fragmentation and breakdown of natural systems worsen where the human population grows denser, which is where the need for the ecosystem services that intact native forests and plants provide is greatest. Eighty percent of the U.S. population, and more than half of the world's, live in or near urban areas. As the population grows from six billion to nine billion by 2050, development and sprawl, and the great unraveling of the natural world, will only increase.

Restoration forestry should be at the top of the environmental agenda in urban and suburban areas. Merely planting trees as we always have done is not enough—we need a more radical approach to reforestation and afforestation (the planting of trees where there weren't any). We shouldn't think of trees as only beautifying a city or suburb, but as a strategically planted ecotechnology, part of a living, versatile, valuable environmental infrastructure that cools the urban heat island, cleans and manages water and air, acts as a natural mood elevator that reduces anxiety and depression, improves property values, mitigates noise, provides wildlife habitat, recreation, and medicines, and grows fruits, nuts, and other nutritious foods. Instead of trees in the cities, we should be thinking about cities in the trees. Just as we wouldn't build new developments without proper roads, sewer systems, and other infrastructure, we shouldn't build new suburbs and other developments without appropriate forest infrastructure.

For forests to continue to carry out these ecosystem services into the future, we must create sustainable urban forests. Precisely how best to do this requires study and analysis of both forests and managed landscapes. It's being done in some areas—in Newark, Delaware, for example, scientists at the University of Delaware's Center for Managed Ecosystems are looking at how best to connect some of the fragments in and around the city. In general it means replanting forests along streams and rivers, and along the ocean in coastal cities. Forests and trees should be planted in and around places where people live and should create corridors to connect to large forest preserves on the edges of town. The construction of strategically located poplar and willow forests—on rooftops, in and around parking lots, near farm fields—can treat agricultural and urban runoff before it makes its way into the oceans as well as provide sewage treatment and biomass for fuel. The list goes on.

There is a global trend to do just this. In hundreds of U.S. cities, the storm drain systems were created so that during severe storms runoff from the streets flows into the sewage system and bypasses treatment. As cities and suburbs have grown, the volume of untreated pollution running into rivers, lakes, and the ocean has grown dramatically. Meanwhile, motor oil, gasoline, lawn chemicals, pet waste, and many other toxic substances wash from the streets directly into waterways. Water pollution is a very serious problem in many cities.

Gray infrastructure, the system of pipes and pumps cities build to handle sewage, is expensive, so many cities are turning to green infrastructure—strategically planted trees and other vegetation. Green infrastructure harnesses the ecosystem services of forests, rain gardens, and other natural filters that intercept, hold, and treat rainwater before it runs into the sewage system. Green roofs, for example, absorb rainwater and hold it during a storm, so that it can be released slowly, rather than simply running off and overburdening treatment facilities.

Urban forests can be employed in other ways as well. In Stuttgart, Germany, officials analyzed the heat island effect from the city's concrete buildings, asphalt roads, and parking lots, which contribute to badly polluted air and high temperatures in the

summer. By planting trees and other vegetation they have created a natural air conditioner—lush wind paths through the
city that draw in cool air from the hills in the country to blow
through the concrete canyons.

In Diana Beresford-Kroeger's bioplan, honey locusts and
other trees would be planted along roads to absorb pollutants,
and black walnuts could be planted in schoolyards, where aerosols will stimulate the immune systems of children and prevent
cancer while the leaves will take in air pollutants and shield children from UV rays. The walnuts, as well as hazelnuts, butter-
nuts, and other nuts, could be served in school lunches, because
they contain omega-3s—nutritionally important oils for brain
development—while apples, peaches, and cherries—fruits from
other trees that would be planted nearby—could provide health-
ful food for kids as well. Woodlots would provide wood for shop
classes and a source of income for school activities. The motto
of agroforestry applies here: "The right tree, in the right place,
for the right reason."

The unplanned chaos of the urban and suburban environment, and the fact that most of it is private property, makes it
difficult to do large-scale restoration, but education, innovation,
and incentives could convince people to roll back the Kentucky
bluegrass and turn their lawns and schoolyards into something
wild. We can use an alternative approach to agriculture called
agroforestry that marries forestry and agriculture, to the benefit
of both. Trees around or over a farm field can reduce soil erosion and dust and keep the fields cool and more moist. And after
the growing season, some trees drop their nitrogen-rich leaves
onto the field, where they become fertilizer. Millions of acres of

barren land in Africa have been reclaimed with nitrogen-fixing trees. Nuts, fruits, and edible oil crops add to the farm's income. The federal government has rediscovered the idea of agroforestry. In 2012 the U.S. Department of Agriculture announced that it intended to renew its agroforestry program and provide incentives for farmers to use trees as a way to manage crops, soil, and water.

To ensure the strength of the forests, we should consider including in our urban forests trees with old-growth genetics, to beef up the overall genetic makeup, or add in genetics from trees that have grown in warmer climates, where the trees have adapted to hotter and drier temperatures. In some cases a tree on the southern edge of its range may have adapted to temperatures as much as ten degrees warmer than those of the rest of the forest.

A sustainable urban forest certainly should mean an end to the planting of exotics, or least some types of exotics. While a Bradford pear or a Tree of Heaven might produce the most beautiful flowers or best autumn colors, these French poodles, as David Milarch calls them, are built for a few years of show, not for survival over the long haul, and may not do well as the climate changes. Douglas Tallamy, a professor of entomology and wildlife ecology who studies ecosystems in the eastern United States, says these exotics are hastening the collapse of the biodiversity around us. The majority of insects in this country can't eat the trees most Americans plant. The bugs here evolved to live on oak and hickory and hemlock, and as the trees have disappeared, the insects that eat them have also disappeared. And trees are by far the single biggest generators of biodiversity. Tallamy studied

1,345 plant genera, native and non-native. The top twenty generators of moths and butterflies in the study were trees—first was
oak, then cherry, willow, and birch. A native oak species supports 534 species of native Lepidoptera in the mid-Atlantic region
alone. On the other hand, ginkgos support four species of caterpillars, dawn redwoods support no species, and Bradford pears
sustain just five species. "Ninety-six percent of terrestrial birds
eat insects," Tallamy says. With so many exotics, there are far too
few insects—too little protein to sustain the birds. "One-third of
our bird species are endangered," says Tallamy. "It's a wake-up
call." Birds are not the only species affected. The overall deficit
of native trees and other plants have led to a decline in a range of
species that are beneficial. Exotics aren't always wrong, says Bill
Libby, but their use needs to be strategic.

We also need a commitment to research the ecotechnology known as trees. It's unforgivable how little we know about
them. They will be on the front lines in a changing world, and
we need to study their genetics, ecosystem services, survivability, and other attributes. It's estimated that over a fifty-year lifetime, a tree provides $162,000 in ecosystem services, including
$62,000 in air pollution control and $31,250 in soil erosion,
and that is a very conservative estimate because things like
atmospheric cooling and protection from ultraviolet radiation
cannot be valued. Even with this limited valuation, though, we
can't afford not to plant trees.

The possibility that planting new forests might change the
world on the macro scale has not been well researched. But that
hasn't kept people from trying. The fisherman of Japan who
formed the organization "Forests Are the Lovers of the Sea" to

plant trees to restore fisheries along the coast are one example. Another is Bishop Frederick Shoo, who is called the "tree bishop" of Tanzania. He has led his half million parishioners to plant tens of thousands of trees to create new forests that they hope will save the glaciers on Mount Kilimanjaro. The bishop believes the glaciers have been melting because of deforestation, which has made the winds that blow toward the mountain hot and dry. If the snow and ice disappear there will be less water for farming. Planting new trees will increase moisture and cool the air, the bishop says, and slow the decline of the snows of Kilimanjaro.

David Milarch, with the help of the Archangel Ancient Tree Archive, is well under way on his quixotic campaign to protect the genetics of the old-growth trees and to create supergroves that will perpetuate the genetics around the world. That idea was his inspiration, and to his credit he has executed it through thick and thin. We won't know for a long time whether he and his vision are correct—if indeed, these genetic qualities are superior or important to the long-term survival of forests. But beyond that, Archangel has joined the growing conversation about, and effort toward, the planting of trees. Planting more trees has been advocated for a long time by a host of organizations and individuals, from American Forests to Trees for Life to Wangari Maathai, the woman who founded the Green Belt Movement in Africa, which focuses on planting trees and women's rights, and who won the Nobel Peace Prize for her efforts. What David Milarch and his colleagues have brought to the discussion is a hard look at what we plant on a changing planet, even if we don't have the science yet to say what is most important, along with a more expansive view of the role of trees and forests.

"Because of the way we have treated the forests, trees—or the lack of them—are the headwaters of all our problems," says Milarch. "Protecting what we have isn't enough, not nearly enough. We need to restore the forests, big time, and help the planet heal itself. It's about restoring the filter system. Instead of spending so much tax money for war and armaments it would be wise to use the army and equipment to reforest the planet as soon as possible. As crazy as that sounds, that is exactly what we need to do, that's the big fix solution. Reforesting and healing Earth is the only answer, and it does a lot more than the science can tell us. That's how we deal with the future—by taking action. Human beings and our machines will not save us. Our government will not save us. And science will not save us. If we wait for their solutions, we will run out of time. But if we harness some of the nearly boundless energy of the planet and the universe by planting trees, it starts into motion the healing and cleansing of the oceans and the atmosphere. And that's what trees do. They benefit every living thing, and it's a gift to our children and grandchildren.

"The big giants of the West Coast, the sequoias and the redwoods, which are so beloved around the world and grow fast, and between them will grow just about anywhere, are the best carbon stackers in the world. They are the ones that will lead us out of this mess. Forty percent of these trees is carbon, and they weigh a thousand tons. That means when they are fully grown they will hold four hundred tons of carbon per tree, and in a forest there are thousands of them, spaced fifteen feet apart. Do the math."

Recently, David was excited about a trip to California, where he had given a talk to NASA, as part of their TEDx speakers series featuring innovative thinkers; he had spoken about the importance of cloning one hundred of the world's landmark trees, planting them in archives, and making their genetics part of the reforestation effort. Some of the scientists from NASA who heard the talk were very interested. "I think it's a fantastic idea," said Steve Craft, the deputy director in the strategic relationships office at NASA's Langley Research Center, who was planning to research it further. "If you are going to plant a tree, why not plant trees genetically you know will survive?" And *Outside* magazine named David one of their innovators of the year in their December 2011 issue.

But there was also troubling news just as this book was going to press. Due to severe budget cutbacks at Archangel, Milarch and his sons were laid off; out of eighteen employees, there are now just a handful. Milarch the elder, at sixty-two, continued to volunteer at Archangel in the hope that more funding would come through to continue the mission of cloning the collection of the world's hundred largest trees, and that others, including universities, industry, and government agencies, would take up the task of collection and research. Soon after, Leslie Lee left the organization, leaving it in charge of Jared Milarch, who was named the new CEO.

IF ONE MAN and his family living in the middle of nowhere, with no financial resources, no political connections, no formal education, with little but a vision of making the world a healthier, safer place for his grandchildren and their grandchildren, can bring us closer to a more hopeful and viable future, imagine what we all can do. As scientists admit, science has, for the most part, failed to understand and appreciate the myriad roles of trees and forests even as our planet heads into a dramatically uncertain future. Government has created little or no legislation regarding the planting of trees. It appears that the gap will be filled only by individuals who believe in their—in our—ability to make a difference. The man—or the woman, or the child—who planted trees is potentially everyone.

"*The Man Who Planted Trees* is an illustration of the power each of us has," wrote Frédéric Back, the Academy Award–winning filmmaker who made a film of Jean Giono's book. "If hands and minds come together, we can have an important beneficial effect. We have children and we have grandchildren. Every reasonable person should have a reaction of this kind, to care for the future. It is about the power of work that is life-giving."

We can wait around for someone else to solve the problem of climate change and the range of other environmental problems we face, from toxic waste to air pollution to dead zones in the oceans to the precipitous decline in biodiversity, or we can take matters into our own hands and plant trees. It may not be the best time to plant a tree, but, as the proverb says, there is no better time.

Afterword

After the initial publication of this book, David Milarch spent fourteen months collecting unemployment, tending to the thousands of cloned trees growing in the warehouse, and hoping there might be another angel in the wings. And there was. Toward the end of 2012 a generous and anonymous donor sent Archangel enough money to keep the organization afloat for a year or so.

So in early December 2012, Milarch traveled to Port Orford, in southern Oregon, to plant the first new old-growth forest, with clones from redwood and sequoia trees 280 to 300-plus feet tall. On a rainy, wind-whipped day, he reunited with his former Champion Tree partner Terry Mock and, with the help of several foresters, dug holes in the mud on a steep slope and planted the trees that were grown at the Archangel propagation facility in Copemish. There were clones of fifty different two-thousand-year-old giant coastal redwoods, including thirteen from stumps of trees far bigger than anything else alive today, as well as clones of eleven different three-thousand-year-old giant sequoias, including both the Stagg and Waterfall trees from the

Lost Grove. "There's some real celebrities there that we brought back from the dead," said Milarch. The planting, on Mock's land just north of the current range of redwoods, is also a way, as the planet warms, to assist the trees' migration north, to the cooler temperatures and fog that the old giants thrive in.

The planting was written about in the London *Sunday Times*, *Der Spiegel,* and publications across the United States, and was featured on National Public Radio's *Morning Edition*. "People from around the world have been calling and asking, 'When can we get the trees? We need to plant them.'" Milarch said.

Other plantings have followed. Some two-thousand-year-old old-growth redwood clones were planted in a park in Bandon, Oregon, as well as in seven different countries. In October 2014 Milarch was making plans to plant twenty clones of the Field-brook Stump at the Eden Project, a massive conservatory and research and education center that contains the largest collection of plants useful to humankind, built on the site of a former clay mine in Cornwall, England. Archangel is also planning to replant at Eden the first redwood old-growth forest in England, from three hundred to five hundred clones of seventy different coastal giants.

Sir Tim Smit, founder of the Eden Project, told me that he is collaborating with Archangel as well as working on a massive project in Northern Ireland. "We have a plan to merge three big estates on the banks of the River Foyle at Derry," he said, "to make it the Irish center for ancient oak propagation, alongside a crafts center for all things to do with wood." *Derry* is Gaelic for "oak grove"; 1,600 Irish towns have *Derry* in their name. He hopes the new propagation center will help heal not only Derry, a city at the heart of the "Troubles," but also much of Ireland, the most deforested country in Europe. "The river has always been ignored despite being among the most beautiful in the world," he said. "It is also home to the largest population of unemployed young people in Europe. It would be perfect to put all these things together into a project that is powerfully good for the environment, creates numerous jobs, and which gets international attention for the right reasons."

And Sir Ted Green, known as the "Ancient Tree Man," will assist the joint venture between Archangel and Eden by locating the largest and oldest of the United Kingdom's champion trees, which will then be cloned at Eden's facility.

Meanwhile, Milarch's efforts inspired the University of Michigan to plant ancient sequoia clones in the campus arboretum on Arbor Day 2014, to see how new old-growth forests might offset the university's carbon footprint. And on Earth Day 2014, with students and faculty from the renowned Interlochen Arts Academy—which is an archival living library for many of the Archangel trees—Archangel planted its first old-growth giant sequoia grove. Two Interlochen teachers have developed a curriculum about climate change, afforestation, and reforestation, available on the Archangel website.

In other words, many of the things Milarch had only dreamed about when he took his first champion tree cuttings with his young sons more than twenty years ago have come to pass. "Every week we have people from all over the world walk through the door and want us to do a planting," said David. "All of the struggle and all of the sacrifice are coming to fruition."

It's been an epic journey and a difficult challenge for David Milarch and his family since *The Man Who Planted Trees* was first published. They have spent the past few years working hard, refining their process, establishing the Research, Development, and Education facility, and continuing to develop ways to propagate massive quantities of ancient cloned trees. David has been spreading his inspirational story far and wide, Jared has been volunteering his time running the nonprofit, Jake has been keeping the factory churning out trees, and countless tireless volunteers and donors have kept the doors open. There are currently five thousand clones of the largest and oldest redwoods, sequoias, and champion trees growing indoors and outdoors, attracting visitors from around the world; and the Milarchs are waiting and praying for the right donor to facilitate their propagation and planting so they can do their job helping to mitigate climate change.

Today, Archangel—www.ancienttreearchive.org—has incorporated a place-based model of education. They have been working with select schools, teaching hands-on skills in tree propagation, tissue culture, and agroforestry, while initiating large-scale restoration projects all over the world. This initiative is teaching K–12 students, college students, and adults how to do what Archangel has been doing for more than twenty years. The educational programs "We Are the Forest" and "Tree School" offer the world a replicable model, through hands-on education and action. "We are here to propagate the propagators," Jake told me, "empowering students and teachers of all ages with the spirit of nature and the skills needed to help save the planet, all while demonstrating and implementing innovations in ecological restoration, educational programming, and economic development. Archangel is creating and empowering a new generation of nature-based problem solvers."

"We're heading into the thick of the climate change thing," David said. "The vise is tightening. It's time to get as many trees in the ground as we can. We are all working for our grandchildren."

Notes

5 **Most of these diseases are zoonotic:** Felicia Keesing et al., "Impacts of Biodiversity on the Emergence and Transmission of Infectious Diseases," *Nature*, December 2010.

14 **Los Angeles, for example, has a campaign:** Linda McIntyre, "Treeconomics," *Landscape Architecture*, February 2008.

14 **The floods caused by deforestation:** Corey Bradshaw et al., "Global Evidence that Deforestation Amplifies Flood Risk," *Global Change Biology*, August 2007.

17 **the Wye Oak:** "The Quiet Giant, The Wye Oak," Maryland Department of Natural Resources, www.dnr.state.md.us/forests/trees/giant.asp.

22 **The human-induced drought killed the trees:** "Temperature Sensitivity of Drought-Induced Tree Mortality Portends Increased Regional Die-Off Under Global Change Type Drought," *Proceedings of the National Academy of Sciences*, April 28, 2009.

23 **The most recent forecast for the mean:** "Climate Change Science Compendium," United Nations Environment Programme, September 2009.

23 **by 2100, *half* of all plant and animal species:** E. O. Wilson, *The Future of Life* (New York: Alfred A. Knopf, 2005).

24 **This one is different:** Niles Eldredge, "The Sixth Extinction," action bioscience.org.

27 **By the time the outbreak ends, British Columbia:** "Lands and Natural Resource Operations Fact Sheet," Ministry of Forests, Province of British Columbia, April 2011.

28 **a violent storm swept through the region:** American Geophysical Union, "Staggering Tree Loss from 2005 Amazon Storm," *Science Daily,* July 13, 2010.

28 **In 2010 another, even more severe drought:** University of Leeds, "Two Severe Amazon Droughts in Five Years Alarm Scientists," *Science Daily,* February 3, 2011.

30 **So much forest has died in British Columbia:** "B.C. Forests No Longer a Carbon Sink," report on the Canadian Broadcasting Corporation website, December 9, 2010.

31 **"With many trees now gone":** Richard Macey, "Fewer Trees, Less Rain: Study Uncovers Deforestation Equation," *Sydney Morning Herald,* March 4, 2005.

31 **Trees are also home to an unusual microorganism:** Jim Robbins, "From Trees and Grass, Bacteria that Cause Snow and Rain," *New York Times,* May 24, 2010.

32 **In spite of the lack:** Jim Robbins, "What's Killing the Great Forests of the American West?" *Environment 360,* March 15, 2010.

33 **"These recent die-offs":** Craig D. Allen, "Climate-Induced Forest Dieback: An Escalating Phenomenon?" *Unasylva,* vol. 60, 2009.

35 **But the tree keeps a small strip of living tissue:** Ronald M. Lanner, *The Bristlecone Book: A Natural History of the World's Oldest Tree* (Missoula, Mt.: Mountain Press Publishing, 2007).

35 **In 1964, a graduate student in geography:** Michael P. Cohen, *A Garden of Bristlecones: Tales of Change in the Great Basin* (Las Vegas: University of Nevada Press, 1998).

36 **The study of tree rings from the ancient trees:** "One for the Ages: Bristlecone Pines Break 4,650-year Growth Record," *Scientific American,* November 24, 2009.

37 **Compounding the attack of the bark beetles:** Jim Robbins, "Old Trees May Soon Meet Their Match," *New York Times,* September 28, 2010.

46 **On a warm day in 1970:** A. Kukowka, "The Hazard of the Yew (*Taxus baccata*)," *Zeitschrift für Allgemeinmedizin,* March 10, 1970.

48 **In California's Sierra Nevada:** D. Helmig and J. Arey, "Organic Chemicals in the Air at Whitaker Forest/Sierra Nevada Mountains, California," *Science of the Total Environment,* March 1992.

48 **In French Guiana, researchers sampled compounds:** E. A. Courtois et al., "Diversity of the Volatile Organic Compounds Emitted by 55 Species of Tropical Trees: A Survey in French Guiana," *Journal of Chemical Ecology,* November 2009.

48 The chemicals act in the environment: Stephen Harrod Buhner, *The Lost Language of Plants: The Ecological Importance of Plant Medicines to Life on Earth* (White River Junction, Vt.: Chelsea Green, 2002).

49 Studies of the boreal forest: D. V. Sprackler et al., "Boreal Forest Aerosols and the Impacts on Clouds and Climates," *Philosophical Transactions of the Royal Society*, 2008.

49 These aerosols play a micro role as well: Rick J. Willis, *The History of Allelopathy* (New York: Springer, 2007).

53 Most significant, though, is its role in cancer: M. N. Gould, "Cancer Chemoprevention and Therapy by Monoterpenes," *Environmental Health Perspectives*, June 1997.

54 brain tumors that don't respond: C. Fonseca, "New Therapeutic Approach for Brain Tumors: Intranasal Administration of Ras Inhibitor Perillyl Alcohol," *Neurosurgery* 976, August 2010.

54 Analysis from the samples taken: Q. Li et al., "Effects of Phytoncide from Trees on Human Natural Killer Cell Function," *International Journal of Immunopathology and Pharmacology*, October–December 2009, 22(4):951–59.

56 the effects of green space on children: University of Illinois at Urbana-Champaign, "Science Suggests Access to Nature Is Essential to Human Health," *Science Daily*, February 19, 2009.

57 Green spaces, the researchers wrote: J. Maas et al., "Morbidity Is Related to a Green Living Environment," *Journal of Epidemiology and Community Health* 15, October 2009.

60 The medicinal properties of the willow: Daniel E. Moerman, *Native American Ethnobotany* (Portland, Ore.: Timber Press, 1998).

61 a bitter yellowish crystal from willow bark: Sunny Auyang, "From Experience to Design: The Science Behind Aspirin," philpapers.org, December 22, 2010.

62 Aspirin remains something of a miracle drug: Peter M. Rothwell et al., "Effect of Daily Aspirin on Long-Term Risk of Death Due to Cancer: Analysis of Individual Patient Data from Randomised Trials," *The Lancet*, December 7, 2010.

68 I'd written a piece about George McMullen: George McMullen, *One White Crow* (San Francisco, Calif.: Hampton Roads Publishing, 1994).

79 "It seemed to me I was high up in space": Carl Jung, *Memories, Dreams and Reflections*, rev. ed. (New York: Vintage, 1989).

79 A 1992 Gallup poll estimates: Near Death Experience Research Foundation, www.nderf.org.

80 Dr. Pim van Lommel, the respected Dutch cardiologist: Pim van Lommel et al., "Near Death Experience in Survivors of Cardiac Arrest: A Prospective Study in the Netherlands," *The Lancet*, December 15, 2001.

85 **Lumber from old-growth redwoods:** Michael Barbour et al., *Coast Redwood: A Natural and Cultural History* (Los Olivos, Calif.: Cachuma Press, 2001).

89 **Another factor in the survivability of forests:** Bruce Dorminey, "Trees Migrating North Due to Warming," *National Geographic News,* February 9, 2009, news.nationalgeographic.com.

96 **The global tree canopy is a similar story:** H. Bruce Rinker, "Conservation from the Tree Tops: The Emerging Science of Canopy Ecology," actionbioscience.org, October 2000.

97 **DNA is now believed to be mutable:** Ethan Watters, "DNA Is Not Destiny," *Discover,* November 2006.

105 **"Finding a living dawn redwood is at least":** William Gittlen, *Discovered Alive: The Story of the Chinese Redwood* (Berkeley, Calif.: Pierside Publishing, 1999).

112 **"fundamental mistake would be to assume":** Gary Moll, "Trees, Environment, and Genes: In the Evolutionary Battle to Survive and Thrive, a Species' Parentage Is Just the Beginning," *American Forests,* Summer 2003.

112 **she believed Milarch had stolen their idea:** Jim Robbins, "A Tree Project Helps the Genes of Champions Live On," *New York Times,* July 10, 2001.

115 **Jared Milarch and his team set out:** Rick Weiss, "Taking Chips off the Oldest Blocks," *Washington Post,* June 16, 2003.

116 **The Czechs nicknamed the seedling Methuselah Jr.:** "Tree of Life," *Prague Post,* September 13, 2006.

129 **Many people cite the fact that trees create oxygen:** David J. Nowak et al., "Oxygen Production by Urban Trees in the United States," *Arboriculture and Urban Forestry* 2007, 33(3): 220–26.

129 **American urban forests alone sequester:** Linda McIntyre, "Treeconomics," *Landscape Architecture,* February 2008.

129 **Trees also mitigate some obstructive lung diseases:** Gina Schellenbaum Lovasi, "Children Living in Areas with More Street Trees Have Lower Asthma Prevalence," *Journal of Epidemiology and Community Health,* May 1, 2008.

130 **the intact native forest also provides a host:** Gretchen Daily and Katherine Ellison, *The New Economy of Nature: The Quest to Make Conservation Profitable* (Washington, D.C.: Island Press, 2002).

131 **One of the most egregious examples:** David A. Farenthold, "Failing the Chesapeake Bay," *Washington Post* series, December 2008.

132 **A study of sixteen tributaries:** Bernard W. Sweeney et al., "Riparian Deforestation, Stream Narrowing, and Loss of Stream Ecosystem Ser-

vices," *Proceedings of the National Academy of Sciences*, September 28, 2004.

133 **poplar and willow trees to remediate toxic waste:** Andrew Revkin, "New Pollution Tool: Toxic Avenger with Leaves," *New York Times*, March 6, 2001.

135 **the city has replaced the plant with a willow field:** I. Dimitriou et al., "Willows for Energy and Phytoremediation in Sweden," *Unasylva* 221, vol. 56, 2005.

138 **The importance of iron led one path-breaking scientist:** T. Kawaguchi, "The Influence of Forested Watershed on Fisheries Productivity: A New Perspective" *Thalassas* 2003, 19(2): 9–12.

140 **There may be yet another reason to value the tree:** G. Strobel et al., "The Production of Myco-Diesel Hydrocarbons and the Derivatives by the Endophytic Fungus *Gliocladium roseum*," *Society of General Microbiology*, September 2, 2008.

143 **much of northern Europe could be at serious risk:** Robert B. Gagosian, Woods Hole Oceanographic Institution, "Abrupt Climate Change: Should We Be Worried?" Talk given at World Economic Forum, January 27, 2003.

144 **diseases could wipe out stressed forests:** Emily Beament, "Now Britain's Oaks Face Killer Disease," *The Independent*, April 28, 2010.

146 **The forest and the native culture:** William E. Klingshirn, *Caesarius of Arles: The Making of a Christian Community in Late Antique Gaul* (Cambridge, U.K.: Cambridge University Press, 1994).

146 **one of the planks in the Sinn Féin platform:** Paul Gallagher, "What Is Sinn Fein? The American System vs. British Geopolitics in Ireland," *American Almanac*, January 9, 1995.

146 **they started to mine the vast oak woods:** Rebecca Solnit, "The Lost Woods of Killarney—Old-growth Oak Forest in Ireland," *Sierra* 29, August 2011.

148 **Shortly afterward, in what seemed a miracle:** Gordon Deegan, "Clare Fairy Tree Vandalised," *Irish Times*, August 14, 2002; "Fairies Defy Chainsaw Attacker to Sprout New Leaves on Thorn Bush," *Irish Times*, June 2, 2003.

151 **native forests across the Continent:** "Global Forest Resources Assessment," Food and Agriculture Organization of the United Nations, 2010.

157 **One of the largest and most beautiful exceptions:** "Kingley Vale National Nature Reserve," Wikipedia.

159 **the teachings of the Austrian mystic Rudolf Steiner:** Lawrence Edwards, *The Vortex of Life: Nature's Patterns in Space and Time* (Floris Books, 2006).

160 **Other scholars have noted a link:** Otto Janik and Leonid B. Starosiel-ski, eds., "Supernovae und Baumwachstum" (Supernovae and Tree Growth), in *Exakt: Exklusiv-Informationen aus Wirtschaft, Wissenschaft, Forschung und Technik in der Sowjetunion (Exakt: Exclusive Information from Industry, Academia, Science, and Technology in the Soviet Union)* (Stuttgart: Deutsche Verlagsanstalt, 1976).

160 **"consistent and statistically significant relationship":** Matt Walker, BBC, October 19, 2009.

165 **In 2009, researchers at the University of Washington:** Roberta Kwok, "A Light in the Forest: Wireless Sensors Draw Energy from Trees," *Conservation,* January 2009.

170 **In John Vaillant's 2002 *New Yorker* article:** John Vaillant, "Letter from British Columbia: The Golden Bough," *The New Yorker,* November 4, 2002. Readers who would like to read more about the golden spruce can read John Vaillant's book *The Golden Spruce: A Tale of Myth, Madness, and Greed* (New York: W.W. Norton & Company, 2005).

184 **This Lost Grove is one of the:** "List of giant sequoia groves," Wikipedia.

189 **the tale of the giant trees that grew:** Joseph H. Engbeck, *The Enduring Giants: The Epic Story of Giant Sequoia and the Big Trees of Calaveras* (Berkeley, Calif.: California State Parks, 1976).

199 **Water that transpires from forests:** George A. Ban-Weiss et al., "Climate Forcing and Response to Idealized Changes in Surface Latent and Sensible Heat," *Environmental Research Letters,* 2011.

205 **over a fifty-year lifetime, a tree provides $162,000:** Kathleen Alexander, "Benefits of Trees in Urban Areas: Colorado Trees," which cites David J. Nowak, "Benefits of Community Trees: Brooklyn Trees" (USDA Forest Service General Technical Report, in review).

Index

PHOTO: © PETER KUPFER

JIM ROBBINS has written for *The New York Times* for more than thirty years. He has also written for magazines including *Audubon, Condé Nast Traveler, Smithsonian, Vanity Fair, The Sunday Times,* and *Conservation.* He has covered environmental stories across the United States and in far-flung places, including Mongolia, Mexico, Chile, Peru, the Yanomami Territory of Brazil, Norway, and Sweden.

Robbins is the author of *Last Refuge: The Environmental Showdown in the American West* (1993) and *A Symphony in the Brain: The Evolution of the New Brain Wave Biofeedback* (2000). He is also the co-author of *The Open-Focus Brain: Harnessing the Power of Attention to Heal Mind and Body* (2007), about the critical and overlooked role of attention, and of *Dissolving Pain* (2010), about the role of attention in pain.

He has lived in Helena, Montana, for thirty-five years.

www.jim-robbins.net.